D0982591

WEATHERMAN

Edited by Harold Jacobs

Dedicated to the Vietnamese people

Table of Contents

Preface   xi

Chronology   xv

   PART ONE: THE EMERGENCE OF WEATHERMAN

Introduction   1

The Real SDS Stands Up   15
   Andrew Kopkind

* Hot Town: Summer In The City   29
   Jim Mellen and Bill Ayers

* More On Youth Movement   39
   Jim Mellen

* You Don't Need A Weatherman To Know Which Way
   The Wind Blows   51
   Karin Ashley, Bill Ayers, Bernardine Dohrn, John Jacobs,
   Jeff Jones, Gerry Long, Howie Machtinger, Jim Mellen,
   Terry Robbins, Mark Rudd and Steve Tappis

* Toward A Revolutionary Women's Militia   91
   Cathy Wilkerson

Hand-Me-Down Marxism In The New Left   97
   David Horowitz

New Left: Old Traps   105
   Todd Gitlin

Weatherman   111
   Jack Weinberg and Jack Gerson

1969   119
   Carl Oglesby

   PART TWO: ACTION IN THE STREETS

Introduction   137

A. Toward The National Action

* Who Do They Think Could Bury You?   147
   Lorraine Rosal

* Break On Through To The Other Side   152
   Motor City SDS

* The Motor City 9   161

* Women's Militia   163

B. *Days Of Rage*

Look At It: America 1969   166

* Bringing The War Home: Less Talk, More
   National Action   175
   Kathy Boudin, Bernardine Dohrn and Terry Robbins

* A Strategy To Win   183
   Bill Ayers

The Second Battle Of Chicago   196
   Tom Thomas

* You Do Need A Weatherman To Know Which Way
   The Wind Blows   227
   Shin'ya Ono

C. *Fall Offensive: Washington Action*

* Washington, November 15, 1969   275
   Cartoon

D. *Aftermath*

Going Down In Chicago   283
   Andrew Kopkind

On Weatherman   293
   Eldridge Cleaver

Justice In The Streets   296
   Tom Hayden

PART THREE: INSIDE THE WEATHER MACHINE

Introduction   301

* Honky Tonk Women   313

* Inside The Weather Machine   321
   "A Weatherwoman"

Weatherman Politics And The Women's Movement   327
   Bread and Roses collective

* National War Council   337

Stormy Weather   341
   Liberation News Service

* Weatherman Songbook   351

PART FOUR: GOING UNDERGROUND

Introduction   359

A. *An End?*

Weatherman: A Lot Of Thunder But A Short Reign   379
   James Weinstein

Reply to REP   394
   James Weinstein

Weatherman: The Politics Of Despair   400
   Michael P. Lerner

* It's Only People's Games That You Got To Dodge   421
   Inessa, Victor Camilo, Lilina Jones, Norman Reed

B. Or A Beginning?

* Everyone Talks About The Weather . . .   440
* Revolution In The 70's   448
* Affinity Groups   452
* Weather Letter   456
* Letter To The Movement   462
   Linda Evans

Unsettled Accounts   464

Ted Gold: Education For Violence   470
   J. Kirk Sale

Untitled Poem In Memory Of Ted Gold   484
   Nelson Temple

For Diana Oughton   484

Memories Of Diana   485

For Terry Robbins   489

Where The Fuse On That Dynamite Leads   491
   I. F. Stone

The Radical Bombers   496
   Andrew Kopkind

How Does It Feel To Be Inside An Explosion . . .   504
* Communique #1 From The Weatherman Underground   509
* Communique #2 From The Weatherman Underground   512
Notes To The Underground   513
* Communique #3 From The Weatherman Underground   515
* Communique #4 From The Weatherman Underground   516
Letter From Timothy Leary   517

* Indicates that the material consists of official Weatherman documents, or that it was written by people who are now, or were once, in Weatherman.

Preface

Weatherman stands second only to the Black Panthers in
its ability to conjure up the spectre of Revolution within
America. Just as the Panthers are taken to be the unseen
hand behind most acts of violent rebellion inside the black
colony, so Weatherman is held responsible for most acts of
violent sabotage inside the mother country.

Weatherman advocates armed struggle and the overthrow
of established power. It is taken seriously, however, not so
much for what it espouses as for what it has done. Weatherman had led extremely militant street demonstrations and
has taken credit for bombings against major capitalist institutions. Owing to Weatherman's efforts and those it has inspired, there is hardly a symbol of racist and imperialist oppression secure from violent attack. John Mitchell and
J. Edgar Hoover have declared Weatherpeople to be outlaws
in America and have mobilized the vast police powers of the
state against them. Nevertheless, Weatherman carries out its
underground activities with relative impunity: as the level of
repression has grown, so too has the number and sophistication of Weatherman bombings. And this is likely to continue.

This book is about these mother country revolutionaries.
It describes and analyzes who they are, how they emerged,
the actions they have taken, and the nature of their politics.
This book is not a "Weatherman" book, although it strives to
make an honest presentation of Weatherman politics. It

should be viewed as a medium through which Weatherman confronts, however indirectly, its critics on the Left.

For some time now, there has been a scarcity of serious theoretical debate within the Movement. Disagreements over theory have tended to degenerate into polemical squabbles, leaving in their wake a deplorable lack of clarity and a great deal of factionalism. The hope here is to raise issues to a notable level of discussion, to avoid the Old Left's characteristic use of slander as a political ploy, and to induce the New Left to take responsibility for its rhetoric.

Even with its relatively short history, Weatherman has provoked much controversy and has challenged the Left to rethink its politics. While Weatherman's strategy and tactics, forms of organization, and life style have a sensational quality about them, my concern is not to exploit that, but instead to treat Weatherman with the gravity it deserves. It would be as unfortunate and irresponsible for the Left to fail to confront the major issues Weatherman has raised as it would be for Weatherman not to welcome the chance to subject its politics to close scrutiny and criticism.

When this book was first conceived, Weatherman was given the opportunity both to suggest material to be included and to answer the major criticisms of its views. An extensive interview with Weatherman leaders was planned as well, which would have enabled them to discuss their errors, elaborate on the issues in contention, and fill in the latest developments in Weatherman strategy and tactics. But once Weatherman went underground, my contact with the Weatherman leadership (minimal to begin with) ceased altogether, and these plans had to be dropped. I have, however, discussed the book with Weatherman sympathizers, ex-Weatherpeople, and some aboveground people "close to" or "in" Weatherman. As a result, this book contains all available Weatherman documents and articles of importance. Whenever a question arose over the value of a particular piece, I chose to include it, even at the risk of making the book unduly long and repetitious, to give Weatherman the greatest possible latitude in the presentation of its ideas. At the same time, I tried to include substantive criticisms of Weatherman to provide as genuine and useful a confrontation of ideas as possible.

The introductions to the four sections of this book contain a capsule history of Weatherman's activities as well as a brief —sometimes critical—description of the material in each section. Reading through all the introductions should provide an over-all perspective on the book, and some idea of how it might be read selectively.

The first section deals primarily with Weatherman's early theoretical formulations and the critical response they engendered. Section two traces Weatherman's organizing techniques and street actions with special emphasis on the "Days of Rage." The third section explores the problems Weatherpeople faced in attempting to remake themselves into committed revolutionaries. The final section contains major criticisms of Weatherman praxis; it concludes with a description of Weatherman's underground activities.

Some readers might prefer to begin this book by reading the section on Weatherman's dramatic and provocative street actions before going through the relatively abstract, sometimes arduous, but extremely important theoretical debate in the first section. The last two sections, however, should be read as they are presented, and only after the material in the first two sections has been digested.

I wish to thank David Horowitz of *Ramparts* magazine for patiently working with me on this book. He criticized early drafts of the introductions and made many valuable suggestions which were incorporated into the book. Thanks also go to Judy Hirsch of Ramparts Press who saw to it that the book emerged relatively free of printing errors. Most of all, I want to express my gratitude for the help I received from people in the Movement, especially those in and around Weatherman. Given the repressive political climate in the country at this time, I believe it best that these people remain anonymous. It should be understood, however, that they had a major impact on much of what eventually went into this book. I am, of course, responsible for the content of the introductions as well as the selection and editing of the collection.

Chronology of Events

1960

Spring

Students for a Democratic Society founded.

1962

June

SDS issues 60 page <u>Port Huron Statement</u>, which calls for an alliance of blacks, students, peace groups, liberal organizations and publications—to bring about a progressive "realignment" of the Democratic party.

1963

June

SDS approves the document <u>America and the New Era</u>, which criticizes the inadequacy of the Kennedy Administration's New Frontier program to solve the problems of disarmament, social justice, and racial equality. As an alternative to collaboration with liberal groups, the document calls for the independent organization of emerging insurgent forces within the civil rights, peace, and student movements.

December

SDS sets up the Education Research Action Project (ERAP), consisting of local community organizing projects aimed at poor whites and blacks in ten Northern cities.

1965

April

SDS organizes the first national anti-Vietnam war march in Washington, drawing over 15,000 people, most of them students. In the following three months, the number of local chapters triples to well over 100 and the national membership of SDS grows to several thousand.

October

Carl Oglesby, then president of SDS, openly attacks corporate liberalism in a speech at an anti-war march in Washington.

1966

August

SDS National Convention at Clear Lake, Iowa, calls for a "student power" strategy and re-emphasizes the need to do political work on the campuses.

December

SDS pushes radical draft resistance as the dominant thrust of its political organizing. It also calls on its campus chapters to protest or disrupt appearances of representatives of the military-industrial complex.

1967

June

At the SDS National Convention in Ann Arbor, Michigan, a "new working class" perspective is counterposed to the Progressive Labor party's stress on the industrial working class being the crucial agency of revolution.

1968

April-May

Columbia University is occupied by black and white students. The demonstrators were able to close the campus in protests attacking University expansion into the black community of Harlem, C.I.A. funded and supported research institutes and programs, and University subservience to the interests of large corporations. Mark Rudd, later to emerge as a major leader of Weatherman, becomes nationally prominent for his role in the Columbia revolt.

June

At the SDS National Convention in East Lansing, Michigan, PL can only muster a minority of delegates. Outright conflict develops between PL and the rest of SDS. The majority of the delegates at the convention stand up, raise their clenched fists, and chant "PL Out."

October

At the SDS Boulder, Colorado, National Council (NC) meeting a major PL-WSA resolution on student-labor action projects (known as the SLAP proposal) is rejected.

December

At the Ann Arbor, Michigan, NC, PL-WSA demonstrates that it is gradually gaining ascendency by winning passage of its resolution on racism. The RYM resolution, "Toward a Revolutionary Youth Movement," is passed. The resolution is presented by a group operating out of Chicago which included Mike Klonsky (then National Secretary of SDS) and Les Coleman (from Chicago Region SDS). It is supported by a number of people who later were to set up Weatherman, including Bernardine Dohrn, Jim Mellen, Mark Rudd, Bill Ayers, John Jacobs, and Howie Machtinger.

March

At the Austin, Texas, NC, the anti-PL forces reverse the PL resolution on racism passed the previous December. The SDS alliance with the Black Panther party is substituted for the overturned PL resolution. Internal differences are beginning to emerge within the group favoring the RYM resolution passed the previous December.

June 18-22

The SDS National Convention in Chicago witnessed the PL-SDS split. The RYM II statement is presented as a refinement of the original RYM resolution by the same people who had authored the original RYM proposal. The "Weatherman" statement ("You Don't Need A Weatherman . . .") also is presented by those who were to emerge as leaders of Weatherman. Weatherman is elected to control of the SDS National Office, with Jeff Jones, Mark Rudd, and Bill Ayers filling the top three positions.

Summer

SDS summer programs in Michigan and Ohio develop as proto-types of Weatherman collectives.

August 29-September 1

A three day mass meeting was held in Cleveland to build support for the upcoming SDS National Action, during which Bill Ayers gave a major speech.

September 3

Weatherman action in Pittsburgh organized and led by women.

September 24

The "Conspiracy 8" trial opens in Chicago. A violent Weatherman action takes place outside the courthouse, resulting in 19 multiple felony arrests of Weatherman.

October 8-11

The SDS National Action takes place in Chicago. The Weatherman "Days of Rage" result in the arrest of hundreds of Weatherman activists and major felony indictments, both local and federal, against Weatherman leaders.

October 29

Bobby Seale is gagged during the "Conspiracy 8" trial.

December 4

Black Panthers Fred Hampton and Mark Clark murdered by Chicago police.

December 27-30

Weatherman "National War Council" takes place in Flint, Michigan.

March 6

Greenwich Village, New York, town house explosion in which Ted Gold, Diana Oughton, and Terry Robbins are killed.

April 3

Twelve Weatherman are indicated by a federal grand jury on 13 counts (one count each for crossing state lines intending to incite a riot and one count of conspiring to do the above).

April 15

Linda Evans and Dianne Donghi are arrested by the F.B.I.

May 21

The Weatherman underground issues its first communique.

June 9

The New York City police headquarters is bombed. Weatherman takes credit in its second communique from underground.

July 23

Thirteen Weatherman are indicted by a federal grand jury on charges of conspiring to engage in acts of terrorism and sabotage against police stations and other institutions.

July 26

Weatherman underground issues communique #3 in response to Justice Department indictments.

July 27

A branch of the Bank of America is bombed in New York for which Weatherman takes credit.

September 15

The Weatherman underground issues its fourth communique. Dr. Timothy Leary issues major statement from the underground after his escape from prison.

Part 1
The Emergence Of Weatherman

Introduction

Students for a Democratic Society grew during the 1960s from an insignificant radical study group to the largest, most vigorous national white organization on the Left. Today SDS is for all intents and purposes dead. Only a short time ago it had an estimated national membership of 70,000 to 100,000 and commanded the allegiance of countless other young activists; now it is no more than an empty shell of its former self. There is, in fact, only a Progressive Labor Party-controlled faction functioning in the name of SDS but without the politics or style of work of its no longer living predecessor. Yet from the destruction of SDS something new was created—a small, tightly organized revolutionary fighting force of white youth called Weatherman.

I

SDS was founded in 1960 by young radical intellectuals most of whom subscribed to some variant of socialism. They did not, as is sometimes claimed, reject Marxist analysis. Rather, they sought to avoid the stereotyped thinking and glaring irrelevancy of traditional Left groups, both Communist and Trotskyist, which had enjoyed their heyday in the 1930s. SDS attracted essentially liberal and idealistic students whose disenchantment with America sprang more from a sense of moral outrage than from the dictates of an "ideological party." If many of them were to become revolutionaries before the decade was over, it was because their liberal reformist orientation and anti-ideological bias proved futile in the face of America's exploitative structure of wealth and power.

SDS became a major national force as it led white students to take "direct action" against racism, poverty, and war. The failure of legal and non-violent protests to eradicate social injustice coupled with the unexpected rigidity of the corporate liberal establishment drove young activists towards greater militancy. A new radicalism made its appearance. It was nurtured by the sons and daughters of the affluent, rooted in the universities and emerging youth culture, inspired by the Cuban revolution, and pushed forward by the black movement. With each additional United States escalation of the Vietnam war, the New Left multiplied in size and expanded its vision. The civil rights movement became a struggle for black liberation; anti-poverty crusades produced opposition to the capitalist system and its welfare-warfare offspring; the peace movement gave rise to an anti-imperialist consciousness. Marxist and anarchist ideas began to assert themselves throughout the Movement.

By mid-1966, SDS was developing in a revolutionary Marxist direction with the following two distinguishing attributes: first, far more of SDS theory grew out of its practice than did SDS practice derive from theory borrowed from the past or other historical contexts; secondly, white youth was coming to be recognized as a revolutionary force in its own right whose oppression could not be overcome except through the total transformation of society. The rudiments of an exclusively New Left revolutionary position began to emerge. It revolved around a new understanding of how the composition of the work force had been drastically changed by modern industry and technology, giving rise to a "new working class" in which students and workers were, more or less, one and the same. Furthermore, SDS was committed to a style of work that rejected Stalinism, elitism, and manipulation. SDSers were insisting that the revolution concerned their lives and that people's personal and political lives could not be separated without doing harm to both.

About this time Progressive Labor, a self-styled Marxist-Leninist-Maoist party, entered SDS. Some have argued that PL encouraged SDS to develop a more sophisticated class analysis and anti-imperialist perspective and that PL helped to broaden SDS' view from concern with an exclusively student movement to one rooted in the working class. PL, however, dealt with SDS in an irresponsibly manipulative manner from the start. Although it intended to build SDS along anti-imperialist lines, it primarily was concerned with recruiting cadre from the organization into its own projects. While only incidentally fostering Marxist ideas and concern for the working class in SDS, PL actually entered the organization because it had been unable to organize a mass base on its own. Its presence became objectively obstructionist as resentment grew within SDS to PL's politics as well as to its uptight and secretive style. PL eventually decided to take control of SDS or, if that proved impossible, to prevent SDS from functioning effectively. For these reasons, there was little basis for any kind of fruitful relationship between the two organizations.

PL, nevertheless, had a jump on its SDS rivals. When PL fought for its politics it had the advantage of disciplined organization and greater facility with Marxist terminology over its loosely organized and ideologically heterogeneous SDS counterparts. Even more important, PL had a self-conscious concept of an anti-imperialist student organization and a vague idea about how those students could eventually become cadre in a working-class movement. Although crude and ultimately wrong, the very systematic quality of PL's perspective caused the debate over program inside SDS to be conducted on PL's own vulgar Marxist terms. Most SDS cadre had no idea of how a revolution in the United States would unfold. PL, in contrast, had a metaphysical belief in the industrial proletariat as *the* agency of socialist revolution. The result was that SDS national leaders found themselves adopting PL's Marxist-Leninist-Maoist rhetoric in order to regain the initiative while, simultaneously, rejecting PL's political line.*

The bulk of the SDS national membership were put off by what appeared to them to be sectarian squabbles. The dogmatic and mechanical quality of the polemics at national meetings (soon to be reflected at the local level as well) promoted factionalism. Most SDSers chose to ignore these ideological debates and to work instead on organizing projects in their local and regional areas against the war in Vietnam and racism. The SDS national leadership, however, recognized the need for a systematic strategy for revolution. They therefore continued to give priority to the problem of coming to grips ideologically with PL, in spite of their growing isolation from the membership. By the fall of 1968, SDS was racked by an inner divisiveness which not only prevented important political work at the national level from getting done, but soon sapped the entire organization of its vitality.

Almost all of the non-PL national leadership of SDS were themselves relative newcomers to the organization. While

* Also significant is the fact that developments in the white movement have followed upon those in the black movement. The rise of the Black Panther party, a Marxist-Leninist party heavily influenced by Maoist teachings, helped foster the impression among white radicals that all serious revolutionary organizations must be Marxist-Leninist-Maoist in orientation. Unquestionably, the Black Panthers have been able to demonstrate the relevance of Maoist theory to conditions in the ghettos. This is owing in large part to their intelligent adaptation of Maoist maxims to the concrete experience of the black community and especially to the anti-colonial nature of the black struggle.

Weatherman first appeared as only one more of the non-PL factions in SDS, some of the eventual Weatherman leadership had been fighting PL for years, having been part of the anti-PL faction in the defunct May 2nd Movement. This small, anti-imperialist student organization, formed in 1964 and disbanded in 1966, had a strong internationalist orientation: it adhered to Lin Piao's belief that Third World nationalist revolutions would play a decisive role in the destruction of United States imperialism. Inside of SDS, these future Weatherman were among those who led the Columbia University rebellion and built the New York, Michigan, and Ohio Regions of the organization. Two months prior to the fateful SDS National Convention in June, 1969, former M2M members and others created a caucus of ten people to produce a policy resolution. They were to become the leadership collective known as the Weather Bureau.

II

Weatherman, then, emerged after a year of factionalism so intense that SDS was splintered into a number of warring sects at both national and local levels. This dissension culminated at the tumultuous June 1969 National Convention in Chicago, where two groups—one dominated by PL, the other a diverse alliance of those opposed to PL—bitterly severed their ties. In fact, the anti-PL alliance ousted PL and, by extension, the persons it had organized into "worker-student alliance" caucuses. This was done without regard to regular SDS procedures and only after the Black Panther party had denounced PL and declared it would judge SDS by the company it kept.

The PL-WSA caucus may actually have constituted a voting majority at the convention. The anti-PL caucus met in closed session for twenty-four hours at a nearby hall and decided there was no longer any basis for unity between PL and SDS. This caucus, whose size varied from 700 to 1200 members, returned to the convention hall (where there were approximately 1000 PL-WSA delegates) and announced the ouster of PL. The anti-PL caucus then marched out of their own convention, reconvened the next day, and proceeded to set programs, elect officers, and adjourn.*

The split between the factions was a result of irreconcilable political differences. The major accusation against PL was that it fostered white supremacy and did not adequately support black liberation. This was said to be manifested most clearly in its declaration that all forms of nationalism were reactionary, including those of oppressed minorities within oppressor nations: specifically, PL had attacked most of the struggles of black students (including their demands for open admissions and black study programs), community control of the police, the Black Panther party and its "breakfast for children" program, and the Detroit-based League of Revolutionary Black Workers.

Another related but more comprehensive accusation was that PL defended the chauvinist "interests" of the white American working class against the class interests of the international proletariat. Many people in SDS had found PL's attacks on the revolutionary governments of Cuba and the Democratic Republic of Vietnam extremely onerous. PL also refused to support the National Liberation Front of South Vietnam, calling its leadership, along with that of the DRV, "sell-outs" and branding Ho Chi Minh a "traitor."

SDS refused to condone such politics within its own organization. It did not take long for it to conclude, in the words of former SDS vice president Carl Davidson, "that it could no longer have a double standard, making major political demands (such as support for the NLF) outside its ranks which were not only not supported, but attacked by persons within its ranks."† The split, which existed *de facto* at least six months prior to the convention, came when it did largely because SDS feared that its leading organizational principle— the development of a revolutionary youth movement—would

* For further details, see Jack A. Smith, "SDS Ousts PL," *Guardian*, June 28, 1969.

† See "Why SDS Expelled the PLP," *Guardian*, July 5, 1969.

be irreparably sabotaged if PL-WSA politics were allowed to continue in the organization. The issue ceased to be academic as SDS faced the likelihood of a political and organizational takeover by the PL-WSA faction at the relatively unrepresentative convention in Chicago.

Both PL and its enemies emerged from the split claiming to be the "real" SDS. It was clear, however, that the political tendencies aligned against PL had the generalized support of an overwhelming majority of the SDS national membership, if not of the delegates at the national convention. Within the anti-PL alliance, Weatherman appeared to represent the majority tendency; its advocates were elected to control of the SDS National Office as well as of many regional offices, allowing Weatherman to consolidate its position inside the organization in the months that followed.

For a while it seemed as if the competing tendencies within SDS, having eliminated the most destructive, could move forward on the basis of enough consensus on political principles to hold the organization together. That hardly turned out to be the case. Eliminating PL from SDS did not lead to fewer or less intense ideological disputes.

In fact, the ousting of PL actually marked a turning point in SDS's drift toward total collapse. The two dominant factions in the anti-PL alliance, RYM II and Weatherman, not only had different reasons for excluding PL, but also had their own distinct and basically conflicting political analyses.

PL's perspective called for building a Worker-Student Alliance, by which it meant that students would be organized around issues that "serve the interests of the working class." SDS, according to PL, was supposed to limit its activities to the campus, leaving off-campus political organizing to PL— except during summer months when students would be encouraged to "work in" factories to learn about the working class.

The "Weatherman" statement, "You Don't Need a Weatherman to Know Which Way the Wind Blows," was part of the evolving body of theory aimed at defeating PL. This body of theory, based on revolutionary youth movement politics (known as RYM), was developed by leadership drawn from members of SDS national and regional staffs, which came to be known as the National Collective.

RYM, in contrast to PL, sought to make SDS into a mass revolutionary organization of youth which would fight against imperialism and in support of the black liberation struggle. RYM itself, however, was composed of two contending political tendencies—Weatherman and RYM II—which only united temporarily to fight PL.

The essential difference between the two RYM factions concerned the role of violence in building a mass-based anti-imperialist movement. RYM II agreed with PL's view of the industrial proletariat as *the* agent of revolutionary change and defined students merely as members of the petite bourgeoisie who, at best, were only capable of giving support to a socialist revolution. Aggressively militant demonstrations by students were viewed by RYM II as part of the petite bourgeoisie's natural inclination toward violence. RYM II argued that such violence alienates workers who have not yet achieved revolutionary consciousness. Hence, by curbing student violence against the state, they hoped to build a broad anti-imperialist movement composed of students and workers.

Weatherman, however, argued in this debate that most all Americans are workers in the Marxist sense and that socialist revolution was in almost everybody's objective interest. Instead of seeking to curb student violence, Weatherman saw the onset of a sustained armed struggle against the state as the best means of creating revolutionary consciousness among the mass of American people.*

The continuing centrifugal forces within the anti-PL alliance prevented what remained of SDS from developing any organizational coherence. Arguments over the strategy and tactics of SDS's October 8-11 National Action only widened

---

* The Radical Education Project collective has compiled the relevant documents in a packet entitled "Debate Within SDS: RYM-II vs Weatherman." Those who wish to pursue this debate in detail should study the packet.

the internal conflicts—which finally grew to the point where they undermined any common adherence to a broadly conceived RYM perspective. By the end of the summer SDS had completely disintegrated, Weatherman and RYM II each going their separate ways.

III

The first section of this book begins with Andrew Kopkind's account of the June, 1969, SDS convention; it includes a brief history of the politics behind the purging of PL from SDS. His remarks are indicative of the guarded optimism which swept through the Movement once SDS had rid itself of PL's disruptive influence. Along with other left commentators Kopkind understood the split at the National Convention not as "a death rattle but a life struggle" to preserve the "radical sensibility of . . . the 'New Left.' " Besides describing the raucous events of the convention, Kopkind highlights some key points of the "Weatherman" statement, thus providing a guide to the document itself.

"Hot Town: Summer in the City . . .," an SDS resolution passed at the March 1969 National Council, is an early formulation of Weatherman strategy. It contains the first set of political policies Weatherman formed around. Weatherman's central concern at this time was to transform SDS from a student movement to one including youth of the entire working class. This was to be done by a network of tight collectives which would organize young people in schools, the army, hip communities, and working-class neighborhoods.

"More on Youth Movement," the "Weatherman" statement, and "Toward a Revolutionary Women's Militia" provide Weatherman's own explication of its theoretical perspective. The programmatic thrust of Weatherman theory calls for building an internationalist fighting force among white working class youth to provide material support for wars of national liberation against United States imperialism. The specifics of Weatherman theory have given rise to much controversy (the reaction in and around SDS was, at best, mixed), but Weatherman's general orientation, stressing the primacy of struggles against imperialism and racism, has been widely accepted.

The issues of racism and imperialism had not been ignored by the white Left. But most groups tended to deal with these issues in an *ad hoc* manner rather than as overriding priorities. RYM politics in general, and Weatherman's impact in particular, helped put an end to that. Over the last two years, the debate within the Movement has shifted to questions of how to bring the struggles against imperialism and racism programmatically to the fore, how to organize around these issues within different strata of the working class, how to relate these issues to women's liberation and youth culture, and how to move in the tactically most appropriate manner to provide maximum support for the Vietnamese and the blacks.

Critics of the "Weatherman" statement have not restricted themselves to attacks on its basic propositions. Some have questioned the Maoist model of world revolutionary process upon which Weatherman theory is premised. David Horowitz takes both the PL and Weatherman factions of SDS to task for subordinating their native American radicalism to the dogmas of old-line Marxism. He specifically objects to their mechanical application of Maoist ideas to conditions in advanced capitalist societies. This criticism, however, is somewhat more germane to PL than to Weatherman. Horowitz tends to emphasize Weatherman's Maoist tendencies because he overlooks the manner in which Maoist language and ideas entered SDS in the first place. Once Weatherman cut itself free of PL and RYM II (which also has a strong Maoist orientation), Weatherman language and theory ceased to reflect what Horowitz refers to as "hand-me-down Marxism" quite so strongly.

In part, Horowitz's criticism of the Maoist turn taken by leading factions of SDS reflects his disappointment over the New Left's failure to breathe new life into the best part of the buried tradition of Marxism and American radicalism. Moreover, his major objection to the "Weatherman" statement still stands: its specific theoretical formulations derive from its basic Maoist premises, which—while compelling on the basis of Chinese experience and exigencies—tend to obscure more than they clarify when adopted uncritically to provide strategy for revolutionaries in advanced capitalist countries.*

Todd Gitlin reiterates this point from another direction by stressing the uniqueness of the New Left without glossing over its history of liberal illusions, elitist practices, and shallow analyses. He warns against a one-sided response to what Weatherman refers to as white skin privilege; he refuses to succumb to the despair implicit in Weatherman's belief that the majority of whites in this country might be too racist, too defeated, and too self-indulgent to make a revolution for themselves. Most importantly, Gitlin argues that the New Left must not renounce its post-scarcity origins and identity. Instead, it must connect its vision that "a new world is possible—free of material misery, hierarchy, useless work" to the more traditional but no less significant concerns of all oppressed peoples.

Jack Weinberg and Jack Gerson maintain that Weatherman has no program for the mass of American workers that speaks to their class interest as workers. They criticize Weatherman for responding in moral rather than political terms to the outrageous crimes perpetrated against people of color by United States imperialism. They back up their argument by pointing to Weatherman's view of itself as primarily a support group for someone else's revolution—blacks and other Third World people. Weinberg and Gerson further claim that Weatherman will be incapable of building a base of sufficient weight to support Third World struggles as long as it refuses

---

* To avoid any misunderstanding, neither my remarks nor those of Horowitz ought to be taken as a disparagement of the thought of Marx, Engels, Lenin, and Mao. These brilliant revolutionary thinkers, were they to view the work of many of their present emulators in the mother country, would have to declare, as Marx himself once did, "Je ne suis pas un Marxiste." What Horowitz is comparing to the disadvantage of "old-line Marxism" is a revitalized Marxism that concretely deals with nationally and historically specific conditions instead of invoking old formulas, out of context.

to organize the American working class around its perceived oppression and material interests.

Carl Oglesby concludes this section with reflections on some of the leading events of 1969. In the course of analyzing the San Francisco State strike, the Berkeley People's Park movement, and the Black Panther Party's call for a United Front Against Fascism Conference, he comes to conclusions that place him at odds with much of Weatherman's political policies.

Weatherman has applied its notion of white skin privilege to the university and hip communities. It views the struggles of white youth around their own social and spiritual needs—such as fights for "student power," rent strikes, People's Park confrontations—as basically attempts by whites to carve out even more privilege than they already derive from the imperialist nexus. Oglesby tries to demonstrate that such struggles can be objectively progressive. Weatherman insists, however, that struggles must be explicitly internationalist and anti-imperialist in content or they become objectively reactionary.

Oglesby goes on to evaluate trends inside SDS leading up to and including the June, 1969, National Convention, anticipating the growing isolation of all major factions—PL, Weatherman, RYM II—from the mass of young people in the Movement. He extends his analysis of the Black Panther party to include a critique of the "Weatherman" statement, especially the part dealing with the black liberation movement. He concludes by summarizing the points of clarification he has tried to make of Movement praxis during the course of the past year.

*   *   *

What then is the significance of this confrontation of ideas? Regardless of the actual merits of Weatherman theory, it has provoked people to think through their own politics. The major issues raised by Weatherman are being faced with a new seriousness and urgency. Revolutionaries are learning through experience that theoretical positions when translated into actions have practical consequences—increasingly of a life and death nature. The ensuing symposium is part of the dialogue going on in the Left. Out of it may emerge, for the first time in American history, a truly indigenous American Marxist theory of revolution.

From
The Fire Next Time, Nov. 1969

The Real SDS Stands Up

Andrew Kopkind

There have been many acts of rebellion in the American
Sixties, and countless scenes of insurgency, but for white
radicals, the Students for a Democratic Society has always
been the only show in town. Like all political shows, it is
both shadowy and substantial, plagued by missed cues and
tardy prompts. But SDS still speaks the lines of the young
white Left in this country. The material of movement is
stored in its wings, and the running plays out front reflect
that unique collection.

What happened in SDS' convulsive convention last week
was not a death rattle but a life struggle. At stake was the
survival of the radical sensibility of what used to be called the
"New Left"—until its immediacy overcame its newness. For
reasons buried in the root-mass of American culture and
society, this generation was seized with a new vision of the
revolutionary possibilities of its future. Now, for almost a
decade, that vision has been contained within SDS. And
although the politics and ideologies constructed over it have
changed with experience, the basic urge has not. SNCC organizing, Vietnam protest, draft resistance, wars of liberation,
Berkeley and Columbia, the international new student revolt,
repression and black liberation have drawn different responses. But the genius of the Movement so far has been its
ability to imagine its own slogans and create its conceptions.

"Participatory democracy" and "Let the People Decide"
did not define the generational vision: Those ideas—and the
politics which grew around them—were expressions appropriate to a time. In the same way, "Power to the People" and

From *Hard Times*, June 30, 1969. Reprinted with permission of the
author. Copyright 1969 by The New Weekly Project, Inc.

"Two, three, many Vietnams" fit today's experience, but may seem inappropriate in another year. There is certainly no value in mindless rejection of ideology; but SDS has always had the sense to let its ideology develop from the experience of its members—in Southern rural counties, urban ghettoes, industrial slums, campuses, streets, and parks.

From the beginning, SDS has been attacked at close quarters for its self-confident, often smug independence from older and wiser heads. The League for Industrial Democracy, a moribund social-democratic (now Humphrey-Democratic) pamphleteering society, expelled SDS as its youth branch for refusing to follow an anti-communist line. Over the years, Trotskyists, Communists and the range of Left sects have spent much of their energies bad-mouthing the growing SDS organization. But the greatest challenge of all has come from the Progressive Labor Party, which decided four years ago to take over SDS as a youthful base for power.

To an untrained eye, PL people look much like their SDS counterparts. Although there are fewer beards, shorter hair, and straighter clothes seen in PL caucuses than in SDS ones, the differences in appearance are not enormous. Distinctions begin to grow on the level of attitude and style: Against SDS types, PL cadres seem mechanistic and dour, with a tone more suited to the street-corner than the street.

But the real clash comes in terms of basic views of how the world works (or doesn't). SDS people seem intuitively to recognize the variety of insurgency in the US, and while they may prefer some kinds to others, they feel a bond with the insurgents and attempt to fit their politics to a wide range of needs. Beneath all the definitions of line and strategy, SDS has always had the ability to look at radicals in their movements and say: "Us." The black rebellion, women's liberation, culture freakdom, workers' struggles, students' strikes, GI demonstrations: Obviously, some must be more strategic than others, but all have a reality which PL seems determined to overlook.

PL derives its ideology not from its experience up against the American empire but (it often seems) from a detailed study of late nineteenth century Europe combined with an analysis of the wall-posters in East-is-Red Square. No doubt post-industrial capitalism in the US has something in common with German and Russian society in the time of the kaisers and czars. Doubtless, too, the American Movement can learn a great deal from the development of the Chinese Revolution—the most cataclysmic political event in the history of the modern world. But there is more to fighting the empire than the application of a labor metaphysic and a position on the Sino-Soviet split. PL peoples a Tolkien middle-earth of Marxist-Leninist hobbits and orcs, and speaks in a runic tongue intelligible only to such creatures. It is all completely consistent and utterly logical within its own confines. But that land at last is fantasy. The real world begins where PL ends.

PL has inherited many of the worst traits of the Old Left and only a few of its virtues, but it is not its ideology and derivative politics which give the most trouble: There's enough wrong-thinking all around in every part of the Movement. What is so destructive is the way in which the doctrine is applied. For some time now, PL has been organizing young people into its Worker-Student Alliance caucuses inside SDS chapters. Trained by and responsive to PL, the WSA members divert much of the Movement's energy from outside action to internal hassling. Because of its emphasis on working-class revolution—and its own rigid definition of what that class is and how it functions—PL discourages support of the Black Panthers, of organizations of black workers, of black and brown community control campaigns, of anti-racist protests on campus, of Cuba and the NLF, of "people's parks," of women's liberation organizations: in short, all the activities that the Movement finds most important and attractive.

SDS has been fighting hundreds of local skirmishes with PL since the "take-over" process began, and in a few areas—Boston and the Berkeley campus, for two—the Movement tradition has lately been very much on the defensive. PL overwhelms newly politicized students with its sophisticated Marxism-Leninism on the one hand, and its simple promises of workable "work-in" programs on the other. It proclaims the inevitability of revolution in America given conditions now at hand. Like Calvin's state of grace, PL's state of socialism requires patience for salvation, not sacrifice for action (although both Calvinists and PL people feel a curious urge to work in spite of its irrelevance). In that, PL denies the central existential agony at the core of the Movement of this generation.

With its simple strategy of instant revolution by the working class and its logical and disciplined structure, PL appeals to young people who are tired of the tentative experimentalism and undiscipline of SDS organizing. More than that, the distracted and contradictory leadership of SDS' National Office plays into the hands of PL's rationalized leader-base relationship: In a stormy season, a disciplined Party is a comforting port for repair.

In a few instances, such as the Harvard strike, PL has had real successes by taking over SDS issues and SDS turf. But in its own area—the factories and the shops—PL politics remain largely rhetorical. But PL's promises have real attraction. It does offer young radicals the hope of joining a broader agency of change—the international proletariat—than they may see in a "transitional" youth movement. It has a program that is far beyond the street fighting actions to which, in the past, SDS people have been confined. And it provides a sophisticated theory against which organizers can test their practice, and see how it is working. In fighting PL organizationally, SDS itself has moved to fit its operations into some of the framework which PL has built rhetorically: particularly, working-class organizing.

On the national level, PL has been gearing up for its major drive to take control of SDS' organization. Implicitly, it has challenged SDS to build a rational Marxist ideology based on a national program; it dares SDS to integrate all the Movement activity in the US in one political schema. And until this week, SDS has failed to respond.

A year ago at the SDS summer convention in East Lansing, PL was able to muster only a minority of the delegate votes.

Last winter at the interim council in Austin, PL was on the way to ascendancy. WSA caucuses work hard to send all their members to conventions in disciplined blocs, but whether the young WSA people know exactly what they're into is another matter. In Chicago last winter, for instance, newly organized WSA members were told they should raise money to go "fight racism" at some vaguely described student meeting in Texas; it turned out that they were really being dispatched to fight SDS at the winter council. Some WSA caucuses sincerely believe themselves independent from PL control—just as many people in PL's earlier front organization, the May 2nd Movement, did. But that feeling is inevitably illusory: WSA is simply the device that PL uses to recruit young naifs for Party cadres and SDS control.

To see the divisions at last week's convention—and the eventual split between SDS and PL into rival organizations—as merely factional fights is to ignore their historical context and underlying meaning: the Movement fighting off a destructive force. To succeed, SDS had to reaffirm the traditions of native American radicalism of which it is the guardian, without losing the sense of worldwide revolution that had driven people into the streets in the first place. In mechanical terms, it had to throw off the PL incubus and accept the challenge to define its own self-conscious revolutionary ideology. Whether SDS can survive that struggle and remain a viable political organization is hard to predict now with any certainty. But what is more certain—and entirely exhilarating to the Movement "side"—is that SDS has at least taken the challenge seriously.

From the beginning, there was a "High Noon" quality to the convention week, a promise of shoot-it-out on the Coliseum floor: If not with guns, then at least with low-caliber word-bullets and ideological grenades. For there were two bodies approaching each other from opposite ends of the street, and there wasn't room enough in the center of town for both.

The delegates assembled in desultory Movement style, fashionably late by six hours for the opening session on

Wednesday. They were not entirely at fault for the delay: They had to push into the hall past rows of well-suited reporters and police agents, then join slow-moving registration and frisking lines (no guns, cameras, knives or dope). At least, the strict security (which still let some snoopers through) reflected the individual sense of siege that many of the activists and organizers feel in their own locales.

Inside the ratty, batty old auditorium, the scheduled boredom of agenda-making and vote-jockeying eventually got underway, and it was not long before the first test of strength between PL and SDS developed. The issue was procedural, but it contained an attractive substantive twist: Delegates had to vote speaking permission for Chris Milton, a young American who went to school in China and joined a platoon of Red Guards in a "long march" through the countryside. PL was against the idea: Milton apparently espoused a "bad line" on American politics, although few of the non-PL delegates were able to tell just what was the trouble.

The most vociferous bloc in favor of Milton was the "Action Faction" of the Ohio-Michigan SDS region. At one heated point in the debate on Milton, the entire bloc—50 people or more—jumped on their chairs, whipped out their Little Red Books, and began a joyful parody/performance of a Red Guard rally: "Ho, Ho, Ho Chi Minh: NLF is Gonna Win!" and "Mao Tse-tung, Mao Tse-tung: Dare to Struggle, Dare to Win!" Those in the hall who could not yet identify the factions were puzzled and perhaps appalled; but the obvious hilarity on the chanters' faces placed them clearly outside the dead-serious PL style. It was the best kind of guerrilla theater, in which the action means something both for itself and for a lesson, and the spirit is both enlivening and instructive.

The Action Faction never lost its prominence as the funny, tough and spirited pep squad of the SDS regulars. At key moments, its leaders surfaced in catalytic roles: Terry Robbins introduced a procedural point Friday night which set in motion the eventual SDS "walkout"; Bill Ayers drew up the statement to "exclude" PL from the SDS organization. Ayers later was voted one of the three national secretaries on SDS' slate of officers.

The Ohio-Michigan group was only one of a dozen or more major factions, tendencies and caucuses on the SDS regulars' side. To tell the players, or at least tell the plays, scorecards of a kind were provided in the appearance from time to time of proposals, resolutions, papers and uncategorizable ideological documents representing the various caucuses. The San Francisco Bay Area Revolutionary Union (called the RU) distributed its "Red Papers"; an SDS National Office *group-uscule* (known as Klonsky-Coleman) passed out its "Revolutionary Youth Movement—II" proposal; and there were papers from anarchists, left-social-democrats, Harvard Marxist intellectuals, campus coalitions and local action projects.

But the most significant ideological force with SDS was a group of 11 New York and Midwestern activists and intellectuals who had drawn up an analytical and programmatic thesis called, simply, "You Don't Need a Weatherman to Know Which Way the Wind Blows" (the title is from Dylan—a characteristic weapon for that group to use against PL). "Weatherman" was a 16,000-word paper which made the first and crucial attempt at defining an ideology and a program for SDS as a movement of the most aggressive part of white radical youth. As a basic platform, it was the first major overhaul SDS has had since the "Port Huron Statement" and "America and the New Era," long ago (five years seems like a century) in the organization's post-liberal infancy and puberty.

Weatherman was both too short and too long, too rambling as an action guide and too sketchy for a coherent work of political philosophy. It was assertive in places where reasoned explanation was needed, and obtuse in other places where definition and delineation were required. A viscous rhetoric suffused the whole. But despite all those disabilities, Weatherman produced a valuable and honest set of notes for a native American revolutionary youth movement, in a setting of worldwide liberation struggles.

In simple summary (Weatherman itself is a barely reducible

summary), the paper presented this argument: Opposition to US imperialism is the major international struggle today, and the "primary contradiction" of capitalism. Those who are leading the fight are the guerrillas of the Third World (principally, now, the Vietnamese and the Latin American guevaristas) and those of the "internal" black colony within the US. The empire will lose its grip as its resources are over-extended in dealing with the combined foreign and domestic rebellion: The US military and economic system cannot successfully maintain itself against intensive, expanded, and protracted insurgency.

That central idea implies several consequences: First, the black liberation movement in the US is the most important element of the whole process. As part of the Third World opposition, it could eventually bring down the imperial system; the role of white radicals is primarily (although importantly) supportive and extensive.

Second, the way in which the various foreign and domestic colonies arrive at the revolutionary stage is through their own fights for "self-determination." Of course, the nature of that process is vastly different in Vietnam and black America, but in both cases the colonized community must become conscious of its own identity: That is, blacks will organize themselves separately from whites, and form whatever alliances they need on their own terms.

Third, the youth movement did not spring full-blown from abstract idealism, but is a specific response to the black movement and the worldwide "war" against the American empire; it must now reach out of its middle-class origins to a base in the white working class and the permanent drop-out culture—without giving up what it has already done to organize students at all the "best" schools. For as the lower classes come increasingly up against the system (often symbolized by police or military authorities), they can move to fight it more surely than the "privileged" students higher up on the class ladder. Strategically, work should concentrate on building city-wide movements, based on intensive youth organizing across a whole range of issues.

Fourth, the several community "movements" should begin to think of themselves as cadres and collectives in the first stages of formation of a revolutionary political party.

In concept, Weatherman's chief distraction seemed to be in its specific reference to PL ideology. It was written in Aesopian style: Each section meant something in itself, and another thing in reaction to PL. The treatment of the idea of black people in the US as a "caste" and a "colony" contained an implicit reference to PL's notion that blacks have no functional quality outside their "class" condition as super-exploited workers. The emphasis on the Third World was specifically aimed at PL's arrogant, carping criticism of the Vietnamese and Cuban revolutions.

Weatherman's ideological point-making did not grow out of an intellectual construct (as PL ideology does), but from the real concerns of SDS organizers—in their local fights with PL as well as their organizing work. PL has frustrated SDS' attempts to develop and energize the anti-war movement around the identification its members feel with the NLF. In the same way, the document tried to justify the natural inclination of SDS people to ally with the Black Panthers (and counterpart chicano groups, such as the Young Lords in Chicago)—against the opposition of PL, which finds the Panthers and the Lords guilty of "chauvinistic nationalism." There was some attempt—not very complete—to integrate women's liberation into the theoretical whole; for it is a movement which SDS people now find immensely important. The idea of city-wide, neighborhood-based youth organizing comes out of the Action Faction's work in the cities and campuses of Ohio, and similar operations in the New York and New Jersey area.

If it was difficult to understand Weatherman without knowing its referents in SDS' experience, it was just as hard to understand the many levels on which the convention seemed to be operating. Every procedural debate contained ideological implications and one-upmanship games that only a handful of the delegates could fathom. For instance, an SDS proposal to have the three outgoing national secretaries give reports to the body was primarily a (not very subtle) attempt to pit the two forceful SDS-leaning secretaries against the weaker WSA partisan.

In that atmosphere, the "panel discussions" of the first three days degenerated into polemic-slinging contests between PL and SDS, at a rock-bottom level of debate. The one on women's liberation was a gross horror show; another on racism was little more than a screaming match between PL's Jared Israel and SDS' Mike Klonsky ("Klonsky's an authoritarian motherfucker," one SDS type in the audience said during the debate; "but he's *our* authoritarian motherfucker").

But what went on off the platform—the things that are never reported in the straight press and rarely even in Movement papers—was the exact antithesis of the events on-stage. Many of the caucuses and informal workshops on the SDS side and within WSA as well—where they were not dominated by PL cadres—worked in the close, undogmatic style which is the best tradition SDS keeps. And although very little about ideas and ideology could be learned from listening to the speakers at the podium, people did glean a great deal of understanding by bouncing ideas off one another.

The low point in the official proceedings was reached early Thursday night, when a clutch of Black Panthers arrived to speak. PL's sullen reception turned to noisy hostility when the first of the Panther speakers began baiting the delegates about women's liberation, and proceeded to promote "pussy power" as a revolutionary tactic. White delegates from the two sides all but shouted him down; a second Panther tried to retrieve the situation, but drew even sharper cat-calls from the audience. Finally, the third Panther combined part of an apology with an attack on white radicals' intellectual game-playing, and seemed to salvage some part of the disastrous performance. Typically, SDS people treated the affair as a healthy opening of criticism between allied movements; PL kept crying "male chauvinism"—in part, surely, as an opportune defense against the same charge SDS makes against PL ideology.

The Panthers' alliance with SDS, formalized by the white organization last winter in Austin, is a fragile affair at best. But it is the best attempt since the break-up of the "integrated" Southern student movement four years ago to align black and white radicals for joint action: this time on the basis of separate organizations with socialist ideas. Both the Panthers and SDS are anxious to preserve the relationship; the Panthers agreed to come to the convention to advance it, despite the predictable hostility from anti-white militant forces in the black community. PL, naturally, saw the Panthers' appearance as a bald power play by Mike Klonsky, the spearhead of SDS' alliance with both the Panthers and the Young Lords. And PL's perception was reinforced Friday night, when—in an atmosphere of growing rivalry between the two sides—the Panthers reappeared for the specific purpose of attacking the PL contempt for black self-determination.

PL people screamed at SDS for its "racist" use of the Panthers as a weapon of debate; SDS shouted back that that very argument revealed PL's "racist" notion that blacks cannot arrive at their own independent politics. PL's Jeff Gordon and a wedge of supporters seized the platform. The noise level in the hall rose to new peaks of intensity, along with the tension. Mark Rudd moved to recess for the evening, and when that motion failed, the SDS walkout began. As the delegates left, PL's cheerleaders began their last chant: "No split, no split, no split!"

Somewhat less than half the people in the meeting hall filed into the dark, dusty sports arena next door, and arranged themselves in rows of bleachers. SDS security guards were posted at the passageway connecting the adjoining rooms. No one then had the slightest idea of how the walkout would resolve itself, but some kind of order in the "caucus" was assembled, and speakers paced the boarded floor as they shouted to the bleachers what sense they made of the move. Jim Mellen, a solemn, analytical "Weatherman," conceded that the SDS side had not acquitted itself impressively in the tactics of the split; for a while, some of the national leaders seemed to entertain fantasies of doing the whole business over again, only this time more cleanly and clearly. Several speakers argued that the break had come squarely on the principle of SDS' support for the Panthers and PL's "racism." But most people had the feeling that the split was more contextual than pretextual.

It was true that neither side had acted with much nobility during the final stages of the confrontation. But if fault could be assigned in broader context, it seemed to lie with PL. Gresham's Law applies in paraphrase: Bad politics drives good politics out. PL had made contributions to the Movement in its association with SDS (nobody loses all the time) but its overall effect had been deformative: It forced SDS into two years or more of reactive maneuvers, inevitably hypocritical and unproductive. So the discussion dragged on in both halls until midnight.

When the SDS side met again in the arena late Saturday morning, spirits were sailing. All night, meetings of regional groups and political blocs had given people the idea that the split was not only inevitable, but somehow liberating. "We feel like we did inside one of the Columbia buildings," a girl told the crowd.

It was left to Bernardine Dohrn, one of SDS' three national secretaries, to sum up the meaning of the break and suggest a course of action. In what was obviously the outstanding political speech of the whole week, she explained the split with PL in the stream of Movement history, and claimed legitimacy for SDS as the keeper of a tradition that now was finding increasingly radical expression. The youth movement in America, she said, was spawned by black student sit-ins in the South, and energized by the guerrillas of Vietnam and Cuba. It was not now going to deny its sources for the sake of PL's metaphysic. It was a thorough, tight—and devastating—job. "We are not a caucus," she said at the end. "We are SDS." And suddenly it all became true to the crowds in the bleachers, and they knew that there was no going back.

By evening, the strategy of "exclusion" was developed (it was impossible on short notice to arrive at an opposite strategy of unity: No set of principles could be found to please all the disparate elements within SDS). It contained a bill of particulars against PL, a list of all the ways in which, nationally and locally, PL and WSA had put blocks in the way of what SDS wanted and needed most to do. There was not much worry about the parliamentary legality, or lack of it, in the move: The glue which had stuck the two bodies together had long ago disintegrated, and there was no basis at all for parliamentary trust. People were more worried about a construction of SDS "anti-communism" which might be placed on the exclusion, which in form—not content—was somewhat too reminiscent of the "expulsions" of radicals from liberal organizations two decades ago. To disarm that criticism, SDS speakers affirmed their pro-communism and in the exclusion statement construed PL to be "objectively anti-communist" because of its scorn for particular liberation struggles. When the order was done and approved, the bleachers emptied and the SDS delegates filed silently back into the hall for the reading-out of Progressive Labor.

Bernardine Dohrn presented the bill of particulars, which now seemed more like a bill of divorcement. The SDS delegates stood in aisles on the perimeters of the auditorium. The PL cadres sat scowling; the WSA kids sat uncomprehending. At the end of the order, PL people responded with a planned mass nervous giggle. Then, flanked by a dozen SDS delegates (chicks up front) who stood Panther-style on the podium, Bernardine Dohrn started to speak in explanation of the exclusion. But after initial attempts to quiet hecklers, the PL leaders began to cheer-lead the heckles themselves, and the speech sputtered to its conclusion: "Long live the victory of the people's war!" From Dylan to Lin Piao in 48 hours.

For the last day of the convention, PL met in the Coliseum to ponder the most perplexing strategic question in its history: What to do about its coveted "mass base," which had suddenly cut out? PL never had an interest in SDS except as a supplier of troops. It will no doubt try for a while to establish its legitimacy as the true SDS and build up WSA chapters on those terms; as a mass student organization it has much less of a chance now of survival than SDS.

In a church across town, around the corner from its national office, SDS met in a much more up-beat mood. A tentative list of unity "principles" was drawn up for circulation and discussion at the local chapter level; national demonstrations against the war were set for Chicago in late September, to coincide with the opening of the conspiracy trial of eight white and black radicals accused of fomenting the fights at last summer's Democratic National Convention. Delegates reopened the continuing problem of leader-base relations between the SDS National Office and the local chapters. Finally, a slate of three national secretaries and an eight-man National Interim Committee was elected. All three secretaries—Mark Rudd, Jeff Jones and Bill Ayers—had been "Weathermen."

The significance of their election lies in that document. Although it never came up for convention action of any kind, it was an expression (chief among many) of the crucial theme of the week: the attempt to begin work on a New Left revolutionary socialist ideology and program. SDS' main problems have grown up in the failure to do that job. Is has never really defined what it is—and how it differs from, say, Progressive Labor. And for that neglect, SDS "alumni" have strayed, because SDS could not identify itself as the critical center of the Movement.

The reasons SDS has failed so far in those respects are for the most part good ones. The original tensions within the Movement between personal liberation and political mobilization still play themselves out at every level. SDS contains both traits. What has to happen finally for SDS to survive is an integration of those traditions, probably in response to outside challenge and as a result of internal synthesis. Only then will the New Left become an American liberation movement.

Hot Town: Summer In The City Or I Ain't Gonna Work On Maggie's Farm No More

Bill Ayers and Jim Mellen

I. TOWARD A REVOLUTIONARY MOVEMENT

Over the past few months, SDS has developed a correct transitional strategy for itself. That strategy is based on an understanding of the class nature of this society; on an understanding that the sharpest struggles against the ruling class are being waged by the oppressed nations against U.S. imperialism, and that all our actions must flow from our identity as part of an international struggle against U.S. imperialism. It is a strategy that understands the need for SDS to tie itself to these struggles, and to make itself something more than it is: to transform itself into a student movement into a working class youth movement.

It is clear that, although a successful revolution in this country is in no way inevitable, any revolution—to have even a small chance of success—would have to be a revolution of

From *New Left Notes*, April 4, 1969. (Bill Ayers and Jim Mellen were both founding members of Weatherman. This is the text of a resolution passed at the March 1969 National Council meeting. It is a revised version of a proposal for a summer program passed earlier by the Michigan Regional Conference.)

the working class. This is not to say that SDS as an organization should move immediately to organizing workers, or that we have, at this point, a precise enough understanding of the various segments and characteristics of the working class. It is only to assert an understanding of the fact that the struggle for freedom that we are involved in can never succeed without the total, fundamental economic and social transformation in which the working class overthrows and liquidates the ruling class.

Up until recently, SDS has been exclusively a student movement. Furthermore, it has been a student movement concentrated primarily on the elite campuses of Harvard, Chicago, Berkeley, Michigan. This is beginning to change. San Francisco State replaces Berkeley, Michigan State replaces Michigan, as the important centers of struggle. And SDS begins to spring up in the high schools and off the campus altogether.

But more importantly, the movement begins to happen in these places. In most cities, high schools are blowing up so fast that SDS organizers can't keep up with them. Community and junior colleges are increasingly the scenes of struggle and confrontation. And the army has become the time bomb of the ruling class.

We're faced with two realities: that, in the past, SDS has been primarily an elite student group, and that, at this point in history, young people in the schools generally, and in the army, are actively resisting the special oppression they face. Given what SDS is, what is happening in this society, and what the movement must become in order to have even a chance of success, it is clear that SDS must begin to consciously transform itself from a student movement into a working-class youth movement. That is, SDS must become more than itself, must move, in the only organic way open to it, to become a self-conscious working-class movement. And it must do this by emphasizing the commonality of the oppression and struggles of youth, and by making these struggles class conscious.

This is possible because of the material basis of the oppression of youth. The majority of young people in America today are either in school, in the army, or unemployed. Specifically in the schools and in the army, young people perform tasks that have no relevance to their own needs but are key to the functioning of capitalism: training young people to fit into a more highly skilled work force, forcing them to defend imperialism and the Empire in struggles against national liberation movements, and, in all cases, deferring young people for longer and longer periods of time from the productive work force. Thus, there is significant class content to the oppression of the vast majority of young people. This is not to say that youth is a class—or that young people's struggles are always in the interest of the working class as a whole. While it's true that youth aren't hardened into class positions and generally reflect all the different class interests, it is clear that the oppression of youth by imperialism hits hardest on working-class youth, especially black and brown youth. We must attack this oppression in a class way, that is, raise the interests of the most oppressed sectors first. That is the only basis that exists for revolutionary class unity. Our task must be to understand the class content of youth's oppression, to specify it in practice, and to build class consciousness through struggle.

DISCIPLINE NEEDED

In order for SDS to succeed at this task it will take tremendous self-consciousness and discipline from the membership. It will involve high school organizers consciously organizing among the lowest tracked kids. It will involve organizers consciously developing bases in community colleges. And it will involve disciplined cadre entering the armed forces and work places as organizers.

There are two important developments that would help this process. These should be seen as urgent tasks. First, is the development of cadre. Seriousness and self-consciousness inside the organization are essential as SDS begins to transform itself into a revolutionary movement. Through collective political experience and study, cadre can be developed who can bring these things to SDS. The function of cadre—through exemplary action and through political education—is to broaden the movement and build class consciousness in a self-conscious way, as well as help consolidate growth and fight uneven development.

A second important task is the concretization of our politics through practice. The development of our politics in the past few months leaves us with an understanding of the oppression of youth, only in a general way. We see that working-class youth are oppressed in specific ways and that the existing base of SDS in colleges and universities has much in common with youth in all sectors of the working class. We must now learn more about the issues which face city youth especially, the kind of consciousness which is developing there, and the organizational forms which can make struggle around those issues and that consciousness coherent. In order to make SDS, now basically a student movement, something more than it is, a revolutionary youth movement, we must learn more about city youth and the class content of their struggle. We must bring organizers from our existing constituency more directly into organizing situations of our potential constituency, thereby creating a material force for the further development of our politics.

The task of developing cadres, as well as the task of broadening our constituency to other sections of white working-class youth, both have a special urgency at this time. This is due to the advanced level of political struggle of the black liberation movement. To recognize the vanguard character of the black liberation struggle means to recognize its importance to the "white" movement. The black liberation struggle has been instrumental in winning much of the white movement to a clearer understanding of imperialism, class oppression within the U.S., the reactionary nature of pacifism, the need for armed struggle as the only road to revolution, and other essential truths which were not predominant within our movement in the past. It must be clear that setbacks to the vanguard are tremendous setbacks to the people's movement as a whole.

WHITE FIGHTING FORCE

Yet repression at this time is very serious against the political vanguard of the black liberation struggle, the Black Panther Party. And this repression is facilitated by the absence of substantial material support—power—by the white movement. Unless we recognize the urgency of fighting white supremacy by building the material strength of the white movement to be a conscious, organized, mobilized fighting force capable of giving real support to the black liberation struggle, we will be deserting the most advanced leadership of that struggle to the free hand of ruling-class repression.

Thus the urgency of broadening the movement to more proletarian sections of white industrial workers and youth is not because in some way concern with the white working class is an alternative political direction from the support for the black struggle. Rather, it is a necessary extension of the support. Nor is "white working-class organizing" an alternative to the struggle within the "student movement" against pacifism and social democratic and revisionist ideas, which feed on the isolation of the student movement from the masses of working people. In both cases, we seek to expand our base not in conflict with the black liberation struggle or "student organizing" but because of it.

In terms of cadre development, an investigation of and intimacy with the real life situation and struggles of the oppressed sections of working-class youth will give formerly "student" cadres a clearer identification with and understanding of the interests of the class as a whole. Thus, on return to a campus situation, they will be better equipped to fight the go-slowism of student provincialism.

II. PROGRAM

A large number of SDS people should come to Detroit to participate in a summer of work and study. A program that calls for SDS people to work as a group in the cities should first understand the history and failures of past SDS programs. While it is beyond the scope of this paper to develop a detailed critical history of SDS programs relating to the cities, we will make a couple of general comments that are particularly relevant.

In our past organizing we incorrectly thought that SDS people should totally follow the direction of the people with whom they were working. This on two levels: first, we assumed that SDS people were foreign elements who had to transform their identities, emulate others; and second, we thought that SDS people should totally take political direction from the people with whom they were organizing. Both of these are incorrect. The task should be to retain one's sense of identity, retain a sense of struggle from the campus, and at the same time build a movement which includes a broader constituency. This process may lead to SDS people undergoing fundamental changes, but consciousness must develop dialectically, not mechanically (like by getting a haircut).

SELECTION AND TRAINING

Participation in the summer program will be based primarily on self-selection, but we will emphasize that those who do become involved should see themselves as full-time SDS cadre, willing to work intensively for the development of the summer collective.

In preparation for the summer, we will continue our program of movement schools which we've developed over the past few months in Michigan. This is a program which involves chapters in intensive weekends of study around questions such as racism, imperialism, and corporate power. This program will intensify as we come closer to this summer.

Furthermore, we will set up special training sessions in Detroit for those who plan to participate in the summer program. These special sessions will include resource people leading discussions on such topics as the history of labor struggles in Detroit, the role of law in society and legal rights, and the political economy of the city. These special sessions will concentrate on preparing people for the summer experience and will be attended by people from all over the state who are coming to Detroit.

JOBS

People involved in the program will try to get jobs in the city. They will be made aware of the job situation in Detroit and urged to seek employment where it will provide the best experiences. Participants will get jobs in bars, restaurants, taxicabs, and shops, as well as a few working out of day-labor slave markets. Women will be urged to work in jobs where the employment of women is high: specific factories, as secretaries, waitresses, maids. The selection of the job place should be done on the basis that it is preferential for our people to work where there are either a great number of young workers, or a great number of unskilled workers; a company union or no union, or where there is rank and file dissent or black caucuses, etc. This is to be done so that the people involved are involved in the most relevant political experiences and for the greatest possible time. The jobs will be necessary to maintain the summer program financially, as well as to provide practical experience necessary toward the concretization of our politics.

STUDY

Workable study groups will be organized which will help people develop political perspective and intellectual background. Study will include revolutionary theory and organizaton, the political economy of monopoly capitalism, the history an development of racism, the history of the labor movement, as well as more specific areas of study, like Vietnam, the Middle East, and Cuba. A major area of study, which will involve some original research, will be the translation of economic power into political power in the city of Detroit. Toward the end of the summer study groups will be tying together their intellectual and practical work and attempting to make specific plans for fall strategy. This will include some campus work as well as GI organizing, high schools, and some on-the-job work.

SKILL-BUILDING

The summer should provide an opportunity to develop much-needed skills that SDS people have had neither the time nor the organization to develop in the past. We will organize groups to learn self-defense skills, printing, propaganda, auto mechanics, and how to do research. More groups will develop depending on the needs and interests of those involved.

LIFE IN THE CITY

People will be living in small groups throughout the city. There should be involvement by SDS people in the neighborhood issues as they come up: a fight in the park, a protest against the pigs. Further, the group as a whole can anticipate certain issues it will become involved in. For instance, we're sure that we'll have to deal with racism in a number of concrete situations. Detroit, with its giant auto corporations and sprawling universities, has created one of the largest ghettos in the country. Detroit is also the home of a large Panther organization and other militant black groups. Working out a relationship with these groups and becoming involved in issues to fight racism will be of primary importance.

The labor situation in Detroit will, almost certainly, be in intensive turmoil this summer. The existence of militant black caucuses in auto [unions] (DRUM, FRUM, ELRUM, etc.) has created a tense situation for the corporations and union bureaucracies, and has provided an alternative for workers. Some people from the SDS project will be in shops as will organizers from Detroit's National Organizing Committee and will be relating to these struggles on a day-to-day basis. The project as a whole must work out ways to support the struggles of revolutionaries in the shops.

Some people, especially those who've been drafted or plan to enter the armed forces soon, will be working around Fort Wayne handing out Vietnam GI and The Bond. They will try to develop an understanding of GI problems that will be valuable in the future.

Others are planning to work with high school kids around the Grande ballroom, hippy capitalist center of Detroit. They hope to develop in these kids an understanding of the ways in which revolutionary rhetoric and hippy culture can be made into commodities by the capitalists.

There will of course be other types of involvement in community issues which we can't foresee. But with this amount of activity going on, it's clear that logistics and coordination are going to be a problem. We will try to have a large meeting weekly to keep people in touch with what overall things are going on, and to maintain a sense of the strength and dynamic of the group.

An important tension should develop in a program between the collective life and training among the SDS people and the political outreach into the community. It will be important to maintain this tension and each person should adjust to the duality. Merely living together and studying would promote isolation and elitism (the value of study undirected by practical political activity is also questionable). Merely working in the community without a self-conscious development of cadre skills and organizational training would promote an undirected activism and lack of concrete political development.

Clearly, an important part of the white movement's fight against white chauvinism is the propaganda effect of the very existence of whites who are on the side of the blacks against the system. This begins to show the masses of white working people that the struggle is a class and political struggle, not a racial struggle. Thus, open, overt, visible political activity of our movement in support of the black struggle must be prominent in our priorities for the summer. Yet we must also understand that this "action propaganda" is not a substitute for going among the working masses, learning directly what their experiences and ideas are about, and doing direct propaganda among them. To correctly balance these two needs will be a central task of our summer effort.

The whole program should be seen as a step towards a strong revolutionary youth movement in Michigan. It should not be seen as an attempt to organize all of Detroit. After the summer, many people will probably return to their campuses to continue on-going SDS work. Many will stay in Detroit to help build a strong movement there, and some will be going into the armed forces and other constituencies to begin work. That this program develop is of crucial importance for the advancement of all this work, and the development of these organizers.

More On Youth Movement

Jim Mellen

At the Austin NC, it became clear that important differences existed among the people who had supported the "Revolutionary Youth Movement" proposal in Ann Arbor. For my part, I could not support the "May Day" resolution nor the "Schools Must Serve the People" resolution. Further, an amendment that I opposed was made to the "Summer Program" proposal. It is difficult to tell how important these differences will be in the future or whether they will work themselves out in practice, but at this point it is clear that they are based on differing theoretical conceptions of U.S. society. Rather than go over the specific arguments on the proposals, I would like to discuss those theoretical conceptions.

The points of difference fall into two broad groups: I) those concerning a class analysis of American society, and II) those concerning the specific nature of the crisis in capitalism in this period of history. I will deal with these two groups by laying out some of my own analysis as well as by discussing some questions that are raised in my mind about the subject. I hope this will provoke further discussion in New Left Notes.

CLASS ANALYSIS

I) Class Analysis of American Society. Marx's prophecy of the development of capitalist society into two classes, a large working class and a small ruling bourgeoisie, has nearly come

From *New Left Notes*, May 13, 1969

true. Stated another way, the complete socialization of production and the concentration of production into the private ownership of a tiny number of people is very nearly complete in the USA. If class membership is determined by relationship to the means of production, in a Marxist fashion, then the vast majority of the people of this country, who own no means of production, and are forced to sell their labor power to someone who does, are members of the working class. This is not to ignore the vast differences among working people in terms of wages, working conditions and relative control over the work process. It is not to ignore the central fact of privilege which divides the masses of the working class and promotes false consciousness of particular interest as opposed to general class interest. It is, rather, to point out that the socialization of the ownership and control of the means of production is in the objective class interests of the overwhelming majority of the people at this time—which is a radically different situation than has ever existed previously.

The bourgeoisie, for its part, is divided into the large corporate (liberal) monopoly bourgeoisie and the petit bourgeoisie, the latter of which is in our time very small and declining. If the bourgeoisie is defined as those who own and control means of production and who live by the exploitation of the labor of others, then the petit bourgeoisie is that group which employs and lives off small numbers of laborers. Throughout the development of capitalism, this petit bourgeoisie has seen its interests as opposed to the large bourgeoisie, whose developing monopolism threatens to wipe out the petit bourgeoisie as a class. The petit bourgeois consciousness has been an anti-monopolist consciousness. In this country, this group is almost entirely defeated. Monopoly capitalism dominates almost all lines of production and the petit bourgeoisie are staging a small but futile resistance. When Wallace says that "pointy-headed intellectuals in Washington think they can tell us how to live," and that he would "throw their briefcases into the Potomac," he is expressing the anti-monopolist sentiment that exists. But it is clear that he cannot win without winning over a vast segment of the working class, which will, of course, require a great deal of duplicity.

In the formal structure of U.S. Government, drawn up two centuries ago, the petit bourgeoisie appear to have power disproportionate to their numbers or economic strength, especially at the local and Congressional levels. If one followed day-to-day politics in U.S. newspapers, he might be convinced that the petit bourgeoisie were indeed powerful. A sophisticated view of U.S. politics, however, would indicate that the important decisions are not made at these levels, but are made at the top by agents of monopoly power.

In speaking of students, middle level management, highly skilled labor and professionals, many radicals would like to create a residual middle category and call it the petit bourgeoisie. First, this is a non-Marxist classification—not being based on relationship to the means of production. Second, the ideology which characterizes these groups is certainly not petit bourgeois anti-monopolist consciousness, but (to the extent that it is not proletarian ideology) it is ruling class, monopolist (what has come to be called corporate liberal) ideology.

Many radicals would also like to use the terms *"middle class"* to describe these groups. It is important to understand that the term "middle class" has little meaning in Marxist analysis. Marx himself was occasionally translated into English as saying that the petit bourgeois and professionals were middle class (a better translation would be intermediate classes), but in the bulk of his analysis he very carefully delineated objective class position based upon relationship to the means of production. In this country, the vast majority of the people generally referred to as "middle class" are objectively of the working class, and the socialization of the owhership and control of the means of production is objectively in their class interests.

There is one further reason for discarding the term "middle class." It tends to reinforce the notion put forward by liberal social scientists that this country has reached a period of calm based on an end of class antagonisms. Since there is one big happy class which anyone, from skilled worker to corporation executive, can be a member of, then there is no real reason to struggle. There are, of course, petty differences and small problems, but nothing really to be excited about, certainly nothing to be violent about. Things can be worked out over coffee, downtown. This notion must be smashed. One way to begin to smash it is to be clear about what class interests different people have. It does not help clarify objective interests when we use liberal terminology which describes an invented class.

Aside from the working class, the petit bourgeoisie and the monopoly bourgeoisie in the U.S., there are a small number of intermediate people, namely, self-employed professionals who live mainly off their own labor and not off labor that they hire. The class position and resulting ideology of these people is admittedly confused, but today they are a very small group. In addition, it must be understood that increasing numbers of professionals are not self-employed, but work for wages in law firms, clinics, and other large institutions. (Correspondingly, it should be recognized that many petit bourgeois merchants and others have mitigated their class position through franchise and other arrangements which leave them as mere agents of monopoly capital.)

BLACK VANGUARD

After pointing to the objective class position of most Americans, it is important to speak to the question of privilege. The central fact of privilege within the American class structure is nowhere more clearly seen than in the oppression of the black nation within the borders of the U.S. The fact of systematic preferential treatment of white workers over black and the resulting better conditions of white workers lay a material basis for a feeling that black workers threaten white privilege—and the resulting racist ideology which is fostered by that feeling of threat. This is the most important way in which the U.S. working class is divided and weakened. Two things result: 1) The participation by white workers in the oppression of the black nation gives an anti-colonial aspect—

in addition to the working-class aspect—to the struggle for black liberation. Fighting white supremacy is our first task. These two conditions, in addition to the high level of consciousness and militancy of the black colony, mean that at our point in history the black liberation struggle is the vanguard of the working-class movement.

One of the reasons for the confusion in class analysis which many radicals experience is the failure to distinguish between objective class position and prospects for the development of consciousness. That many (a majority) of our people are objectively of the working class does not necessarily mean that they will immediately become conscious of their class interests. The privileges that some workers have achieved are impediments to the development of working-class consciousness and class solidarity. But these privileges in no way change objective class interests. Privileged workers under capitalism can never acquire wages equal to their productivity and can never gain enough control over their lives and the productive forces to be able to avoid alienated labor as long as capitalism exists. Hence, they too are exploited, they too would benefit from the destruction of American imperialism.

The factors which determine the development of class consciousness and of the need for revolutionary socialism are the subject of a separate analysis. Marx and, especially, Lenin argued that the vanguard in the development of class consciousness would be the industrial workers in the large consolidated and rationalized manufacturing industries. This was for various reasons. Mainly, the need for cooperation and organization in the productive process of such plants—which was uncommon in capitalist society of that day—meant that these workers had a greater organizational ability and consciousness of the need for cooperation. (One thing must be clear: Marx and Lenin never argued that these workers would be in the vanguard because they were the most oppressed. They were certainly not the most oppressed and, further, the most oppressed are not always the most conscious of their oppression and of the revolutionary alternatives.) Marx and Lenin were proven correct by the Russian workers in the factories in Petrograd and Moscow who led the Russian Revolution.

Today, almost everyone in society works in a productive process involving a sophisticated division of labor. Further, the industrial workers in the U.S. have undergone a peculiar experience of relative success in organizing for and achieving higher wages and near failure in the development of the consciousness of a political role for the working class. The process by which the CIO was built and then emasculated and turned into an imperialist front should be the subject of great study by the left. What is clear is that a deal of sorts was struck between the labor bosses and the ruling class that 1) no communists would be allowed in union leadership, 2) CIO unions would assist imperialism in every way possible, including the fostering of anti-communist ideology, and 3) organized workers in U.S. factories would (for a while, anyway) be allowed certain gains in real wages (crumbs from the imperialist table, as Lenin put it) which would hopefully lay the material basis for support of the system. The effect of this bribery is a subject of great debate, but it is clear that class consciousness among U.S. workers is lower than almost anywhere in the world.

NEED FOR THEORY

We need a theory which will help us understand which segments of the working class can develop class consciousness and lead the rest. It is not enough merely to say that some segments of the working class are necessary to the construction of socialism—as surely the industrial workers are—but some reason must be offered as to why that segment is likely to break out of the mystification and particularism in which it is now bogged down.

What can be clearly seen in U.S. society today is that a vanguard role in developing working-class consciousness (at least to the very primitive extent to which it is developing at all) is being played primarily by the blacks, as well as the youth. Many of the industrial labor struggles today are an extension of the black community's struggle for self-determination into the factories. To answer the question of the U.S. working class requires an analysis and an argument. To continue irrationally to insist on the vanguard role of factory workers in our changed circumstances is mere assertion of orthodoxy, and not an argument.

For our part, SDS has committed itself to the development of a Revolutionary Youth Movement. In the present transitional period, we intend to organize among youth, penetrate the working class as much as possible with revolutionary ideas, and develop our analysis concerning who will be the vanguard of the working class. The revolutionary youth movement proposal was conceived of as a transitional strategy for the development of a specifically working-class movement. It recommends the transcendance of SDS from a radical students organization to a class-conscious movement of the youth of the entire working class. It is distinguished from the Worker-Student Alliance by its recognition of revolutionary youth as a part of the working class.

POSITION OF YOUTH

In this context, before turning to the nature of capitalist crisis in our time, it is necessary to discuss the class position of youth and especially students. The overwhelming majority of American youth (say 18-24) are students, soldiers and unemployed. Also, the overwhelming majority come from working-class backgrounds—no matter how comfortable, mystified, or bourgeois an ideology they may have. The overwhelming majority, further, are destined for jobs and positions within society which are securely within the working class—no matter how conscious they are of the privileges their specific future positions offer. I would argue, however, that what gives specific class content to the struggles of youth—in the schools and in the army specifically—is the proletarianization of the roles youth play in those institutions.

In the army, coerced though he may be to join and intangible though his product may be, the soldier provides a very necessary labor for capitalism—no different than any other service labor. In the schools, the training of labor which cannot be done by individual capitalists, is done by that agent of monopoly capital—the State. The student, by studying, creates value within himself in the form of skilled labor power, and in so doing performs an exploited and alienated labor. The nature of the specific labor of the student gives his struggles to control or change the conditions of that labor a class content. The struggles of students to break out of their alienated labor and destroy the class institutions in which they exist are part of the class struggle.

Some argue that students are intellectuals in the classic sense that Lenin and Mao conceived of revolutionary intellectuals imbuing the masses with the idea of socialism. It must be understood that Lenin and Mao were writing about societies more than 80% illiterate. Students then participated in more mass communications and were able to carry ideas from one sector to another. The student today is in a totally different role. All of society is literate and heavily saturated with mass communications. The student is merely a worker in training and is as mystified as the general population. Besides, anyone who has any experience in our organization knows that it is not an intellectual movement and does not pretend to be.

Others argue that when students support working-class struggles they are working class, and when they do not, they are not. This garbles the entire analysis. The class content of the students' struggle is determined by their objective class position. This does not mean there is never any false consciousness. Clearly, the demand for student power is analogous to the skilled workers' struggle to protect privileges—say to constrict access to the skill in keeping out blacks. This kind of struggle for protection of privilege must be opposed. But neither the student seeking student power nor the skilled worker seeking exclusion is thereby outside the working class—he is struggling for a particular, rather than a class, interest based on a false consciousness. To overcome this false consciousness it is necessary to continue to raise issues concerning the most oppressed sectors of the working class—especially the Vietnamese and the blacks—and to emphasize that their struggle is the same one.

CRISIS OF CAPITALISM

II) The Nature of the Current Crisis in Capitalism. The classical Marxist concept of capitalist crisis was based upon a system of competitive capitalism, in which a large number of small capitalists were competing with one another on the basis of price. The basic contradiction of capitalism—that between the price of labor and its productivity—manifested itself at the level of the whole economy as a total production of goods produced by labor greater than the demand for the goods based on the wages paid to labor. This contradiction could be forestalled as a crisis by investment in production of machines which produce goods, but this only led to a greater productivity of labor and thereby a greater crisis. Periodically, this crisis led to a depression in which the weaker firms were either bought out or failed altogether and production was consolidated into fewer hands. Marxists argued that this would lead to succeedingly more severe crises leading to the eventual breakdown of capitalism. In this model, the struggle of workers over their wages and working conditions was central to the crisis. Demands for higher wages related directly to the capitalists' competitive position. The crisis in capitalism, then, manifested itself at the point of production.

Two things developed out of competitive capitalism: the system of monopoly capitalism and imperialism. The concentration of production into fewer and fewer hands means that competition in terms of price has nearly been eliminated. Monstrous firms, then, have no longer the problem of cutting costs in order to remain competitive. On the contrary, cutting costs while maintaining price means merely the expansion of profit margins, resulting in huge amounts of surplus capital requiring absorption in new investment outlets. In addition, wage demands by workers can be passed on to consumers by monopolies as price increases. The result is that a general increase in the money wages of the whole working class means only a general price increase and no increase in real wages. In this situation, the specific crisis of monopoly capitalism manifests itself not at the point of production but in ever increasing amounts of surplus capital requiring investment outlets. The manner and form of the absorption of this capital surplus is what gives character to the crisis of our society.

Vast investments in the production of military hardware and research, combined with imperialism's need to create a world-wide repressive military network, have resulted in the development of a military-industrial complex within the ruling class which continues to waste resources and forge a militarized, authoritarian regimen.

Vast investments in the system of higher education provide military research, produce a highly skilled labor force, and defer the entrance of surplus labor into the labor force. The draft, the tracking system and other instruments of channelling force the young people into these institutions, where they suffer severe alienation. The youth rebellion stems from these conditions.

The increasingly high ratio of capital to labor means that less unskilled labor is required and a large section of the working class, mainly black, is perpetually unemployed. The containment of this surplus labor in ghettoes is a result.

Since investments in social services and welfare do not produce the return or the accelerator effect on the economy of military hardware investments, many social institutions are starving for funds. The school systems, welfare systems, distribution systems, medical care, transportation systems, etc. of the large cities are nearing collapse, and severe social strains result. Rebellion among the masses of urban dwellers is only barely repressed.

The driving thrust of imperialism to control and develop suitable investment opportunities means a steadily deteriorating quality of existence for the workers of the whole world—and the struggles against that thrust do not occur mainly at the point of production. The struggle of Third World peoples for liberation is primarily a nationalist struggle—and it occurs primarily as a military struggle. The struggle of blacks for liberation in this country is also a nationalist struggle, and is led primarily not by blacks who are industrial workers, but by the street people, unstable workers that Panthers refer to as "field niggers." For the youth of the mother country, the class struggle manifests itself around issues like the draft, the ruling class uses of the university, police and other agents of the ruling class for social control. Throughout society, institutions designed to stabilize and serve capitalism are breaking down, and struggle ensues.

If the breakdown of the U.S. capitalist system is not necessarily going to come as a huge depression but as a gradual deterioration of the social structure, then our revolutionary movement must be prepared for the eventuality, not just of a general strike, but of a gradual raising of the level of struggle around various issues resulting in a general protracted civil war.

Dogmatic applications of Marxism to the U.S. make two important errors: 1) They attribute to the struggle of industrial labor a centrality to the class struggle, or worse, they say that only industrial labor struggles are the class struggle. Since industrial labor is only a segment of the broader working class and since it is not yet playing a vanguard role in the class struggle, a proper perspective on labor struggles requires that they be seen as only one front on which we are fighting. What we need is an analysis and an argument concerning what sectors of the total working class can develop consciousness and lead the rest. 2) Dogmatic applications of Marxism to the U.S. also fail to attribute to the struggles of youth a significant class content. When youth support the struggle of the Vietnamese and the blacks and simultaneously fight the class nature of the schools, they are waging class war. When they do not wage these struggles, they impede the class struggle. Any argument that students can struggle only on the basis of their immediate needs for an improved education—with the implication that when the struggle moves beyond anti-imperialism to the construction of socialism itself, the students will have no further progressive role to play and must yield to the industrial workers—is based on a faulty class analysis and a faulty understanding of capitalist crisis in our time.

SDS Convention, June 1969. Bernardine Dohrn speaks to the anti-PL delegates prior to official split with PL. Photo: David Fenton/LNS

You Don't Need A Weatherman To Know Which Way The Wind Blows

Submitted by Karin Ashley, Bill Ayers, Bernardine Dohrn, John Jacobs, Jeff Jones, Gerry Long, Howie Machtinger, Jim Mellen, Terry Robbins, Mark Rudd and Steve Tappis.

I. INTERNATIONAL REVOLUTION

> *The contradiction between the revolutionary peoples of Asia, Africa and Latin America and the imperialists headed by the United States is the principal contradiction in the contemporary world. The development of this contradiction is promoting the struggle of the people of the whole world against US imperialism and its lackeys.*
>
> —Lin Piao, Long Live the Victory of People's War!

People ask, what is the nature of the revolution that we talk about? Who will it be made by, and for, and what are its goals and strategy?

The overriding consideration in answering these questions is that the main struggle going on in the world today is between US imperialism and the national liberation struggles against it. This is essential in defining political matters in the whole world: because it is by far the most powerful, every other empire and petty dictator is in the long run dependent on US imperialism, which has unified, allied with, and defended all of the reactionary forces of the whole world. Thus, in considering every other force or phenomenon, from Soviet imperialism or Israeli imperialism to "workers struggle" in France or Czechoslovakia, we determine who are our friends and who are our enemies according to whether they help US

From *New Left Notes*, June 18, 1969

imperialism or fight to defeat it.

So the very first question people in this country must ask in considering the question of revolution is where they stand in relation to the United States as an oppressor nation, and where they stand in relation to the masses of people throughout the world whom US imperialism is oppressing.

The primary task of revolutionary struggle is to solve this principal contradiction on the side of the people of the world. It is the oppressed peoples of the world who have created the wealth of this empire and it is to them that it belongs; the goal of the revolutionary struggle must be the control and use of this wealth in the interests of the oppressed peoples of the world.

It is in this context that we must examine the revolutionary struggles in the United States. We are within the heartland of a world-wide monster, a country so rich from its world-wide plunder that even the crumbs doled out to the enslaved masses within its borders provide for material existence very much above the conditions of the masses of people of the world. The US empire, as a world-wide system, channels wealth, based upon the labor and resources of the rest of the world, into the United States. The relative affluence existing in the United States is directly dependent upon the labor and natural resources of the Vietnamese, the Angolans, the Bolivians and the rest of the peoples of the Third World. All of the United Airlines Astrojets, all of the Holiday Inns, all of Hertz's automobiles, your television set, car and wardrobe already belong, to a large degree to the people of the rest of the world.

Therefore, any conception of "socialist revolution" simply in terms of the working people of the United States, failing to recognize the full scope of interests of the most oppressed peoples of the world, is a conception of a fight for a particular privileged interest, and is a very dangerous ideology. While the control and use of the wealth of the Empire for the people of the whole world is also in the interests of the vast majority of the people in this country, if the goal is not clear from the start we will further the preservation of class

society, oppression, war, genocide, and the complete emiseration of everyone, including the people of the US.

The goal is the destruction of US imperialism and the
achievement of a classless world: world communism. Winning
state power in the US will occur as a result of the military
forces of the US overextending themselves around the world
and being defeated piecemeal; struggle within the US will be
a vital part of this process, but when the revolution triumphs
in the US it will have been made by the people of the whole
world. For socialism to be defined in national terms within so
extreme and historical an oppressor nation as this is only
imperialist national chauvinism on the part of the "movement."

II. WHAT IS THE BLACK COLONY?

Not every colony of people oppressed by imperialism lies
outside the boundaries of the US. Black people within North
America, brought here 400 years ago as slaves and whose
labor, as slaves, built this country, are an internal colony
within the confines of the oppressor nation. What this means
is that black people are oppressed as a whole people, in the
institutions and social relations of the country, apart from
simply the consideration of their class position, income, skill,
etc., as individuals? What does this colony look like? What is
the basis for its common oppression and why is it important?

One historically important position has been that the black
colony only consists of the black belt nation in the South,
whose fight for national liberation is based on a common
land, culture, history and economic life. The corollary of this
position is that black people in the rest of the country are a
national minority but not actually part of the colony themselves; so the struggle for national liberation is for the black
belt, and not all blacks; black people in the north, not actually part of the colony, are part of the working class of the
white oppressor nation. In this formulation northern black
workers have a "dual role"—one an interest in supporting the
struggle in the South, and opposing racism, as members of

the national minority; and as northern "white nation" workers whose class interest is in integrated socialism in the north. The consistent version of this line actually calls for integrated organizing of black and white workers in the north along what it calls "class" lines.

This position is wrong; in reality, the black colony does not exist simply as the "black belt nation," but exists in the country as a whole. The common oppression of black people and the common culture growing out of that history are not based historically or currently on their relation to the territory of the black belt, even though that has been a place of population concentration and has some very different characteristics than the north, particularly around the land question.

Rather, the common features of oppression, history and culture which unify black people as a colony (although originating historically in a common territory apart from the colonizers, i.e., Africa, not the South) have been based historically on their common position as slaves, which since the nominal abolition of slavery has taken the form of caste oppression, and oppression of black people as a people everywhere that they exist. A new black nation, different from the nations of Africa from which it came, has been forged by the common historical experience of importation and slavery and caste oppression; to claim that to be a nation it must of necessity now be based on a common national territory apart from the colonizing nation is a mechanical application of criteria which were and are applicable to different situations.

What is specifically meant by the term caste is that all black people, on the basis of their common slave history, common culture and skin color are systematically denied access to particular job categories (or positions within job categories), social position, etc., regardless of individual skills, talents, money or education. Within the working class, they are the most oppressed section; in the petit bourgeoisie, they are even more strictly confined to the lowest levels. Token exceptions aside, the specific content of this caste oppression is to maintain black people in the most exploitative and oppressive jobs and conditions. Therefore, since the lowest class is the working class, the black caste is almost entirely a caste of the working class, or [holds] positions as oppressed as the lower working-class positions (poor black petit bourgeoisie and farmers); it is a colonial labor caste, a colony whose common national character itself is defined by their common class position.

Thus, northern blacks do not have a "dual interest"—as blacks on the one hand and "US-nation workers" on the other. They have a single class interest, along with all other black people in the US, as members of the Black Proletarian Colony.

III. THE STRUGGLE FOR SOCIALIST SELF-DETERMINATION

The struggle of black people—as a colony—is for self-determination, freedom, and liberation from US imperialism. Because blacks have been oppressed and held in an inferior social position as a people, they have a right to decide, organize and act on their common destiny as a people apart from white interference. Black self-determination does not simply apply to determination of their collective political destiny at some future time. It is directly tied to the fact that because all blacks experience oppression in a form that no whites do, no whites are in a position to fully understand and test from their own practice the real situation black people face and the necessary response to it. This is why it is necessary for black people to organize separately and determine their actions separately at each stage of the struggle.

It is important to understand the implications of this. It is not legitimate for whites to organizationally intervene in differences among revolutionary black nationalists. It would be arrogant for us to attack any black organization that defends black people and opposes imperialism in practice. But it is necessary to develop a correct understanding of the Black Liberation struggle within our own organization, where an incorrect one will further racist practice in our relations with the black movement.

In the history of some external colonies, such as China and Vietnam, the struggle for self-determination has had two stages: (1) a united front against imperialism and for New Democracy (which is a joint dictatorship of anti-colonial classes led by the proletariat, the content of which is a compromise between the interests of the proletariat and nationalist peasants, petit bourgeoisie and national bourgeoisie); and (2) developing out of the new democratic stage, socialism.

However, the black liberation struggle in this country will have only one "stage"; the struggle for self-determination will embody within it the struggle for socialism.

As Huey P. Newton has said, "In order to be a revolutionary nationalist, you would of necessity have to be a socialist." This is because—given the caste quality of oppression-as-a-people-through-a-common-degree-of-exploitation—self-determination requires being free from white capitalist exploitation in the form of inferior (lower caste) jobs, housing, schools, hospitals, prices. In addition, only what was or became in practice a socialist program for self-determination—one which addressed itself to reversing this exploitation—could win the necessary active mass support in the "proletarian colony."

The program of a united front for new democracy, on the other hand, would not be as thorough, and so would not win as active and determined support from the black masses. The only reason for having such a front would be where the independent petit bourgeois forces which it would bring in would add enough strength to balance the weakening of proletarian backing. This is not the case: first, because much of the black petit bourgeoisie is actually a "comprador" petit bourgeoisie (like so-called black capitalists who are promoted by the power structure to seem independent but are really agents of white monopoly capital), who would never fight as a class for any real self-determination; and secondly, because many black petit bourgeoisie, perhaps most, while not having a class interest in socialist self-determination, are close enough to the black masses in the oppression and limitations on their conditions that they will support many kinds of self-determination issues, and, especially when the movement is winning, can be won to support full (socialist) self-determination. For the black movement to work to maximize this support from the petit bourgeoisie is correct; but it is in no way a united front where it is clear that the Black Liberation Movement should not and does not modify the revolutionary socialist content of its stand to win that support.

IV. BLACK LIBERATION MEANS REVOLUTION

What is the relationship of the struggle for black self-determination to the whole world-wide revolution to defeat US imperialism and internationalize its resources toward the goal of creating a classless world?

No black self-determination could be won which would not result in a victory for the international revolution as a whole. The black proletarian colony, being dispersed as such a large and exploited section of the work force, is essential to the survival of imperialism. Thus, even if the black liberation movement chose to try to attain self-determination in the form of a separate country (a legitimate part of the right to self-determination), existing side by side with the US, imperialism could not survive if they won it—and so would never give up without being defeated. Thus, a revolutionary nationalist movement could not win without destroying the state power of the imperialists; and it is for this reason that the black liberation movement, as a revolutionary nationalist movement for self-determination, is automatically in and of itself an inseparable part of the whole revolutionary struggle against US imperialism and for international socialism.

However, the fact that black liberation depends on winning the whole revolution does not mean that it depends on waiting for and joining with a mass white movement to do it. The genocidal oppression of black people must be ended, and does not allow any leisure time to wait; if necessary, black people could win self-determination, abolishing the whole imperialist system and seizing state power to do it, without this white movement, although the cost among whites and blacks both would be high.

Blacks could do it alone if necessary because of their centralness to the system, economically and geo-militarily, and because of the level of unity, commitment, and initiative which will be developed in waging a people's war for survival and national liberation. However, we do not expect that they will have to do it alone, not only because of the international situation, but also because the real interests of masses of oppressed whites in this country lie with the Black Liberation struggle, and the conditions for understanding and fighting for these interests grow with the deepening of the crises. Already, the black liberation movement has carried with it an upsurge of revolutionary consciousness among white youth; and while there are no guarantees, we can expect that this will extend and deepen among all oppressed whites.

To put aside the possibility of blacks winning alone leads to the racist position that blacks should wait for whites and are dependent on whites acting for them to win. Yet the possibility of blacks winning alone cannot in the least be a justification for whites failing to shoulder the burden of developing a revolutionary movement among whites. If the first error is racism by holding back black liberation, this would be equally racist by leaving blacks isolated to take on the whole fight—and the whole cost—for everyone.

It is necessary to defeat both racist tendencies: (1) that blacks shouldn't go ahead with making the revolution, and (2) that blacks should go ahead alone with making it. The only third path is to build a white movement which will support the blacks in moving as fast as they have to and are able to, and still itself keep up with that black movement enough so that white revolutionaries share the cost and the blacks don't have to do the whole thing alone. Any white who does not follow this third path is objectively following one of the other two (or both) and is objectively racist.

V. ANTI-IMPERIALIST REVOLUTION AND THE UNITED FRONT

Since the strategy for defeating imperialism in semi-feudal colonies has two stages, the new democratic stage of a united front to throw out imperialism and then the socialist stage, some people suggest two stages for the US too—one to stop imperialism, the anti-imperialist stage, and another to achieve the dictatorship of the proletariat, the socialist stage. It is no accident that even the proponents of this idea can't tell you what it means. In reality, imperialism is a predatory inter-national stage of capitalism. Defeating imperialism within the US couldn't possibly have the content, which it could in a semi-feudal country, of replacing imperialism with capitalism or new democracy; when imperialism is defeated in the US, it will be replaced by socialism—nothing else. One revolution, one replacement process, one seizure of state power—the anti-imperialist revolution and the socialist revolution, one and the same stage. To talk of this as two separate stages, the struggle to overthrow imperialism and the struggle for social-ist revolution, is as crazy as if Marx had talked about the proletarian socialist revolution as a revolution of two stages, one the overthrow of capitalist state power, and second the establishment of socialist state power.

Along with no two stages, there is no united front with the petit bourgeoisie, because its interests as a class aren't for replacing imperialism with socialism. As far as people within this country are concerned, the international war against imperialism is the same task as the socialist revolution, for one overthrow of power here. There is no "united front" for socialism here.

One reason people have considered the "united front" idea is the fear that if we were talking about a one-stage socialist revolution we would fail to organize maximum possible sup-port among people, like some petit bourgeoisie, who would fight imperialism on a particular issue, but weren't for revo-lution. When the petit bourgeoisie's interest is for fighting imperialism on a particular issue, but not for overthrowing it and replacing it with socialism, it is still contributing to revo-lution to that extent—not to some intermediate thing which is not imperialism and not socialism. Someone not for revolu-tion is not for actually defeating imperialism either, but we still can and should unite with them on particular issues. But this is not a united front (and we should not put forth some joint "united front" line with them to the exclusion of our own politics), because their class position isn't against imperialism as a system. In China, or Vietnam, the petit bourgeoisie's class interests could be for actually winning against imperialism; this was because their task was driving it out, not overthrowing its whole existence. For us here, "throwing it out" means not from one colony, but all of them, throwing it out of the world, the same thing as overthrowing it.

VI. INTERNATIONAL STRATEGY

What is the strategy of this international revolutionary movement? What are the strategic weaknesses of the imperialists which make it possible for us to win? Revolutionaries around the world are in general agreement on the answer, which Lin Piao describes in the following way:

> US imperialism is stronger, but also more vulnerable, than any imperialism of the past. It sets itself against the people of the whole world, including the people of the United States. Its human, military, material and financial resources are far from sufficient for the realization of its ambition of domination over the whole world. US imperialism has further weakened itself by occupying so many places in the world, overreaching itself, stretching its fingers out wide and dispersing its strength, with its rear so far away and its supply lines so long.
>
> —*Long Live the Victory of People's War*

The strategy which flows from this is what Che called "creating two, three, many Vietnams"—to mobilize the struggle so sharply in so many places that the imperialists cannot possibly deal with it all. Since it is essential to their interests, they will try to deal with it all, and will be defeated and destroyed in the process.

In defining and implementing this strategy, it is clear that the vanguard (that is, the section of the people who are in the forefront of the struggle and whose class interests and needs define the terms and tasks of the revolution) of the "American Revolution" is the workers and oppressed peoples of the colonies of Asia, Africa and Latin America. Because of the level of special oppression of black people as a colony, they reflect the interests of the oppressed people of the world from within the borders of the United States; they are part of the Third World and part of the international revolutionary vanguard.

The vanguard role of the Vietnamese and other Third World countries in defeating US imperialism has been clear to our movement for some time. What has not been so clear is the vanguard role black people have played, and continue to play, in the development of revolutionary consciousness and struggle within the United States. Criticisms of the black liberation struggle as being "reactionary" or of black organizations on campus as being conservative or "racist" very often express this lack of understanding. These ideas are incorrect and must be defeated if a revolutionary movement is going to be built among whites.

The black colony, due to its particular nature as a slave colony, never adopted a chauvinist identification with America as an imperialist power, either politically or culturally. Moreover, the history of black people in America has consistently been one of the greatest overall repudiations of and struggle against the state. From the slave ships from Africa to the slave revolts, the Civil War, etc., black people have been waging a struggle for survival and liberation. In the history of our own movement this has also been the case: the civil rights struggles, initiated and led by blacks in the South; the rebellions beginning with Harlem in 1964 and Watts in 1965 through Detroit and Newark in 1967; the campus struggles at all-black schools in the South and struggles led by blacks on campuses all across the country. As it is the blacks—along with the Vietnamese and other Third World people—who are most oppressed by US imperialism, their class interests are most solidly and resolutely committed to waging revolutionary struggle through to its completion. Therefore it is no surprise that time and again, in both political content and level of consciousness and militancy, it has been the black liberation movement which has upped the ante and defined the terms of the struggle.

What is the relationship of this "black vanguard" to the "many Vietnams" around the world? Obviously this is an example of our strategy that different fronts reinforce each other. The fact that the Vietnamese are winning weakens the enemy, advancing the possibilities for the black struggle, etc. But it is important for us to understand that the interrelationship is more than this. Black people do not simply "choose" to intensify their struggle because they want to help the Vietnamese, or because they see that Vietnam heightens the possibilities for struggle here. The existence of any one Vietnam, especially a winning one, spurs on others not only through consciousness and choice, but through need, because it is a political and economic, as well as military, weakening of capitalism, and this means that to compensate, the imperialists are forced to intensify their oppression of other people.

Thus the loss of China and Cuba and the loss now of Vietnam not only encourages other oppressed peoples (such as the blacks) by showing what the alternative is and that it can be won, but also costs the imperialists billions of dollars which they then have to take out of the oppression of these other peoples. Within this country increased oppression falls heavier on the most oppressed sections of the population, so that the condition of all workers is worsened through rising taxes, inflation and the fall of real wages, and speedup. But this increased oppression falls heaviest on the most oppressed, such as poor white workers and, especially, the blacks, for example through the collapse of state services like schools, hospitals and welfare, which naturally hits the hardest at those most dependent on them.

This deterioration pushes people to fight harder to even try to maintain their present level. The more the ruling class is hurt in Vietnam, the harder people will be pushed to rebel and to fight for reforms. Because there exist successful models of revolution in Cuba, Vietnam, etc., these reform struggles will provide a continually larger and stronger base for revolutionary ideas. Because it needs to maximize profits by denying the reforms, and is aware that these conditions and reform struggles will therefore lead to revolutionary consciousness, the ruling class will see it more and more necessary to come down on any motion at all, even where it is not yet highly organized or conscious. It will come down faster on black people, because their oppression is increasing fastest, and this makes their rebellion most thorough and most dangerous, and fastest growing. It is because of this that the vanguard character and role of the black liberation struggle will be increased and intensified, rather than being increasingly equal to and merged into the situation and rebellion of oppressed white working people and youth. The crises of imperialism (the existence of Vietnam and especially that it's winning) will therefore create a "Black Vietnam" within the US.

Given that black self-determination would mean fully crushing the power of the imperialists, this "Vietnam" has certain different characteristics than the external colonial wars. The imperialists will never "get out of the US" until their total strength and every resource they can bring to bear has been smashed; so the Black Vietnam cannot win without bringing the whole thing down and winning for everyone. This means that this war of liberation will be the most protracted and hardest fought of all.

It is in this context that the question of the South must be dealt with again, not as a question of whether or not the black nation, black colony, exists there, as opposed to in the North as well, but rather as a practical question of strategy and tactics: Can the black liberation struggle—the struggle of all blacks in the country—gain advantage in the actual war of liberation by concentrating on building base areas in the South in territory with a concentration of black population?

This is very clearly a different question than that of "where the colony is," and to this question the "yes" answer is an important possibility. If the best potential for struggle in the South were realized, it is fully conceivable and legitimate that the struggle there could take on the character of a fight for separation; and any victories won in that direction would be important gains for the national liberation of the colony as a whole. However, because the colony is dispersed over the whole country, and not just located in the black belt, winning still means the power and liberation of blacks in the whole country.

Thus, even the winning of separate independence in the South would still be one step toward self-determination, and not equivalent to winning it; which, because of the economic position of the colony as a whole, would still require over-throwing the state power of the imperialists, taking over production and the whole economy and power, etc.

VII. THE REVOLUTIONARY YOUTH MOVEMENT: CLASS ANALYSIS

The revolutionary youth movement program was hailed as a transition strategy, which explained a lot of our past work and pointed to new directions for our movement. But as a transition to what? What was our overall strategy? Was the youth movement strategy just an organizational strategy because SDS is an organization of youth and we can move best with other young people?

We have pointed to the vanguard nature of the black struggle in this country as part of the international struggle against American imperialism, and the impossibility of anything but an international strategy for winning. Any attempt to put forth a strategy which, despite internationalist rhetoric, assumes a purely internal development to the class struggle in this country, is incorrect. The Vietnamese (and the Uruguayans and the Rhodesians) and the blacks and Third World peoples in this country will continue to set the terms for class struggle in America.

In this context, why an emphasis on youth? Why should young people be willing to fight on the side of Third World peoples? Before dealing with this question about youth, how-ever, there follows a brief sketch of the main class categories in the white mother country which we think are important, and [which] indicate our present estimation of their respective class interests (bearing in mind that the potential for various sections to understand and fight for the revolution will vary according to more than just their real class interests).

Most of the population is of the working class, by which we mean not simply industrial or production workers, nor those who are actually working, but the whole section of the population which doesn't own productive property and so lives off of the sale of its labor power. This is not a metaphysical category either in terms of its interests, the role it plays, or even who is in it, which very often is difficult to determine.

As a whole, the long-range interests of the non-colonial sections of the working class lie with overthrowing imperialism, with supporting self-determination for the oppressed nations (including the black colony), with supporting and fighting for international socialism. However, virtually all of the white working class also has short-range privileges from imperialism, which are not false privileges but very real ones which give them an edge of vested interest and tie them to a certain extent to the imperialists, especially when the latter are in a relatively prosperous phase. When the imperialists are losing their empire, on the other hand, these short-range privileged interests are seen to be temporary (even though the privileges may be relatively greater over the faster-increasing emiseration of the oppressed peoples). The long-range interests of workers in siding with the oppressed peoples are seen more clearly in the light of imperialism's impending defeat. Within the whole working class, the balance of anti-imperialist class interests with white mother country short-term privilege varies greatly.

First, the most oppressed sections of the mother country working class have interests most clearly and strongly anti-imperialist. Who are the most oppressed sections of the working class? Millions of whites who have as oppressive material conditions as the blacks, or almost so: especially poor southern white workers; the unemployed or semi-employed, or those employed at very low wages for long hours and bad conditions, who are non-unionized or have weak unions; and extending up to include much of unionized labor which has it a little better off but still is heavily oppressed and exploited. This category covers a wide range and includes the most oppressed sections not only of production and service workers but also some secretaries, clerks, etc. Much of this category gets some relative privileges (i.e. benefits) from imperialism, which constitute some material basis for being racist or pro-imperialist; but overall it is itself directly and heavily oppressed, so that in addition to its long-range class interest on the side of the people of the world, its immediate situation also constitutes a strong basis for sharpening the struggle against the state and fighting through to revolution.

Secondly, there is the upper strata of the working class. This is also an extremely broad category, including the upper strata of unionized skilled workers and also most of the "new working class" of proletarianized or semi-proletarianized "intellect workers." There is no clearly marked dividing line between the previous section and this one; our conclusions in dealing with "questionable" strata will in any event have to come from more thorough analysis of particular situations. The long-range class interests of this strata, like the previous section of more oppressed workers, are for the revolution and against imperialism. However, it is characterized by a higher level of privilege relative to the oppressed colonies, including the blacks, and relative to more oppressed workers in the mother country; so that there is a strong material basis for racism and loyalty to the system. In a revolutionary situation, where the people's forces were on the offensive and the ruling class was clearly losing, most of this upper strata of the working class will be winnable to the revolution, while at least some sections of it will probably identify their interests with imperialism till the end and oppose the revolution (which parts do which will have to do with more variables than just the particular level of privilege). The further development of the situation will clarify where this section will go, although it is clear that either way we do not put any emphasis on reaching older employed workers from this strata at this time. The exception is where they are important to the black liberation struggle, the Third World, or the youth movement in particular situations, such as with teachers, hospital technicians, etc., in which cases we must fight particularly hard to organize them around a revolutionary line of full support for black liberation and the international revolution against US imperialism. This is crucial because the privilege of this section of the working class has provided and will provide a strong material basis for national chauvinist and social democratic ideology within the movement, such as anti-internationalist concepts of "student power" and "workers control." Another consideration in understanding the interests of this segment is that, because of the way it developed and how its skills and its privileges were "earned over time," the differential between the position of youth and older workers is in many ways greater for this section than any other in the population. We should continue to see it as important to build the revolutionary youth movement among the youth of this strata.

Thirdly, there are "middle strata" who are not petit bourgeoisie, who may even technically be upper working class, but who are so privileged and tightly tied to imperialism through their job roles that they are agents of imperialism. This section includes management personnel, corporate lawyers, higher civil servants, and other government agents, army officers, etc. Because their job categories require and promote a close identification with the interests of the ruling class, these strata are enemies of the revolution.

Fourthly, and last among the categories we're going to deal with, is the petit bourgeoisie. This class is different from the middle level described above in that it has the independent class interest which is opposed to both monopoly power and to socialism. The petit bourgeoisie consists of small capital—both business and farms—and self-employed tradesmen and professionals (many professionals work for monopoly capital, and are either the upper level of the working class or in the dent class interests—anti-monopoly capital, but for capitalism rather than socialism—gives it a political character of some opposition to "big government," like its increased spending and taxes and its totalitarian extension of its control into every aspect of life, and to "big labor," which is at this time itself part of the monopoly capitalist power structure. The direction which this opposition takes can be reactionary or reformist. At this time the reformist side of it is very much mitigated by the extent to which the independence of the petit bourgeoisie is being undermined. Increasingly, small businesses are becoming extensions of big ones, while professionals and self-employed tradesmen less and less sell their skills on their own terms and become regular employees of big firms. This tendency does not mean that the reformist aspect is not still present; it is, and there are various issues, like withdrawing from a losing imperialist war, where we could get support from them. On the question of imperialism as a system, however, their class interests are generally more for it than for overthrowing it, and it will be the deserters from their class who stay with us.

VIII. WHY A REVOLUTIONARY YOUTH MOVEMENT?

In terms of the above analysis, most young people in the US are part of the working class. Although not yet employed, young people whose parents sell their labor power for wages, and more important who themselves expect to do the same in the future—or go into the army or be unemployed—are undeniably members of the working class. Most kids are well aware of what class they are in, even though they may not be very scientific about it. So our analysis assumes from the beginning that youth struggles are, by and large, working-class struggles. But why the focus now on the struggles of working-class youth rather than on the working class as a whole?

The potential for revolutionary consciousness does not always correspond to ultimate class interest, particularly when imperialism is relatively prosperous and the movement is in an early stage. At this stage, we see working-class youth as those most open to a revolutionary movement which sides with the struggles of Third World people; the following is an attempt to explain a strategic focus on youth for SDS.

In general, young people have less stake in a society (no family, fewer debts, etc.), are more open to new ideas (they have not been brainwashed for so long or so well), and are therefore more able and willing to move in a revolutionary direction. Specifically in America, young people have grown up experiencing the crises in imperialism. They have grown up along with a developing black liberation movement, with the liberation of Cuba, the fights for independence in Africa and the war in Vietnam. Older people grew up during the fight against fascism, during the Cold War, the smashing of the trade unions, McCarthy, and a period during which real wages consistently rose—since 1965 disposable real income has decreased slightly, particularly in urban areas where inflation and increased taxation have bitten heavily into wages. This crisis in imperialism affects all parts of the society. America has had to militarize to protect and expand its empire; hence the high draft calls and the creation of a standing army of three and a half million, an army which still has been unable to win in Vietnam. Further, the huge defense expenditures—required for the defense of the empire and at the same time a way of making increasing profits for the defense industries—have gone hand in hand with the urban crisis around welfare, the hospitals, the schools, housing, air and water pollution. The State cannot provide the services it has been forced to assume responsibility for, and needs to increase taxes and to pay its growing debts while it cuts services and uses the pigs to repress protest. The private sector of the economy can't provide jobs, particularly unskilled jobs. The expansion of the defense and education industries by the State since World War II is in part an attempt to pick up the slack, though the inability to provide decent wages and working conditions for "public" jobs is more and more a problem.

As imperialism struggles to hold together this decaying social fabric, it inevitably resorts to brute force and authoritarian ideology. People, especially young people, more and more find themselves in the iron grip of authoritarian institutions. Reaction against the pigs or teachers in the schools, welfare pigs or the army, is generalizable and extends beyond the particular repressive institution to the society and the State as a whole. The legitimacy of the State is called into question for the first time in at least 30 years, and the anti-authoritarianism which characterizes the youth rebellion turns into rejection of the State, a refusal to be socialized into American society. Kids used to try to beat the system from inside the army or from inside the schools; now they desert from the army and burn down the schools.

The crisis in imperialism has brought about a breakdown in bourgeois social forms, culture and ideology. The family falls apart, kids leave home, women begin to break out of traditional "female" and "mother" roles. There develops a "generation gap" and a "youth problem." Our heroes are no longer struggling businessmen, and we also begin to reject the ideal career of the professional and look to Mao, Che, the Panthers, the Third World, for our models, for motion. We reject the elitist, technocratic bullshit that tells us only experts can rule, and look instead to leadership from the people's war of the Vietnamese. Chuck Berry, Elvis, the Temptations brought us closer to the "people's culture" of Black America. The racist response to the civil rights movement revealed the depth of racism in America, as well as the impossibility of real change through American institutions. And the war against Vietnam is not "the heroic war against the Nazis"; it's the big lie, with napalm burning through everything we had heard this country stood for. Kids begin to ask questions: Where is the Free World? And who do the pigs protect at home?

The breakdown in bourgeois culture and concomitant anti-authoritarianism is fed by the crisis in imperialism, but also in turn feeds that crisis, exacerbates it so that people no longer merely want the plastic '50s restored, but glimpse an alternative (like inside the Columbia buildings) and begin to fight for it. We don't want teachers to be more kindly cops; we want to smash cops, and build a new life.

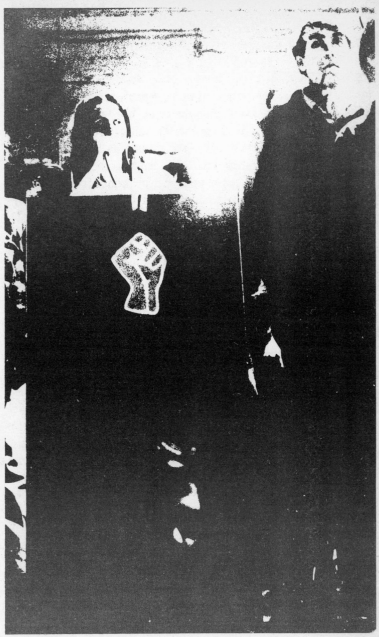

Bernardine Dohrn announces the expulsion of PL from SDS.

The contradictions of decaying imperialism fall hardest on youth in four distinct areas—the schools, jobs, the draft and the army, and the pigs and the courts. (A) In jail-like schools, kids are fed a mish-mash of racist, male chauvinist, anti-working class, anti-communist lies while being channelled into job and career paths set up according to the priorities of monopoly capital. At the same time, the State is becoming increasingly incapable of providing enough money to keep the schools going at all. (B) Youth unemployment is three times average unemployment. As more jobs are threatened by automation or the collapse of specific industries, unions act to secure jobs for those already employed. New people in the labor market can't find jobs, job stability is undermined (also because of increasing speed-up and more intolerable safety conditions) and people are less and less going to work in the same shop for 40 years. And, of course, when they do find jobs, young people get the worst ones and have the least seniority. (C) There are now two and a half million soldiers under thirty who are forced to police the world, kill and be killed in wars of imperialist domination. And (D) as a "youth problem" develops out of all this, the pigs and courts enforce curfews, set up pot busts, keep people off the streets, and repress any youth motion whatsoever.

In all of this, it is not that life in America is toughest for youth or that they are the most oppressed. Rather, it is that young people are hurt directly—and severely—by imperialism. And, in being less tightly tied to the system, they are more "pushed" to join the black liberation struggle against US imperialism. Among young people there is less of a material base for racism—they have no seniority, have not spent 20 years securing a skilled job (the white monopoly of which is increasingly challenged by the black liberation movement), and aren't just about to pay off a 25-year mortgage on a house which is valuable because it's located in a white neighborhood.

While these contradictions of imperialism fall hard on all youth, they fall hardest on the youth of the most oppressed (least privileged) sections of the working class. Clearly these youth have the greatest material base for struggle. They are the ones who most often get drafted, who get the worst jobs if they get any, who are most abused by the various institutions of social control, from the army to decaying schools, to the pigs and the courts. And their day-to-day existence indicates a potential for militancy and toughness. They are the people whom we can reach who at this stage are most ready to engage in militant revolutionary struggle.

The point of the revolutionary youth movement strategy is to move from a predominant student elite base to more oppressed (less privileged) working-class youth as a way of deepening and expanding the revolutionary youth movement—not of giving up what we have gained, not giving up our old car for a new Dodge. This is part of a strategy to reach the entire working class to engage in struggle against imperialism; moving from more privileged sections of white working-class youth to more oppressed sections to the entire working class as a whole, including importantly what has classically been called the industrial proletariat. But this should not be taken to mean that there is a magic moment, after we reach a certain percentage of the working class, when all of a sudden we become a working-class movement. We are already that if we put forward internationalist proletarian politics. We also don't have to wait to become a revolutionary force. We must be a self-conscious revolutionary force from the beginning, not be a movement which takes issues to some mystical group—"THE PEOPLE"—who will make the revolution. We must be a revolutionary movement of people understanding the necessity to reach more people, all working people, as we make the revolution.

The above arguments make it clear that it is both important and possible to reach young people wherever they are— not only in the shops, but also in the schools, in the army and in the streets—so as to recruit them to fight on the side of the oppressed peoples of the world. Young people will be part of the International Liberation Army. The necessity to build this International Liberation Army in America leads to certain priorities in practice for the revolutionary youth movement which we should begin to apply this summer. . . .

IX. IMPERIALISM IS THE ISSUE

> *The Communists are distinguished from the other working-class parties by this only: 1. In the national struggles of the proletariat of different countries, they point out and bring to the front the common interests of the entire proletariat, independently of all nationality. 2. In the various stages of development which the struggle of the working-class against the bourgeoisie has to pass through, they always and everywhere represent the interests of the movement as a whole."*

—Communist Manifesto

How do we reach youth; what kinds of struggles do we build; how do we make a revolution? What we have tried to lay out so far is the political content of the consciousness which we want to extend and develop as a mass consciousness: the necessity to build our power as part of the whole international revolution to smash the state power of the imperialists and build socialism. Besides consciousness of this task, we must involve masses of people in accomplishing it. Yet we are faced with a situation in which almost all of the people whose interests are served by these goals, and who should be, or even are, sympathetic to revolution, neither understand the specific tasks involved in making a revolution nor participate in accomplishing them. On the whole, people don't join revolutions just because revolutionaries tell them to. The oppression of the system affects people in particular ways, and the development of political consciousness and participation begins with particular problems, which turn into issues and struggles. We must transform people's everyday problems, and the issues and struggles growing out of them, into revolutionary consciousness, active and conscious opposition to racism and imperialism.

This is directly counterposed to assuming that struggles around immediate issues will lead naturally over time to struggle against imperialism. It has been argued that since people's oppression is due to imperialism and racism, then any struggle against immediate oppression is "objectively anti-imperialist," and the development of the fight against imperialism is a succession of fights for reforms. This error is classical economism.

A variant of this argument admits that this position is often wrong, but suggests that since imperialism is collapsing at this time, fights for reforms become "objectively anti-imperialist." At this stage of imperialism there obviously will be more and more struggles for the improvement of material conditions, but that is no guarantee of increasing internationalist proletarian consciousness.

On the one hand, if we, as revolutionaries, are capable of understanding the necessity to smash imperialism and build socialism, then the masses of people who we want to fight along with us are capable of that understanding. On the other hand, people are brainwashed and at present don't understand it; if revolution is not raised at every opportunity, then how can we expect people to see it in their interests, or to undertake the burdens of revolution? We need to make it clear from the very beginning that we are about revolution. But if we are so careful to avoid the dangers of reformism, how do we relate to particular reform struggles? We have to develop some sense of how to relate each particular issue to the revolution.

In every case, our aim is to raise anti-imperialist and anti-racist consciousness and tie the struggles of working-class youth (and all working people) to the struggles of Third World people, rather than merely joining fights to improve material conditions, even though these fights are certainly justified. This is not to say that we don't take immediate fights seriously, or fight hard in them, but that we are always up front with our politics, knowing that people in the course of struggle are open to a class line, ready to move beyond narrow self-interest.

It is in this sense that we point out that the particular issue is not the issue, is important insofar as it points to imperialism as an enemy that has to be destroyed. Imperialism is always the issue. Obviously, the issue cannot be a good illustration, or a powerful symbol, if it is not real to people, if it doesn't relate to the concrete oppression that imperialism causes. People have to be (and are being) hurt in some material way to understand the evils of imperialism, but what we must stress is the systematic nature of oppression and the way in which a single manifestation of imperialism makes clear its fundamental nature. At Columbia it was not the gym, in particular, which was important in the struggle, but the way in which the gym represented, to the people of Harlem and Columbia, Columbia's imperialist invasion of the black colony. Or at Berkeley, though people no doubt needed a park (as much, however, as many other things?), what made the struggle so important was that people, at all levels of militancy, consciously saw themselves attacking private property and the power of the State. And the Richmond Oil Strike was exciting because the militant fight for improvement of material conditions was part and parcel of an attack on international monopoly capital. The numbers and militancy of people mobilized for these struggles has consistently surprised the left, and pointed to the potential power of a class-conscious mass movement.

The masses will fight for socialism when they understand that reform fights, fights for improvement of material conditions, cannot be won under imperialism. With this understanding, revolutionaries should never put forth a line which fosters the illusion that imperialism will grant significant reforms. We must engage in struggles forthrightly as revolutionaries, so that it will be clear to anyone we help to win gains that the revolution rather than imperialism is responsible for them. This is one of the strengths of the Black Panther Party Breakfast for Children Program. It is "socialism in practice" by revolutionaries with the "practice" of armed self-defense and a "line" which stresses the necessity of overthrowing imperialism and seizing state power. Probably the American Friends Service Committee serves more children breakfast, but it is the symbolic value of the program in demonstrating what socialism will do for people which makes the Black Panther Program worthwhile.

What does it mean to organize around racism and imperialism in specific struggles? In the high schools (and colleges) at this time, it means putting forth a mass line to close down the schools, rather than to reform them, so that they can serve the people. The reason for this line is not that under capitalism the schools cannot serve the people, and therefore it is silly or illusory to demand that. Rather, it is that kids are ready for the full scope of militant struggle, and already demonstrate a consciousness of imperialism, such that struggles for a people-serving school would not raise the level of their struggle to its highest possible point. Thus, to tell a kid in New York that imperialism tracks him and thereby oppresses him is often small potatoes compared to his consciousness that imperialism oppresses him by jailing him, pigs and all, and the only thing to do is break out and tear up the jail. And even where high school kids are not yet engaged in such sharp struggle, it is crucial not to build consciousness only around specific issues such as tracking or ROTC or racist teachers, but to use these issues to build toward the general consciousness that the schools should be shut down. It may be important to present a conception of what schools should or could be like (this would include the abolition of the distinction between mental and physical work), but not offer this total conception as really possible to fight for in any way but through revolution.

A mass line to close down the schools or colleges does not contradict demands for open admissions to college or any other good reform demand. Agitational demands for impossible, but reasonable, reforms are a good way to make a revolutionary point. The demand for open admissions by asserting the alternative to the present (school) system exposes its fundamental nature—that it is racist, class-based, and closed—pointing to the only possible solution to the present situation: "Shut it down!" The impossibility of real open admissions—all black and brown people admitted, no flunk-out, full scholarship, under present conditions—is the best reason (that the schools show no possibility for real reform) to shut the schools down. We should not throw away the pieces of victories we gain from these struggles, for any kind of more open admissions means that the school is closer to closing down (it costs the schools more, there are more militant blacks and browns making more and more fundamental demands on the schools, and so on). Thus our line in the schools, in terms of pushing any good reforms, should be, Open them up and shut them down!"

The spread of black caucuses in the shops and other workplaces throughout the country is an extension of the black liberation struggle. These groups have raised and will continue to raise anti-racist issues to white workers in a sharper fashion than any whites ever have or could raise them. Blacks leading struggles against racism made the issue unavoidable, as the black student movement leadership did for white students. At the same time these black groups have led fights which traditional trade-union leaders have consistently refused to lead—fights against speed-up and for safety (issues which have become considerably more serious in the last few years), forcing white workers, particularly the more oppressed, to choose in another way between allegiance to the white mother country and black leadership. As white mother country radicals we should try to be in shops, hospitals, and companies where there are black caucuses, perhaps organizing solidarity groups, but at any rate pushing the importance of the black liberation struggle to whites, handing out Free Huey literature, bringing guys out to Panther rallies, and so on. Just one white guy could play a crucial role in countering UAW counter-insurgency.

We also need to relate to workplaces where there is no black motion but where there are still many young white workers. In the shops the crisis in imperialism has come down around speed-up, safety, and wage squeeze—due to higher taxes and increased inflation, with the possibility of wage-price controls being instituted.

We must relate this exploitation back to imperialism. The best way to do this is probably not caucuses in the shops, but to take guys to city-wide demonstrations, Newsreels, even the latest administration building, to make the Movement concrete to them and involve them in it. Further, we can effect consciousness and pick up people through agitational work at plants, train stops, etc., selling Movements, handing out leaflets about the war, the Panthers, the companies' holdings overseas or relations to defense industry, etc.

After the Richmond strike, people leafleted about demonstrations in support of the Curaçao Oil workers, Free Huey May Day, and People's Park.

SDS has not dealt in any adequate way with the women question; the resolution passed at Ann Arbor did not lead to much practice, nor has the need to fight male supremacy been given any programmatic direction within the RYM. As a result, we have a very limited understanding of the tie-up between imperialism and the women question, although we know that since World War II the differential between men's and women's wages has increased, and guess that the breakdown of the family is crucial to the woman question. How do we organize women against racism and imperialism without submerging the principled revolutionary question of women's liberation? We have no real answer, but we recognize the real reactionary danger of women's groups that are not self-consciously revolutionary and anti-imperialist.

To become more relevant to the growing women's movement, SDS women should begin to see as a primary responsibility the self-conscious organizing of women. We will not be able to organize women unless we speak directly to their own oppression. This will become more and more critical as we work with more oppressed women. Women who are working and women who have families face male supremacy continuously in their day-to-day lives; that will have to be the starting point in their politicization. Women will never be able to undertake a full revolutionary role unless they break out of their woman's role. So a crucial task for revolutionaries is the creation of forms of organization in which women will be able to take on new and independent roles. Women's self-defense groups will be a step toward these organizational forms, as an effort to overcome women's isolation and build revolutionary self-reliance.

The cultural revolt of women against their "role" in imperialism (which is just beginning to happen in a mass way) should have the same sort of revolutionary potential that the RYM claimed for "youth culture." The role of the "wife-mother" is reactionary in most modern societies, and the disintegration of that role under imperialism should make women more sympathetic to revolution.

In all of our work we should try to formulate demands that not only reach out to more oppressed women, but ones which tie us to other ongoing struggles, in the way that a day-care center at U of C [University of Chicago] enabled us to tie the women's liberation struggle to the Black Liberation struggle.

There must be a strong revolutionary women's movement, for without one it will be impossible for women's liberation to be an important part of the revolution. Revolutionaries must be made to understand the full scope of women's oppression, and the necessity to smash male supremacy.

X. NEIGHBORHOOD-BASED CITY-WIDE YOUTH MOVEMENT

One way to make clear the nature of the system and our tasks working off of separate struggles is to tie them together with each other: to show that we're one "multi-issue" movement, not an alliance of high school and college students, or students and GIs, or youth and workers, or students and the black community. The way to do this is to build organic regional or sub-regional and city-wide movements, by regularly bringing people in one institution or area to fights going on on other fronts.

This works on two levels. Within a neighborhood, by bringing kids to different fights and relating these fights to each other—high school stuff, colleges, housing, welfare, shops—we begin to build one neighborhood-based multi-issue movement off of them. Besides actions and demonstrations, we also pull different people together in day-to-day film showings, rallies, for speakers and study groups, etc. On a second level, we combine neighborhood "bases" into a city-wide or region-wide movement by doing the same kind of thing; concentrating our forces at whatever important struggles are going on and building more ongoing interrelationships off of that.

The importance of specifically neighborhood-based organizing is illustrated by our greatest failing in RYM practice so far—high school organizing. In most cities we don't know the kids who have been tearing up and burning down the schools. Our approach has been elitist, relating to often baseless city-wide groups by bringing them our line, or picking up kids with a false understanding of "politics" rather than those whose practice demonstrates their concrete anti-imperialist consciousness that schools are prisons. We've been unwilling to work continuously with high school kids as we did in building up college chapters. We will only reach the high school kids who are in motion by being in the schoolyards, hangouts and on the streets on an everyday basis. From a neighborhood base, high school kids could be effectively tied in to struggles around other institutions and issues, and to the anti-imperialist movement as a whole.

We will try to involve neighborhood kids who aren't in high schools too; take them to anti-war or anti-racism fights, stuff in the schools, etc.; and at the same time reach out more broadly through newspapers, films, storefronts. Activists and cadres who are recruited in this work will help expand and deepen the Movement in new neighborhoods and high schools. Mostly we will still be tied in to the college-based movement in the same area, be influencing its direction away from campus-oriented provincialism, be recruiting high school kids into it where it is real enough and be recruiting organizers out of it. In its most developed form, this neighborhood-based movement would be a kind of sub-region. In places where the Movement wasn't so strong, this would be an important form for being close to kids in a day-to-day way and yet be relating heavily to a lot of issues and political fronts which the same kids are involved with.

The second level is combining these neighborhoods into city-wide and regional movements. This would mean doing the same thing—bringing people to other fights going on—only on a larger scale, relating to various blow-ups and regional mobilizations. An example is how a lot of people from different places went to San Francisco State, the Richmond Oil Strike, and now Berkeley. The existence of this kind of cross-motion makes ongoing organizing in other places go faster and stronger, first by creating a pervasive politicization, and second by relating everything to the most militant and advanced struggles going on so that they influence and set the pace for a lot more people. Further, cities are a basic unit of organization of the whole society in a way that neighborhoods aren't. For example, one front where we should be doing stuff is the courts; they are mostly organized city-wide, not by smaller areas. The same for the city government itself. Schools where kids go are in different neighborhoods from where they live, especially colleges; the same for hospitals people go to, and where they work. As a practical question of staying with people we pick up, the need for a city-wide or area-wide kind of orientation is already felt in our movement.

Another failure of this year was making clear what the RYM meant for chapter members and students who weren't organizers about to leave their campus for a community college, high school, GI organizing, shops or neighborhoods. One thing it means for them is relating heavily to off-campus activities and struggles, as part of the city-wide motion. Not leaving the campus movement like people did for ERAP [Education Research Action Project] stuff; rather, people still organized on the campus in off-campus struggles, the way they have in the past for national actions. Like the national actions, the city-wide ones will build the on-campus movement, not compete with it.

Because the Movement will be defining itself in relation to many issues and groups, not just schools (and the war and racism as they hit at the schools), it will create a political context that non-students can relate to better, and be more useful to organizing among high school students, neighborhood kids, the mass of people. In the process, it will change the consciousness of the students too; if the issues are right and the Movement fights them, people will develop a commitment to the struggle as a whole, and an understanding of the need to be revolutionaries rather than a "student movement." Building a revolutionary youth movement will depend on organizing in a lot of places where we haven't been, and just tying the student movement to other issues and struggles isn't a substitute for that. But given our limited resources we must also lead the on-campus motion into a RYM direction, and we can make great gains toward city-wide youth movements by doing it.

Three principles underly this multi-issue, "cross-institutional" movement, on the neighborhood and city-wide levels, as to why it creates greater revolutionary consciousness and active participation in the revolution:

(1) Mixing different issues, struggles and groups demonstrates our analysis to people in a material way. We claim there is one system and so all these different problems have the same solution, revolution. If they are the same struggle in the end, we should make that clear from the beginning. On this basis we must aggressively smash the notion that there can be outside agitators on a question pertaining to the imperialists.

(2) "Relating to Motion": the struggle activity, the action, of the Movement demonstrates our existence and strength to people in a material way. Seeing it happen, people give it more weight in their thinking. For the participants, involvement in struggle is the best education about the Movement, the enemy and the class struggle. In a neighborhood or whole city the existence of some struggle is a catalyst for other struggles—it pushes people to see the Movement as more important and urgent, and as an example and precedent makes it easier for them to follow. If the participants in a struggle are based in different institutions or parts of the city, these effects are multiplied. Varied participation helps the Movement be seen as political (wholly subversive) rather than as separate grievance fights. As people in one section of the

Movement fight beside and identify closer with other sections, the mutual catalytic effect of their struggles will be greater.

(3) We must build a Movement oriented toward power. Revolution is a power struggle, and we must develop that understanding among people from the beginning. Pooling our resources area-wide and city-wide really does increase our power in particular fights, as well as push a mutual-aid-in-struggle consciousness.

XI. THE RYM AND THE PIGS

A major focus in our neighborhood and city-wide work is the pigs, because they tie together the various struggles around the State as the enemy, and thus point to the need for a Movement oriented toward power to defeat it.

The pigs are the capitalist state, and as such define the limits of all political struggles; to the extent that a revolutionary struggle shows signs of success, they come in and mark the point it can't go beyond. In the early stages of struggle, the ruling class lets parents come down on high school kids, or jocks attack college chapters. When the struggle escalates the pigs come in; at Columbia, the left was afraid its struggle would be coopted to anti-police brutality, cops off campus, and said pigs weren't the issue. But pigs really are the issue and people will understand this, one way or another. They can have a liberal understanding that pigs are sweaty working-class barbarians who over-react and commit "police brutality" and so shouldn't be on campus. Or they can understand pigs as the repressive imperialist State doing its job. Our job is not to avoid the issue of the pigs as "diverting" from anti-imperialist struggle, but to emphasize that they are our real enemy if we fight that struggle to win.

Even when there is no organized political struggle, the pigs come down on people in everyday life in enforcing capitalist property relations, bourgeois laws and bourgeois morality; they guard stores and factories and the rich and enforce credit and rent against the poor. The overwhelming majority of arrests in America are for crimes against property. The pigs will be coming down on the kids we're working with in the schools, on the streets, around dope; we should focus on them, point them out all the time, like the Panthers do. We should relate the daily oppression by the pig to their role in political repression, and develop a class understanding of political power and armed force among the kids we're with.

As we develop a base these two aspects of the pig role increasingly come together. In the schools, pig is part of daily oppression—keeping order in halls and lunch rooms, controlling smoking—while at the same time pigs prevent kids from handing out leaflets, and bust "outside agitators." The presence of youth, or youth with long hair, becomes defined as organized political struggle and the pigs react to it as such. More and more everyday activity is politically threatening, so pigs are suddenly more in evidence; this in turn generates political organization and opposition, and so on. Our task will be to catalyze this development, pushing out the conflict with the pig so as to define every struggle—schools (pigs out, pig institutes out), welfare (invading pig-protected office), the streets (curfew and turf fights)—as a struggle against the needs of capitalism and the force of the State.

Pigs don't represent State power as an abstract principle; they are a power that we will have to overcome in the course of struggle or become irrelevant, revisionist, or dead. We must prepare concretely to meet their power because our job is to defeat the pigs and the army, and organize on that basis. Our beginnings should stress self-defense—building defense groups around karate classes, learning how to move on the street and around the neighborhood, medical training, popularizing and moving toward (according to necessity) armed self-defense, all the time honoring and putting forth the principle that "political power comes out of the barrel of a gun." These self-defense groups would initiate pig surveillance patrols, visits to the pig station and courts when someone is busted, etc.

Obviously the issues around the pig will not come down by neighborhood alone; it will take at least city-wide groups able to coordinate activities against a unified enemy—in the early stages, for legal and bail resources and turning people out for demonstrations, adding the power of the city-wide movement to what may be initially only a tenuous base in a neighborhood. Struggles in one part of the city will not only provide lessons for but [will] materially aid similar motion in the rest of it.

Thus the pigs are ultimately the glue—the necessity—that holds the neighborhood-based and city-wide movement together; all of our concrete needs lead to pushing the pigs to the fore as a political focus:

(1) making institutionally oriented reform struggles deal with State power, by pushing our struggle till either winning or getting pigged;

(2) using the city-wide inter-relation of fights to raise the level of struggle and further large-scale anti-pig movement-power consciousness;

(3) developing spontaneous anti-pig consciousness in our neighborhoods to an understanding of imperialism, class struggle and the State;

(4) and using the city-wide movement as a platform for reinforcing and extending this politicization work, like by talking about getting together a city-wide neighborhood-based mutual aid anti-pig self-defense network.

All of this can be done through city-wide agitation and propaganda and picking certain issues—to have as the central regional focus for the whole Movement.

XII. REPRESSION AND REVOLUTION

As institutional fights and anti-pig self-defense off of them intensify, so will the ruling class's repression. Their escalation of repression will inevitably continue according to how threatening the Movement is to their power. Our task is not to avoid or end repression; that can always be done by pulling back, so we're not dangerous enough to require crushing. Sometimes it is correct to do that as a tactical retreat, to survive to fight again.

To defeat repression, however, is not to stop it but to go on building the Movement to be more dangerous to them; in which case, defeated at one level, repression will escalate even more. To succeed in defending the Movement, and not just ourselves at its expense, we will have to successively meet and overcome these greater and greater levels of repression.

To be winning will thus necessarily, as imperialism's lesser efforts fail, bring about a phase of all-out military repression. To survive and grow in the face of that will require more than a larger base of supporters; it will require the invincible strength of a mass base at a high level of active participation and consciousness, and can only come from mobilizing the self-conscious creativity, will and determination of the people.

Each new escalation of the struggle in response to new levels of repression, each protracted struggle around self-defense which becomes a material fighting force, is part of the international strategy of solidarity with Vietnam and the blacks, through opening up other fronts. They are anti-war, anti-imperialist and pro-black liberation. If they involve fighting the enemy, then these struggles are part of the revolution.

Therefore, clearly the organization and active, conscious, participating mass base needed to survive repression are also the same needed for winning the revolution. The Revolutionary Youth Movement speaks to the need for this kind of active mass-based Movement by tying city-wide motion back to community youth bases, because this brings us close enough to kids in their day-to-day lives to organize their "maximum active participation" around enough different kinds of fights to push the "highest level of consciousness" about imperialism, the black vanguard, the State and the need for armed struggle.

XIII.   THE NEED FOR A REVOLUTIONARY PARTY

The RYM must also lead to the effective organization needed to survive and to create another battlefield of the revolution. A revolution is a war; when the Movement in this country can defend itself militarily against total repression it will be part of the revolutionary war.

This will require a cadre organization, effective secrecy, self-reliance among the cadres, and an integrated relationship with the active mass-based Movement. To win a war with an enemy as highly organized and centralized as the imperialists will require a (clandestine) organization of revolutionaries, having also a unified "general staff"; that is, combined at some point with discipline under one centralized leadership. Because war is political, political tasks—the international communist revolution—must guide it. Therefore the centralized organization of revolutionaries must be a political organization as well as military, what is generally called a "Marxist-Leninist" party.

How will we accomplish the building of this kind of organization? It is clear that we couldn't somehow form such a party at this time, because the conditions for it do not exist in this country outside the Black nation. What are these conditions?

One is that to have a unified centralized organization it is necessary to have a common revolutionary theory which explains, at least generally, the nature of our revolutionary tasks and how to accomplish them. It must be a set of ideas which have been tested and developed in the practice of resolving the important contradictions in our work.

A second condition is the existence of revolutionary leadership tested in practice. To have a centralized party under illegal and repressive conditions requires a centralized leadership, specific individuals with the understanding and the ability to unify and guide the Movement in the face of new problems and be right most of the time.

Thirdly, and most important, there must be the same revolutionary mass base mentioned earlier, or (better) revolutionary mass movement. It is clear that without this there can't be the practical experience to know whether or not a theory, or a leader, is any good at all. Without practical revolutionary activity on a mass scale the party could not test and develop new ideas and draw conclusions with enough surety behind them to consistently base its survival on them. Especially, no revolutionary party could possibly survive without relying on the active support and participation of masses of people.

These conditions for the development of a revolutionary party in this country are the main "conditions" for winning. There are two kinds of tasks for us.

One is the organization of revolutionary collectives within the Movement. Our theory must come from practice, but it can't be developed in isolation. Only a collective pooling of our experiences can develop a thorough understanding of the complex conditions in this country. In the same way, only our collective efforts toward a common plan can adequately test the ideas we develop. The development of revolutionary Marxist-Leninist-Maoist collective formations which undertake this concrete evaluation and application of the lessons of our work is not just the task of specialists or leaders, but the responsibility of every revolutionary. Just as a collective is necessary to sum up experiences and apply them locally, equally the collective interrelationship of groups all over the country is necessary to get an accurate view of the whole movement and to apply that in the whole country. Over time, those collectives which prove themselves in practice to have the correct understanding (by the results they get) will contribute toward the creation of a unified revolutionary party.

The most important task for us toward making the revolution, and the work our collectives should engage in, is the creation of a mass revolutionary movement, without which a clandestine revolutionary party will be impossible. A revolutionary mass movement is different from the traditional revisionist mass base of "sympathizers." Rather it is akin to the Red Guard in China, based on the full participation and involvement of masses of people in the practice of making revolution; a movement with a full willingness to participate in the violent and illegal struggle. It is a movement diametrically opposed to the elitist idea that only leaders are smart enough or interested enough to accept full revolutionary conclusions. It is a movement built on the basis of faith in the masses of people.

The task of collectives is to create this kind of movement. (The party is not a substitute for it, and in fact is totally dependent on it.) This will be done at this stage principally among youth, through implementing the Revolutionary Youth Movement strategy discussed in this paper. It is practice at this, and not political "teachings" in the abstract, which will determine the relevance of the political collectives which are formed.

The strategy of the RYM for developing an active mass base, tying the city-wide fights to community and city-wide anti-pig movement, and for building a party eventually out of this motion, fits with the world strategy for winning the revolution, builds a movement oriented toward power, and will become one division of the International Liberation Army, while its battlefields are added to the many Vietnams which will dismember and dispose of US imperialism. Long Live the Victory of People's War!

From *New Left Notes*, August 29, 1969

Toward A Revolutionary Women's Militia

Cathy Wilkerson

The inability of the Weatherman proposal to include an organic analysis of male supremacy stems from weaknesses in the basic analysis. Nowhere does the paper confront head on how we specifically determine who in the mother country (although it deals with the colonies) are our friends and enemies, or how we might affect which side they come down on. The section on class analysis says there is an upper and lower strata of the working class and a middle strata, none of whom own or control any of the means of production, and who are differentiated on the basis of differing amounts of "privileges (i.e., benefits)" which they acquire partly as a result of the imperialist pillage of the colonies' labor and natural resources. This gives us some beginning way of judging the material basis for the existence of "racism and loyalty to the system." But it certainly does not help us solve the immediate task of determining the cutting-edge element of consciousness which will determine which loyalty in fact will develop and prevail in sectors of working-class youth, and how we can specifically affect that development.

Young people can be most easily won to a revolutionary perspective precisely because they are most affected by the progressive aspects of contradictions. We can say to working-class youth who have few material benefits that the privilege of access to protection by the ruling class that is held out to them is a shuck because that same ruling class will nonetheless increasingly exploit and oppress them. We can point to the schools, courts, pigs, jobs to concretize that. We can build struggles which focus on these forms of oppression and ex-

Excerpted from *New Left Notes*, July 8, 1969.

ploitation, and the specific aspects of these forms of oppression which try to win allegiance to the oppressor.

A close look at the condition of women will help clarify these things because women are affected by these contradictions, not in a different way from or additional way than men, but in a sharper, more extreme, way than men.

Where the noose is getting tighter it is especially tight around the necks of women. Most women identify primarily with the home and the family. In their roles as provider, wife, and mother they are pushed by even more forces than men to ally with the oppressors. They feel more immediately the need to maintain stability so as to keep stomachs full, children clothed; they feel the threat to the stability of their position even more acutely. Secondly, having been taught to feel passive and defenseless, especially in physical ways, they are more threatened by the spectre of black struggles as defined by the mass media, the ruling class through the PTA, women's magazines, etc.

On the other hand, it is women's jobs that are disappearing fastest. Textile mills, for instance, were originally concentrated in New England, exploiting the labor of immigrant European women. Then, as working people in New England gained minimum protection from slavish working conditions, the mills moved to the South, where women were in plentiful supply as unorganized, unprotected cheap labor. Now these mills are being moved to colonies to use the labor of colonized women. The move of small parts assembly plants to Third World nations is another example. As unemployment, job instability, and working conditions worsen, they deteriorate fastest for women.

Also, women's family roles as wives and mothers force them to rely much more than men on social services, such as schools, hospitals, transportation, welfare, etc. As these public services are less and less able to meet the material needs of the people, women are most affected. They are the most conscious of the real increase in their oppression. As the family is defined more and more on bourgeois values, and serves more and more a pig function in relation to kids, young girls are the hardest hit.

In these ways, the forces which push working-class people toward allegiance with the ruling class are less strong on young women than on men, and yet those forces which point out the necessity of allying with Third World struggles are clearer and more compelling.

It must therefore be clear that "women's issues" cannot be considered or dealt with separately from an understanding and strategy of the way the major contradictions affect the whole proletariat of the mother country. Attacks on male supremacy must be a major focus of all our work. When we talk to young working people in the shops, in the schools, or on the streets, it is one of the first notions we raise, and we begin very quickly to stress the importance of changing the practice of male supremacy into more communist forms of relationships. Because male supremacy is one of the major ways, along with racism, that the ruling class wins allegiance, we must break down the practice in order to destroy the material basis for that allegiance.

Further, male supremacy as an ideology is one of the most important ways that the Man defines individuals and societies in such a way that it makes it difficult to understand how socialism and communism could work, let alone how the forces of people struggling to win these ends could ever be successful. It demoralizes the people, and is a critical force in promoting bourgeois individualism through false separation of men from women, preventing collective practice. All of this discourages the people from allying with the struggles of the international proletariat and encourages them to be cynical and thus to ally with the ruling class to try to maintain as much stability and access as possible.

Within the Movement it is crucial that men and women both begin to fight against the vestiges of bourgeois ideology within themselves, to break down existing forms of social relationships. Only by developing forms in which we can express love in non-exploitative and non-competitive ways will men and women develop their full human and revolutionary potential for struggle.

Men who claim to be fighting imperialism in any form must fight against their own supremacist practices and notions. Not to do so undercuts their own legitimacy as revolutionaries. We have just expelled PL and WSA from our organization because we could not tolerate within our organization people who in practice worked against that struggle to which we are trying to win people. In regional and local struggles we must begin to take the same attitude toward those who comply with male supremacy.

PROGRAM

This basic analysis of the function and manifestations of male supremacy leads us in certain strategic directions. First, we must concentrate much more heavily on winning more women to the fight against imperialism. Second, we must initiate an attack on male supremacy as an essential part of our attack on those forces which push mother country working people to ally with the ruling class.

We have failed badly in the first task in the last year because of our mistaken notion that there were somehow analogous or equivalent "issues" around which to organize women to those laid out in the entirely male-oriented RYM paper. We now understand that we cannot organize separately around "women's issues"—unless it is a tactic (e.g., equal wages for black and brown women) within a larger strategy for liberation. Men, and especially women, must focus the work on winning women to all of our struggles. By explaining the material basis of male supremacy and the way the ideology is used to promote allegiance to the ruling class, women will be able to understand more clearly the nature and cause of their oppression, and will be won to fighting. We must go into training schools for women, e.g. nursing, beauty, and secretarial. In the schools we must focus on the especially high rate of dropouts among women. We can expose the way young women are tracked into the most oppressive jobs, trained to function as a reserve labor force, prepared for exploitative family roles. We will attack the ideology of consumerism as the false front of the unreal myth of upward mobility.

As we win more and more women into the fight against imperialism through an understanding of their real position in society, we must form women's caucuses within each struggle. We must see these caucuses as fighting groups to push the theoretical understanding of male supremacy. They can also devise ways for ensuring individual and collective improvements in practice among the progressive forces.

Clearly these two fronts of struggle must be waged simultaneously. In high schools, for instance, we must organize girls to fight along with men against the tracking system in general, as well as the way it affects girls in particular. Girls will also struggle against pigs and against the war. At the same time we can form women's militias of high school girls which directly attack male supremacy and the broader set of bourgeois values upon which it rests. We have seen that one of the greatest oppressions of young working-class women is the restriction and surveillance of parents. "The family" is constantly trying to define their identity as submissive, mate-able, and skilled in family tasks. Most girls have repressive restrictions on how late they can stay out and must report where they are at all times. Further, if the parents disapprove of the guy they are going out with they will impose even more restrictions and harass the girl continually at home. Militias can band girls together to fight collectively for collective freedom; they can, for example, confront the parents of each girl from the basis of power. These militias can also serve an educational and agitational role in the community as a whole. These girls could easily relate to friends who were working in plants or service industries and bring these young women into the struggle against imperialism.

Thus, women are not in particular demanding equality with men under the current conditions, but are demanding a whole new set of values—socialist values—by which people relate to each other in all forms of individual and collective relationships. It is true that while we fight these battles for socialist practices, we can't be clear as to the exact content of the demand. These struggles must be seen as the beginning of a long, protracted struggle for socialism, and we will only gradually be able to perceive the positive content of the demands.

But, it is also clear that there are real dangers and problems with struggles which focus only on the principle of equality within the mother country. White women workers who voted for Wallace could easily wage a national chauvinist struggle for equal wages with men, without understanding the relationship between their oppression and the oppression of Third World people, and therefore without understanding the relationship between their struggle and the struggles for national self-determination. Further, unless women are brought into a movement that is, in practice, fighting male supremacy, they will be prevented, by their oppressive obligations, from playing a large or important role in struggles.

Hand-Me-Down Marxism In The New Left

David Horowitz

The rafters of the Chicago Coliseum had hardly ceased to reverberate with the chants of the rival factions, when the ghost of Karl Marx was being heaped with blame for the SDS debacle. "Alas," mourned Establishment pundits in ill-concealed triumph, "the New Left has finally gone the primrose way of the Old. Marxism has at last cursed it with factional wars and historical irrelevance. The apostles of ultra-democratic revolution and 'power to the people' (the most incendiary notion in the modern world) have shown themselves ready, if inept, practitioners of the art of political manipulation. The idol-smashing revolutionary vanguard has again been revealed as a latter-day religious cult prostrating itself before patron saints and overseas meccas, while suppressing the heresy of thought with mind-gluing incantations from holy scriptures. R.I.P."

But the smug obituaries are, to say the least, premature. The "Movement," first of all, is larger than any of its organizations. The virility of the New Left, the sheer vitality of its actions and the deep, deep roots of its culture of rebellion will surely bypass the martinets of any bible-toting, icon-worshiping elite, should such a group seek to impose its Law—whether from the closeted cells of a Maoist sect or through the once-open forum of SDS. For the time being, at least, this is still the revolution that can't be taken over.

Nonetheless, the still-unfolding fate of SDS—until now the central organization of (white) student struggle—cannot remain a matter of indifference to the radical movement from which it draws its strength and which it, in turn, inspires. Too

From *Ramparts,* September, 1969. (David Horowitz is an editor of *Ramparts* and the author of *Empire and Revolution.*) Copyright 1969 by Ramparts Magazine Inc.

much of the tried and tested leadership, too much of the best and most militant energies of the left are caught up in the current enthrallment of SDS, for the outcome not to have significance for the movement as a whole.

What is at the source of SDS's descent into a politics at once so claustrophobic and incomprehensible as to virtually insure the isolation and defeat of those who adopt it? A politics so antagonistic to the imaginative, open spirit and creative action that has informed and powered the New Left since its emergence from the ashes of the Old a decade ago? (The present vanguard seems to have forgotten that the New Left had to midwife its own birth precisely *because* the old line toeing, Lenin/Stalin/Mao-quoting vanguard had finally encased itself in a sectarian, sterile solitude where it had only its own self-righteousness for company.)

One can readily appreciate why liberals would rush to attribute the difficulties of America's New Left (and the demise of the Old) to "Marxism." Liberalism's Great American Celebration of the Fifties has all but disappeared in the Great American Disintegration of the Sixties. The bankruptcy of the liberal world-view has become more and more self-evident with each new stage of the social crisis. Who can still put credence in the basic tenets of the postwar liberal faith: the essential harmony and pluralistic democracy of America's "affluent" society, the alleged solution of the fundamental problems of the industrial revolution, the end of class-based struggle and its revolutionary ideologies? If the new generation has absorbed one lesson, it has been that of the vacuity of liberal analysis, the hypocrisy of liberal preachment and the collusion of liberal practice in the imperialist and racist world system of U.S. corporate capital.

How lucid Marxism—with its focus on the inequities and irrationalities of the status quo—now looks, in comparison to the soothing obfuscations of the liberal mind. For what is Marxism but the recognition of the class pivot of history and the class basis of social oppression, coupled with a clear commitment to one side of the social struggle: the side of the oppressed against their oppressors? Far from being a handicap, the discovery of Marxism by the movement has put within its grasp the possibility of becoming a serious revolutionary force for the first time. A long-range perspective on real social forces (not illusory promises, superficial harmonies and surface stabilities) is essential to the development and success of any movement for social change and transformation, and it is Marxism above all other ideologies that has shown itself capable of providing such a perspective for the capitalist era.

But there is Marxism and there is Marxism. A Marxism which is developed in a concrete social context; which is flexible, open, and unafraid to rethink its revolutionary perspectives according to specific conditions; and which fashions its language as a means of communication, analysis and mobilization, rather than employing it merely as ritualistic invocation, can be just the powerful instrument that a revolutionary movement requires.

But there is also Marxism of the hand-me-down variety, where an ideological perspective and vocabulary developed in a different epoch or a different political-cultural environment is transposed whole and adopted as an all-embracing wisdom. This attempt to don the ideological cloth of the victims of imperialism and their vanguard may satisfy many egos and assuage much guilt, but it doesn't help to build radical constituencies and revolutionary forces in the United States. Yet such a direction appears to be developing in SDS, where both major factions at the Chicago convention spoke in the language of Maoism and put forth a Maoist model of the world revolutionary process as their own.

The self-styled Marxist-Leninist-Maoists of SDS would do well to remember that the New Left grew out of two bankruptcies—not just liberalism, but old-line Marxism as well. The failure of Marxist (or Marxist-Leninist, or Marxist-Trotskyist) vanguard parties to build revolutionary movements in the advanced capitalist countries is an historic fact that no revolutionary can afford to ignore. The "Marxist-Leninist" groups which exist in these countries have either isolated themselves as sterile sects, or transformed themselves into basically reformist organizations like the Italian and French Communist parties. A careful analysis of these failures will show that hand-me-down Marxism and overseas mecca-watching played a significant role in each.

Can Maoism, the new vogue in SDS ideology, itself provide a reliable guide to the causes of the impasse in Western revolutionary Marxism? There is little reason to think so. According to Maoist theory, the key to all contemporary developments in the international revolutionary movement is Khrushchev's denunciation of Stalin in 1956, which marks the emergence of "modern revisionism" and its doctrines of "peaceful coexistence" and "peaceful transition" to socialism (in certain "favorable" circumstances). But the historical record shows that the reformism of the Western Communist parties (not to mention most of those in the Third World) predates Khrushchev's denunciation of Stalin by at least two and probably three decades, as does the promulgation of the so-called "modern revisionist" doctrine of peaceful coexistence between the systems.

Of course, this is not merely a case of error in historical interpretation on the part of the Chinese. The fact is that the Chinese Communist Party, in order to pursue its ideological struggle with the Kremlin, has deliberately re-written the history of even its own movement to obscure the role of Stalin both in obstructing the Chinese Revolution and in transforming the Communist parties in Europe and elsewhere into reformist organizations.

A theory such as Maoism, in which the answers to key questions are based on the re-writing of history, can hardly provide a sound guide to revolutionary practice in the long run. Sooner or later the manipulation of facts will lead to a gap which cannot be bridged by administrative measures and historical legerdemain. Perhaps the gap will not be as large as that which developed in the Stalin era and which discredited and disoriented a whole revolutionary generation in the West. However, the very existence of the gap will prove crippling to a party which tries to build a revolutionary program across it, for *truth* is a basic weapon in the revolutionary arsenal just as the ability to grasp real social relationships and forces is its greatest strength. A revolutionary movement thrives on truth just as surely as a ruling class lives by deception.

The penchant for ideological manipulation is not peculiarly Chinese. To some extent, any revolutionary party which achieves power in an underdeveloped country must itself become a ruling stratum. The problems of industrialization, education and democratization (including the liberation of internal nationalities) still lie before it, and it must deal with these problems in the face of encirclement and armed hostility from imperialist forces. Moreover, the urban proletariat in such a country is itself so underdeveloped as to be incapable of providing the leadership prescribed for it in the classic Marxist conception. Historically, therefore, the revolutionary party has tended to substitute itself for the revolutionary classes and, as a consequence, to resort to the techniques of manipulation and deception reminiscent of (but by no means equivalent to) the techniques used by the ruling classes of old. (The practice tends to vary: in some revolutionary countries, like Cuba, the level of revolutionary candor has been extraordinarily high; in others such as Russia, the reverse has been true.) In any event, because of these distortions, the attempt to transplant uncritically such revolutionary ideologies into the revolutionary movement in the United States serves to weaken the movement in a profound way.

A further element of distortion in the official ideologies of underdeveloped revolutionary regimes is introduced by the contradictions arising from the conservative character of the nation-state itself, a factor which has received little attention from Marxist theoreticians to date. Thus China's support for the reactionary military dictatorship in Pakistan (and its silence during the repression of working-class strikes and student demonstrations after the fall of Ayub Khan) may be understandable from the point of view of the state interests of China and the diplomatic support it received from the Ayub regime; but from the point of view of the international revolutionary movement, which Peking aspires to lead, it can only be seen in a very different light.

These are not academic points. The "weatherman" state-ment of the majority faction in the new SDS leadership (non-PL) is built around the strategic concept of "people's war" as laid down by China's Lin Piao. The concept envisages a united people's front of third world liberation forces encir-cling the principal metropolis of imperialism—the United States. The concept is derived from China's own revolution, which was fought as a national war of liberation against the Japanese and progressed from its peasant base in the country-side to the towns.

The inadequacy of such a concept for a world character-ized by uneven levels of development in which nationalism and its offspring, the nation-state, are still vital historical fac-tors needs no emphasis. One has only to look at the contra-diction between China's policy and Pakistan's revolution, or even more obviously at the Sino-Soviet split (neither the Soviet Union nor the Sino-Soviet split receives any mention in the 15,000-word global analysis called "weatherman") to see how abstract and unrealistic such a projection can be.

No doubt, a consistent perspective in the Maoist vein can still be constructed by ignoring the tensions between revolu-tionary policy and *raison d'état*, and by assigning the Soviet Union to the imperialist camp (a ploy which makes a mirage both of the arms race between Russia and the U.S. and of their military support for opposing sides in revolutionary struggles such as in Viet-Nam and Cuba). There are obviously more things on revolutionary earth than are dreamt of in Maoist and "weatherman" philosophy; things, moreover, which a revolutionary movement ignores at its peril.

The main consequence so far of SDS's new-found orienta-tion is its essentially fifth-column mentality and its largely negative vision of revolution in its home environment. It is not surprising that Lin Piao and the Chinese should see the struggle against U.S. imperialism in negative terms (get off our backs), but the transposition of this attitude to the sup-posed revolutionary vanguard inside the imperialist powers renders it self-defeating, not to say absurd. Thus the "weatherman" program in effect proposes approaching American workers with the argument that everything they possess is plundered from the Third World (a false proposition in any case: it is the imperialists and not the workers who benefit from imperialism), and that a revolution should be made in this country so that they can give it back.

No revolution was ever built on a negative vision. Moreover, there is no reason even to attempt to build the American revolution as a negative act, a program of social demolition. At a time when the industrial engine has reached a point in its development where it opens up a vista of material plenty and free time (i.e., freedom) for all, America's imperialist system saddles its people and all mankind with militarism, war, pollution, deprivation, exploitation, racism and repression. America now possesses the means to a humane, liveable, democratic future for all its citizens, but only if they are ready to seize the means of production and overthrow the system which dominates their lives just as surely as it dominates the lives of those in the Third World who suffer under its aggression and rule. That is the revolutionary foundation and the internationalist bond as well. It is certainly true that the liberation of the Third World will hasten the liberation of the U.S. But it is no less true that the American revolution is the key to the liberation of mankind. This is the insight that was missing in Chicago; let us hope that it returns to SDS before long.

New Left: Old Traps

Todd Gitlin

The New Left of the Sixties was specifically of the American Sixties. It was born in action and vision—action to create a decently responsible life in the twentieth century; vision to recover the nation's soul from the bankrupt imitative leftism and the end-of-ideology liberalism of the gray Fifties. Instead of the soapbox harangue, patient, everyday work *with* people; instead of frozen hierarchy, organization by real contributions, participation, democracy. "Put your body on the line" and "let the people decide" were rallying cries, from the Mississippi Delta to Berkeley and the Newark ghetto. New generations, born into affluence and cynicism, rattling around in the hollowness of the American Century, learned that the world was in revolution and that American power was finally the enemy of all dreams, discovered that blacks wanted out of their chains and felt unselfconscious in demanding that the society conform to their vision of a civilization beyond scarcity and in beginning to be that vision (traces of it at least) themselves.

The Good Old Days weren't all that good, although people did seem to care more about each other then. The New Left was elitist, narrowly built on the education acquired in the hated but elite educational factory itself. It was self-righteous and vague enough in its rhetoric to see the slogans of Port Huron and the Free Speech Movement co-opted by the Peace Corps and the university pacification programs; it was tentative at a time when everything began to cry for clear explanations.

The New Left had to discard its lingering illusions of American flexibility with every broken black body, every butchered Vietnamese and every broken white head. The rad-

From *Ramparts*, September, 1969. (Todd Gitlin is a past president of SDS.) Copyright 1969 by Ramparts Magazine, Inc.

ical disappointment with which we began the decade, the bitter discovery that America had defaulted on her own liberal promises, had to yield to something that felt like a revolutionary imperative. Suddenly in the middle of the decade, there was a mass resistance—resistance against the war, against the war university, against white supremacy. Finally, whether in so many words or not, against capitalism itself, against class society and the empire, which are its logical outgrowths. The very success of that mass resistance—a dead end against its own limits—has thrown the movement for a loop. The young radicals, increasingly the radical young, driven from all the institutions of control and management, had to make a new life, necessarily a life of political opposition, out there in the space between institutions.

The interface between "hippies" and "politicals" melted into a new creature: the hairy, anarchic, activist, implacable, creatively desperate "street person" whose life conditions admit no chance of reform solutions, who says with his actions: "Your schools, your offices, your shops, your army have vomited me up, and now your cops come to mop me up, but you can't take from me the only place you have left me, the place where I live and breathe my being, the base from which I launch my assault on your barbarism; I *will fight.*" He is a new creature living in a new political culture; he feels like a nigger and the coercive powers-that-be treat him like one.

Through all this, from Stop the Draft Week to Chicago, the Movement felt its strength in the streets. But precisely at the moment it discovered its strength, it also comprehended its weakness. Although it grew numerically as a social force, including high school kids and soldiers as well as "students" and "dropouts," and became recognizable, even to the universal sign of the flashed "V," it was still painfully far from even the shadow of revolutionary change. Not only that; at the peak of its energy it was more brutally attacked by the police, the courts, the entire repressive apparatus, than ever before. Moreover, first-hand encounters with Vietnamese and Cubans made imperialism and its Third World opposition concrete. The stakes of success or failure had never seemed so fatefully present.

In this sequence, most sharply at the time of the Chicago battles, an inescapable choice presented itself: Either the post-scarcity left would comprehend its own unprecedented identity as a social force, elaborate that identity into a vision and program for the campus and the youth ghettoes, and use its reality as a strength from which to encounter anti-colonial and working-class energy and to devise common approaches—or it would turn from its identity, throw the vision out with the narrowness of the class base, and seek an historically pre-packaged version of revolution in which students and *déclassés* intellectuals are strictly appendages or tutors to the "real" social forces. Either it would take itself seriously as a visionary force, conscious of post-scarcity potentials with revolutionary and democratic goals, or it would buy clarity on-the-cheap, taking refuge in mirror-models of the underdeveloped socialisms of Russia and the Third World. Either it would accept the awesome risk of finding new paths—or it would walk the beaten trails, pugnacious and sad. A grave choice, where the stakes are immense; but the pounding pressure of the State leaves no time for placid reflection.

Since Chicago, there has been a fundamental failure of nerve throughout the white movement, which is too widespread to be pinned on any agency, individual, or faction. We could obsess ourselves infinitely with the horror stories of this collective failure: assuming you are the revolution if you say so; getting to like the taste of the word "dictatorship" (of the proletariat, over the proletariat, over anyone); getting so pleased with being correct that you don't like being corrected; substituting rhetoric and slogans for analysis and appeals; kicking your friends as practice for your enemies. It is easier to obscure the real achievements of the past year (and it is again progress which is the property of no faction): the dozens of militant campus movements; the broaching of questions of class within the movement itself; the self-direction of a Women's Liberation movement which refuses to be pigeonholed; the development of the movement's own institutions, including the underground press, Newsreel, communes; the explosion of energy in the high schools and the stirrings in the working-class junior colleges; the identification of the enemy as the global imperialist system. But make no mistake. Most of that growth, numerical and political, is an enormous tribute to what Marxists call the objective conditions; much of the rest, like the weight of a tumor, is canceled out by the attending pathologies.

Fortunately, this impossible society creates the left faster than the organized left can destroy itself. Little question about it—regardless of the fate of the left, all signs are that the monster will continue to sap itself of its own strength, keep itself off-balance. It will lose the loyalty of students, blacks and other colonized minorities by failing to meet their most elemental needs. Soldiers will continue to desert, blacks to revolt, white students to reject the withering carrot and fight the big stick, millions of others to look, at least, for ways to make sense of the madness. Even deprived of its revolutionary scapegoats, this society will disrupt itself.

At the same time, the society digs the foundations of the police state. Not only the police, but all the skilled and privileged whites who are squeezed to finance the failures of capitalism, all those forced to occupy the front lines of racism while the Rockefellers and Cliffords are secure in their bunkers—they are the shock troops for a desperate system. Whether the left can survive is finally a question of whether it can inject its dreams so deeply into the lifestream of the society that millions of people across class and race lines will fight to vindicate the revolutionary promise. Right now it is a question of whether the living consciousness that a new world is possible—free of material misery, hierarchy, useless work—can encounter the more traditional needs of the rest of the American people and the rest of the world, without abandoning its integrity. For underneath the new, pre-packaged, clenched-teeth optimism complete with symbols, language, heroes and unquestioning allegiances, is a fundamental despair about this country, whether it can make—or even *deserves*—its own revolution.

But that revolution, if fought with an international sensibility, would be the best contribution we could make to the rest of the world. If the wealth that America loots from the Third World, and wastes (on arms, packaging, trivial work, etc.) were liberated, how much of the economic pressure could be taken off the Third World, whose own best energies are now absorbed in the struggle for brute industrialization? How might the continents now entering history be spared the agonies of primitive capital accumulation? There are no answers yet because we have not asked urgently, because we have been satisfied to try to tie down American troops on domestic battlefronts—to break the will of the Leviathan by depriving it of the loyalty of its work force, its managerial apprentices, its reluctant soldiers and its literal children. Good; but not enough.

The left must be *conscious* of its visionary prerogative as well as of its privilege; it must find ways of working on the other side of both hope and despair because there is no other way to live and because Americans must be confronted with the practicality of a new way of life. It must make models of that life, like People's Park, while at the same time explaining itself and constantly probing outward from its roots in the middle classes. It must be patient while urgent, and it must do all this without transforming itself into a scatter of "vanguards," each defined by its imperious distance from the Americans from whom at least one piece of the world revolution is to be made.

Plainly, there is much more to be said. But the old civil rights song said the important thing: "Keep your eyes on the prize. Hold on."

Weatherman

Jack Weinberg and Jack Gerson

Taking a close look at "Weatherman," we find that nationalism and national struggles play for Weatherman precisely the same central role that the struggle of the working class plays for Marxists. We are told, with regard to "the principal contradiction" (between the revolutionary Third World and U.S. imperialism), that: "The primary task of revolutionary struggle is to solve the principal contradiction on the side of the people of the world. It is the oppressed peoples of the world who have created the wealth of this empire and it is to them that it belongs; the goal of the revolutionary struggle must be the control and use of this wealth in the interests of the oppressed peoples of the world." Then, a little further on, just in case the message isn't clear, we read: ". . . your television set, car and wardrobe already belong, to a large degree, to the people of the rest of the world."

The message of Weatherman to the American working class is not that the workers are robbed by the capitalist class of the surplus value they create, that the level of technology and potential productivity already obtained in this country are such that by doing away with the outmoded capitalist relations of production, prosperity and plenty is possible not only for Americans, but for the people of the entire world. No; Weatherman says, by implication, that the workers themselves are robbers.

Weatherman reinforces reactionary prejudices by telling the American workers that SDS, and in fact all militant and progressive struggles in the world, have, as their ultimate goal, taking away from the workers what they already have. They put themselves forward as the world tax-collector. Unfortunately for Weatherman, only a very small section of the

Excerpted from "SDS and the Movement: Where Do We Go From Here?," *Independent Socialist,* September, 1969 (Jack Weinberg and Jack Gerson are members of International Socialists).

American population is afflicted with liberal guilt. Weatherman would do better to revive the Kingdom of Heaven, for they have nothing to offer the mass of the American population here on Earth.

Weatherman polemicizes very strenuously against ". . . any conception of 'socialist revolution' simply in terms of the working people of the United States . . ." They denounce it as "imperialist national chauvinism" to define socialism "in national terms within so extreme and historical an oppressor nation." They state: "Any attempt to put forth a strategy which despite internationalist rhetoric, assumes a purely internal development to the class struggle in this country, is incorrect. The Vietnamese (and the Uruguayans and the Rhodesians) and the blacks and Third World peoples in this country will continue to set the terms for class struggle in America."

Against whom are they polemicizing? Who is it that defines socialism *"simply"* in national terms? Who is using "internationalist rhetoric" to mask a secret belief that the class struggle in the US is a *"purely* internal development"? It becomes clear that the words "simply," "purely" and the like are included only for the sake of appearances and that what is really being said is that one should not at all conceive of socialism in terms of the working people of the United States; one should not assume any internal development of the class struggle. They are polemicizing against any conception that white American working people have any decisive role to play in socialist revolution, against any conception that it is at all internationally progressive for workers to struggle in their own class interest.

This is made quite explicit in an amendment submitted by one of the Weatherman authors during the discussion of unity principles. After a variation on the above theme revolving around the word "simply," we read: "The socialist revolution must have the specific content of serving the needs and interests of the oppressed peoples of the world. This means that conscious full support for the international struggle is the *key element* [our emphasis] of socialist consciousness. To not uphold this as the basis of the American revolution is necessarily to uphold white supremacist privilege and to separate oneself from the international revolutionary movement."

The underlying assumption seems to be that socialist revolution will be visited upon the bulk of the American people as retribution for their sins and corruption. It will be in their interest, but only in a moral, not in a material, sense. Our job then must be, as it were, to gather together the elect and hasten the judgment day.

Weatherman does recognize that the workers in the shops face problems. They realize that: "In the shops the crisis in imperialism has come down around speed-up, safety, and wage-squeeze—due to higher taxes and increased inflation, with the possibility of wage-price controls being instituted." What programs do they offer in response to these problems? "We must relate this exploitation back to imperialism. The best way to do this is probably not caucuses in the shops, but to take guys to city-wide demonstrations, Newsreels, even the latest administration building, to make the Movement concrete to them and involve them in it. Further, we can effect consciousness and pick up people through agitational work at plants, train stops, etc., selling Movements, handing out leaflets about the war, the Panthers, the companies' holdings overseas or relations to defense industry." If a black caucus exists in the shop, Weatherman advocates: ". . . perhaps organizing solidarity groups, but at any rate pushing the importance of the black liberation struggle to whites, handing out Free Huey literature, bringing guys to Panther rallies, and so on."

In short, Weatherman's "industrial program" seems to be: whatever you do with workers, for God's sake, don't build anything in the shops—don't organize workers to struggle against their oppression as members of the working class.

For a moment, let us relate the Weatherman strategy to the May-June events in France. After massive street demonstrations and street-fighting carried out primarily by students, the French working class went out on general strike. It was the general strike which transformed the very significant student demonstrations into an event of explosive international revolutionary significance. The student movement triggered a response by the working class, which then shook the very foundations of French society.

During those events, a large number of the most militant young French workers were out in the streets fighting side by side with students. Meanwhile, there was far too little (often none at all) radical organization or organizing in the shops, and as a result there was no militant force in the shops which could effectively counter the influence of the CGT (the CP trade union federation) and the other sell-out French unions. They were able to isolate the bulk of the workers from the infectiousness of the movement in the streets, were able to conservatize the situation and blunt the revolutionary potential, were able to destroy the impulses toward class unity and class power, and as a result were able to trick the various shops into separate settlements and lead the workers back to work. And when the workers went back to work, for all intents and purposes that round of the struggle was over all across France.

It is a fine thing for young workers to mix with radical students and participate in their demonstrations. It is, however, a grave error if their immersion in the student movement is counterposed to playing a role in or organizing a radical working-class movement—particularly in the shops. When a revolutionary situation develops, it is the activity, or lack thereof, of a revolutionary movement in the shops which is ultimately decisive. But according to Weatherman, young workers who are affected by speed-up, safety hazards, wage freeze, etc., should not be encouraged to respond by organizing and struggling around these issues in the shops.

Why can the young worker best learn the relationship between speed-up and imperialism by participating in a student struggle at a college administration building, rather than participating in a struggle against speed-up? Part of their answer flows from Weatherman's general methodology: "... the particular issue is not the issue, is important insofar as it points to imperialism as an enemy that has to be destroyed. Imperialism is always the issue. . . . The masses will fight for socialism when they understand that reform fights, fights for improvement of material conditions, cannot be won under imperialism. With this understanding, revolutionaries should never put forth a line which fosters the illusion that imperialism will grant significant reforms."

Making this more concrete, they say: "What does it mean to organize around racism and imperialism in specific struggles? In the high schools (and colleges) at this time, it means putting forth a mass line to close down the schools rather than reform them so they can serve the people."

The essence of the Weatherman line seems to be that the reason one orients toward those who are oppressed and exploited is that it is they who are likely to be angry enough to tear the motherfucker down. To organize in the shop in an attempt to force immediate concessions from the boss is reformist, economist, and fosters illusions. Since such organizing is a necessary ingredient in the building of a revolutionary movement and revolutionary consciousness in the shops, that too is prohibited. The notion that by collective struggle one can wrest from the rulers concessions which better the lives of oneself and one's fellows, is a notion that Weatherman is intent on destroying. But it is that notion, not despair, which among the masses generalizes to revolution.

One might conclude that Weatherman is overzealous in its opposition to reformism. But the demand for workers' control is clearly not reformist. It is the logical extension of workers' opposition to speed-up, unsafe practices, and the prerogative of the company to maintain dictatorial control on the shop floor. It is the demand which most easily leads to a very clear understanding of the capitalist relations of production. And it is a demand which cannot be in any meaningful sense achieved short of the workers' seizure of state power. It is a demand, moreover, which epitomizes the interest of the working class, and makes clear the meaning of workers' power. To Weatherman, workers' control is an "anti-internationalist" concept which represents "national chauvinist and social democratic ideology within the Movement."

Weatherman sees itself and the movement it is trying to build as the agents within Babylon of the oppressed peoples of the world. In fact they consider themselves even less than agents. They consider the black movement to be the real agents, and themselves to be its supporters. We read: "In defining and implementing this strategy, it is clear that the vanguard (that is, the section of the people who are in the forefront of the struggle and whose class interest and needs define the terms and tasks of the revolution) of the 'American Revolution' is the workers and oppressed peoples of the colonies of Asia, Africa, and Latin America. Because of the level of special oppression of black people as a colony they reflect the interests of the oppressed people of the world from within the borders of the United States; they are part of the Third World and part of the international revolutionary vanguard."

At precisely the time that the Panthers, who originated the colonial analysis of blacks in America, and the League of Revolutionary Black Workers are seriously discussing the relationship between black workers and the rest of the American working class, Weatherman denies that black workers are a part of the American working class, and almost even implies that class divisions do not exist within the black community. They say: "Thus, northern blacks do not have a 'dual interest'—as blacks on the one hand and 'US-nation workers' on the other. They have *a single class interest along with all other black people in the US*, as members of the Black Proletarian Colony."

The Weatherman view of revolution is expressed in their discussion of black liberation. ". . . If necessary, black people could win self-determination, abolishing state power to do it, without this white movement, although the cost among whites and blacks both would be high. Blacks could do it alone if necessary because of their centralness to the system, economically and geomilitarily, and because of the level of unity, commitment and initiative which will be developed in waging a people's war for survival and national liberation. . . .

To put aside the possibility of blacks winning alone leads to the racist position that blacks should wait for whites and are dependent on whites' acting for them to win. Yet the possibility of blacks winning alone cannot in the least be a justification for whites' failing to shoulder the burden of developing a revolutionary movement among whites. If the first error is racism by holding back black liberation, this would be equally racist by leaving blacks isolated to take on the whole fight—and the whole cost—for everyone." The task is "to build a white movement which will support the blacks in moving as fast as they have to and are able to, and still itself keep up with the black movement enough so that white revolutionaries share the cost and the blacks don't have to do the whole thing alone." We are then told that any white that doesn't follow this path is "objectively racist."

One might ask what would be the nature of the state or at least what social and economic relations in the US would be like, following a revolution in which the blacks did it alone. But somehow, that question seems to miss the point. One feels that to Weatherman the revolution is Armageddon, and all that follows is the judgment day.

The central driving force behind Weatherman is desperation. Its adherents see the state power of decaying American capitalism playing an increasingly reactionary and brutal role throughout the world and at home. They see it viciously suppressing the legitimate desires and aspirations of oppressed people everywhere. They know that it is willing to use the most barbaric means to protect its own interest, and fear the worst. The response of Weatherman comes from its combined feelings of outrage and impotence. It generates such a great sense of urgency that suddenly in its mind the urgency itself is translated into a material force capable of tipping decisively the balance in favor of its deep desires.

How does Weatherman justify its belief that, if necessary, blacks can make the revolution alone? "The genocidal oppression of black people must be ended, and does not allow any leisure time to wait." Throughout history, the most noble of wishes and sentiments, no matter how imperative, have not, in and of themselves, countered barbarism and oppression. Rather, when sentiment stands in the way of an analysis of material relations and forces, it impedes the development of programs which can begin to deal with the crisis, and as a result functions counter to its original desires. We noted Weatherman's systematic substitution of national antagonisms for class antagonisms as the decisive social and historical dynamic. The result begins to resemble a patriotic movement in negation—flag and mother country become, rather than the objects of veneration, the anathemas. Meanwhile, Weatherman seems, at least in theory, to be moving away from its petit bourgeois origins toward the development of a political base among what has classically been called the lumpenproletariat. Many of its adherents have come to extol as a virtue, in and of itself, violence and political gangsterism. . . . It is difficult to predict in what direction the Weatherman tendency in SDS will go, or how long it will hold together. It will almost immediately begin to face one serious difficulty. A large and central part of its theory is based upon adaptations of politics that have been put forward by the black movement, particularly by the Panthers. But the Panthers and other leading black groups are rapidly moving away from those ideas. At least in rhetoric, they are moving increasingly toward a class-oriented analysis and program. Though Weatherman emerged at the convention by far the dominant tendency in SDS, it seems quite doubtful that without a severe metamorphosis it can maintain that position for more than a year.

1969

Carl Oglesby

The leading events so far: The SF State strike and the structurally similar conflicts that erupted across the country, the People's Park showdown in June, the SDS convention, and the Black Panther call for the Oakland conference.

San Francisco State: I want to make just two observations on this much-studied event.

First, the movement's characteristic attitude toward partial victories—more particularly, toward what is disparaged as "student power"—is mechanistic. It appears that every change which is not yet The Revolution is either to be airily written off as no change at all, or further than that, to be denounced as co-optation into the counter-revolution. People should only try to remember that the SF State strike did not materialize out of thin air, that it had a background, that it was that particular moment's culmination of a long conflictual process, and that just as with Columbia, where political work had been sustained at a generally intense level at least since May 1965, the explosive strike at State was made possible, maybe even necessary, by a long series of small moves forward, any one of which could have been attacked as "bourgeois liberal reform." More precisely, it was in large part those incremental "reforms" of curriculum and student-teacher and teacher-administration relationships carried out under the unseeing eyes of President Summerskill that created the general conditions in which the strike could take place. As with Columbia, the atmosphere had long been thoroughly politicized—that is to say, charged with consciousness of national issues. And a long reign of liberalism had, in effect, already *legitimated* the demands around which the strike was fought through, just as a long reign of reform-

Excerpted from "Notes on a Decade Ready for the Dustbin," *Liberation,* August-September, 1969. (Carl Oglesby is a past president of SDS and an author of *Containment and Change.*) Reprinted with permission of the author. Copyright, 1969, by Carl Oglesby.

ism had created the institutional means of the strike. In the same way, the fact that the Third World Liberation Front leadership did after all negotiate the "nonnegotiable" demands, the further fact that this leadership then moved to *consolidate these bargaining-table victories within the changing structure of the institution itself*—this meant not that the fight was over, not at all that "capitalism" had suffered a tactical defeat only to secure a strategic victory, but rather that the stage was—and is—being set for another round of conflict at a still higher level of consciousness within a still wider circle of social involvement. For the net result of the strike's victories is still further to break down the psychological, social, and political walls that had formerly sealed off the academy from the community. This is a big part of what we are about—the levelling of all these towers, the redistribution of all this ivory, the extroversion of these sublimely introverted corporate monstrosities: and not just because we have willed it, whether out of malice or chagrin or a blazing sense of justice, but rather because capital itself, in all its imperial majesty, has invested these schools with its own trembling contradictions. Necessarily demanding a mass consciousness of and for its technological and political ambitions, it necessarily produces a mass consciousness of the servility of the first and the brutality of the second. Necessarily demanding an army of social managers, pacifiers of the labor force, it necessarily produces an army of social problem solvers, agitators of that same labor force. Necessarily demanding an increasingly sophisticated corps of servicemen to the empire, it necessarily produces a cosmopolitanism to which this empire's shame is its most conspicuous feature. Necessarily demanding a priesthood to bless its work in the stolen name of humanity, it necessarily produces the moral and social weaponry of its own political condemnation. . . .

So. That's the first "observation"—the winning of a "reform" isn't always a bad business, and Leftists should stop being scared of being reformed out of things to do. The only real strategic necessity is to make sure the reform in question reforms the power configuration so that it becomes the basis for further and still more fundamental challenges to class rule.

The second observation is connected. It has to do with the question of what's called (disparagingly) "student power." The formula attack on the making of demands for such things as curriculum reform and greater student participation in campus government goes like this: "The young bourgeois, privileged already, exhibits here only his desire to extend his privileges still further. This desire must be fought by radicals. If not exactly in the *name* of the working class, we must see ourselves as fighting at least in its *behalf,* and since its interests are hardly served by the abolition of grades or the reduction of required credits, we must oppose such demands."

First, the outlines of a speculation. What if the multiversity is in some substantial part the creation of the advanced world proletariat—not merely the plaything and mistress of the imperialists? What if it is partly in the multiversity that the proletariat has banked and stored up its enormous achievements in technology? What if the multiversity— the highest realization yet of the idea of mass education and the rationalization of productive labor—is in one of its leading aspects the institutional form through which the proletariat continues its struggles for emancipation? Behind how many of these so-called "bourgeois" children, one or two generations back, stands a father in a blue collar, a mother in an apron? The proletariat, says Marx, will have to prepare itself for self-government through protracted struggle. What if this struggle is so protracted that it actually must be seen as taking place, in one of its aspects at least, across *generations?* The revolutionary aspiration of whites in the 1930s manifested itself most sharply in factory struggles. In the 1960s, that aspiration has materialized most sharply on the campuses. What have we made of this fact? The function of a method of social analysis is not to reprimand reality for diverging from its model, but on the contrary to discover in reality the links and conjunctures that make history intelligible and life accessible to effective action. An abstraction is not something to stand behind like a pulpit but a lens to see through more discerningly. Obvious? Then it is high time to confess: At the same time that it has been trying so desperately to live forwards, the New Left everywhere, in West Europe as well as here, has been just as desperately trying to think backwards. If Marxism is any good, and if we can prove it worthy of the moment, then we ought to be able to say what it is about contemporary relations of production that makes the campuses a primary site of contemporary revolutionary motion. Only when that question is answered will we have any right to pontificate about "correct" and "incorrect" lines, and it has not yet been answered. Meanwhile, even if it is good and sufficient, as I am almost sure it is not, to characterize "student power" as a fight for "bourgeois privilege," we would still have to ask: What *kind* of privilege? Assuming that there is nothing here at all but an intra-class struggle against the contemptuous indifference of institutions, against the mindless blather of the dons, the deans, the sycophants and the liars, against authority in particular and authoritarianism on principle, we would still have to say that the political balance of this struggle is *progressive and portentous.* To those who tell me that this fight neither equals, approximates, initiates, nor reveals the form of The Revolution Itself, I answer first, Neither did Nanterre, neither did Watts, neither did anything else in man's social history but a bare handful of uniquely definitive and epochal convulsions, each one of which moreover appeared only at the end of a painfully long train of indeterminate events which escaped their ambiguity only thanks to the denouement; and I answer second, If you are trying to tell me you know already what The Revolution Itself will look like, you are either a charlatan or a fool. *We have no scenario.*

Second, for what it's worth to a movement suddenly infatuated with the words of the prophets, Lenin faced a somewhat similar question in 1908 when certain radicals refused to support an all-Russia student strike on the grounds that "the platform of the strike is an academic one" which "cannot unite the students for an active struggle on a broad front." Lenin objected: "Such an argument is radically wrong. The revolutionary slogan—to work towards coordinated political action of the students and the proletariat—here ceases to be a live guidance for many-sided militant agitation on a broadening base and becomes a lifeless dogma, mechanically applied to different stages of different forms of the movement. Further: "For this youth, a strike on a large scale ... is the beginning of a political conflict, whether those engaged in the fight realize it or not. Our job is to explain to the mass of 'academic' protesters the objective meaning of the conflict, to try and make it *consciously* political."

The People's Park: Those few SDSers, unfortunatley conspicuous this past year, who think Stalinism is more or less right on, ought at least to have admitted that "socialism in one country" is not exactly the logical antithesis of "socialism in one park." But it was the Stalinists, both pure and off-breed, who among all the Bay Area radicals found it hardest to relate to the park before the attacks, were most puzzled by the attack itself, and produced the most opportunistic "support" in the aftermath. Mainly because these curious rumbles of the hip are so hard to focus politically in terms of a mass-and-vanguard model, it's hard for people with old minds to figure out how to relate to them. That fact may be the basis of a touching epitaph; but a living politics for our period will have to understand that "decadence" is as "decadence" does, that the "cultural revolution" is not merely a craven and self-serving substitute for the "political" one, and that if the West has, indeed, a leftwards destiny, then neither its particular ends nor its modes of organization and action will be discovered through archeology. My guess: People's Park was one among many episodes of a religious revival movement—exactly the kind of movement that has heralded every major social convulsion in the United States—and as with all such movements, its ulterior target, its enemy, is the forces of the industrialization of culture. The difference now is that the virtual consummation of the Industrial Revolution, *within the West,* lends a credibility and relevance to such a program that it formerly has not had. That is: The anti-industrialism of early radicals like Blake and Cobbett, though it was fully anti-capitalist, could confront rampant capitalist industrial progress with nothing more powerful than a retiring, improbable, defenseless nostalgia; could argue against the system of "masters and slaves" only in behalf of the older and no doubt mythical system, allegedly medieval, of "masters and men." Every time it became a *practical* movement—whether revolutionary or reformist—socialism had to put forward simply a more rational version of the program of industrialization itself. This is not an irony or tragedy of history, it's just the dialectics of historical process. That it has so far been unsurpassable is in fact the essence of revolutionary socialism's general isolation to the backwards countries, or put differently, this limit merely expresses the wedding of revolutionary socialism to anti-colonialism, and on the other hand, its impotence in countries in which the industrialization process has been carried forward effectively (however ruthlessly) by the bourgeoisie. The thesis of People's Park, rough as it may be to deal with both in terms of our tradition and our current practical needs, is that the essentially *post-industrial* revolution, embodied most fully but still (we must suppose) very incompletely in the hip communities, portends the historically most advanced development for socialist consciousness.

"Most fully" because it goes beyond industrialization, and in doing so, implies (much more than it has so far realized) a genuinely New Man—just as new compared to Industrial Man as Industrial Man was new in comparison to the artisans and small farmers who foreran him.

But it would be useless just to approve of this cultural revolution without being very clear about its terrible limits. I see two limits. First: The "new values" (they are, of course, very old) can claim to be subversive only of the standing values of work, but not really of consumption, there being nothing in the structure and precious little in the texture of "hip leisure" that keeps it from being commercially copied (deflated) and packaged. Thus, in effect, the target of the attack detaches itself, refuses to defend itself, and in offering itself as the apparent *medium* of the attack is able (persuasively to all but the sharpest consciousness) to pose as the "revolution's" friend. There are a thousand examples of this process, whose minimum result is vastly to complicate the cultural critique, and which at the other limit succeeds wholly in disarming it. The quietism of which the hip community is often accused may thus be much less the result of a principled retreat to cosmology than of its flat inability to confront commercialism with a deeply nonnegotiable demand. Second, even though the new anarchism is morally cosmopolitan—affirming in a rudimentary political way the essential oneness of the human community—its values are *practical* only within the Western (imperialist) cities, and are far from being universally practical even there. So the second and bigger problem the cultural revolution needs to overcome is its lack of a concrete means of realizing its ideal sympathy with those globally rural revolutionary movements whose social program necessarily centers around the need for industrialization, not the surpassing of it. A solution of this problem would no doubt also solve the first. This is why it's so important to subject the cultural revolution to a much more profound and critical analysis than what has been produced so far. For the point at the moment is not to be for or against the current reappearance of anarchism. It will be necessary rather to explicate its tradition (too many hippies think they are saying brand new things) and then to try to see if the balance of forces has changed sufficiently that this old movement for a cultural revolution against industrial society has begun to acquire a power which it formerly has not had.

The SDS Convention: I wasn't there, never mind why. At the last SDS thing I was at, the Austin NC, the handwriting was already on the wall. Having determined that SDS must become explicitly and organizationally committed to its version of Marxism-Leninism, PL would continue in its Trotskyist way of identifying organizations with movements and would try to win more power in SDS—that much was already clear in the spring. I didn't think, though, that PL people would force a split. As fiercely indifferent to this country's general culture as they seem to be, I still thought they would understand a split as contrary to their purposes and would therefore seek to avoid it, even if that meant a momentary tactical retreat. Either I was wrong, or PL misunderstood—and misplayed—the situation.

I want to make just one point about the current situation. What is wrong about PL is not its rigidity, its "style," its arrogance or anything like that. Its *ideology* is wrong. And not just in the particulars of emphasis or interpretation or application, but in its most fundamental assumptions about the historical process. Someone else may argue that PL's Marxism-Leninism is a bad Marxism-Leninism, and that is a view which can doubtless be defended. But I see no prosperity in the approach that merely wants to save Leninism from Milt Rosen here and Jared Israel there. The problem is deeper and the task much more demanding. It can be posed this way: Backwards as it is, our practice is more advanced than our theory, and our theory therefore becomes an obstacle to our practice—which is childish and schematic, not free and real enough. The general adoption of some kind of Marxism-Leninism by all vocal factions in SDS means, certainly, that a long moment of intellectual suspense has been resolved—but much less in response to experience than to the pressure of the *tradition.* We have not produced even a general geosocial map of the United States as a society—only as an empire. We have not sought in the concrete historical experience of classes a rigorous explanation of their acceptance of "cross-class" (Cold War) unity but rather have employed a grossly simplified base-and-superstructure model to explain away the fact that labor does not appear to think what we think it ought to think. We have taken a class to be a thing, not a process (or as E.P. Thompson called it five years ago, "a happening"), and have imagined it to be bound, more or less, to behave according to the "scientific laws" which govern the category. Most generally, we have imported a very loose and sometimes garbled theory of pre-industrial revolution, have tightened it without really clarifying it, and are now in the process of trying to superimpose that theory, thus reduced, on our own very different situation. The RYM group does not differ in this respect from PL, the Revolutionary Union or even YSA or ISC. All these groups, opportunistic in widely varying degrees, claim to have the same ace in the hole, and Lenin's phrases (or what's worse, the Chairman's truistic maxims) are gnawed upon by every tooth.

For a long time I was baffled. Last fall the word began to reach me: It was being said that I had "bad politics." How could *that* be, I wondered, since I thought I had no politics at all. But by winter I conceded the point: no politics is the same as bad politics. So there followed a time in which I experimented with only the "mass line." Could Klonsky and Coleman be right? It didn't come to much. My mind and my instincts only became adversaries. By spring I had to deactivate, couldn't function, had to float. What I know now is that this did not happen to me alone. On every quarter of the white Left, high and low, the attempt to reduce the New Left's inchoate vision to the Old Left's perfected remembrance has produced a layer of bewilderment and demoralization which no cop with his club or senator with his committee could ever have induced. And my view of the split at the convention is that it merely caps a series of changes which began at the East Lansing convention in 1968, with the decision to counter PL's move on SDS by means of a political form—the "SDS caucus," i.e., a countervailing faction—which accepted implicitly PL's equation of the social movement with the organizations that arise within it. What walked out of the Coliseum was simply a larger version of 1968's SDS caucus. Certainly it had grown in awareness and self-definition over the year; and knowing that bare opposition to PL is no very impressive gift to The Revolution, it had spurred itself to produce an independent Marxist-Leninist analysis and at least the semblance of a program. My unhappy wager is that even in its RYM incarnation it remains a faction, that it will continue last year's practice of "struggling sharply" against internal heresies, that it will remain in the vice of the old illusions, that it will pay as little attention to what is happening in the country and the world as its predecessor regime did, and that whatever growth the movement achieves will be in spite of its rally cries and with indifference to its strictures. Nor is there a lot that can be done about this. The Western Left is perhaps in the midphase of a long, deep transition, and there is no way for SDS to protect itself from the consequences. They will have to be lived out. Which does not mean there is nothing to do. It means, rather, that any new initiatives will confront a situation very heavily laden with obstacles and limits. It isn't 1963 anymore. . . .

[The Black Panthers:]

The Panthers are in trouble not because they have no white support, but because they have too little black support; not because they have no white allies, but because, in the virtual absence of a wide array of real activities, real social programs in the black communities, there is nearly nothing that white allies can do besides pass resolutions, send lawyers, and raise bail.

SDS will have to take its share of the blame for this. Much more interested in shining with the borrowed light of Panther charisma than in asking all the hard practical questions, much more interested in laying out the metaphysical maxims that identify the "vanguard" than in assuming real political responsibility, this SDS, which so often chews its own tongue for being "petty bourgeois," most shamefully confesses its origins precisely when it tries so vainly to transcend them in worship of "solidarity" which really amounts to so much hero-worship. Bourgeois is as bourgeois does. Marx, Engels, Lenin, Trotsky, Mao, Chou, Ho, Giap, Fidel, Che, Fanon: which one plowed a furrow, ran a punchpress, grew up hungry? That, in the first place, ought to be that. Further, in the second place, it is not lost causes, however, heroic, or martyrs, however fine, that our movement needs. It needs shrewd politicians and concrete social programs. Not theoretical (really theological) proofs that The People Will Win in the End, but tangible social achievements now. Not the defiance of a small, isolated band of supercharged cadre who, knowing they stand shoulder to shoulder with mankind itself, will face repression with the inner peace of early Christians, but a mounting fugue of attacks on political crime of all sorts, on all fronts, at all levels of aspiration, from all sectors and classes of the population, so that repression can never rest, never find a fixed or predictable target. Humble example: Yesterday's *New York Times* carries a full-page political ad—the American Institute of Architects, it seems, has come out against the war. What will the Panther or the SDS national office do? Send a wire? Make a phone call? Investigate the possibility of a combined action? Try to make two or three new friends in order to make a hundred or a thousand later. I guess not. For the AIA is as *bourgeois* as they come, awfully *liberal,* too. When even the Oakland 7 and the Chicago 8 are suspect, what chance do a lot of architects have? So the architects will never hear what we have to say about the empire, about the houses that are being built in Cuba, about what we take to be the extent and causes of the present world crisis.

But this loss is presumably compensated by our clarity about the "vanguard." Clarity! Any close reading of the RYM's Weatherman statement will drive you blind. Sometimes the vanguard is the black ghetto community, sometimes only the Panthers, sometimes the Third World as a whole, sometimes only the Vietnamese, and sometimes apparently only the Lao Dong Party. Sometimes it is a curiously Hegelian concept, referring vaguely to all earthly manifestations of the spirit of revolution. At still other times, it seems to be the fateful organ of that radicalized industrial proletariat (USA) which has yet to make its Cold War-era debut. Mostly, though, it's the poor Panthers, whose want of politics was never challenged by the few SDSers who had access to their leaders; this appointment—Vanguard to the People's Revolution—being, presumably, SDS's to make—and one which is defended, moreover, in terms of a so-called revolutionary strategy (see the Weatherman statement) in which the United States is to experience not a social revolution at the hands of its own people, but a military defeat at the hands of twenty, thirty, many Vietnams—plus a few Detroits.

But perhaps the ghetto = colony analysis means that the Detroits are already included in the category of Vietnams? In that case, for all real political purposes, (North) American = white; and the historical role of these whites, their "mission" in the many-sided fight for socialism, is most basically just to be overcome. The authors of the Weatherman statement are of course perfectly right in trying to integrate what may appear to be *decisive* international factors into a model scenario of domestic change. From no viewpoint can an empire be treated as if it were a nation state. But although they face this problem, they do not overcome it. They might have said that the leading aspect of the US industrial proletariat remains, classically, its exploitation at the hands of US capital, and that it therefore still embodies a momentarily stifled revolutionary potential. Contrarily, they might have said that what we have here is a gigantic "labor aristocracy who are quite philistine in their mode of life, in the size of their earnings and in their outlook . . . [and who are] real channels of reformism and chauvinism" (Lenin, *Imperialism: The Highest Stage of Capitalism*). On its face, neither view is silly, but neither is one more satisfactory than the other. Weatherman's refusal to settle for one or the other seems to me to express a realistic *intuition;* but the problem is not solved simply by asserting one theory here and the other theory there. They cannot both be equally valid. I think the difficulty is embedded in the method of analysis: Weatherman takes class to be a thing rather than a process, and consequently tries to treat class as if it were, in and of itself, *a definite political category.* (That is, labor is fated to be Left.) But Weatherman also has a certain level of historical realism, and this realism always intervenes (happily) to obstruct the mostly theoretical impulse—a kind of social Freudianism—to idealize labor, to strip it of its historical "neurosis" by the simple and fraudulent expedient of viewing its neurosis as *merely* superstructural. In other words, Weatherman's confusions and ambiguities stem from a conflict between its model and its data, and it comes close to escaping this dilemma only when it forgets its static model of class for a moment, and gives freer rein to its sense of history and process. At such moments, it comes close to saying something really important, which I would paraphrase, over-optimistically no doubt, thus: "The labor force we are looking at today is not the one we'll see tomorrow, and the changes it will undergo have everything to do with the totality of its current and forthcoming experiences, which range all the way from the increasingly sensed contradiction between the rhetoric of affluence and the fact of hardship to the blood and money sacrifices it will be asked to offer in the empire's behalf." But this ought to be said up front, and it then ought to lead to the most exhaustive analysis of the real, living forces that impinge upon not just labor but the population as a whole. Everytime something like this starts to happen, Weatherman breaks off and reverts to its concealed paradox: the vanguard of the US (Western would be better) revolution will be those forces which most aggressively array themselves *against* the US, those forces, in other words, which are most *distant* from white culture. Thus, *cause becomes agency:* the living proof of a *need* for change—the Panthers, the NLF, etc.—is defined as the political *means* of change; an almost absent-minded abstraction converts white America's sickness into the remedy itself.

The most succinct case of this kind of bad reasoning I've heard came at the end of a speech Bob Avakian made at the Austin NC. The racism of white workers would have to be broken, he said, because, when the revolution comes, it will be led by blacks, whose leadership whites must therefore be prepared to accept. If this were only an unconsidered trifle, it would by pointless to snap it up, but it appears to represent a serious, persistent, and growing school of thought in the New Left. The problem with it is just that it implies that there could be a revolution in the absence of a profound radicalization of the white working class, in the absence of profound changes in the political character of that class. What would make it possible for white workers to revolt would also make it possible—and necessary—for white workers to help *lead* that revolt. The very idea of a white working-class revolution against capitalism that is, necessarily *presupposes* either that racism will have been overcome or at least that the conditions for that triumph will have been firmly established. The problem with this dreamed-of revolution will not be anti-blackism within its ranks, but the anti-communism of its adversary. "In revolution, there are no whites or blacks, only reds."

But beyond this, Avakian (as with the Weathermen) wants it both ways: blacks are a colony, on the one hand, outside the colonizing political economy and set over against it; and on the other hand, they are in and of the empire's proletariat. In the first mode, they press against the empire from a position which is outside it in every sense but the geographical. In the second mode, they press upwards against the bourgeoisie from within capital's system of social classes. It is of course not impossible that these modes really do coexist and interpenetrate one another. In fact, it is likely that they do. But both modes cannot be represented as simultaneously co-leading aspects of the black situation *vis-à-vis* white society. A white revolutionary strategy requires a decision as to which aspect is dominant and which secondary, *as well as an understanding that what is dominant now may become secondary later, may even disappear.*

So—an attempt at a clarification (which, as with certain other points I've tried to make in this letter, I'll have to elaborate and defend in some other, more ample space):

1. The persistence of integrationism, in a dozen disguises, and nationalism's struggle against it, make a strong circumstantial case for the view that blacks are above all blacks. They are not just another part of the workforce, not even just the main body of the lumpenproletariat. Nor do they make up a *caste.* Industrial societies do not have, cannot afford, castes; castes belong to pre-capitalist formations (or, at latest, to agrarian capitalism) and are in fact destroyed by the imperatives of industrial organization

Obviously, blacks are assigned an important role in the US production-consumption process. So were pre-revolutionary Cubans. So are contemporary Venezuelans. The low-skill aspect of black production and the importance of the credit and welfare systems in black consumption constitute, in themselves, the leading features of a *colonial* relation to a colonizing political economy. It is therefore appropriate to see the black ghetto as a colony. Thus, *true* black nationalism (much "nationalist" rhetoric is merely a Hallowe'en mask for integrationist or even *comprador* demands) is necessarily anti-imperialist, and could consummate whatever military or political victories it might achieve in the independence struggle only through a socialist development of the means of production.

2. No more than the struggle of the Vietnamese can be the struggle of the blacks to play a "vanguard" role in the problematic revolution of white America. *Vietnam and Detroit, the NLF and the Panthers, do not constitute the means of white America's liberation from imperialist capital. They constitute, rather, the necessity of that liberation.* They exist for white America as the living embodiment of problems which white America must solve. There are, obviously, many other such problems: the draft, high taxes, inflation, the whole array of ecological and environmental maladies, Big Brotherism at all levels of government, the general and advanced hypertrophy of the State, the fractionalizing of the civil society. Most of these problems are relatively diffuse; they are not experienced so acutely as the war or the ghetto risings. But they are still real to people, and they all have the same general source in the hegemony of capitalism: What sets Vietnam aflame is the same force that brutalizes the black population and poisons everybody's air.

3. The function of the white Western socialist is therefore, at this moment, to confront white America (white France, etc.) with the truth about the problems that harass it, to explain that these problems cannot be solved merely by repressing those people in whose lives the problems are embodied, cannot be solved by prayer or petition, and above all that they cannot be solved so long as the means of production, the wealth of that production, and the monopoly of political power that goes with those means and that wealth are locked up in the hands of the big bourgeoisie. You would

as wisely ask the bullet to sew up the wound it made as ask the monopoly capitalist to solve these problems. The capitalist cannot do it. But the socialist can. That is the point we have to make.

4. The rebellion of white students is provoked most fundamentally by the general *extrinsic* failure of capitalist production—by the fact, that is, that production has become so conspicuously anti-social. This is what gives the student rebellion both its power and its very real limits. But this extrinsic collapse has not yet been followed by an *intrinsic* collapse: the system of capitalist production is at the moment *both insane and rational.* If a failure of its administration should produce also an *intrinsic* collapse—if suddenly no one could buy and no one could sell—then the people of the West would come again to the crossroads of the 1930s, and would have to decide again whether they would solve their problems by means of war or revolution. It is at that point that the fight for the loyalty of the proletariat will become truly historical instead of merely theoretical, necessary instead of merely right, possible instead of merely desirable. *But no will, no courage, no ingenuity can force this eventuality.* If it develops, and if the crisis is prolonged enough for white American workers to grasp the need for revolution, then with the same motion in which they change their rifles from one shoulder to the other, they will simultaneously *de-colonize* the blacks, the Vietnamese, the Cubans, *the French*—for at such a moment, all the old paralyzing definitions will die and new definitions, revolutionary ones, will take their place. The world proletariat will have achieved, at last, its dreamed-of world unity. This possibility, this towering historical power, is merely the other side of what it means to be a white American. But again: no matter how well it is organized or how combative and brilliant its performance is, no Western socialism has it in its power to force or even to hasten the intrinsic collapse of capitalist production. If you are an unreconstructed Marxist, you believe that it will come about sooner or later; if, like myself, you are not, then you don't know. It could happen: the market seems pale, inventories

are large, the need to fight inflation in behalf of the international position of the dollar may lead to harder money,
more unemployment, and still further slippage in demand;
and if Nixon does not get the ABM, the whole system of the
US Cold War economy will have received an ominous if
mainly symbolic jolt. My view is that if this process starts
unfolding, labor will have scant need of student organizers,
and in the second place, that it will actively seek the support
of student radicals. The "worker-student alliance" will
happen when workers want it to happen, they will want it
when they need it, and they will need it when and if the
system starts coming apart. At such a conjuncture, students
will have a critical contribution to make no matter what
happens between now and then; but their contribution will
be all the greater if they will have employed this uncertain
threshold period to secure some kind of power base in the
universities and such other institutions as they can reach, and
if they will have used the opportunities of their situation to
take the case for socialism to the country as a whole, aware
certainly that class *implies* a political signature, but just as
aware that it does not *necessitate* one. It is mainly to the
extent that the white movement has done just this, in fact,
that it has been of some occasional concrete service to the
black movement, and the same will be true of any forthcoming relationship with a self-radicalized labor force.

Let me put this more bluntly. We are not now free to
fight The Revolution except in fantasy. This is not a limit we
can presently transcend; it is set by the over-all situation, and
it will only be lifted by a real breakdown within the system
of production. Nor will the lifting of the limit be the end of
our fight; it will be just the possibility of its beginning. Meanwhile, there is no point in posing ourselves problems which
we cannot solve, especially when the agony of doing so
means, in effect, the abandoning of humbler projects—
"humbler"! . . . as for example, the capture of real power in
the university system—which might otherwise have been
brought to a successful head. Just look: Very little, even
insignificant effort was invested in the idea of "student

power," and the SDS leadership even debunked the concept as, of all things, "counterrevolutionary." Yet we have just witnessed a moment in which a few key universities very nearly chose to collide head-on with the State over the question of repression of the Left. That would have been a momentous fight, especially coming on the heels of the black campus insurgencies. It's our fault that it didn't happen. The fault may be immense.

This was supposed to be about the future. Thousands of words later, I have still said very little about the future. I'm not really surprised at myself, and I won't apologize, but simply sum it up by saying that if SDS continues the past year's vanguarditis, then it, at least, will have precious little future at all. For what this movement needs is a swelling base, not a vanguard.

Or if a vanguard, then one which would rather *ride* a horse than look it in the mouth. One which wants students to get power and open up the campuses, blacks to win the franchise and elect some mayors, architects to be against the war and advertise that fact in the *Times,* clergy to be concerned and preach heretical sermons, inductees to dodge the draft and soldiers to organize a serviceman's union, workers to have more pay and shorter hours, hippies to make parks on private property, liberals to defeat the ABM, West Europe to escape NATO, East Europe the Warsaw Pact, and the global south the Western empires—and the American people as a whole (by any means necessary!) to be free enough to face their genocidal past for what it was, their bloody present for what it portends, and their future for that time of general human prosperity and gladness which they have the unique power to turn it into. And for being still more "revolutionary" than this implies, let us confess that time alone will tell us what that might mean.

Part 2
Action In The Streets

Introduction

Weatherman actions leading toward the National Action, while highly diverse and of varying success, gradually defined the nature of Weatherman practice and priorities. To begin with, a number of the most significant actions were led, organized, and carried out by Weatherwomen. As Lorraine Rosal summarized it, Weatherman's position on women's liberation emphasized:

> the need to bring women into the movement by organizing them to fight racism and imperialism; that women's liberation will come through the fight for international communism; that the Third World women's liberation front is the vanguard force of all women's liberation; and that it is racist of white women not to fight the struggles led by the women of Cuba, China, Vietnam, and the black and brown colonies of the US.*

Weatherman had said little, however, about the specifics of organizing against male chauvinism and supremacy. The articles in "Toward the National Action" describe how Weatherman first approached this problem in its mass work.

The demonstrations led by Weatherwomen cannot be measured merely in terms of how well they accomplished their stated goals. That women were moving independently—and sometimes against the opposition—of men, and that this was accompanied by the smashing of myths that held women

* See "Who Do They Think Could Bury You," *New Left Notes*, August 29, 1969.

back from developing as revolutionaries, were victories in and of themselves. Moreover, the criticisms made of these early actions forced Weatherman to deal more seriously with male chauvinism within its own ranks. While radical women generally have been critical of the role of women in Weatherman, many have acknowledged the early contribution Weatherwomen made toward the development of an autonomous revolutionary women's movement.

Weatherman's organizing techniques are well-represented in the article by Motor City SDS. Weatherman seeks to organize white youth from all segments of the working class around anti-racist and anti-imperialist struggles. Its approach differs from that of other radical groups in the predominant emphasis it places on putting forward its politics in an open and aggressive manner. For Weatherman, militant struggle is the key to heightening contradictions—it not only strikes concrete blows against the state, but also builds revolutionary consciousness among those involved in the struggle. Weatherman goes so far as to define militancy in terms of physical confrontation with reactionaries in the presence of the very people it seeks to organize. Provoking arguments and fights around anti-imperialist symbols, such as Viet Cong flags, demonstrates Weatherman's allegiance in no uncertain terms and shows its willingness to fight. Having involved people in struggle at a relatively high level in this and other ways, Weatherman maintains it has created situations in which the anti-communist attitudes of young workers can be quickly overcome.

Most people on the Left first became familiar with the thrust of Weatherman's provocative political policies in the course of debating Weatherman street actions—a controversy which reached new levels of intensity in the weeks before and after the "Days of Rage," Weatherman's part of the SDS October 8-11 National Action in Chicago.

Soon after the June, 1969, National Convention, the Weatherman and RYM II factions of SDS began to collectively implement the resolution passed at the convention calling for the National Action as part of an entire fall offensive against the Vietnam war and imperialism. "Look at It: America 1969" illustrates the SDS mass line on the National Action at a time when differences between Weatherman and RYM II had not yet surfaced. The Boudin, Dohrn, Robbins article puts forth a Weatherman perspective on the National Action, which expresses the hope that it "will be as broadly based and widely supported as possible."

By the end of August, serious differences over the strategy and tactics of the National Action had emerged between the two dominant factions of SDS. Mike Klonsky, a leader of the RYM II faction and a member of the steering committee for the SDS fall offensive, publicly resigned from the Weatherman-controlled National Office leadership, charging (among other things) that Weatherman had gone back on the convention's mandate to "win the masses of working people to a united front movement against imperialism."* Mark Rudd and Terry Robbins responded for Weatherman by arguing that priority must be given to building "a fighting, anti-imperialist youth movement, which itself not only raises the issue of imperialism, but also shows people how to fight back . . . , and by fighting back provides material support to the vanguard struggles of Third World peoples for national liberation."†

While this exchange appeared in the pages of *New Left Notes,* Bill Ayers was in Cleveland giving his "A Strategy to Win" speech. It typifies the aggressive tone Weatherman began to adopt towards those in and around SDS who questioned Weatherman politics or plans for the National Action. It best captures the rhetorical flavor of Weatherman on the attack—combative, uncompromising, confident, audacious, and outrageously arrogant.

Weatherman spokesmen toured the country pushing for an extremely militant National Action. The Left, on the whole, did not respond favorably. The criticism throughout the Movement, which had been gaining momentum, reached a

* See "Why I Quit," *New Left Notes,* August 29, 1969.

† See "Goodbye, Mike," *New Left Notes,* August 29, 1969.

climax toward the latter half of September. Carl Davidson, writing in the *Guardian* summarized the doubts that beset most Movement organizations, including many SDS members, over the evolving Weatherman conception of the action:

> The original plan for the action had four objectives: (1) to build a broad-based attack against imperialism; (2) to expand the anti-imperialist movement into the working class and to fight for working-class leadership of the movement; (3) to raise the level of militancy as a response to repression and (4) to make the demand "immediate withdrawal from Vietnam" operative rather than agitational.
>
> At this point, the Weatherman faction ... seems to have scrapped all these objectives except the third—increased militancy.*

To Davidson's accusation that Weatherman was pursuing the path of "left" adventurism, Bill Ayers replied for Weatherman that "there's no such thing as fighting too hard against imperialism."

Despite the fact that as October 8 approached Weatherman found itself increasingly isolated within SDS, the Weather Bureau kept predicting—up to the moment before the action—that thousands of working-class youth would come to Chicago to participate in mass street fighting. "Practice would prove what's what," said Rudd and Robbins in their exchange with Klonsky. As it turned out, not thousands, not even a thousand, but about 800 Weatherman demonstrators showed up, squaring off against over 2000 police. By Saturday, October 11, only 300 people were willing to once again face an overwhelming number of police.

The Weathermen and women who went ahead with the action did so fully realizing, if not expecting, that some of them would be killed or badly injured. The Weather Bureau never seriously considered calling off the action because the

---

* See "SDS Chicago Oct. 8-11 Action Under Fire," *Guardian*, September 13, 1969.

turnout was small. Instead, they transformed the demonstration on the spot from a mass confrontation involving thousands of white working-class youth into an "exemplary" action by a relatively small number of mother country revolutionaries, who would risk death rather than turn back. *

Tom Thomas documents the four days of Weatherman street actions in Chicago; Shin'ya Ono provides the view of an actual Weatherman participant. His article remains one of the clearest statements of Weatherman political policies. It includes a strong defense of the strategy and tactics of Weatherman actions in general and the "Days of Rage" in particular, as well as a detailed account of Weatherman criticism and re-evaluation of the action as it unfolded in Chicago.

Weatherman departed from previous Movement mass street actions during the "Days of Rage" by initiating attacks against symbols of capitalist oppression—the police and private property. This violence was not in retaliation for specific acts of police violence, but part of a publicly announced policy to "raise the level of struggle."

Moving toward armed struggle is part of Weatherman's internationalist approach to revolution in the United States—first, in the sense that the Vietnamese and the blacks need

---

* Bill Ayers was later to remark: "We were talking the other night and we realized that all our heroes are dead. Wow, what a trip! Che, Nguyen Van Troi, the Vietnamese who tried to get McNamara. We're running their pictures in our paper with the line 'Live Like Him!' and they've all been killed. Outtasight, man. We've got a new slogan for the people that are going down to help with the sugar harvest: 'Cuba is for the Living!' " Ayers' remarks typify Weatherman's tendency to define its situation in terms of extremes. Building socialism in Cuba is for the living; overthrowing American imperialism is a death trip. Weatherman, as early as the action in the streets of Chicago, already had begun to live in the shadow of death. Not long after the "Days of Rage," Weatherman would compensate for its death trip mentality with hedonistic orgies. Like a pendulum, moving from one extreme to the other, Weatherman swung from death trips to life trips to death trips. . . . Bill Ayers is quoted in an article by John Kifner, "Vandals in the Mother Country," *New York Times Magazine*, January 4, 1970.

such support and, secondly, because the revolutionary consciousness of the American people will be most affected by the power and impending victory of the Third World over American imperialism. Hence, Weatherman's desire to "Bring the War Home."

This is all predicated on Weatherman's belief that most Americans understand their interests and are alienated from the system and its traditional political values—but that they also feel powerless and unable to act in a manner that will make a difference. People are confused, however, about the causes of their oppression and about who is ultimately responsible for it. Their false consciousness is reinforced by their atomized and destructively competitive lives and especially by their racism and national chauvinism. Weatherman concludes that a good organizing strategy identifies the enemy and shows people they can strike a blow at their oppressors and get away with it.

What Weatherman actually established in Chicago by putting the lives of its members behind its rhetoric was its courage and moral authority; it failed to establish that it could provide material support to the Vietnamese and the blacks. Weatherman, nevertheless, made its presence felt.

The perseverance it exhibited in the streets of Chicago pushed people on the Left toward increased militancy. The articles by Andrew Kopkind and Eldridge Cleaver reflect the admiration Weatherpeople elicited for what they had dared to do. Even those critical of the politics behind the "Days of Rage" could not help but be moved by the spirit and commitment of Weatherman. Radical activists compared their own willingness to fight with that which Weatherman exhibited in Chicago. The white Left brooded and criticized itself for not doing enough, for not openly taking more risks. No doubt part of the heavy trashing that went on during The Day After demonstrations following the verdicts in the Chicago "Conspiracy 8" trial had a lot to do with the need people felt to raise the level of struggle in the face of growing repression. No less important, however, was the impulse to fight as hard as Weatherman did in Chicago.

The same holds true with regard to the militant action against the Justice Department during the national moratorium in Washington—but there were tremendous differences in the number of participants in the TDA and the Justice Department actions as compared with the "Days of Rage." Tom Hayden tries to account for this discrepancy by critically evaluating Weatherman's organizing perspective and tactical sense.

In summary, then, some important lessons emerge from Weatherman's political practice. To distinguish itself from what it took to be the opportunism of RYM II's "Serve the People" line, around the time of the National Action Weatherman began—at first facetiously—to push a "Fight the People" line. The Movement drew the inference that Weatherman thought the vast majority of white people in America were unalterably corrupted by their white skin privilege and ingrained racism. While Weatherman would eventually succumb to this belief by the end of 1969, it did not characterize Weatherman politics in the period leading up to and including the "Days of Rage."* The fact that the Left erroneously believed that it did as early as the fall of 1969 only helped isolate Weatherman from its possible allies even more. Weatherpeople, having mistaken ferociously outrageous rhetoric for strength, must bear the brunt of the responsibility for the misconceptions that grew up around them at this time.

Yet in raising the slogan "Fight the People," Weatherman touched on a dilemma all revolutionaries must eventually face. In all revolutions *some* of the people actively side with the forces of reaction and counter-revolution. There are circumstances in which these people must be fought, often physically. For example, when a proto-fascist force of "hard

* Note, however, that the "Weatherman" statement, contrary to earlier Weatherman position papers, provided the theoretical foundation for Weatherman's later despair at the possibility of a majority revolution when it glibly stated that, if necessary, the blacks could make the revolution in America by themselves. The reasons behind this later shift in Weatherman's politics are discussed in the introduction to the third section of this book.

hat" construction workers physically attacked peaceful anti-war demonstrators (with the apparent connivance of Nixon administration officials, union leaders, and local police), the Movement should have fought back. An anti-war movement that cannot stop vigilantes from chasing it off the streets cannot hope to stop the war. In this context, fighting some of the people makes sense; indeed, it is essential. In general, however, the Left can best demonstrate its willingness to fight on behalf of the people not by pitting itself against them, but by organizing them to smash the repressive state.

More than anything else, the Chicago street actions made Weatherman a national force. The media created a Weather Myth: Weatherman soon became known as the most militant and omnipresent of white revolutionary organizations. The Left, having experienced less aggressive but no less violent street demonstrations, also gave Weatherman its grudging respect. But the "Days of Rage" were, by their nature, unrepeatable. Bond alone for the approximately 300 Weatherpeople arrested came to three-quarters of a million dollars, and the federal conspiracy charges eventually pressed against the leadership could hardly be ignored. A repeat performance by Weatherman, even with fewer casualties, would have left many cadre rotting in jails for lack of bail and facing impending imprisonment after their trials. But the "Days of Rage" did not need to be repeated: they had established Weatherman's reputation as a white fighting force. Weatherman rhetoric about inflicting material damage to major imperialist institutions in Chicago can be discounted; the actual significance of the demonstrations was symbolic. They projected a commitment on the part of white revolutionaries to move into total opposition to the state, regardless of personal cost. Earlier and less one-sided confrontations had lacked such force. In this sense, Weatherman turned a possible debacle into a victory of sorts.

Weatherman's courageous action did severely limit its future options. The leadership still had some latitude in deciding when and how to go underground, but its flexibility was curtailed by the noose the state was tightening around

Weatherman's neck. Despite these difficulties, Weatherman managed to build, in the short time available and under constant surveillance and harassment from the police and FBI, an infrastructure that could sustain a revolutionary underground.

From *The Fire Next Time*, Sept. 20, 1969

BRING THE WAR HOME!

OCCUPATION TROOPS OUT OF VIETNAM, LATIN AMERICA, ALL OTHER FOREIGN COUNTRIES, BLACK AND BROWN COMM-UNITIES, AND THE SCHOOLS.

CHICAGO, OCT 11
ALL POWER TO THE PEOPLE!

From *New Left Notes*, July 8, 1969

Who Do They Think Could Bury You?

Lorraine Rosal

The Ohio Summer Project is Weatherman in practice. . . .

One of our major self-criticisms of the Ohio Project has been that we were internal—i.e., did not practice—for too long after the beginning of the project. All of us, both men and women, came off our campuses timid, physically afraid of moving in the streets, but more importantly psychologically afraid of the people. The more we dwelt on our fear, the more we made the people into monsters; the more we doubted our own ability and knowledge to organize and raise an anti-imperialist, anti-racist consciousness; the more we felt unable to live up to our international duty, and accept our role as urban guerrillas concretely aiding the liberation struggles of the Third World. . . .

The result of our fears and internal emphasis led to all the pitfalls of reactionary liberalism. In the Columbus Project, and particularly in the women's caucus, our growing liberalism had bad effects on our attempts to deal with male chauvinism and male supremacy. Firstly, we dealt with chauvinism simply by attacking chauvinist and paternalist remarks by men. Our criticisms were handled liberally and personalistically. . . . Secondly, we began defending each other in political discussions because we were women, not because we were politically correct. Often if a man criticized a woman for a counterrevolutionary action or statement, another woman would react in a man-hating way against the man who made the criticism. We failed to act upon our understanding that what side any person is on in an ideological struggle should be determined not by one's sex, but by one's understanding of the political differences involved. Thirdly, we often did not criticize each other in front of the rest of the collec-

Excerpted from *New Left Notes*, August 23, 1969

tive. . . . The result of these three things was that we began to use chauvinism as a bludgeon. And this served to hamper the development of political trust and led to disunity within the collective. The woman's caucus we formed had become nothing but a tea group.

Our correct fighting instincts led to a few fistfights when the men's chauvinist baiting reached an unbearable level. Such fights led the men to take us more seriously at first, but because they were in the context of no practice, the political content of such struggles became more and more unclear.

The turning point came one night when the women were invited by a neighbor to a "Stanly" party. Stanly parties for women are run by the Stanly Company at which they push their products. The woman who gives the party gets a certain number of points for giving the party and extra points if her guests buy Stanly products. If you accumulate a certain number of points you get a free gift. The more you screw your friends by getting them to buy products they can't use, the more points you get and the more worthless products you acquire; i.e., the more the Stanly Company screws you.

An all-women's party of young working-class girls, a party where the exploitation of women was crystal clear: there couldn't have been a better push for us. It was the first time we had really organized around women's liberation, and we made lots of mistakes. We were too liberal and we didn't put the women, particularly the representative from the Stanly Company, up against the wall. Our fear of being too aggressive failed to polarize the group, and therefore the whole evening lacked any dynamics of struggle. Also we spoke only about consumption, the family, and women's poor wages and working conditions. We didn't attack racism when it came out in the conversation, and failed to speak strongly enough about white privilege.

However, despite our terrible raps, it was a very important event in our development. Our women's caucus that night was out of sight. For the first time we had criticism/self-criticism based on practice. We criticized each other as political women doing political work, and set up more concretely what our caucus must be. We began to see the caucus working within the larger collective as a place for women to share organizing experiences and to develop an analysis of male chauvinism and supremacy as tools of the ruling class, an analysis of the relationship between white working-class women and the international proletariat, an analysis of the economic ramifications of the oppression of women, particularly young women, caused by the crisis in imperialism, and so on. In light of this, the caucus took responsibility for researching and writing on the women's question. In addition, we decided that women would train in self-defense along with the rest of the project, but that the caucus would see itself as an affinity group, learning how to move well in the streets, and serving as an exemplary fighting unit. Because there are only six women in the Columbus Project, we do not see ourselves setting up a women's collective at this point, but plan to use the caucus as a basis for forming such a collective in the future. The caucus will also be responsible for collecting study material on women's liberation for the study sessions of the whole project.

This first organizing experience proved exemplary for the men and forced them to begin dealing with us as political people. It served as a real impetus for all of us to form political collectives, go out into the streets and the parks, etc., do mass work around the national action, and do some real heavy and consistent organizing. Because of the women's continuing practice, we began to really assume leadership positions.

For the first time, we could really dig on the concept laid down by the women of Long Bow, China, that the best way to combat chauvinism is for women to do not just good, but exemplary revolutionary work. The kids we began organizing came in contact for the first time with strong women whose purpose in life was not to have a home and babies, but to pick up the gun and fight in a communist revolution.

Moving out in our organizing collectives (high school, college and street), on the job (small restaurants, McDonalds, laundromats, etc.), in parks and at community and recreation centers, we organized and raised struggles. On the Fourth of July we answered Governor Rhodes' call for all "patriotic citizens and our military boys to celebrate this great holiday of freedom in the parks of our cities" by charging through the parks with an NLF flag, leafleting and rapping. In the following weeks slogans painted in red appeared on the walls and steps of 5 high schools—Free Huey, Fuck US Imperialism, Off the Pig, Vietnamese Women Are Fighting, Viet Cong Will Win, etc.; carloads of pigs, heated discussions, leafleting, and high school contacts resulted. And in job after job, racists were put literally up against the walls. The political polarization that has occurred through these struggles has been the basis for our organizing success. Every day it becomes clearer that struggle is the only way to build a fighting Movement.

Then came our actions aiding the black rebellion of July 21-23. Our hard raps, especially after the arrests, pig harassments, etc., of the last two weeks, where women played an all-important role, have forced guys we have been organizing to combat their chauvinism, to understand more clearly the fight for women's liberation, and to begin to see their role in aiding that liberation. The fact that one of us, Elizabeth Stanley (no relation to the Stanly Company) was in jail on inciting to riot charge (felony, 1-3 years, $25,000 bail) because she had aided the black struggle organize against racism, did more to combat male chauvinism and bring the idea of female revolutionary leadership home—both to the kids we were working with and to the men in our own project—than all the discussions, criticism sessions, etc., that we had had about racism and male chauvinism all summer.

Through our practice and struggles we ourselves have felt more liberated and have begun to build a women's army within our own movement. We have rejected our programmed bourgeois roles as the bastion of conservative forces in the home, on the job, and in the community; we have attacked our being used as a surplus labor force for imperialist racist dogs; we have attacked our role as chattel, scabbing on the international liberation struggle. Instead, we have accepted a new role—a role of dignity—a role as members of a women's army, fighting not just for our own liberation, but for the liberation of all the people.

Break On Through To The Other Side

Motor City SDS

"Bring the War Home" is a slogan not just for the national action but for here on in. Our aim is to create another front against imperialism in the white mother country itself. We will attack the beast from within as the peoples of the world attack it from without. We are building a fighting force of white working-class youth who see the necessity of fighting with the Vietnamese and the blacks. Until imperialism is smashed and the rest of the world is free, we cannot achieve our own liberation. . . . In Detroit, Motor City SDS has built a solid base for a city-wide Movement and is growing rapidly. We've been organizing for the national action through actions in Detroit—at schools, beaches, drive-ins and rock concerts. The young people we're reaching out to—high school kids, freaks, community college people, bikers, greasers, almost all of whom work in factories around the city when they work— dig the Chicago action and are joining Motor City SDS through the struggles we have initiated. These people will not only come to Chicago, but will bring Chicago back to every city in America.

ON PRACTICE

The "Metro Beach Riot" (as the papers called it) was the first action Motor City SDS undertook in organizing for the national action. Metropolitan Beach is located in one of the white working-class suburbs that surround black Detroit, and is packed with young white kids. One Saturday afternoon in the middle of July, about 30 SDS cadre and people starting to work with us swept the beach in a line distributing Chi-

Excerpted from *New Left Notes,* August 23, 1969

cago leaflets and carrying a red flag. When we planted the flag a crowd of about 200 quickly gathered. Loud arguments began in the center of the crowd, which included many Vietnam veterans. The reaction of the kids was a vehement defense of American myths. The arguments centered around communism, and especially the Viet Cong, upward mobility, and white-skin privilege. Many of us got into good raps with people on the fringe of the crowd who wanted to know what was happening. When we heard that the beach rent-a-pigs had called the sheriff's patrol, we moved to regroup. One Viet vet yelled "Let's get the flag!," and about 40 people charged it. Sticking together as a group, we fought the attackers to a standstill and left the beach chanting.

We created a tremendous impact on the beach because we confronted kids with the fact that it's a political world and that they have to deal with that. The main contradiction is between those who have it and those who don't—between white America and the colored nations of the world. By growing up in white America, we've been fucked into being oppressors, brainwashed and given privileges to secure us on the side of the white ruling class. The kids on the beach were confronted with the fact that we were taking sides with the Vietnamese and the blacks, and acted defensive, confused, sympathetic and uptight in varying degrees and combinations. When they called us "Communists!" we talked about how communism is right-on, how people can cooperate to build a society that's good for everybody, where a few bastards don't get rich off the blood and labor of others. We talked about how we are oppressed in the schools, on the job, in the courts and in the army, and how this fucked-up capitalist system alienates us from our brothers and sisters.

RESPONSE

We got a continuous response from the people who were at the beach and from everybody who heard about it. One of our people talked to a motorcycle dude who fought against us at the beach while they were both waiting in line to apply for a job at Chrysler. He had read the leaflet since the fight and dug on going to Chicago and bringing his friends. The action not only made an impact on the beach but initiated the city-wide fighting presence of Motor City SDS.

The McComb action, now known throughout the country, was an action taken by nine Motor City SDS women at a local community college. We gathered outside a sociology classroom of about 40 or 50 students who were taking a final exam. We entered the classroom chanting, and barricaded the door with the teacher's desk. One woman distributed Chicago leaflets while the rest of us lined up in front of the classroom, and we stopped chanting as one woman began to address the class. She rapped about how American imperialism fucks over the people of the world, and about people's struggles for self-determination. Another woman spoke about how imperialism oppresses the black colony within America. When a third woman began to talk about the material oppression of women and the necessity to break out of subordinate roles and join the struggle, some men got uptight and tried to charge the door in order to get out and call the pigs. These pig agents were dealt with while a fourth woman continued to rap to the people in their seats about Chicago and the necessity to take sides with the peoples of the world. Somehow a teacher managed to get out a back door, and the administration called the pigs. Because of an unclean getaway, we were busted as we left the school on charges of disorderly conduct and assault and battery.

McComb Community College is located in an all-white working-class community and trains the local white youth in the skills necessary for lower managerial jobs, positions that objectively oppress black people. By busting into a classroom during final exams, and by talking to people about what's happening in the world, we confronted them with their dual position in capitalist society. They are oppressors because of their acceptance of privilege, and they are oppressed because of their objective relationship to the ruling class.

On another plane, it was women who made the situation happen. Organizing women through exemplary action is key to the way we do work. It is necessary to struggle to raise consciousness of women's oppression and male supremacy in the context of world revolution. We do not just urge women to become fighters, nor do we just talk to them about taking sides. It is necessary to build a white fighting movement that provides material support for national liberation struggles in the black colony and throughout the world. The force needs fighters—both men and women.

All over the city people talked to us about McComb, and wanted a McComb to happen at their school. Our action spoke to the new role that women have to play, and has helped bring women from McComb and around the city into our fighting movement.

We planned an action at the Henry Ford Community College—Ford's fanciest factory. At Henry Ford we got a chance to talk to a lot of working-class kids and many Vietnam veterans on pension to learn trades. Most of the kids who attend the college are at least partially funded by the motor companies and are trained for lower managerial jobs in factories.

When we reached the school we divided up into small groups and went into every class to announce an SDS rally that afternoon. After all the classes had been covered we regrouped and went into the student union. People there were already talking about our presence on the campus. Within a few minutes the union was transformed from a passive scene with separate groups of individuals to a heated political struggle involving everyone in the room. We moved from the union to the center of campus, bringing with us many kids whom we had involved in conversations; and were met with more kids from the classrooms. We spent the whole afternoon rapping about the national action, imperialism, and SDS in the Motor City, and later that week people came to a meeting we called about Chicago, and they are now organizing for the national action and to join our actions around the city.

ROCK CONCERTS

Huge rock concerts happen all the time in the Motor City.

Hip culture is part of the lives of all white working-class youth. These concerts bring together thousands of freaks, bikers and greasers, digging the music and each other, and turning on to dope. Coming together conscious of their alienation as a group, the kids who go to these concerts are aware of the pigs and ready to fight if they get hassled. We go there and talk to them about the need to organize ourselves as a fighting force against the Man, taking sides with the people of the world.

Our political objective at a rock concert is to rap with as many people as possible and to get out mass propaganda about the national action. We have been distributing at least 10,000 leaflets every weekend, which talk about Chicago and city-wide SDS meetings. We have made a political presence at almost every large gathering of youth this summer, and many of the kids at our city-wide meetings have been people we met at these concerts. Many of the kids we have rapped with are coming along with us on our actions, and some have become full-blown organizers for the national action.

WHITE CASTLE

Drive-ins in Detroit are one of the few places where kids can hang out. We've spent many weekend nights at drive-ins around the city. Our favorite drive-in is the White Castle near the East Detroit Line, which is always packed with about 200 kids from different areas of the city—high school and even junior high school kids, vets, and young freaks. The energy level of the White Castle is high, and the pigs evidently feel that they have to keep it under control. The pigs succeed in making their presence known to everyone. No one is allowed out of their cars for very long, and the parking lot is cleared frequently.

The first night we went to the White Castle, a small group of us started leafleting cars quickly, trying to get as many leaflets out as possible. The drive-in kids helped pass leaflets from car window to car window. While one of our people was passing out literature, the pigs came over to try to stop him. Ignoring the pigs, he finished giving his leaflets away and split out of the parking lot, outrunning the pigs. Kids in the lot jumped on top of their cars, and one group started to chant "Power to the People!" The kids in the lot then helped us find our brother, who by this time was in a side street blocks away from the White Castle.

Before we split the area we talked to the kids who had helped us out. They were into the fact that the pigs were especially uptight about us since we had been passing out SDS leaflets. We exchanged names and phone numbers, and they told us to come back to the White Castle soon.

We went back the next week, and this time we brought many more people, including kids we'd met on other actions and on the first White Castle action. We swamped the parking lot with national action leaflets, running from one side to another in a pack, giving war whoops and chants. The pig scene was heavy and some pigs tried to prevent us from getting back through the parking lot. We had to knock a few down to make it back to our cars. Kids followed us out of the lot, asking for more leaflets to give to their friends and shouting their names and phone numbers.

The next time we went to the White Castle, we decided to work under cover in order to have as much time as possible to talk to people. We knew that the kids had read our leaflets and had a sense of who we were, but we still needed to get into real political discussions of the questions they had. We split up into small groups and drove to the White Castle in a number of different cars. This time we went out from our cars in groups of two to go to other cars and rap. City pigs constantly patrolled the area while we were in the lot, and when we walked up to cars the kids were hip to the fact that the pigs were watching us. Some invited us to sit inside and rap, and we covered every car in the lot and talked to everyone in the drive-in.

The kids we talked to had lots of questions—about the war, about communism, about why we're for black people. Answering these questions is the crucial part of our organizing—when our politics make sense to people they can move with us. The actions we took at first set a struggle tone for the talking we did later, and this combination of tactics is crucial for organizing new people into the Movement.

In our first actions we encountered tactical problems which impaired our ability to move. At Metro Beach at one point some of us made the decision that the group should leave the beach. Those who had made the decision tried to communicate it to all our people, but some people didn't hear the change in plans and didn't notice the group leaving. Much confusion resulted, and it became obvious that the danger of somebody becoming isolated and left behind, with the resulting immobility of the whole group, had to be over-come. It also became clear that situations could frequently arise where there would be no time to discuss changes in plans. In other situations where we had to be able to move quickly together because of pigs, we found it imperative to know the turf. At McComb, since we didn't look over the area thoroughly before our action, we didn't have get-away routes planned, and that resulted in a bust.

Through criticism and correction of these problems, we developed a general method for handling actions tactically. Before any action, two or three people are chosen to be tactical leaders. They scout out the chosen area and develop a comprehensive plan for the action. Immediately before the action a planning meeting is held; for security reasons, only those going on the action can attend the meeting. The tacti-cal leadership explains the plans, using maps which they have drawn up, and our forces are divided into affinity groups. Each group sticks together, protects each of its members, acts as a fighting unit in case of confrontation, and functions as a work team. In a large crowd, for example, each affinity team may be assigned a specific section of the crowd to leaflet and talk to. The tactical leadership operates from a central place, coordinates the action, and makes all tactical decisions. Tac-tical leadership communicates its decisions to the leaders of the affinity groups by signals (whistles, etc.) or runners, if the area is large. Immediately following every action an evalua-tion meeting is held.

Follow-up has been crucial to all of our actions. We have

returned to the scene to rap with kids about what came down and why we had come to their school or drive-in or beach. On our actions and often during follow-up work, we have met kids who want to work with us on Chicago and join struggles all over the city. The first form that we brought our contact into was a regular Monday night meeting. We made sure that every piece of literature we handed out announced open meetings on Monday nights at a set time and place. These Monday night meetings have grown over the summer to about 80 people. They always include some form of political education—films, raps on Cuba and Vietnam, and discussions on Chicago and the politics of the national action. Question and answer sessions usually turn into general political discussions involving many of the people at the meeting. At the end of the meeting we continue talking in smaller groups to get a better sense of who people are, where they come from, and to talk directly to the questions that individuals have.

Our contacts are also involved in the total action process. They plan actions with us, participate in them, and are involved in the evaluation sessions (criticism and self-criticism) held immediately afterward. This process is crucial to political development. People must learn to plan and initiate struggles and learn the need for self-conscious criticisms if we are to be better and more effective in future political struggles. During each action, the new people who come with us actually do organizing work themselves. By trying to explain our politics to other people, their understanding of our politics has deepened.

We are bringing people away from waging struggle only at their particular institutions—their high school, their Community College—and their neighborhoods. We are building a mobile city-wide group which will be the fighting force in the opening of yet another front against imperialism in the Motor City. Our contacts will also be involved in the planning for Chicago. Many of them from Detroit will be coming to the Cleveland conference with us.

We've become fighters this summer. Our study of karate

makes us strong, and our practice makes us real to young people. Fighting understands winning. Our words have content because they are backed up by a growing base of power. Opening a new front here at home can only be achieved by striking blows at the enemy and building a Movement that understands that to aid the Vietnamese and blacks we must develop a white fighting force that FIGHTS!

We are making over-extension a reality—the United States cannot contain rebellions in Vietnam, Laos, Korea, Venezuela, Guatemala, and ten cities at home, but that's what they will have to deal with. Chicago is the beginning stage of a fighting Movement in this country. We're bringing the war home October 8-11, and then back to every city in America. The thousands of Motor City kids who come with us to Chicago will know just what business needs to be done when they get back to Detroit.

POWER TO THE PEOPLE!
BRING THE WAR HOME!

The Motor City 9

POWER TO THE PEOPLE!
BRING THE WAR HOME!

Last week nine women—now the Motor City Nine—walked into a classroom at McComb Community College and barricaded the doors. Inside they interrupted the students writing final exams to talk about the most important things going on in the world today—things that teachers at McComb College never mention or only lie about. They rapped about the war in Vietnam and about how the Vietnamese women carry on armed struggle together with Vietnamese men against US imperialism.

They rapped about the struggle for liberation and the Black Panther Party, and about how McComb College keeps black people out by charging them higher tuition, saying it's because they don't live in the same community.

They spoke about how white people are acting against the people of the world, helping the rich get richer, and how white people must join the revolution now waged by black and brown people across the world to liberate the riches of the world for all the people.

When they began to talk about how women are kept down in this country, two men got up to leave the room. It is reported that the Motor City Nine responded to such an exhibition of male chauvinism and general pig behavior by attacking the men with karate and prevented them from leaving the room. They then continued to discuss how women are used as slave labor in the household, exploited on the labor market, and turned into sexual objects.

One of the men called the pigs and the women were

From *New Left Notes*, August 23, 1969

The Motor City 9

arrested. They were released on bonds totaling $6500 for charges of disorderly person and assault and battery.

The Motor City Nine are part of the Women's Liberation Movement. They understand that the road to women's liberation is not through personal discussions about the oppression of women; nor is it through an appeal to the public conscience through demonstrations or guerrilla theater about the issue of female liberation. It will only come when women act, not only around the issues of women's liberation, but when they act on other issues such as the war and racism. Women's liberation will come when women exercise real power—as is done in Vietnam and in the McComb College classroom.

Women's Militia

Seventy-five women won a victory in Pittsburgh last week. Coming off of a Weatherman conference, women from collectives across the country formed a women's militia to march on Pittsburgh. Pittsburgh, like every city, has been bordering on the brink of race war, and during the past few weeks blacks have been fighting in the streets for an end to the racist hiring practices of large, powerful construction companies.

The women came to the city as an exemplary fighting force, fighting on the side of the black liberation struggle and the Vietnamese struggle, demanding that white kids in Pittsburgh decide which side they're on. Never before in Pittsburgh had there been a white revolutionary fighting force which kids who supported the black liberation struggles could identify with.

On Wednesday night, September 3, when they arrived in Pittsburgh, they commemorated the death of Ho Chi Minh, the leader of the Vietnamese struggle, by taking small guerrilla actions around the city in sections where kids usually hang out. In a hippie part of town one group of women marched around chanting "Ho Lives" and "Free Huey," carrying an NLF flag. From the very start some kids followed them, joining in with the chants. There were several confrontations with the pigs, but no sisters were busted and the flag was defended.

On Thursday all the women went to South Hills High School, which was by then covered with writing on the walls and sidewalks such as "Vietnamese Women Carry Guns," "Ho Lives" and "Jail Break." They arrived at the predominantly white school of 3000 kids during a lunch break, or when hundreds of kids were hanging outside the school. The women marched together around the school, handing out

From *New Left Notes,* September 12, 1969

leaflets about the National Action and rapping with the kids. They ran through the school yelling "jailbreak" and then held a rally outside the school. The pigs came and tried to stop the women from talking to the kids, who were digging it. The pigs attacked and the women fought back, protecting their sisters and the Viet Cong flag. They fought, liberating every sister that the pigs tried to arrest, and left the scene of the struggle chanting "Ho Ho Ho Chi Minh, the Viet Cong is Going to Win."

As people were leaving in cars parked some distance away from the school, the pigs moved and arrested 26 women, now charged with riot and inciting to riot. Two are also charged with assault.

During the action, women moved in affinity groups, each of which had a tactical leadership. The entire action was planned and led by a group of women who made up the tactical leadership for the action. Affinity groups were very important in effectively defending our sisters; however, in a criticism session afterward we understood that we had not used the affinity groups to move offensively against the pigs, and that one of the most important uses of the affinity group is the extra power it gives us for offensive actions.

After the action, people all over the city of Pittsburgh talked about what the women had done. The war had been brought home to white people in Pittsburgh. Pittsburgh freaked out not only because a Red Army had come to town, but because that army was made up of women. The pig newspapers tried to explain the women's action as a nudity show, and announced on the radio that a group of "bare-breasted women" had run through the school. But the kids at the school know that what really happened was that women, speaking in support of the Vietnamese, black and brown struggles, and against the pigs, the teachers and the courts, came to their school, fought the pigs, and won.

Women fought together in Detroit at McComb Community College and they fought in Pittsburgh; the women's militia will come together from all over the country to pull off an action in Chicago during the National Action.

The action in Pittsburgh attacked imperialism and racism, and, because it was carried out by women alone, it dealt a particularly strong blow to male chauvinism in men and women. It challenged the passive, non-political role which women are forced into, a role which only helps to maintain imperialism. Through the collective struggle of the women in Pittsburgh we took one more step in building a fighting force of women, the very existence of which attacks male chauvinism and male supremacy and strengthens the forces fighting imperialism and racism.

Look At It: America 1969

Look At It: America, 1969: The war goes on, despite the jive double-talk about troop withdrawals and peace talks. Black people continue to be murdered by agents of the fat cats who run this country, if not in one way, then in another: by the pigs or the courts, by the boss or the welfare department. Working people face higher taxes, inflation, speed-ups, and the sure knowledge—if it hasn't happened already—that their sons may be shipped off to Vietnam and shipped home in a box. And young people all over the country go to prisons that are called schools, are trained for jobs that don't exist or serve no one's real interest but the boss's, and, to top it all off, get told that Vietnam is the place to defend their "freedom."

None of this is very new. The cities have been falling apart, the schools have been bullshit, the jobs have been rotten and unfulfilling for a long time.

What's new is that today not quite so many people are confused, and a lot more people are angry: angry about the fact that the promises we have heard since first grade are all jive; angry that, when you get down to it, this system is nothing but the total economic and military put-down of the oppressed peoples of the world.

And more: it's a system that steals the goods, the resources and the labor of poor and working people all over the world in order to fill the pockets and bank accounts of a tiny capitalist class. (Call it imperialism.) It's a system that divides white workers from blacks by offering whites crumbs off the table, and telling them that if they don't stay cool the blacks will move in on their jobs, their homes and their schools. (Call it white supremacy.) It's a system that divides

From *New Left Notes*, August 1969

men from women, forcing women to be subservient to men from childhood, to be slave labor in the home and cheap labor in the factory. (Call it male supremacy.) And it's a system that has colonized whole nations within this country—the nation of black people, the nation of brown people—to enslave, oppress and ultimately murder the people on whose backs this country was built. (Call it fascism.)

But the lies are catching up to America—and the slick rich people and their agents in the government bureaucracies, the courts, the schools and the pig stations just can't cut it anymore.

Black and brown people know it.

Young people know it.

More and more white working people know it.

And you know it.

LAST YEAR, THERE WERE ONLY ABOUT 10,000 OF US IN CHICAGO

The press made it look like a massacre. All you could see on TV were shots of the horrors and blood of pig brutality. That was the line that the bald-headed businessmen were trying to run down—"If you mess with us, we'll let you have it." But those who were there tell a different story. We were together and our power was felt. It's true that some of us got hurt, but last summer was a victory for the people in a thousand ways.

Our actions showed the Vietnamese that there were masses of young people in this country facing the same enemy that they faced.

We showed that white people would no longer sit by passively while black communities were being invaded by occupation troops every day.

We showed that the "democratic process" of choosing candidates for a presidential election was nothing more than a hoax, pulled off by the businessmen who really run this country.

And we showed the whole world that in the face of the

oppressive and exploitative rulers—and the military might to back them up—thousands of people are willing to fight back.

SDS IS CALLING THE ACTION THIS YEAR

But it will be a different action. An action not only against a single war or a "foreign policy," but against the whole imperialist system that made that war a necessity. An action not only for immediate withdrawal of all US occupation troops, but in support of the heroic fight of the Vietnamese people and the National Liberation Front for freedom and independence. An action not only to bring "peace to Vietnam," but beginning to establish another front against imperialism right here in America—to "bring the war home."

We are demanding that all occupational troops get out of Vietnam and every other place they don't belong immediately. This includes the black and brown communities, the workers' picket lines, the high schools, and the streets of Berkeley. No longer will we tolerate "law and order" backed up by soldiers in Vietnam, and pigs in the communities and the schools; a "law and order" that serves only the interests of those in power and tries to smash the people down whenever they rise up.

We are demanding the release of all political prisoners who have been victimized by the ever-growing attacks on the black liberation struggle and the people in general. Especially the leaders of the black liberation struggle like Huey P. Newton, Ahmed Evans, Fred Hampton and Martin Sostre.

We are expressing total support for the National Liberation Front of South Vietnam and the newly-formed Provisional Revolutionary Government of South Vietnam. Throughout the history of the war, the NLF has provided the political and military leadership to the people of South Vietnam, and has constantly fought against all enemies of Vietnamese independence. The Provisional Revolutionary Government, newly formed by the NLF and other groups, has pledged "to mobilize the South Vietnamese armed forces and people in order to push forward the struggle against U.S. aggression." Calling for the abolition of the Ky-Thieu clique, the consolidation of the liberated zones, and a thorough intensification of the war in general, the PRG also expressed total international solidarity with "the just struggle of the Afro-American people for their fundamental national rights," and pledged "to actively support the national independence movements of Asia, Africa, and Latin America."

We are also expressing total support for the black liberation struggle, part of the same struggle that the Vietnamese are fighting, against the same enemy.

We are demanding independence for Puerto Rico, and an end to the colonial oppression that the Puerto Rican nation faces at the hands of US imperialism.

We are demanding an end to the surtax, a tax taken from the working people of this country and used to kill working people in Vietnam and other places for fun and profit.

We are expressing solidarity with the Conspiracy 8 who led the struggle last summer in Chicago. Our action is planned to roughly coincide with the beginning of their trial.

And we are expressing support for GIs in Vietnam and throughout the world who are being made to fight the battles of the rich, as poor and working people have always been made to do. We support those GIs at Fort Hood, Fort Jackson and many other army bases, who have refused to be cannon fodder in a war against the people of Vietnam.

IT'S ALMOST HARD TO REMEMBER WHEN THE WAR BEGAN

But after years of peace marches, petitions and the gradual realization that this was no "mistake" at all, one critical fact remains: the war is not just happening in Vietnam.

It is happening in the jungles of Guatemala, Bolivia, Thailand, and all oppressed nations throughout the world.

And it is happening here. In black communities throughout the country. On college campuses. And in the high schools, in the shops and on the streets.

It is a war in which there are only two sides; a war not for domination, but for an end to domination; not for destruction, but for liberation and the unchaining of human freedom.

And it is a war in which we cannot "resist"; it is a war in which we must fight.

National actions against the war have played a tremendous part in building the revolutionary movement in this country and in aiding the struggles of oppressed peoples throughout the world. They have helped concentrate our numbers and strength and thus allowed us a level of militancy impossible in local areas. They have enable us to smash through that liberal web of words, polite protest and impotence that passed for dissent in this country in the Fifties and well into the Sixties. They have focused the attention of the world on the resistance in the United States, thus giving freedom-fighters in other lands encouragement and a sense of world-wide solidarity. (Remember how we were all jolted by the Vietnamese take-over of the American Embassy in Saigon; by the TV pictures of scores of thousands of Germans converging on Berlin, marching rows upon rows, chanting Ho Ho Ho Chi Minh and then taking on the German pigs; by the Watts, Newark and Detroit uprisings—the pictures of battlefields right here in the motherland; by the French uprising last May; and by the Columbia uprising last year?) From the Pentagon and Oakland Induction Center demonstrations in the fall of 1967 to the battle of Chicago last summer, we had that kind of electric effect in Vietnam, Latin America, Cuba and Western Europe. A few pictures demonstrated, as no number of articles, reports and speeches could have, that a movement was growing in the United States and that it was becoming increasingly serious and increasingly identified with the struggles of oppressed peoples in other lands.

Here in the United States those demonstrations set the terms for the struggle and gave the Movement a push in gutsiness and in the targets it chose to attack. Remember the Pentagon and the nearly simultaneous West Coast Oakland Induction Center demonstrations. The slogans, targets and militancy were almost totally new.We moved from individual acts of moral protest—remember the spring before, the draft

card burning had been considered the very limit of the Movement—to massive attacks on the centers of military power in
this country. The Pentagon and the vast Oakland Induction
Center were real; in Oakland the slogan changed from "Hell
No, We Won't Go" to "HELL NO, NOBODY GOES." We
had begun to realize that to stop the war we had to stop the
United States government. In Oakland the Movement controlled the streets for a few exhilarating days.

Before the Pentagon and Oakland, large national actions
had a bad name among some organizers engaged in community work. They said that the most oppressed people
never joined the marches; that they distracted from "real"
organizing, and that they could not help in their work in
"Uptown, Chicago or Newark." They put forward an alleged
dichotomy between local work and national demonstrations.

Arguments couldn't show why this was wrong, but history
did. The Pentagon "organized" thousands of demonstrators
and many thousands of TV, radio and newspaper viewers
who saw in the demonstration the growth of a movement
they wanted to join. The demonstration enabled us to overcome our limited means for propaganda, our restricted access
to new audiences. It reached out to millions where our organizing in the past could only reach thousands. We used the
media and the potential of technology for our ends. We
projected our hatred for the war and an image of strength
and power. We had, in fact, overcome localism, provincialism,
and a tendency for "sewer socialism"—the term for those in
the era of socialist organizing before the First World War who
wanted to concentrate on local issues, prove that socialists
could deliver street lights faster than the bosses could, and to
build socialism in one city. The demonstrations had a double
effect: They spread the word that it was legitimate to fight;
and they helped create a culture of resistance in which GIs
revolted, white working-class gangs turned political, and hippies (sensing the end of the love trip) acting as shock troops
in street actions flourished. And they projected a seriousness
and strength of the Movement which made many not on
college campuses see that there was more to this thing than

just a few white college missionaries in their neighborhood. The irony, of course, is that local projects have come and gone, but now youth across the country are organizing themselves in response to what's happening, and a part of what's happening is that a fighting movement has come to dominate the news in a dramatic way.

The Pentagon and Oakland also began to lay the basis for a new way of looking at organizing. We had often talked of the "decisions that affect our lives," and somehow had all too often become bogged down in bread-and-butter issues. Now our actions began to change some people's minds in the direction that the real issues that affected people were not the most narrow and seemingly immediate ones, but were in fact the large, social, political, moral ones—issues of militarism, racism, hunger, imperialism. In the days of a growing war demanding more and more young men; of a gold crisis threatening to bring down the American Empire; of assassinations of liberal leaders; and of increasing police control of our communities, the problems of stop-lights in the community and questions of *in loco parentis* on campus did not grip people in the manner organizers had assumed they would. Ideologically we began to grasp the idea that the system as a whole was the enemy; tactically we began to try to attack the system as a whole system. We gradually abandoned the notion that if we fought and fought for reforms we might succeed in reforming the system away, or that consciousness would somehow arise out of enough local fights so eventually the local rent-strike group would spring into action as a guerrilla force. Nevertheless, the old view of organizing held on. SDS failed to endorse the Pentagon until the very last moment, when the government failed to give the Mobilization Committee permits, and then it endorsed the action in a hedged manner. Nine months later, at almost the last minute, SDS endorsed the Chicago action in a limited fashion and after much debate.

Last but not least, militant actions affected the liberals. Nineteen sixty-seven to sixty-eight was THEIR year to end THEIR war. After the Pentagon, Allard Lowenstein scurried around the country a little faster looking for a legitimate liberal to defuse the growing movement. The Pentagon convinced Eugene McCarthy that he must enter the race for the Democratic Party nomination for President in order to move the protest from the streets back to electoral politics. On the one hand, 1967-68 witnessed the "Clean for Gene" kids all over New Hampshire and Wisconsin; Senator Fulbright's hearings on TV attacking Johnson's war and vainly trying to stem the war tide; and finally, on April Fool's eve, LBJ dropping out and halting the regular bombing of Vietnam. On the other hand, after the Pentagon came the Hilton-Foreign Policy Association demo in New York, the Dow demonstrations on campuses throughout the country, and finally Columbia. Columbia transferred to a single campus the ideas of the Pentagon: Bring the War Home. Hit where it hurts. We had moved from individual protests to attacks on the centers of power, attacks on the home ground of the war machine. Columbia drew in those whom we hadn't seen since the Pentagon. The action and the realness of the attempt to close down the universities convinced many to join us.

The year which began in Washington ended in and around the Hilton Hotel in Chicago. McCarthy entered the city the hero of thousands of youth; he left, a forgotten dream. McCarthy entered the race to take us out of the streets and back into electoral politics; McCarthy pushed his own kids into the streets, and to dramatically illustrate to the country the bankruptcy of the "legitimate" way of affecting government decisions, Daley had McCarthy campaign workers beaten in their hotel room.

The Pentagon to Chicago: a year of ascending militancy and power for the movement in the United States. Those two events mark the conception and birth of a white mother country anti-imperialist movement. A movement conceived in battle and willing to die in battle. In the next year the example and the experience of those events spread across the country. Revolts in colleges, neighborhoods, and high schools spread throughout the land. Radio reports gave battle reports like baseball scores: hundreds of thousands of black and brown high school students in the streets; San Francisco State College draws on community support; riots in Berkeley, Madison, and Kent State . . . on it went.

The actions on October 8-11 in Chicago will be part of a whole fall offensive against the war and imperialism. The offensive will include:

An action in San Francisco where the richest men in the world will meet at the International Industrialists' Conference September 12-14 to talk about how they can get even richer. We will make it clear to them that the people of the world will no longer stand for their robbery.

The National Action, October 8-11, when people will converge on Chicago to demand the end of the war and political repression, to voice support for the NLF and the black liberation struggle.

The November 8th Movement. November 8th is one year after Nixon was elected, a year that has seen thousands of people come to the movement. We will move in cities and towns throughout this country, leaving the mark of our growing strength at pig stations, draft boards, schools, courts, and on the streets.

On November 15, there will be a mass action called by the New Mobilization Committee; hundreds of thousands of people will move on Washington, demanding the end of the war, racism, and poverty in the United States.

The Venceremos Brigade—a series of two-month trips to Cuba for 300 Movement people to participate in the Cuban people's 10,000-ton harvest.

The fall offensive is only the beginning. Then will come the winter, spring and summer offensives, followed by another next fall—for however long it takes to win.

On October 11, tens of thousands of people will come to Chicago to bring the war home. Join us.

ALL POWER TO THE PEOPLE!

POLITICS AND STRATEGY: BRING THE WAR HOME!

Bringing The War Back Home: Less Talk, More National Action

Kathy Boudin, Bernardine Dohrn and Terry Robbins

One of the most important reasons for calling the National Action lies with the decision SDS made in Ann Arbor last winter that it was possible and necessary to build an anti-imperialist, working-class youth movement in the mother country; a movement that allies with and provides material aid to the people of Vietnam, of the black and brown colonies, and to all oppressed people of the world.

Over the past year, our understanding of the nature of imperialism and the capitalist system has increased tremendously: building the RYM is a programmatic response to that understanding. We know now that the failure of the white mother country movement to expand beyond the limits of bourgeois student consciousness came at least partly from the class base of our movement, and therefore from our own liberalism. We were afraid to bring our politics to the people; afraid to raise the key issues of imperialism and racism in a consistent, aggressive way. Instead, we hid behind the security of "student power," or economism, or "bread-and-butter issues." On campuses and in communities, we thought that if we could trick the people into any kind of struggle—and any level of struggle, no matter how low—they would see the naked teeth of the capitalist monster and join the revolution.

It didn't work. And what became clear to people—through the struggles at Columbia and Chicago, at San Francisco State and at Kent State—was that putting forward our politics in an aggressive way was the ONLY way to organize the masses of people in this country. That only by dealing with the issues of white supremacy, the black liberation struggle, Third World

Excerpted from *New Left Notes*, August 23, 1969

struggles, and the fight against imperialism, only by challenging the consciousness of the people could we ever develop a movement capable of helping topple the imperialist state.

Key to all this is the need for militancy, the need for struggle. A look around shows that the Man understands this. Events like the Woodstock gentleness freak-out and the demonstration at Nixon's home in California indicate that as long as militancy isn't a threat, pig and ruling-class approval is forthcoming. But we learn from every organizing situation that people change from being challenged, and that it is in situations of sharp conflict that people are forced to act. Nixon's policy of Law and Order is the modern-day version of McCarthyism: all those who are orderly, polite, and well-behaved are welcomed to imperialism and will be absorbed.

Our strategy of building a fighting force is being put forth openly for the national action, as well as for local organizing. Because national demonstrations have their major impact on the political issues and tone which is carried back for ongoing work, we put forward a struggle scenario of the action. Because we know that revolutionaries are created in struggle and not through protest or persuasion, we say clearly that this is an action not to register a complaint or to up the percentage points in public opinion polls, but to make a difference, to create the solution.

And more. We must build struggles not only because they are the way to build our own movement—but also because they are the only concrete way to relate to the vanguard struggles of black and brown people in this country, and of colonized people throughout the world. Chicago last year did more damage to the ruling class, helped build our own movement, and aided the Vietnamese in a more concrete and significant way than any mass peaceful gathering this country has ever seen.

The National Action was conceived to speak to the need to build a mass action that ups the level of politics and ups the level of struggle. In the action we will direct ourselves not only against the war, but against the imperialist system that created the war in the first place; not only in support of withdrawal of US troops, but also in support of the heroic fight of the Vietnamese people, the NLF and the PRG, to defeat imperialism and win freedom and independence; not only to demand an end to racism, but in support of the black liberation struggle as part of the world-wide struggle of oppressed colonized peoples.

The National Action is one of the key ways of talking to young people in this country about building a class conscious revolutionary youth movement which has as its primary task the establishment of another front in the international class war—not only to defeat the imperialists in Vietnam but to BRING THE WAR HOME!

Chicago is the site. It is here that thousands of young people faced the blind terror of the military state; where dreams of grandeur and new life turned into the slaughter of innocence. And it was also here that those same people began to fight back—to struggle against the betrayal, the lies, the oppressiveness and the brutality of the state.

We are coming back to turn pig city into the people's city.

THE SCENARIO

As approved by the last NIC meeting, the action will take place over a four-day period, October 8-11. The scenario as it now stands will look like this:

The action will start on Wednesday night, October 8, with a memorial rally for Che Guevara, who was murdered by CIA pigs October 8, 1967, and Nguyen Van Troi, the Vietnamese hero murdered by the US October 15, 1964 for attempting to kill MacNamara. A rally for Che and Troi and all other revolutionaries who have died in the struggle.

On Thursday, October 9, we will join with kids from high schools, community colleges, trade schools, etc., here in Chicago in an offensive against the schools. The action will be something around the idea of a "Jailbreak," and people in the Chicago region are already working with several high schools in the city to develop cadre who will help work out and co-ordinate this action. The need for tactical flexibility on this day is crucial, but it could be one of the most important actions of the week, involving thousands of local kids and getting the word out to thousands more about who we are and what's going on.

Either on Thursday or Friday there will be a women's action, planned by women from functioning political collectives all over the country. Unlike other women's actions—which focused on the symbols of cultural oppression—this action will be an attack on the institutions of racism and imperialism, combatting male chauvinism in large part by being an exemplary women's army.

Thursday night we'll have a youth-rock music festival. (October 9 is the anniversary of the day when Mrs. O'Leary's cow kicked over a lantern and burned half the damn city down.) Fuck hippie capitalism. Build culture in struggle.

Friday we go after the courts. The trial of the "Conspiracy" will be going on at the Federal Building in the downtown Loop area. Our slogan for this action should be "Stop the Trial." Like the slogan "Stop the Convention" last year, it must indicate our commitment to fight back when the Man comes down with repression, to force the ruling class to pay an increasingly heavy price for the farce of "trying" the Conspiracy or any other political prisoners in this country.

And finally, on Saturday, October 11, we'll have the big march. We're starting to work on a route for the march, and will be seeking permits from the city. The permit, however, even if we get it, will be no guarantee of safety. As on all the other days, we must be prepared to defend ourselves in the event of any vicious attacks by the Chicago pigs. . . . The plans for the four days are of course not finalized. Changes will undoubtedly take place; some probably will happen when Daley and the Chicago pigs begin their all-out offensive against the action. In building an action like this one, many factors will remain unknown until the actual event. But if the general strategic outlook for the demonstration is sound, we will be able to use anything that happens between now and October 8 to our own advantage.

SELF-DEFENSE

Recently, both here in Chicago and in traveling around the

country, we've started to get feedback on the plans for the action. Of all the things being said, the one that presents the most serious problem is one that the pig has been spreading. The rumor has been that we are organizing white youth to bring guns to Chicago to provoke an armed confrontation. What this obviously does is give the pig the excuse to bring out his shotguns and shoot people down in the streets like they did in Berkeley. That people in and out of SDS around the country actually believed such bullshit is amazing. . . .

We must begin immediately to put together serious groups on the local level that will work self-consciously to build the action and come to it as a group. When we talk to new kids about the action we should try to get them to come as groups rather than individuals. This involves political implementation deeper than pure tactics. We no longer organize people to participate in actions as individuals because we no longer act out of individual anger or alienation. We reach out to groups because we are building a collective response to collective oppression.

In a mass action made up of many types of groups, there is naturally a wide range of experience. Some are heavy, disciplined collectives, people who are engaged in full-time movement work together and who have gone through demonstrations together before. Others might be just groups of kids who hang together, go to school together, who might never have undergone a self-conscious political experience as a group. What we have seen is that those who have experience in the streets (and other tactical situations) usually provide leadership for the action as a whole. That leadership develops within the situation, and is made real by the fact that in general people's instincts are correct: people follow others who have shown themselves to be together and trustworthy in the context of real struggle. In every action we soon learn whom to look to for leadership. And one of the qualities of street leadership is a sensitivity to the level of struggle of the mass of people. No one except a pig is going to lead people into a slaughter situation because people don't follow leadership that moves beyond their level of militancy and self-confidence. At the same time, correct leadership does not underestimate the level of struggle that the people are willing to engage in.

OTHER ORGANIZATIONS

It is our hope that the National Action will be as broadly based and widely supported as possible. Since the National Convention, we have contacted and spoken with many organizations, asking for their support. The basis for participation in the action by other organizations has been based primarily on willingness to participate in a militant, anti-imperialist struggle.

Soon after the National Convention we met with representatives of the Mobilization Committee and we sent representatives to the Mobilization conference in Cleveland. We laid out what we were attempting to do politically with this action, and we laid out our criticisms of Mobilization actions in the past. We asked for Mobilization support for this action. What followed was a request for co-sponsorship—speakers, marshals, and a "joint" negotiating team to meet with the city.

The Mobilization has come to symbolize and represent the twice-yearly Sunday afternoon anti-war movement. We're not saying that some of those Sunday afternoons weren't heavy, like the Pentagon and Chicago last year. What we're saying is that a movement must be built with people who will fight imperialism at home as well as at national actions. The politics put forward through the Mobilization these past years will not be sufficient this year. The request for co-sponsorship and the request for marshals (who were weak in Chicago and pigs in Washington at the inauguration) could not be met without completely changing the politics of the action. Therefore we declined their offer of support.

Of extreme importance have been our discussions with the Illinois Chapter and National Office of the Black Panther Party, the Young Lords Organization, and the Young Patriots, an organization of working class youth from Uptown Chicago. Of these, only the Patriots were totally opposed to the action, and through discussions with them significant political differences emerged.

The Patriots argued essentially that SDS was a "student" organization that wasn't interested in the people (white people), and "objectified" the people. They criticized the action for "disrupting" their local work, and complained that SDS was only interested in fucking up Chicago, and not in building a movement in the city. We strongly disagreed with this "national-local" argument, as well as with the Patriots' incorrect assessment of where SDS is at, and their tendency to ignore the issue of white supremacy and white-skin privilege in their work.

In our first discussions with the Panthers and the Lords, they raised strong reservations about the action, saying that white people did not have to go through mass struggle in the streets in order to build a revolutionary consciousness. However the National Panther Party, through Bobby Seale and David Hilliard, indicated that they would support the action—though not work actively on it—and discussions with the Illinois Chapter, as well as with the Young Lords, will continue.

What is critical to understand here is that the level of struggle in the black and brown liberation movements is totally different from our own; that black and brown people have reached a level of consciousness where mass demonstrations are no longer so necessary. However, the white movement, riddled by timidity rather than a wealth of experience in struggle, MUST seek to escalate its seriousness and power at this time through the tactic of mass confrontation.

Also, there are hundreds of thousands of kids who are not in SDS, reached by us or able to relate to our politics, but who nonetheless are pissed off, fighting, tearing up the schools, the pigs, their parents, or the army. Many of these kids will be reached in our summer organizing projects. As well, the Yippies are supporting the action, and will be helpful in bringing many of these kids to it. They will be setting up an office in Chicago and producing mass propaganda around the action.

At the September 1 NIC, we will propose that both the Yippies and possibly the Conspiracy, who have also indicated support, co-sponsor the action along with SDS.

Other groups who have indicated support for the action include MDS, Youth Against War and Fascism, and several high school groups around the country. Discussions are in process with others.

A Strategy To Win

Bill Ayers

Last week I went up to St. Johns in New Brunswick with a couple of other people to meet with the people who had come back from Cuba and a meeting with the PRG. The reason we went up there is because we felt they had been out of the country six weeks, that a lot of contradictions had been heightened, especially between us and RYM II, that a lot of changes had taken place all over this country, and we felt that the people might be totally out of it and should be cued in to what was going on.

The first thing that I found out when I got up there was that there wasn't a whole lot of straightening out that needed to be done, because in fact a lot of changes we had gone through here they had gone through also. They had been involved in the process of building cadre just as we had, they had had some confrontations with a few members of the running dogs (RYM II) who were down there, so it wasn't a terrible problem the way we had anticipated it would be.

One of the things I did while I was there was that I talked a lot about the criticisms that have been made of the national action. I talked particularly about the charge that we are adventurist which people hear a lot, that somehow the national office, and Weatherman in particular and the Weather Bureau in specific, are a bunch of adventurist fools who are out to get us all killed. I talked about that, and one of the

From *New Left Notes*, September 12, 1969. Excerpted from a speech by Bill Ayers, Education Secretary, at the Midwest National Action conference held in Cleveland August 29–September 1.

things that I said is that adventurism is when you don't believe that you can organize the people, and lose confidence in
the people, and therefore totally cut yourself off from everything, and you develop a strategy for losing, which of course
is not what we're involved in at all. I also talked about the
fact that if it is a worldwide struggle, if Weatherman is correct in that basic thing, that the basic struggle in the world
today is the struggle of the oppressed peoples against US
imperialism, then it is the case that nothing we could do in
the mother country could be adventurist. Nothing we could
do because there is a war going on already, and the terms of
that war are set. We couldn't be adventurist while there is
genocide going on in Vietnam and in the black community.

Later on in the conversation, people criticized me for that
statement, and they said it was wrong to say that genocide is
being committed in Vietnam, because that communicated a
number of non-struggle things—that the Vietnamese are sad,
tired old people who are persecuted by the evil United States.
In fact that's not what the Vietnamese are about. The Vietnamese are strong, the most heroic and the most incredible
people in the world, and they've beaten US imperialism—
they've defeated the United States. That lesson is very important for us because it teaches us that struggle against US
imperialism is possible, that when we fight US imperialism we
have a chance of winning, that even a small nation, relatively
unarmed, can hold off 500,000 US troops, can defeat them
in every way—that the Vietnamese have won, that they are
strong, that the United States is not indestructible, not some
kind of monolith that can never be changed, that history is
not static, that the people can win.

Bernadette Devlin, when she was here last week, said a
similar thing: that our greatest weakness is our belief in our
weakness, and that's certainly true in the mother country
here. What we have to communicate to people is our
strength, and to show people our strength we have to show
them the strength of fighting on the side of the worldwide
movement. So I was criticized for projecting the image of
weakness. It's a similar thing if people have seen this Wilming-

ton, Delaware thing that Newsreel did. The kind of image that that creates about black people is that they're down-trodden, that DuPont is this heavy thing that is screwing these black people, as if they're so beaten down that they can't move. The film is essentially useless, because it conveys that kind of notion, that imperialism has defeated the people, whereas the Huey Newton film and the first Panther film conveys just the opposite: it conveys strength, it conveys confidence, it conveys positiveness, it conveys all those kinds of things that we have to learn to convey to people, all those kinds of things in terms of the image that the Vietnamese have tried to project to the world. It's no longer that we can make posters about Vietnam with an old man and a little kid who are burned by napalm. The posters that we put out and the truth is the symbol of a woman with a gun, or the picture of Nguyen Van Troi, the hero who was captured and later shot for attempting to assassinate McNamara in 1964. And Van Troi, handcuffed to the post where he was to be shot and screaming at his assassins, screaming "Long Live People's War! Death to U.S. Imperialism!" That's the image of Viet-nam, it's that strength, that confidence, and that's what we have to bring to our own constituency, it's that that we have to integrate into our politics in a positive way. That's one of the major things that we have to deal with in terms of the national action.

We have to deal with the fact that in a lot of ways all of us have elements of defeatism in us, and don't believe really that we can win, don't really believe that the United States can be beaten. But we have to believe it, because defeatism is based on individualism—it is really based on the thought that I can't beat US imperialism, I'm going to die, I'm going to get wiped out. But the Vietnamese people have won, and that fact makes it a lie to say that we can't win or that we won't win. We have won, we won in Vietnam, that was a victory for us and for all people, and we will continue to win, continue to defeat US imperialism. We have to stamp out that individual-ist notion that if I don't make it through the next year, or that if I don't make it to construct socialism within 20 years, that that is a defeat. That's a defeatist and individualist attitude, and we have to beat that attitude, and we have to beat that attitude out of ourselves.

One of the things about the politics of confidence and the politics of victory is that we know that if we have good politics, if we stick closely to Weatherman, if we project that analysis of worldwide struggle and our part in that, that we have essentially the answers to the questions that people are asking us. We have answers for people that other politics don't have. For instance, when people in Detroit go into a drive-in, and talk to those kids about the war and about the international struggle, and talk to those people about racism and male supremacy and pigs, they're not just talking on an intellectual level and saying see, here's what's happening, this is why you're fucked up, because those kids know that already. We don't have to say to people what's wrong, we have to say to people what do you do about it, and what you do about it is you fight, you fight back, and you join together with your brothers and sisters, and you kick ass, that's what you do about it. And that concretely is what actions in Detroit, in Chicago, in Ohio and [in] other places have communicated.

We can't project the phony kind of image that you join the Movement because you get a dollar more an hour, you join it 'cause you get New Left Notes, some bullshit—though that's a good thing, not a bad thing. You join the Movement because you want to be part of that worldwide struggle that's obviously winning, and you win people over to it, and you win people over by being honest to them about the risks, by being honest to them about the struggle, by being honest to them that what they are getting into is a fight: it's not a comfortable life, it's not just a dollar more; it's standing up in the face of the enemy and risking your life and risking everything for that struggle. But it's also being on the side of victory, and that's the essential thing that we have to show people.

In terms of building for the national action, this is what we have to project. We have to build this confidence, and build this power, we have to feel this power, and that's why it was so important to start this weekend off by talking about the Vietnamese, by talking about that power, by talking about that worldwide struggle. At this point I think it is also important to talk about the historical period that we're in, the importance of our job. A lot of people tend to ignore the role we have to play and therefore allow themselves all kinds of luxuries of being sloppy in their work, and not pushing people, and being liberal toward other people because they don't understand the necessity of what we're doing right now, including the total importance of this fall for our politics.

I think that the national action has to be seen in the context of a strategy that's going to win, that's going to support the NLF concretely, that's going to build Weatherman, and that's going to build a fighting revolutionary youth movement. We can't get involved anymore in the kinds of actions that merely say to people that this is wrong, or that is wrong, because that doesn't tell people what to do, that doesn't project the kind of confidence, and the crucial nature and importance of what we're trying to do in this country now. We have to fight and show people through struggle our commitment, our willingness to run risks, our willingness to die in the struggle to defeat US imperialism. We have to convey those things, and October 8-11 is a concrete way that we can do that.

I think people should push out this slogan "Bring the War Home." We're not just saying bring the troops home, bring the US troops home and deploy them some place some other time, we're saying bring the war home. We're saying you're going to pay a price because increasingly guys in the army are going to shoot you in the back, increasingly the guys in the army are going to shoot over the heads of the Vietnamese, shoot over the heads of the blacks, increasingly this country is going to be torn down, and we're not going to bring the troops home to be deployed someplace else, we're going to bring the war home, we're going to create class war in the streets and institutions of this country, and we're going to make them pay a price, and the price ultimately is going to be total defeat for them. That's the kind of thing that we have to convey, and that's the kind of thing that we have to build.

I think people understand how this kind of action at this time, given the whole thing in Paris and the situation the Vietnamese are in now, can concretely aid the Vietnamese. The other thing that people have to get confident about is that we can build a revolutionary youth movement. There's a lot of skepticism in some places about whether this action can come off, and that skepticism comes out of one thing, and that is that people have been listening to so-called "Movement people," and these "Movement people" have been telling them that it won't work, and that it's adventurist, that it's going to hurt people, that it's not right at this time, that we have to build a united front, or some other bullshit. And these Movement people, this kind of right-wing force, this weirdness that's moving around, it's all these old people who came into the Movement at a time when pacifism was important, at a time when there was a total consciousness of defeat, when the only reasons that we were in it were moral reasons, when there was no strategy for victory, for gaining power, so that the people who came into the Movement at that time have a certain kind of consciousness and belief about what is possible, and what we have to do is not listen to the Guardian, or what the Guardian thinks is possible, not listen to other "Movement" groups, like certain local Newsreels, certain local NOCs, and think that they must know what's right because they are "the Movement."

If you think you've been isolated sometimes in your local work, you've got to dig what happened in Detroit, where because of the actions that people were taking, every so-called "Movement group" in the city started to get together in a coalition to stop SDS. When the MC 9 were arrested and put in prison, and Motor City SDS people tried to raise money, they had responses from some of these so-called Movement people that it would be better to leave them in jail, because they'd be dangerous on the streets. But the point is that to judge our actions by what those fucking people have to say about them is crazy. We have to go to the people and see what *they* have to say about the actions. Anybody who has gone out to a high school or to a drive-in, to a community college in an aggressive and assertive way, knows that the people out there loved the fuckin' action, and thought that it was out of sight.

We have to understand that if we're going to build our movement, if our movement is going to go forward and develop a different class basis and fight privilege, and fight on the side of the Vietnamese and the blacks, that a lot of these so-called Movement people are just going to have to get out of the way, drop out, and that's what should happen to them—that's what their class interest is. But we don't have to listen to what they have to say and get defeatist, we have to get out to more and more people. It's not so much that those people as individuals, as people, have to be smashed or destroyed or anything like that; it's that those ideas, those tendencies, those notions have to be totally discredited, smashed and destroyed. And in the process of doing that, some of those individuals will come over. They won't understand if we sit and talk about it, they'll only understand if we smash their ideas.

In places where we smashed ideas and built our movement off of toughness and combatted liberalism in ourselves, we've developed the best struggles in this country. It happened at Columbia, it happened in Michigan-Ohio. The whole region in Michigan-Ohio was built by destroying the right wing in a couple of chapters, and asserting the power to throw them out of the chapters. But in order for us to really accomplish this, in order for us to really gain in this kind of struggle, a lot of the business that we have to be about is transforming ourselves, by getting rid of the things that are slowing us down and holding us back. This means that the only way we're going to gain that confidence and build that fighting movement, and to get rid of those bourgeois things in ourselves is by developing collectives off struggle, and off outreach, and to build them off internal struggle—but the internal struggle only makes sense when there's outreach going on.

MALE SUPREMACY

A lot of the problems that people are going through now have to do with monogamy and its basis in male supremacy What we have to understand in this whole discussion is that we have one task, and that's to make ourselves into tools of the revolution. We know what we have to do, and that means a lot of heavy stuff. It means a lot of invading things that people didn't think should be invaded before, and it means a lot of resisting. Just this morning a guy was saying to me that I know that what I'm saying about monogamy has to do with my own bourgeois hang-ups, but my bourgeois hang-ups are more important to me than being a communist at this point. That's something that just has to be smashed. The reason that this thing comes up at all is not just about people liking to be house-wreckers or some shit, it's got to do with the fact that people have come to see the need to build collectives that can fight, the need to build collectives that are strong and tough, and in order to do that a lot of individualism has to be worked out of every one of us. Any notion that people can have a primary responsibility for one person, that they can have that "out"—we have to destroy that notion in order to build a collective, we have to destroy all "outs" to destroy the notion that people can lean on one person and not be responsible to the entire collective.

It's heavier than that, too, because it has to do with male chauvinism and male supremacy, and the development of women's leadership, the development of women as communists. A lot of what's going on is people resisting the notion that in a collective everyone is equal. A lot of resistance comes from men, from men who have a privileged situation in that relationship, from men who dig the fact that they have control over another person. It comes from men who are involved in a classical pattern of male chauvinism, of finding a woman who they can control, trying to teach that person, build that person up, take credit for building them

up, begin feeling a lot of contempt for them, a lot of competition with them, and maintain that relationship to maintain their dominance. We have seen concretely that there is
not an instance of a relationship that we've seen that doesn't
have some kind of dominance in it, some kind of control over
someone's acts—and for the most part, it's the woman who is
held back. In practice, when people are operating in collectives and those relationships break down, the women begin to
get strong, begin to assert themselves, begin to come out as
leaders—not as political people who work through another
individual, but as political people who build collectives and
lead struggles. I think every one of us could run down instances like this. I'm from Michigan and could run down five
or six instances, and I think that the women in Detroit are
the strongest, most exemplary people in our movement right
now, and I think it's precisely because they grappled with
this issue early, they dealt with it four months ago, they got
through it and understood the need to take the initiative in
changing those relationships, and they did. That's an example, the most heated example of the job that we have to
do. We have to organize ourselves in collectives, fight our
individualism, we have to see that the Mellon-Hegel formula
is true: freedom is the recognition of necessity, that we become free when we realize the tasks that we have to do and
go about changing ourselves into the instruments that can do
those tasks.

The other thing that's clear around that whole action is the
question that Klonsky raised at the NIC when he said you
guys aren't into serving the people, you're into fighting the
people, and we kind of just sat there and said that that's
wrong. We thought about the whole thing of serve the
people, and we thought that you don't serve the people by
opening a restaurant, or by fighting for a dollar more; you
serve the people, that means *all* the people—the Vietnamese,
everybody, by making a revolution, by bringing the war
home, by opening up a front. But the more I thought about
that thing "fight the people," it's not that it's a great mass

slogan or anything, but there's something to it. What's true about it is that we've never been in a struggle where we didn't have to fight some of the people. For instance at Michigan State we had to fight jocks, we had to fight a lot of them, and in the process of the next couple of weeks, we won over a number of these jocks. We understood that they weren't our enemies, but we also understood that when they objectively acted like our enemies they had to be fought, and that that was the best way to deal with them.

There's a lot in white Americans that we do have to fight, and beat out of them, and beat out of ourselves. And that part of it is true—we have to be willing to fight people, and fight things in ourselves, and fight things in all white Americans—white privilege, racism, male supremacy—in order to build a revolutionary movement. We know there's going to be polarization, but we also know that through that polarization there's going to be change. In Detroit, the whole question of creating a presence, of polarization, has come to a halt because they've polarized the whole city. They've been to every drive-in, every high school, and people have an opinion of SDS. How many places has anybody even heard of it? When you say SDS in Detroit, they say Oh, those are those broads who beat up guys, or those are those people who come into drive-ins, and that polarization is an important thing. Of course, the pole of the city that hates us is all these old "Movement people."

ADVENTURISM?

The major criticisms of the action have to do with adventurism, have to do with leading people to a slaughter, have to do with the pig rumor that we've been telling people that we're bringing guns to Chicago, and these things must be smashed, and it's a tricky thing to smash. It's a good rumor for them to pass around, because it does three things, highly contradictory. First they say we have guns, and that sets people up, so that they can attack us. It also scares people away, it makes people scared to get into it. But the third thing it does is that it forces us to take a defensive and a weak position on guns, it forces us to say No, we're not asking people to bring guns to Chicago. Do we dig guns? Well, no . . . it forces us into that defensive position. And when we make clear that we're not urging anybody to bring guns to Chicago, we're not urging anybody to shoot from a crowd, but we're also going to make it clear that when a pig gets iced that's a good thing, and that everyone who considers himself a revolutionary should be armed, should own a gun, should have a gun in his home.

Since our militance is going to obviously lead to a military confrontation, maybe not this year, then the fact that most of us in here don't even know karate makes us fools, and whoever doesn't own a gun and doesn't know how to use a gun is a fool. So we should state publicly that we believe in, we support, and we are preparing for armed self-defense, because that's what we have to do in order to win.

Our politics deals well with the question of adventurism, and we don't have to be defensive about the action. It's clear that the opposition to the action comes from right-wing "Movement people." The unity of the opposition to the action is incredible, because people are uniting who have totally different positions. Anti-communists are uniting with people who call themselves Stalinists, are uniting with people who believe there's a black nation only in the South, are uniting with people who don't believe there's any black nation, and that whole unity is basically around one thing, and that's fear, basically around an inability to understand that we have to continue to move forward, and that we have to continue to build a fighting movement, and take that fight to the streets of Chicago, and take it back from Chicago to our local cities, and make them pay a price by involving thousands and thousands of kids in militant, out-of-sight destructive actions in every city in this country. So that this whole fall we begin to chip away at imperialism in the most concrete way that we can, and all the right-wingers who are united around this one thing, we should just ignore them—they're not our base, they never were, and they never could be. A strategy that talks about power is a strategy that ignores them and goes to the youth in the cities and begins to build among them.

I want to deal with one last criticism of the action, and that's what Klonsky puts forward in his famous article "Why I Quit." What Klonsky says is that we didn't act on the mandate of the Convention and build a united front action against the war. In the first place that's a lie, and a lot of the running dogs (RYM-II) are going around saying we support the action except not really, the same way that PL says well, we dig struggle except where it really is. It's a lie to say that that was passed at the Convention because the paragraph that talked about the united front was debated at the Convention and was dropped out of the resolution.

WEATHER BUREAU

It's also important to understand that even if it passed, we wouldn't implement it because we understand that what we have to do is to build a movement that's geared toward power—and we're not going to be involved in obeying mandates that tell us to do something that's a losing strategy. For the first time in SDS a coherent leadership was elected, with stated politics, with coherent politics, stated before they were elected, and they're united on that. Not only are they united on that, but they're in a collective that has a base in probably the most important regions in the country, and that bigger collective, the Weather Bureau, makes political decisions, moves in a political way, and moves for victory, and it would be insane for anyone to expect leadership to organize around the mandates and drop their own politics.

In the national office we're building a political collective for the first time. And it's a collective that understands that it has a primary responsibility to Weatherman, to the Weather Bureau, that its job is the implementation of those politics. And the people who don't believe that, or can't understand that, have been fired, or will be fired, because we're building a political movement, we're building a movement of revolutionaries, and we have to do that in a coherent way. The same is true of New Left Notes, which is looking better and better. The political content of the articles in New Left Notes has to speak to the best politics in the organization. And I think that's important—that we have to organize around our politics, not around some mushy, directionless student movement, but around a movement of revolutionary youth, and we must begin to build revolutionaries in the Movement, not just anyone who wants to join the club, not just "Movement people."

The criticisms of the action have to be dealt with in that honest way, in a very up-front way, have to be totally smashed, and people have to begin to get a sense that the politics of this action can win, are winning, can be built and are being built all over this country. In every city in the Midwest where we've got a summer program, people are predicting thousands and thousands of people coming out in October for the action, and that's thousands and thousands of people that we've never reached before—vets, greasers, bikers. At the Metro Beach action, Motor City SDS got into a fight with a gang. But a week later the gang sent a message that they sure did dig beating up SDS but they also dig going to Chicago to beat up some pigs.

Strategically, in the long run, it's our overwhelming strength that we have to play off of and that we have to win people to, and we have to communicate to people, and that's the only way people are going to come to understand the reality of the fact that we can, and will, and beginning in October are going to bring that war home in Chicago, build off that to bring the war home in Detroit, in San Francisco, in Columbus, and New York, and everywhere all over the country.

The Second Battle Of Chicago 1969

Tom Thomas

SDS members began arriving in Chicago Tuesday afternoon. They arrived in groups of threes and fours, many having driven from the east and west coasts, others hitching rides from nearby areas. Their destinations were designated Movement centers at which organization was to be developed on a regional basis. The Movement centers, however, were not anticipating arrivals until Wednesday and the youths consequently spent Tuesday night scattered throughout the city.

The atmosphere in Chicago was hostile before the first demonstrators ever arrived. The preceding day, Chicago's monument to police officers was destroyed by a dynamite blast. Mayor Richard Daley termed the bombing "an attack on all the citizens of Chicago."

The Haymarket Square statue was the only police monument in the United States. The figure of a nineteenth century vintage officer, commemorating seven policemen killed during a riot in 1886, was toppled from its base at 11:10 Monday night in an explosion that shattered hundreds of windows in the surrounding area.

Police officers reacted angrily to the destruction. "An obvious declaration of war between the police and SDS and other anarchist groups," said Sgt. Richard M. Barrett, president of the Chicago Police Sergeants Association.

"We now feel that it is kill or be killed, regardless of the Jay Millers, Daniel Walkers, and the so-called Civil Rights Act" (Miller is head of the Illinois branch of the American Civil Liberties Union, which has frequently criticized Chicago police; Walker headed a study commission which declared a "police riot" occurred at the 1968 Democratic Convention).

Other police organization spokesmen agreed that the act

was part of an organized attack on law and order in Chicago. Lt. James A. O'Neill, president of the Police Lieutenants Association, said the bombing showed the "mentality of the people who are causing strife in the streets." He said, "It is time for the people of Chicago and the nation to wake up to what we are opposing. These are not harmless kids with firecrackers."

*   *   *

Posters appeared Wednesday afternoon announcing actions planned for the coming four days. The posters, circulated by the Weatherman faction, were headed "SDS Handwriting on the Wall." They heralded the slogan "Bring the War Home." The announced activities included a rally in Lincoln Park Wednesday night, an attack by the "women's militia" on the Chicago Armed Forces Induction Center and demonstrations at high schools scheduled for Thursday, a "move on the courts" for Friday, and a massive march Saturday through the Chicago Loop.

The posters proclaimed, "We move with the people of the world, to seize power from those who now rule, we . . . expect their pig lackeys to come down on us. We've got to be ready for that. This is a war we can't resist. We've got to actively fight. We're going to bring the war home to the mother country of imperialism. AMERIKA: THE FINAL FRONT."

"If you think you are in the middle, then you are on the wrong side. When you participate in and benefit from the American system, you are helping to keep it together."

Under the heading "Sister Stomp," the poster read "More and more women are fighting on the right side now. They are realizing the strength within themselves and in women who are free and complete human beings, fighting out of love for all the people."

And finally, "All these wars are really one big war. People refuse to have their countries run by the US any more, and that is what the war is all about."

Weatherman movement centers opened Wednesday at

three locations. Demonstrators from Wisconsin, Michigan, New York, and New England reported to Garret Theological Seminary in Evanston; those from New York City, Ohio and Pennsylvania assembled at the University Disciple Church in Hyde Park; and groups from Illinois, Indiana, Colorado, and Pacific Northwest, Washington, D.C., and the South (originally intending to form at St. Luke's Lutheran Church) moved into the gymnasium of McCormick Theological Seminary. The group at McCormick, led by the Chicago SDS collective, was to be by far the largest contingent.

Youths arrived prepared for street action. Nearly everyone carried some kind of a helmet, many were holding wooden clubs and other weapons, and a Baltimore group brought more than a score of gas masks. Men and women alike were dressed in combat boots, jeans, and heavy, protective clothing.

The Chicago police were prepared as well. Unmarked cars and plainclothesmen continuously patrolled the area while another unit systematically read license numbers into a tape recorder.

Security guards were immediately stationed by the Weathermen. Every person entering the centers had all possessions thoroughly scrutinized, down to every identification card in their wallets, and each person was carefully frisked. All weapons were left at the "security desk" and no one was allowed to possess illegal drugs. Only those prepared to "run with us in the street" were allowed to enter and even representatives of the underground press were barred admittance. Items confiscated included a can of lighter fluid, a pair of scissors, and a butane cigarette lighter.

At one point, several underground photographers tried to get in and an hour-long debate followed between the photographers and leaders of the Chicago collective. The leaders objected to the photographers because "if you're carrying a camera you can't fight and that's what we're here for. . . . It's all which side you are on, because if you're not fighting with us, you're fighting against us, no matter what else you are doing."

The photographers objected, pointing out that they felt it

necessary to have the "media present, in order to build the Movement."

"You can't talk about the Movement, because we have to crush the Movement to build the revolution," one leader told them. "The Movement only co-opts people and you aren't going to bring down 'the Man' by some pansy-ass demonstration.

"We start to build a Red Army by fighting in the streets now. We're going to knock the pig on his ass in those streets. Sure there's going to be pigs hitting people like before, but this time there's going to be people hitting pigs.

"The focal point is here in Chicago. We've got to show people that white kids are willing to fight on the side of black people and on the side of revolution around the world. If you're not going to fight then you're not part of us. It's as simple as that." . . . By late Wednesday afternoon, preparations for the Weatherman action were underway at the McCormick Seminary. In an atmosphere that lies somewhere between a National Guard armory and a football locker room, grim-faced radicals checked their first-aid kits, tried on helmets, and adjusted straps on gas masks. In one corner, a group discussed the effects of different kinds of tear gas.

Youths wrote key phone numbers on their arms and several people were carefully polishing goggles.

At about five o'clock two people entered carrying 2x2 wooden poles about five feet in length. Viet Cong flags were affixed to one end. In a voice not unlike that of an army drill instructor, a leader announced, "We are now going to learn how to smash pigs. Listen up!" He then proceeded to give a short demonstration in various techniques of stick fighting: jab, lunge, thrust, swing. "Always advance on your opponent, keep him moving back, surprise him."

Soon, in groups of eight, people began to practice the basic moves, some awkwardly, others with obvious experience. Against walls, against imaginary opponents—shouting as they moved—the radicals swung their poles. Others began to practice karate kicks and judo holds.

By six o'clock they were taping their wrists and padding

their arms. One youth of about 17 said, to no one in particular, "It's amazing that in a couple of hours I might be dead."

Shortly after six the regional leadership group arrived. It was explained that the contingent would march to Lincoln Park, there to be joined by the other groups at a rally in honor of Che Guevara and Nguyen Van Troi, a Vietnamese revolutionary. From the rally, the group would then move into the streets of Chicago and "tear apart Pig City."

Leaders again went over medical and legal information. A medical cadre would be on the street, it was explained. No one was to go to a hospital except in extreme circumstances. "If you have anything short of a mortal wound, you are expected to fight on," said one leader. "We're going to off [kill] the pig."

Leaders explained that people should "run with their affinity group of five or six people." The affinity groups should stay together, and help each other. The contingent was told that national leadership would be at the rally and that it was only then that it would be announced exactly what was to happen. The meeting then broke into affinity groups to prepare for the action.

In Lincoln Park, a crowd of about 200 gathered in anticipation of the rally scheduled for 7:30. A fire was started with pieces of wood torn from park benches. No uniformed [police] were in sight, although 300 were deployed in the area, over 100 of them stationed in the nearby Lincoln Park Cultural Arts Center. Several plainclothes officers mingled with the crowd. One officer later told newsmen he had thought, "Maybe we won't even have to tell them to leave."

After about an hour's wait, 150 Weathermen arrived chanting, "Ho, Ho, Ho Chi Minh, the Viet Cong are going to win." This was the McCormick Contingent. As the helmeted marchers approached the bonfire, one elderly gentleman asked who they were. From somewhere in the crowd came the answer, "It's the riot squad, *our* riot squad."

As the rally got underway, a girl with a bullhorn, one of the leaders of the Chicago Collective, proclaimed "This rally is to honor the memory of Che Guevara and Nguyen Van Troi. And the way to honor them, there is only one way, is to move into the streets and tear the city apart."

She went on to explain that the group would wait until the groups from the other Movement centers arrived and then move out to "tear down the mother country." The other contingents did not arrive immediately and the intervening time was filled with speeches, songs and chants of "Power to The People" and "Off the Pig." After about an hour's wait the crowd began to get nervous, wondering if anyone else was going to come. "This is an awful small group to start a revolution," commented one helmeted student from Oregon.

Between 9:45 and 10:15 two more groups entered the park, neither numbering over 30 members. They marched up to the bonfire and joined the rally.

Three defendants in the Conspiracy Trial were in the park—Tom Hayden, Abbie Hoffman, and John Froines. Hayden told the rally "People have been saying the Conspiracy Eight are against this demonstration. That is not true. While there are some differences among the 'Eight,' we are all united in the need to intensify the struggle to end the war."

"We are glad to see people back in Lincoln Park. We are glad to see the militancy of Chicago increased," Hayden added.

At 10:15 a member of the Weather Bureau (the national office of Weatherman/SDS) announced himself under the pseudonym of Marion Delgado and told the crowd they were going to march on the Drake Hotel, "where the rich people live." "Judge Hoffman (who is presiding in the Conspiracy Trial) is up at the Drake, and Marion Delgado don't like him and the Weatherman don't like him, so let's go get him."

With a shout, the Weathermen, numbering now about 250, moved out of Lincoln Park and down Clark Street, past policemen now forming outside of the Cultural Arts Center. The first large building the crowd passed was the North Federal Savings and Loan. A rock went through one of the building's large plate-glass windows and the crowd was electrified.

As they broke into a run, now shouting and screaming, smashing windows on both sides of the streets and in parked cars, police watched with incredulous expressions. One officer gasped, "I just don't believe it."

A squad of about 40 plainclothesmen ran on the sidewalks but did nothing to stop the Weathermen. As a window broke over the head of newsmen also running on the sidewalk, one member of the press shouted, "Hey watch it." "Get in the street you motherfucker!" someone said. "The next rock will be for you."

As the crowd turned east on Goethe, one passerby said, "I don't know what your cause is, but you have just set it back a hundred years." At the corner of Goethe and State, a Rolls Royce was parked in front of a hotel. It became an instant symbol of the "ruling class." Every window was smashed and the interior was destroyed. Similarly, the Weathermen singled out windows of businesses and banks for particular destruction. Many bricks and clubs, however, went through apartment windows into private homes.

"This is it baby, tear the fucker down," someone shouted. "Smash the State."

One individual tried to protect his car from the youths. He was beaten to the ground and left bleeding on the street. One man, looking at his smashed car, sobbed. Another shouted "Are these the ones you're protecting freedom for, the ones whose windows you're smashing? You're pigs, all pigs."

The Weathermen turned south on State Street, still encountering no opposition from the police. At State and Division, having come over eight blocks, the demonstrators ran into a forming police line. They charged straight into it. A brief battle followed and the leadership ranks, swinging clubs and chains, broke through the police. They were followed by only a handful of others. As police and demonstrators lay bleeding in the street, some still fighting, someone released a smoke bomb. The demonstrators turned back shouting "Gas, run for it."

The crowd broke into several large groups and headed east towards Lake Shore Drive on several side streets. Though disorganized, the group reformed briefly and moved south on Lake Shore. As they passed a construction site, bricks and concrete reinforcing rods were grabbed by the Weathermen.

Before they had gone a block, they were met head-on by police coming north on Lake Shore. The police released tear gas and the crowd turned back into the side streets. Although leaders pleaded, "Walk, don't scatter, stay together," the crowd again divided. Police began to arrive in unmarked cars and sealed off the intersections of side streets and Lake Shore. Several officers drew guns and began to fire into the crowd.

Two students attacked an officer and knocked him unconscious. The officer, Patrolman John Thompson, pulled his revolver and shot one of the students, John Van Veenendaal of Seattle, through the neck. Van Veenendaal was left in the street and later taken to a hospital in Evanston by fellow demonstrators. He said later, "I thought I was going to die." Seven other demonstrators were also shot during the night.

The crowd, which formed briefly one last time, moved into the Old Town area. Another battle with police came at Eugenie and LaSalle after the crowd had started to move back to Lincoln Park. As the crowd moved toward the park, people shouted, "It's a trap," and the crowd turned. There was a brief skirmish with police and then the demonstrators again moved to dark side streets. It was about 11:15.

The crowd moved northwest, presumably heading back toward McCormick Seminary. There were only about 60 people left in the main group. The crowd moved north to North Avenue, and then west. As they reached Menomonee, several police cars drove straight toward the group. One car actually drove into the crowd at a speed of about 25 miles per hour, knocking several persons down. Officers jumped from the cars and some carried revolvers. The crowd turned to Orleans Street, overturned a car and smashed more windows, then scattered into the night.

Behind them remained over 75 arrested demonstrators, 21 injured policemen, and streets full of shattered glass and shocked onlookers. The action had occurred in what is known as Chicago's Gold Coast, one of the wealthiest and most exclusive sections of town.

"We never expected this kind of violent demonstration," said Stephen Zicher, an assistant corporation counsel. "There has always been a big difference between what they say and what they do."

Richard D. Elrod, another assistant corporation counsel, told newsmen that the violence was "the worst possible thing you could imagine." Deputy Superintendent of police James M. Rochford, Jr., said, "We were faced with revolutionaries."

* * *

Many Chicagoans had scarcely finished reading the Thursday morning newspaper account of the Gold Coast battle when the second Weatherman action began. This was to be the action of the women's militia, who had announced that they would destroy the Chicago Armed Forces Induction Center.

A rally was called for 9:30 at the General Logan statue in Grant Park. At the announced time, about fifty women moved into the park carrying Viet Cong flags and clubs, and wearing helmets. Most of the women had been in the street the previous night. The group seemed disorganized and it was apparent that the national leadership had yet to arrive. The women clustered in a group near the statue.

Again, few police officers were in sight. Four patrol cars were parked on Michigan Ave., which runs next to the park, and several unmarked cars were also in the area, manned by undercover police. The Weatherwomen were almost outnumbered by the more than fifty newsmen present. Many of the newsmen, however, turned out to be either members of the Chicago Police Intelligence Unit or undercover policemen. Police took both still and moving pictures and tape recorded the entire event.

At about 10:15, the women were joined by a second contingent numbering about twenty and including Bernardine Dohrn, former Interorganizational Secretary of SDS and a member of the Weather Bureau. After several speeches by other leaders Miss Dohrn announced herself as Marion Delgado and told the group, "We are born in 1969 in America behind enemy lines."

"People are determined to fight here," she said. "We are here to tell the people that this is not a women's movement of self-indulgence. This is not a movement to make us feel good."

"We are here to teach the people the lesson of what it means to be a 'good German.' There are people fighting every minute of every day here in America. We are going to be part of that fight."

"We are here to go there (the Induction Center) and say there is a new army being formed. The new army is being built . . . the old one is falling down, crumbling from within."

"There is a war going on and we are not the ones who started that war. We're here to bring that war home!"

The demonstrators then headed north in Grant Park toward the corner of Michigan and Balboa. Police officers jumped out of their cars and helmeted officers who had previously been out of sight appeared and formed a line at the intersection. Deputy Chief of Patrol James J. Riordan, who commands officers in the Loop area, directed his men through a bullhorn device. As the police quickly formed their line, one officer said, "Remember, when you get in there, lay it on heavy."

As the women approached the police line, Riordan ordered them to "Hold it right there!" Approximately ten women, led by Miss Dohrn, charged into the police line. The officers, using clubs and mace, quickly subdued the women after about a four-minute scuffle. One policeman, holding a demonstrator in a double armlock, asked, "Now are you going to behave like a nice lady?" She turned and spit in his face.

Twelve women were arrested, including Miss Dohrn, who was charged with battery, mob action, and resisting arrest.

Five policemen reported having suffered cuts and bruises and assistant corporation counsel Zucker said he was bitten on the hand. The arrested women were immediately taken away in waiting paddy wagons.

Riordan then told the remaining Weatherwomen they would be arrested if they stepped onto the sidewalk. "You are armed and carrying weapons," he said. "Lay down your helmets and your weapons or you will be arrested."

As police formed a ring around the demonstrators, one woman asked how a helmet could be considered a weapon. Riordan replied that they could keep their helmets if they took them off. Police then confiscated clubs, four six-inch sections of metal pipe, and a length of chain.

Riordan told the women that they could file any complaints if they wished and Zucker came forward. One woman complained of having been hit with a camera by an undercover policeman.

The women were allowed to continue their march unarmed and on the sidewalk. They abandoned their plans to go to the Induction Center, however, and instead, escorted by police, marched to State and Harrison, where they boarded CTA subway trains and returned to McCormick Seminary.

Shortly following the arrests, Jonathan Lerner, Assistant National Secretary of SDS, held a press conference at the Civic Center Plaza. He announced that the Weathermen's planned invasion of the schools set for Thursday was to be postponed until Friday. The Weathermen had received word that over a thousand police would guard the high schools at which they planned the action. Lerner announced that instead the group would join the rally at the Federal Building scheduled for noon that day by the RYM II–Black Panther–Young Lords coalition.

The rally at the Federal Building, site of the trial of the Conspiracy Eight, was the first action scheduled by the RYM II group. As was typical throughout the week, the rally did not start on time. By 12:15, however, over five hundred people were congregated in the Plaza. This time police were very much in evidence, with helmeted squads completely surrounding the area.

Although the crowd was extremely nervous, there was a marked difference between this gathering and the Weathermen. Few helmets were in evidence and people passed through the area selling underground newspapers and distributing leaflets. Many of those present discussed the Weatherman action of the previous night and most condemned it.

The mid-day rally attracted large numbers of older people in addition to the expected young radicals. Many were there on what appeared to be a lunch break.

Banners were displayed reading "Racist Pig Daley, Stop Fascist Raids, Free Panthers Now," and "Free Bobby Seale, Free the Conspiracy Eight, Jail Judge Hoffman." (Seale is National Chairman of the Black Panther Party.)

A sizable group of Weathermen arrived at about 12:30. Police officers arrested several who were identified as having participated in the Wednesday night street-fighting. "They know who we are and they are just picking us off," said one Weatherman.

The rally was opened by Mike Klonsky, former National Secretary of SDS and a leader of the RYM II faction. Klonsky reiterated the RYM II slogan of "US Get Out of Vietnam Now!" and told the crowd that RYM II sought to "unite the struggle of the people of Vietnam with the struggles here in America" in a "year of solidarity with the Vietnamese people." As Klonsky spoke, federal marshals moved through the crowd and formed a protective ring around the Federal Building.

Klonsky introduced Fred Hampton, chairman of the Illinois Black Panther Party. Hampton, who drew loud cheers, began by condemning the Weathermen. "We do not support people who are anarchistic, opportunistic, adventuristic, and Custeristic," said Hampton, referring at the end to Custer's last stand.

"We do not believe in premature so-called acts of revolution. We support the actions of RYM II and no other faction of SDS. We've got to spend our time now on revolutionary education."

Hampton told the audience, however, that there would soon be a time for the people to take power. "No matter how many pigs there are, there are more people than there are pigs. We want power of people, by the people, for the people! Fuck this shit of the pigs, by the pigs, for the pigs!"

"Right on, brother!" the crowd responded.

Yoruba, a New York leader of the Young Lords, and Carl Davidson, a former SDS officer, also spoke at the rally. Klonsky then spoke again and told the crowd "The pigs are going to try to provoke a riot. Don't let them. There are not enough of us here to start the revolution now. We are going to go in an orderly and disciplined way to a demonstration at International Harvester. We will go in small groups. This is not a march." Those at the rally then split into groups of about twenty and headed for bus stops and subway stations.

Although there was some confusion, over four hundred demonstrators arrived at the International Harvester plant within a surprisingly short time. As demonstrators walked toward the plant from a subway station, police vans passed in which chanting officers shouted "Police Power" and "We're going to get you commie bastards."

The International Harvester plant is located across the street from the Cook County jail. As demonstrators arrived, over sixty sheriff's deputies, carrying three-foot-long riot batons, surrounded the jail. In front of the plant itself, over two hundred policemen formed in units while many more were held in reserve. The Chicago Daily News reported that policemen with rifles were stationed on rooftops.

The rally was opened by a worker from the plant who identified himself as "Slim." He told the crowd that at 9:00 that morning workers in four departments had walked out. He claimed that at 11:00, most of the rest of the workers left. "There's some people left in there, but there ain't no production going on now." Harvester officials later reported attendance was normal.

"Without firing a single shot, we cost International Harvester over a quarter of a million dollars." Slim went on to explain that the workers were protesting the fact that International Harvester was planning to close down the plant, taking jobs out of the area. An addition to the jail is to be built on the present plant site, and the existing factory is to be replaced by a new plant being built in a suburban location.

The new location is in a predominantly white area and black workers claim that they will not be able to find housing in the vicinity. Although International Harvester is encouraging workers to seek jobs at the new site, present workers will lose their seniority when they transfer to the new location.

The black workers were also protesting being "sold out" by their union, the UAW. A black worker, identified as Jake, told the crowd, "Eighty thousand people need work in Chicago and they're tearing down this plant to build a jail." "The union ain't doing a thing about it."

Slim spoke again and protested discrimination in hiring policies for skilled jobs. "When this plant opened, it was established that white guys got skilled jobs and black workers got unskilled jobs—and the union didn't do nothing against it then and it hasn't done nothing yet."

Jake added, "You can die with the white man in Vietnam, but you can't work with him in this plant."

A speaker from the Buffalo, N.Y., Chevrolet plant spoke of the strength in a worker-student alliance. "What happens when kids meet up with the pigs—people generally get messed up. But when seven hundred workers are standing across the street, shouting, 'On strike, shut it down,' the pigs don't mess with nobody." He was referring to a recent strike at the Buffalo plant.

The group then sang "Solidarity Forever," a traditional union song, and then peacefully dispersed.

*   *   *

On Thursday, Gov. Richard B. Ogilvie announced that 2,633 National Guardsmen were being called to Chicago to back up police officers. Ogilvie termed the call-up a "precautionary move."

After Wednesday night's Weatherman action, Police Superintendent James B. Conlisk asked Mayor Daley to request the guard. Ogilvie disclosed, however, that he had been contacted as early as Tuesday by Daley concerning the call-up possibility.

Conlisk apparently feared police ranks would be thinned

by the necessity to station precautionary forces at area high schools. He said "We have the potential for problems in the schools" until the SDS demonstrations end.

Brig. Gen. Richard T. Dunn, commander of the Illinois Emergency Operation Headquarters, was sent to Chicago by Ogilvie to assess the situation. Dunn reported that police had done "an excellent job" in controlling SDS demonstrators.

After the call-up, Dunn told newsmen that the Guardsmen, on readiness alert in six armories, would be called out "only on the request of civil authorities."

Earlier in the day Mayor Daley held a press conference at which he condemned the "senseless and vicious behavior" of the Wednesday night demonstrators. Daley lauded the police, who, he said "manifested the highest dedication to duty and professional conduct when, in the face of great personal danger, they preserved and protected the rights of our citizens."

Commenting on the women's action, Daley said police did "what I think they should do." "No one should be permitted to march and walk through the streets with clubs and chains and iron pipes in their hands. So, at the Logan Monument this morning, when they refused to surrender their weapons, they were arrested."

"When they are carrying clubs and pipes and chains, you know they are not playing hockey—unless they are playing hockey with someone's head, particularly a policeman's."

When asked about police preparations for the Wednesday night action, Daley said, "How are you going to be prepared for guerrilla tactics when they run in all different directions?"

*   *   *

Thursday night the Weathermen had scheduled a "Wargasm" rally in Lincoln Park. The rally never came off. There was, however, a crowd of about one thousand in the park, consisting of detectives, plainclothes police, newsmen, and "riot watchers."

Several individuals were arrested for "refusing to obey police orders." One youth was arrested when police found several new bricks in the trunk of his car. He told police the bricks were intended for a bookshelf. They were not convinced. Several people were also arrested after police identified them as having participated in the Wednesday fighting. The park cleared when heavy rains fell later in the evening.

Meanwhile, over two hundred Weathermen and national leaders gathered at Garret Theological Seminary in Evanston for a "strategy session." The group discussed actions that had taken place and laid plans for Friday and Saturday. While the Weathermen met in Evanston police attempted to gain entry to the McCormick Movement Center. They were kept out by Weatherman security guards.

As the meeting at Garret began, leaders from the national office asked for comments and criticisms on actions so far. This opened what was to be a more than six-hour meeting.

Much of the resultant criticism was levelled at the national leadership, the Weather Bureau. Demonstrators said that they felt the leadership did not have enough confidence in them. Specifically, it was pointed out that almost no one knew exactly what was to happen Wednesday night. This included the affinity group leaders, who were expected to keep their groups together and direct them in the action.

The group also complained that they should have had an opportunity to discuss the tactics with the leaders before the action began, as several had reservations as to whether the action was a proper one.

It was mentioned that national leadership had shown up late at both the Wednesday night rally and the women's action. It was felt that this furthered the disorganization and disoriented atmosphere of the actions.

Demonstrators discussed the fact that in Wednesday night's fight, the leadership contingent had broken through the police lines, but when others did not follow, the main group was cut off. Students said that this was in part due to the fact that leaders had not prepared the group for what was expected and in the confrontation situation, people were not sufficiently organized to follow through.

The Weather Bureau acknowledged that a number of mistakes had been made. They pointed out, however, that the entire concept of "offensive action" was a new one, having been developed only in the four months since the summer SDS conference.

The leaders explained the secrecy in terms of needed security and pointed to the apparent surprise on the part of police officers at Wednesday's actions. By keeping plans secret, the Weather Bureau said, the group was able to catch the police off guard. This is in marked contrast to previous radical actions when police have been thoroughly prepared for militant actions.

Leaders also said that those who broke through the lines Wednesday night were showing "exemplary action" and had been expecting that others would follow.

The leaders spent considerable time discussing the entire concept of revolutionary struggle in America. The goal of the national action, they said, was to "build a Red Army, to show that white kids are really ready to fight."

"We showed them that Wednesday night. It was like unfurling a gigantic Viet Cong flag in the heart of Chicago." The important goal of the action, said one leader, was to "establish our presence in the nation's mind."

In fighting a war, said a member of the Weather Bureau, one must "think in terms of losses." The losses in battle are expected to be balanced by political gains.

Wednesday night definitely raised the level of struggle in America, the leadership maintained. It was the first time white students had been the aggressors. It was a demonstration that the group was "out to win."

Leaders felt that all previous movements had failed in their attempts to build a revolutionary movement. Said one person, "We are the most progressive group in the country." He went on to say that because of the Weathermen's progressive nature, they had few models to follow. Thus, actions had to be experimental. It was pointed out that there had never before been a revolution in the "mother country of imperialism."

The Women's Militia march was considered as one such

experimental action. Although the affair was a military defeat, many of the marchers confessing that they felt humiliated, the group believed the march, in total, was a success. Both political and tactical gains were cited.

The Weathermen felt that the mere fact that women armed themselves and attacked police was a significant advance. Newspaper headlines of "SDS Women Fight Police" would establish the presence of a women's fighting force, armed and ready to participate in revolutionary struggle. This fulfilled both the goals of "establishing presence" and "raising the level of struggle." It was also possible to observe how police functioned in that kind of situation. The significant changes in operational procedure from the Democratic Convention, for example, were important.

It was also observed, however, that the fact that only a small number of women demonstrators followed the leadership into the police line indicated again the need to more adequately prepare individuals for confrontations. "You have to completely understand the political reasons for your actions before you ever go into the street," said one Weatherman. "If you don't know exactly what you have to do and why, you shouldn't be there."

The Weathermen extensively discussed the concept of "white-skin privilege." They felt that most people in America would never fight on the side of revolution, as they were not oppressed by the conditions felt elsewhere in the world. This situation was contrasted with the position of a Vietnamese, who experiences American oppression on a day-to-day basis.

One leader said that for this reason, mass support of the Weatherman action must be discounted. "Most people will be turned off, you have to expect that. They are going to be fighting on the side of pigs if they ever fight at all."

Therefore, the group abandoned most efforts to appeal to the working class, a traditional source of revolutionary support. The working class, too, it was contended, can exist under their white-skin privilege and do not have to suffer the oppression levelled against black, brown, and yellow peoples.

Similarly, most college students were discounted in another departure from traditional revolutionary strategy. The college students were seen as too secure in their present position to be willing to "lay their lives on the line" for the cause of revolution.

The basis of appeal must be directed toward the "alienated youth culture, particularly working-class youth." From among the youth who are not yet part of the system and who are totally alienated by it must be drawn the fighting force. From this segment of the population the Weathermen hoped to find youth committed to "smashing the State" so that "we can build something better in its place."

The meeting finally turned to a discussion of activities for the remainder of the national action. Leaders announced that the demonstrations at high schools, originally scheduled for Thursday afternoon and postponed until Friday, were to be called off entirely. Heavy losses at the high schools, which were to be guarded by hundreds of police, would prevent the group from being at full strength for the Saturday march, the Weather Bureau said.

Demonstrators were encouraged to go into the city on Friday in groups of two or three and "scout out" the march route in order to be thoroughly familiar with the area. Wall posters were also being printed, which the group was to paste up Friday night.

As the meeting closed, it was emphasized that "nobody should consider tomorrow a day off." "We're going to win by not thinking of losing!"

Seminary officials objected to the radicals' meeting. They had previously made arrangements for about thirty SDS members to stay in the seminary during the National Action in an effort to "keep them off the streets at night."

John Morin, president of the Garret Student Association, said, "We accept full responsibility for their presence. We affirm their right to be here. We believe that fundamental change in American society is necessary. However, that does not mean we believe that all the tactics currently used by SDS contribute to the creation of a more humane society."

SDS refused to confer with school officials, but spent the

six hours during the meeting negotiating with a committee of students. The SDS members refused to allow Garrett students into the meeting and frisked all students who entered the building.

Garret President Orville H. McKay said, "We thought we could make some contribution, so that they wouldn't have to sleep in the streets and avoid confrontations with the police." The Garret Dean of Students said, "They have violated all agreements with us."

When the meeting concluded, shortly after 2 a.m., all but thirty students left the seminary. Arrangements were made to house the students at churches in the Evanston area. . . .

Earlier on Friday the Weathermen moved out of their main Movement Center at McCormick Seminary. A carefully worded, neatly typed note explained "An arrangement has been reached by the National Action Committee (NAC) of SDS and the McCormick Theological Seminary, whereby no further use of these facilities will be made during the National Action by SDS." A Weather Bureau member later said simply, "We were forced to give up the center."

The Weatherman central office told demonstrators to go to two new movement centers in Evanston, the Wheeden Methodist Church and the Covenant Methodist Church. Students had stayed at the churches the previous night after leaving the Garrett Seminary.

A contingent of about sixty Weathermen was at the Wheeden Church under the leadership of the Ohio collective. The groups with the Chicago collective, now numbering over two hundred, moved to the Covenant Church.

At the Covenant Church a seven-hour general meeting took place as demonstrators debated both tactics and philosophy in preparation for the Saturday action. The discussion was not as well organized as the previous night's, due mainly to the absence of national leadership.

The Weathermen began by reiterating much of the philosophy of their faction for the benefit of several new members who had only recently arrived.

The demonstrators again evaluated previous actions and

sought to understand the necessity for following through with the planned march on Saturday although they were certain to face suicidal odds. One collective leader pointed out that the newspapers had led the public to believe the Weathermen had been crushed by the police. "It's important to show them that that is not true. We've got to show them that even those of us who have been busted or messed up are ready to go back out on the streets and off the pig. Many of the people in this room are out on bail and face four or five charges already, but that isn't going to stop them. We're going to go out tomorrow and tear the motherfucker down."

A leader from the New York collective said, "The fact that they have called out the National Guard is a victory. Why is it a victory—because for every soldier they bring in here, that's fewer than can vamp on our brothers in Vietnam, our brothers in Latin America, in the ghetto. For every soldier they bring in here, that's more breathing space for our brothers."

"In a funny sort of way," he added, "the more they vamp on Weatherman, the more they oppress us, the more Weatherman wins."

A former soldier who had served in Vietnam commented, "We've got to win little by little. That's what the Viet Cong do. They hit a little here, a little there, and that's how they win."

Many of the demonstrators expected that several of the group would be killed in the next day's action. One youth from Baltimore said, "Probably a lot of us will get shot. But for every one of us that goes down, there'll be five to take his place."

Another radical commented that, "If you [go] back to your home, and you've had your arm shot off, or your best friend has been killed—let's consider the possibilities—but if this happens and you still want to fight, that's going to impress the hell out of them."

Other Weathermen felt that it was unlikely that many people would be seriously hurt. People referred to the concept of "white-skin privilege," under which many white people hide to avoid true commitment to the revolutionary struggle. "In a strange sort of way," it was explained, "we can exploit that white skin privilege."

"If a bunch of black brothers marched down the street and got shot, it wouldn't make much difference to people in this country. But if they shot a bunch of us, even if the people hated us, they wouldn't stand for it because we're white."

About halfway through the meeting, one of the students who had been shot in the Wednesday night fight entered the room, still wearing Cook County Hospital pajamas. He told the group, "The next time I come to Chicago, I'm going to bring a gun, and if I get shot I'm going to take a couple of pigs with me."

Several youths immediately responded that such a position was "not correct." "That's an individualistic, terroristic thing. We must think in terms of the group, in terms of furthering the revolution."

Leaders explained that individual terrorism or action by small groups was not the proper strategy for Saturday. "We must remember that the purpose of this action is to build a Red Army. There is not much difference between black terrorism and brown terrorism and white terrorism. Blowing up a few things or shooting a few pigs from rooftops may do more damage, and we may get into that later, but not at this time."

"The action tomorrow has to demonstrate that white people are willing to join the struggle, willing to fight. To do that, we have to be on the streets, in the Loop."

The direction of debate changed when a girl from Iowa told the group that although she could accept the Weatherman philosophy in principle, she could not get over the emotional hurdle of going into the street with the intention of killing a policeman. "Although I know he's a pig and I should hate him for it, I can't help but think of him as a person."

The group agreed that this was a problem that many seemed to have. A girl from Michigan said, "We don't like to hit people, to hurt people. We don't like to get hurt either. But the pig, whether he's a person or not, is the only thing that is holding the Man up, and the pig must be smashed. The way to tear down the Man is to off the pig."

Chicago, October 8, 1969. SDS Weatherman march down street from Lincoln Park. Photo: Pterodactyl

Another student added, "We must fight because it is correct. You hate the pigs so much you want to kill them. We may lose militarily, but by smashing pigs, we will win in the eyes of the people of the world. We will win in the worldwide revolutionary struggle."

The girl from Michigan added, "Offing a pig is more than just hate; it's love. Love for the revolution, love for the oppressed people."

When asked if she thought the Viet Cong should fight, the girl from Iowa replied that she did. She added, however, that she believed that there "could be an alternative for people living in America in 1969."

A Vietnamese in the crowd rose and delivered a bitter attack. "That is exactly the hiding behind the white-skin privilege that we have been talking about," he said. "She can just sit there and say the Vietnamese should fight but she doesn't have to. She is a nationalist chauvinist racist. The Viet Cong would kill her. She shouldn't even be here. We should kick her out."

The girl was allowed to remain but it was decided that the group was wasting its time talking with a pacifist and should return to the problems it would face the next day, as the bulk of the group intended to fight.

Several leaders said that they felt that there was a defeatist attitude in the group. "You can't go into the streets tomorrow thinking that," said a New York leader. "You've got to go out there knowing you're going to win, knowing you're going to win even if you die."

A Chicago organizer told the group, "The kids in this town are digging us like hell." She said, "They think we've got an out-of-sight thing going."

A demonstrator with her arm in a sling told the group everywhere she went people identified her as a Weatherman. "I got on the subway and the whole car was uptight. People think every fucking kid in this town is a Weatherman, and that messes their minds."

The meeting continued until about three a.m. when Chicago and Evanston police broke down the door. The raid was intended, according to police spokesmen, to seize six Weathermen for whom warrants were obtained after a police spy had been beaten at another Evanston church.

The spy had entered the Movement Center at Immanuel Methodist Church where members of the New York Collective were having a meeting Friday morning. Members of the Weather Bureau were also present at the church.

One of the demonstrators who had been arrested Wednesday claimed he recognized the spy, having seen him at the police station. Weathermen debated what to do with the spy, then decided to "work him over and kick him out."

As the pastor of the church arrived, the Weathermen threw the spy out of the church. The group then decided, for obvious reasons, to leave the Immanuel Church. The collective moved into the streets that afternoon in small groups. The demonstrators later joined the group at the Covenant Church.

The police arrived at the Covenant Church at about 3:15 a.m. and were met by that church's pastor. "I asked them to wait and let the janitor open the door with keys, but they just broke down the door," he said afterward.

As the police burst into the meeting room, several of the radicals successfully fled into the night. Others had left only a short time before to put up new wall posters. The policemen ordered the remaining two hundred Weathermen "up against the wall."

Demonstrators were told to keep their heads down and to look straight ahead. The group was caught completely by surprise and there was almost no resistance. Three of the youths for whom warrants were obtained were immediately seized. Another forty were recognized as having participated in Wednesday night's action and were also arrested. As the group was frisked, officers removed money from individual's wallets, [money] which was never returned. Many of the helmets and other items of equipment were taken by the officers as they left.

Approximately one hundred fifty Weathermen remained in the church after the raid. The group spent the remainder of the evening discussing the effect of the raid. Many were obviously disturbed by the fact that the police had so easily broken into the center. Several thought that the group should have fought the police. Others thought resistance would have been suicidal.

As a consequence of the ease with which the police had subdued the group, several of the demonstrators decided not to participate in the Saturday march. The Weathermen did not sleep that night but continued the discussion through the dawn and up to the time when they departed for the march.

The final Weatherman march was called for 12:00 noon at Haymarket Square, site of the destroyed police monument. At 12:00 not a Weatherman was in sight. About fifty policemen were present, none of them wearing helmets.

At about 12:10, a group of approximately twenty Weathermen moved into the Square and formed near the remains of the statue. The group included several members of the Weather Bureau.

About five minutes later, a squad of fifteen policemen dressed in heavy jackets, old clothes and boots, entered the Square and quickly walked toward the assembled group. Their arrival was hidden from the Weathermen by the many newsmen who walked about the area. The policemen mingled in with the Weathermen (at least one officer wore an SDS button) and then suddenly attacked five leaders with clubs. No warning was given, and only the five were beaten.

The leaders fought back and a violent struggle filled half the Square for about two minutes. The arrested Weather Bureau members were immediately placed in waiting paddy wagons and carried away. One of those seized was Mark Rudd, National Secretary of SDS.

Assistant corporation counsel Stephen Zucker said those arrested would be charged with "inciting to riot." "We're not looking for leaders," claimed Zucker, "we're looking for ones who broke the law."

He also said that many of the over one hundred and twenty Weathermen previously arrested were out on bails, some as high as $5,000.

About twenty minutes following the arrests more than one hundred Weathermen arrived in the Square, only about half with helmets. Many of those present had been on the street Wednesday. This time, however, few weapons were in evidence.

John Jacobs of the national office, wearing a red football helmet, began the rally. As he spoke, other contingents arrived, bringing the total to more than three hundred and twenty-five demonstrators. After about thirty minutes of speeches, the group, which had obtained a parade permit earlier, moved into the street. They marched at a rapid pace for more than eight blocks east on Randolph Street. As the crowd moved out of Haymarket Square, led by a squad car, a half-dozen unmarked cars pulled into the street behind them. The officers who had patrolled the Square also formed behind the marchers.

As the march moved east, squads of police who had lined the street joined the officers behind the crowd. Uniformed and plainclothes police kept pace on the sidewalk. The march then turned south on LaSalle, according to the prescribed route. By this time, over seventy-five officers were following the demonstrators. As the three hundred and twenty-five Weathermen passed one policeman, he muttered incredulously, "Is this it? Are these all?" A woman bystander said angrily, "They should not leave them alone, they know what they are going to do."

After marching south for two blocks, a leader suddenly yelled "Break!" With a shout the Weathermen turned east on Madison, off the official route. One policeman was immediately thrown through a plate-glass window at the Railway Express office at the corner of Madison and LaSalle. Demonstrators charged down Madison, battling police as they went.

Over one hundred police in full riot gear almost immediately closed in behind the Weathermen, joining those who had followed the march. They pursued the demonstrators as they headed east past Clark and Dearborn, where they were met head on by another contingent of police.

At Dearborn, the Weathermen split into three groups, one

heading east on Madison toward State Street, the other heading north and south on Dearborn. "Follow them, get them," officers shouted to their men. As police began to round up the marchers, several discarded their helmets and were able to avoid detection.

At Clark and Madison, a demonstrator was felled, unconscious, at the center of the intersection. Police first allowed a member of the "medical cadre" to treat the youth, then carried the unconscious demonstrator to a waiting squad car by his arms and legs. The medic was also arrested and taken away in a paddy wagon.

A more serious casualty occurred earlier in the fight when assistant corporation counsel Richard Elrod attempted to arrest a demonstrator. He was knocked to the ground and kicked in the neck. When assistant counsel Zucker attempted to come to his aid, he, too, was attacked before police arrived and subdued the Weathermen. Elrod, a close personal friend of Mayor Daley, was taken to a hospital immediately, where it was later announced that his neck was broken and that he was paralyzed from the neck down.

The fighting lasted about fifteen minutes, principally in the three-block area on Madison between LaSalle and State. Some demonstrators managed to avoid the police by merging with the crowds that jammed the street corners. Others fled the area or boarded buses and subways. A total of more than one hundred and eighty demonstrators were arrested. Over thirty policemen were injured.

Relatively little material damage occurred. Aside from the Railway Express windows, only the large plate-glass front of Maxim's Restaurant and a handful of small shop- and car-windows were broken. A large brick was hurled at a window of the First National Bank, but it only chipped the glass.

By 2:30 the police were attempting to clear the area. "All persons move out of this area," announced one officer. "If you do not do this, you are violating police orders and will be arrested."

As the streets cleared, a Weatherman leader walked down the sidewalk, unnoticed by the police. "We're not finished yet," he said. "If you see any of our people, tell them groups of twos and threes."

. . . . A large crowd began to gather in Grant Park. By 4:00 over two hundred were present, many surrounding the statue of General Logan. At one end of the park, members of the Ameican Nazi Party demonstrated, carrying signs proclaiming "Gas the Red Traitors," "Support White Police," and "We Killed Ho Chi Minh."

National Guard vehicles circled the area. A large squad of helmeted police stood in formation across Michigan Avenue, which borders the park. Throughout the nearby Loop area, police officers stood guard at every block and a cordon of police surrounded City Hall.

Shortly after 4:00 Deputy Chief of Patrol James Riordan arrived with several squads of police and about fifteen detectives. Riordan approached the crowd with a portable loudspeaker and announced:

"There are people in this crowd who will be identified by officers as being guilty of assault. Those people will be arrested. It is expected that they will surrender with no resistance. If there is resistance or if anyone tries to aid a prisoner, there will be further arrests. There is no need to run or to panic."

It had been rumored that the Weathermen would hold one last rally at Grant Park. Riordan had with him officers who had been in the fighting little more than an hour before.

The squad of about seventy-five officers, in formation, moved up to the statue. Another group of police formed a wider ring about the entire crowd. The officers identified no one and left after about five minutes as the youths about the statue sang "Mickey Mouse" and blew soap bubbles.

Another contingent of officers moved in and one person was arrested. A somewhat ludicrous scene followed, as fifty grim-faced, helmeted officers, formed in double file, escorted the youth to a paddy wagon. Again the officers drew loud jeers. Most of the police departed from the area a short time later.

About fifteen minutes following the arrest, a Weatherman

spokesman addressed the crowd. "In the last four days," he began, "we have learned some important lessons."

"The most important lesson is that we can fight, too—that we have a role to play—that's a tremendous lesson."

"We have learned that the spirit of the people is greater than the Man's technology."

People in the crowd, at least one of them an undercover policeman, began to heckle the speaker. He ignored them. "We did what we have to do every time," he continued.

"We have shown the pigs that we can fight. We have shown the pigs that they have to overextend themselves on another front. We have taken the movement a qualitative step forward."

"We are now going to split into groups of four and five and take to the subways and buses. We are going to take the lessons we have learned here in Chicago home with us as we go back; we are going to bring the war home!"

New Left Notes, August 29, 1969

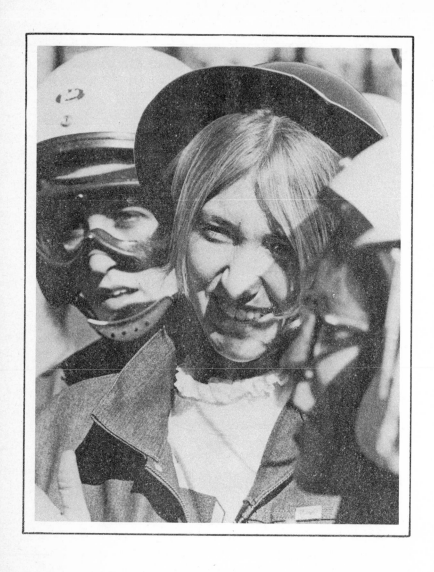

Chicago, October 9, 1969. Weatherman Women's Militia in Grant Park.
Photo: Pterodactyl

A Weatherman: You Do Need A Weatherman To Know Which Way The Wind Blows

Shin'ya Ono

In September, I attended the Cleveland Conference on the National Action as an anti-Weatherman representative from the New York Movement for a Democratic Society. A month and a half later, a photograph of me being fucked over by three Chicago pigs appeared on the Guardian cover, and I came back with charges amounting to more than ten years. My non-Weatherman comrades ask me: Was it worth it? The answer is yes, yes—wholeheartedly, yes. How I, a firm anti-Weatherman, felt compelled—after a tremendous resistance— to become a Weatherman, is important, but mostly in a personal way. What I would like to go into here is how the Chicago action, and the Weatherman logic behind it, made, and still makes, compelling sense for an old-timer like myself with the usual "credentials."

THE WEATHERMAN PERSPECTIVE

Three key points divide the Weathermen from all other political tendencies:

First: the primacy of confronting national chauvinism and racism among the working-class whites; the necessity to turn every issue, problem, and struggle into an anti-imperialist, anti-racist struggle; the assertion that organizing whites primarily around their own perceived oppression (whether it be women's liberation, student power, the draft and the stockades, the crisis of the cities, oppression at the point of production) is bound to lead in a racist and chauvinist direction.

From *Leviathan*, December 1969

Second: the urgency of preparing for militant, armed struggle now; the necessity of organizing people into a fighting movement, not primarily by critiques, ideas, analyses, or programs, though all these are important, but by actually inflicting material damage to imperialist and racist institutions right now, with whatever forces you've got.

Third: the necessity of building revolutionary collectives that demand total, wholehearted commitment of the individual to struggle against everything that interferes with the revolutionary struggle, and to struggle to transform oneself into a revolutionary and a communist: collectives through which we can forge ourselves into effective "tools of necessity" and through which we can realize, concretely, in our day-to-day lives, such well-known Maoist principles as "Politics in command," "Everything for the revolution," "Criticism—self-criticism—transformation."

The Weatherman did not pick up these three points from Mao or the classics abstractly. These points arose out of, and are situated within, a broader revolutionary strategy specific to the conditions prevailing within the imperialist mother country.

As we see it, US imperialism has already entered a period of organic crisis, in the Gramscian sense of that term. And this crisis is of such intensity, depth, and immediacy as to make the destruction of imperialism and socialist revolution both possible and necessary *in our generation,* that is, in the order of twenty to thirty years, as opposed to fifty or one hundred years. But since the US is neither a colony nor a semi-colony (like China, Cuba, or Vietnam), nor an ordinary capitalist country (like Denmark), nor an ordinary imperialist country (like France or Britain), but the hegemonic imperialist country of the entire capitalist world, there are conditions peculiar to it that give the revolutionary process here its specific characteristics.

The political economy of US imperialism has reached an advanced stage of monopoly capitalism whose development is determined primarily by the problems of absorption of surplus capital and of reproduction of capital and of labor power, rather than those related to the point of production. (See the discussion by Ernest Mandel and Martin Nicolaus, Leviathan, September 1969.) More concretely, U.S. imperialism is an integrated international politico-economic system in which the peoples of the Third World, and to a much smaller degree the workers of other capitalist countries, are forced into the position of the proletariat of US political economy, while the white workers of the mother country itself find themselves in the position of a relatively privileged stratum of the imperialist US working force as a whole.

So, looking at the imperialist beast as a totality, we become aware that the primary contradiction within the US imperialist political economy is not one between the working class and the bourgeoisie within white North Amerika, but one between the oppressed people of the Third World and the US imperialist ruling class. We adduce this primacy of the Third World not merely from an objective-structural analysis of US imperialism, but, more importantly, from the actual liberation wars that are being waged in the post-World War II period by the peoples of Asia, Africa, and Latin America (and within the ghettoes of Amerika by the black and brown peoples). Furthermore, in the development of this primary contradiction, we see that the victory of the Chinese, Cuban, and especially the Vietnamese, revolutions, constitute a dramatic turning point; that is, the people of the Third World have already become, on the worldwide level, the principal and the predominant aspect which will determine the course and the ultimate resolution of this antagonistic contradiction. The coming decisive US defeat in Vietnam, the Chinese Cultural Revolution and the achievement of a usable Chinese nuclear force, the highly probable liberation war in Korea, the utter inability of US imperialism to forge a capitalist alternative in the developing nations, and the surging liberation struggles in Laos, Burma, Thailand, Malaya, India, Palestine, in Africa and Latin America, and in the ghettoes of the imperialist homeland itself, make the eventual and total defeat of US imperialism in this generation a certainty. What is not so clear is the role that whites in the mother country can play in this anti-imperialist struggle and the nature of the revolutionary strategy that will enable us to maximize their active participation in the coming revolution, both qualitatively and quantitatively.

How do we situate the class position of whites in Amerika within the context of this worldwide revolutionary war, and within the context of the political economy of monopoly capitalism at its more advanced imperialist stage? How one answers this question shapes the specifics of one's entire revolutionary strategy here in the mother country.

The class position of white people in this country is determined by two contradictory aspects. On the one hand, by the classical Marxist definition, the overwhelming majority of whites belong to the working class in the sense that they neither own nor control the means of production. Furthermore, they are materially, psychologically, and in every other way, concretely oppressed by the imperialist political economy and by its concomitant superstructure. This implies that the destruction of imperialism and socialist revolution are objectively in the interests of the vast majority of white Amerikans.

On the other hand, we confront the fact that the white workers do not constitute the main or the most oppressed sections of the work force within the worldwide political economy of US imperialism: on the contrary, they form a tiny, and the most privileged, sector of that proletariat. More, Racially and politically they are members of the oppressor nation in relation to the Third World, including as always the blacks and the browns here; and as such they experience concrete benefits, both material and spiritual. They are the best paid, most comfortable, and the least oppressed, among the proletariat of the US imperialist political economy.

They also derive invidious sick satisfaction out of their feeling that they belong to the top nation in the whole world. Just as the rulers' self-esteem is largely based on their sense of superiority vis-à-vis "lowly and stupid" masses, so the white masses of Amerika base a large part of their self-definition on their membership in the "superior race" and the "greatest nation." And in the short run, as long as they remain a reliable mass base for imperialism, these material and spiritual privileges will be allowed by the ruling class.

The classical contradiction at the point of production is to a large degree superseded by more crucial contradictions rising out of surplus absorption and reproduction. On the level of the individual white worker's consciousness, chauvinism and racism, which have a real short-range material basis, are superimposed upon his class consciousness which, if fully developed, would conflict with imperialism. At present, racism and national chauvinism form the predominant aspect of contradictory consciousness for the overwhelming majority of white workers. In the short run, then, the development of consciousness of most working-class whites will be decisively shaped by the fact that they share in the fruits of the imperialist domination and plunder; and any attempt to politicize them in a revolutionary direction must deal with this fact in a real, and not a rhetorical or a cerebral, way. Not to make the distinction between the long-term class interest which we can infer from an objective structural analysis of people's relationship to the means of production, and the concretely experienced, short-term, privileges that determine their consciousness at present, is to fall into a pure dogmatism about the centrality of the role of the industrial workers. (See Jim Mellen, "More on Youth Movement," *New Left Notes,* May 13, 1969.)

YOUTH ON THE MOVE

Given this understanding of the forces at work in the development of the white working class consciousness, what we must ask now is: Of the many segments that make up this working class, which ones are most likely to develop full (i.e., internationalist) class consciousness at the present time, and lead the rest into anti-imperialist, anti-racist revolutionary struggles? In other words, which segments of the white working class are least privileged, or have the least stakes and roots in the system of privilege, and are most immediately and acutely oppressed? We answer: Youth, and especially the working-class youth. To summarize the arguments:

1. They are least tied down materially to the system of oppression and relative privilege (marriage and children, mortgage, stable lifetime jobs, pension plans, etc.).

2. They grew up when the people's struggle was on the upsurge (Cuba, Black Liberation, Vietnam), and when imperialism entered its most decadent, hypocritical, and transparently chauvinist phase (thereby negating many bourgeois norms and values).

3. They were socialized when important socializing media and mechanisms were disintegrating (the breakdown of the bourgeois family, deterioration of social services like the school, the plasticity and the transparent manipulativeness of the TV-advertisement-culture, sexual-psychoanalytic-cultural revolution, etc.).

4. They experience in the most acute way the oppressive conditions engendered by the imperialist crisis. (The schools, the draft and the army, unemployment, draggy jobs, the pigs and the courts who come down on their anti-authoritarian modes of living and expression.)

These forces generated by the imperialist crisis, and lived through by every youth of our generation, have produced a youth culture and potentially explosive, anti-authoritarian motions in the past decade. We ourselves are both products and creators of these motions and forces. What we need to do now is to coalesce all these fragmented motions into an effective, anti-imperialist fighting force, with explicit revolutionary goals and with the most oppressed working-class youths as its core.

But how?

The problem is not primarily one of creating the consciousness among youth that they are oppressed: working-class youth knows much better than we that they are fucked over by this system in all kinds of ways. It's not even a question of "teaching" them to fight. Most of these kids have done much more of that (even fighting the pigs) than most Weathermen can hope to do in the near future. In fact, there are but two obstacles preventing their acute awareness of oppression and of oppressive social order from developing into a fully revolutionary direction: first, their racism and chauvinism; second, their basic defeatism about their ability, not merely to "beat the system" once in a while, but actually to destroy it totally.

We've already dealt at some length with racism and chauvinism as the chief impediments to the development of revolutionary consciousness among the white workers. The situation is essentially the same, though to a significantly lesser degree, among white youth. In the practice of our collectives in Michigan, Ohio, and New York, we've encountered many working-class youths who know very well that they are oppressed, and who hate this system, and who yet fight both the pigs and the blacks. In the emerging race war in many New York high schools, many of the same whites who vamp on the blacks went out on the "45-minute" high school strike last year, and this spring ripped up the schools with the blacks. These kids know they are being fucked over by the tracking system in the school and the class society outside the school. As the crisis of Amerikan imperialism deepens in the next few years, there will be more and more working-class kids who want to fight their oppression, but who will be in motion primarily against the blacks and the Vietnamese because their racism and chauvinism prevent them from seeing the imperialist ruling class as the true and the common enemy.

The correct way to deal with this racism and chauvinism in a polarized situation is to confront it directly and show a real alternative. To hand them a leaflet or pamphlet or merely to rap, with explanations as to how racism is not in their long-term interest, is not a way to do either. Words, words, words. Mere words, however persuasive, mere ideas, however true, can not make even a dent in an ingrained psychic structure like racism that not only reaches into the very depth of whites' souls, but also has a material basis to sustain it. The only way to make our anti-racist ideas and analyses real is for these white kids to be confronted with a group of other whites who are willing to actually fight on the side of the blacks (and not just talk, hand out leaflets, picket, march, or give money for black liberation). Make oppressed and racist white working-class youth really grapple with the existence of such a white fighting force. To see a group of other whites willing to fight to the very end on the side of the blacks will be a shocking experience for most whites. The existence of such whites, and actually seeing them fight, will hit hard at the core of their racist being in ways no words or analyses alone can do. The resulting fluidity in their consciousness will provide us with a radical space through which we can begin to communicate a class analysis of their own oppression. Without the reality of white groups actually fighting on the side of the blacks, the racism of whites could never be broken through, let alone overcome systematically.

While you confront their racism in this manner, you also must show a concrete alternative by identifying and actually attacking the real enemy, that is, the various imperialist institutions implicated in their class oppression, such as schools, draft boards, army, banks, pigs, courts, big corporations, local and national enemies of the people, etc. You also show a concrete alternative by the very existence of a communist fighting force which they can join on various levels of struggle.

The second obstacle to the revolutionization of white working-class youth is their basic defeatism. In the last few years, hundreds of thousands of youths in and out of the Movement have fought against this imperialist system in various ways, but only a handful have become revolutionaries. Why? Because most of us are basically defeatists about our ability to destroy the system ("You can't fight city hall"). No matter how hard or how often we fight, we slide back to non-revolutionary bourgeois holes, because, at the basic core of our psychic life, we too have internalized the strongest ideological bulwark of US imperialism, i.e., the chauvinist idea that US imperialism, and its social order at home, is permanent and invincible. If most of us radicals and "revolutionaries" in the movement have not overcome this US imperialist-chauvinist myth, how can we expect working-class youth, who are not as familiar as we supposedly are with the experience and the victories of the Third World peoples, not to share this basic presumption about the permanence and invincibility of this social order?

A WHITE FIGHTING FORCE

The only way to confront and change this basic defeatism, which again is no mere idea but an essential element of their psychic structure, is by creating the presence of a white fighting force. A few hundred or a few thousand white revolutionaries who understand that US imperialism is really a paper tiger, that the oppressed people of the world are really fighting and winning, that this imperialist mother is going to come down within our generation, must form themselves into a disciplined fighting force, and with the forces they now have, fight to inflict the maximum material damage to imperialism and racism. Under the leadership of blacks and Vietnamese, this force must fight not primarily for this specific demand or for that particular reform, but to disrupt the functioning of this imperialist country, and to smash it. And they must fight in a tight and together way, appropriate to the seriousness and protracted nature of the struggle. Again, to see such a group of whites actually doing it is a thousand times more effective in shaking up the whites' chauvinist defeatism about the permanence of this system than the most incisively argued pamphlet on the "inevitability of the collapse of U.S. imperialism," etc.

If every rebellious white working-class youth in this country was compelled to really grapple with the possibility that this social order might be brought down, that we may be able to really change things, then the revolutionary movement in this country will have made a qualitative leap to a much higher level of struggle. Before this is done, all else is talk and words, no leap in consciousness. Without this leap, the movement will continue to be a mere aggregate of individuals who wish things were otherwise, or who may even put in many hours of routinized political work, but who really have no concrete idea of how to make a revolution.

Note that in all of the preceding I said nothing about "turning people on" to the revolution or to communism. Weatherman is not about "turning people on." People don't become revolutionaries because it's groovy or nice. People are *compelled* to turn towards revolution and communism because there is no other way out of their predicament. What Weatherman is about is showing the white working class that they're really up against the wall, like the Vietnamese and the blacks, though not so immediately or so intensely now; that, ultimately, their only choice is either joining the world revolution led by the blacks, the yellows, and the browns, or being put down as US imperialist pigs by the people of the Third World, as has already happened to three hundred thousand working-class Amerikans in Vietnam. What Weatherman is about is breaking through the racism and chauvinism at its core by forcing white people to grapple with the existence of a white fighting force that understands that this imperialist mother country will come down, and actually fights on the side of the blacks, yellows, and the browns of the world. If our actions, struggle and words often put white working-class people (and movement people, too) up against the wall forcing them to fight us, so be it. They're dealing with the ideas of anti-chauvinism, anti-racism, and the coming revolution much more seriously by fighting us than when they threw our leaflets into garbage cans, or passed good resolutions without any practical consequences.

The time is past when tens of thousands of "movement" or left-liberal people can "dig" revolution, Che, Malcolm, Cleaver, put revolutionary posters on their walls and listen to revolutionary songs, "enjoy" the "Battle of Algiers" and consider themselves to be "hip" and on the right side of the revolutionary struggle—while living bourgeois, chauvinist, racist, white-skin privileged lives with six, seven, fifteen thousand dollars a year. If they dig the Panthers, the very least they can do is live on $5,000 and give the other $4,000 to the Panther bail fund. Weatherman has been accused of "guilt-organizing." Well, that is inaccurate. But there is nothing wrong with white Amerikans feeling guilty for sharing the blood money and psychic "superiority" sucked and looted out of the Third World. If they are truly experiencing that guilt, they would begin to struggle against their blood-stained white-skin privilege, and turn that guilt into hatred of the imperialist ruling class. And by thus lowering themselves to the position of the Vietnamese and the blacks in terms of material comforts and repression, and by joining in the revolutionary struggle, they can attain that communality and universality of human struggle for liberation, and thus raise themselves to the level of the Vietnamese and the blacks.

Although the Weatherman is not out to "turn people on," it is no accident that the people who have begun the process of becoming revolutionaries through collectives really dig themselves and other people, and are among the most live and spirited people around. The two months of my struggle, such as it was, in and out of the collective, has given a revolutionary significance to an old Asian saying: "By denying oneself, one realizes oneself." I became aware for the first time of the day-to-day significance of Chairman Mao's dictum that: "Not to have correct politics is like having no soul."

BRING THE WAR HOME!
THE LOGIC OF THE ACTION

The Chicago National Action was conceived by the Weather Bureau as an anti-imperialist action in which a mass of white youths would tear up and smash wide-ranging imperialist targets such as the Conspiracy Trial, high schools, draft boards and induction centers, banks, pig institutes, and pigs themselves. The main reason why we chose such a wide range of targets was our desire to project the existence of a fighting force that's out, not primarily to make specific demands, but to totally destroy this imperialist and racist society. Two sets of objectives were stipulated. The first set of objectives arose out of our general strategy. The specific tactic chosen (that is, mass street-fighting attacking imperialist targets) was intended to accomplish several aims to fulfill our strategic goal for the immediate future:

a. To take the first step towards building a new Communist Party and a Red Army: the toughening and transformation not only physically and militarily, but also politically and psychologically, of the old cadre; and the recruiting and training of new people as cadres.

b. To compel every youth in the country to become aware of and grapple with the existence of a group of pro-VC and pro-black white youths who effectively fight against imperialism and the pigs, on the basis of their understanding that this country not only needs to be, but can be, brought down. Also, to identify in a dramatic way some of the institutions that oppress these youths.

c. To do material damage so as to help the Viet Cong.

d. To push the entire movement to a new level, to sharpen its "cutting edge," to give militant shape to struggles undertaken by various sectors of the movement in the coming year, so that every struggle and all political work will be defined and judged by what happens in Chicago.

The second set of objectives arose out of our understanding as to how we can concretely push the political crisis confronting the US imperialist ruling class over the Vietnam question:

Militarily, US imperialism has already been defeated in Vietnam. Diplomatically, too, it is clearly on the defensive everywhere, and in some key places, the US conduct in Vietnam has created major setbacks (e.g., Sweden's agreement to extend $40 million to the DRV; the tremendous resurgence of anti-imperialist, revolutionary movements in Japan; etc.). From the standpoint of the worldwide US imperialist strategy, the war has severely limited its ability to pacify and/or suppress the Third World and the blacks and the browns at home; and even its sole reliable rear—the whites of the mother country itself—has begun to loosen up because of inflation, taxes, war casualties, youth rebellions—all attributable in some measure to the war.

Seeing all this, the US ruling class appears to have decided that a strategic retreat from Vietnam is highly desirable, in fact imperative. (Hence Johnson's decision not to run, the cessation of bombing, the Paris talks, the phony withdrawals, Vietnamization, etc.) But this strategic retreat is still conceived of as "extrication"; it is not squarely accepted as a defeat. So the war drags on and on. During the conference between the Vietnamese and SDS leaders this summer, the Vietnamese told us in no uncertain terms what our responsibilities to the world revolution were: "Look, we've won, but we can't physically kick out the US bases right now. So the war could drag on for a long time. Whether it will end in six months or drag on for ten more years will be, to a large degree, determined by the kind of struggle you people carry on in the heart of the imperialist mother country."

Within this broad understanding of the Vietnam situation, how did the Weatherman place the Chicago action? We saw that the majority sentiments in Amerika had turned against the war. We saw, too, the signs of the vast resurgence of frustration and anger among left-liberal segments for the first time in three years. There were several mass actions already planned: the September offensive in San Francisco (which failed to explode), the October 15 Moratorium, and the November 15 marches in Washington and San Francisco. All this was very good and constituted a powerful material support to the Viet Cong. Then, why Chicago?

The answer can be stated in two different ways, though in the end they amount to the same thing. To begin with, a minority of militants fighting on the streets and smashing imperialist targets would reinforce, rather than detract from, the value of the majority of peaceful dissenters who are holding candles. The ruling class would have to consider the probability that the longer they drag their feet in admitting defeat and getting out of Vietnam, the more the candle-holding type will join the ranks of the crazies on the streets. The dialectic of prolonged imperialist war, if further pushed out, could change the power balance now existing between the anti-imperialist and left-liberal camps of the peace movement; that is to say, the candle-holders may end up being the diminishing minority, and the street-fighters might emerge as the expanding majority. This very thought would have a tremendous impact on the ruling class, if they are foolish enough to contemplate the "option" of dragging the war on indefinitely. So, Chicago was intended in part as a warning and a deterrent to the ruling class, and also as a reinforcer to more low-keyed mass actions of the Moratorium and Mobilization type.

More concretely, Chicago was conceived of as a model and a training ground for the militant, fighting the anti-imperialist core of the peace movement. A couple of thousand kids, fighting in a together way, smashing up induction centers, pig institutes, etc., and having been toughened psychologically, militarily, and politically, would go back to their home cities and regions to create "two, three, many Chicagos" during November 8-14, and then go to Washington, several tens of thousands strong, to tear apart that pig capital of US pig power. In a few months after Chicago, we thought it possible to build a core of ten to twenty thousand anti-imperialist fighters tearing up ROTCs, pig institutes, research institutes, draft boards, stockades, on every major campus, in every city, in every region all over this imperialist motherland. All these motions—local and national mass kick-ass anti-imperialist street fights, as well as precise cadre actions—in the context of the majority anti-war sentiments and massive left-liberal anger, would give the ruling class a tremendous kick; in fact, such a strong kick that when combined with further defeats at the hands of the heroic Viet Cong, diplomatic setbacks at the hands of people in Europe and Japan, and the long-range worldwide strategic disadvantages incurred by the war, the US ruling class could be put under an irresistible pressure to admit defeat and pull out as early as six months following the Chicago action. Our understanding of the immediate and specific political crisis engulfing the imperialist ruling class made Chicago not only absolutely imperative, but also boundlessly exciting.

For five years now, since the founding of the May 2nd Movement, student radicals of this imperialist mother country pledged their internationalist solidarity with the Viet Cong. We petitioned, marched, sent medicine to Vietnam, conducted teach-ins, stopped troop trains, marched again, worked full summers on immediate withdrawal campaigns, attacked Dow and ROTC, ran independent anti-war candidates, and even fought on the streets once in a while. In retrospect, all this did help the Viet Cong some. But we never had a clear sense of how what we did day-to-day concretely helped to get the US out. Now, for the first time, we had a clear strategy which, in the context of Viet Cong-Third World-black-Japanese-European struggles, could defeat US imperialism in Vietnam in an all-round way, and get its aggressor troops out, in several months rather than ten years, thus saving millions of Asian and American lives. Within this framework, Chicago was the key focus, the model, the training ground, and the divining rod for everything else. It was indeed going to be the first battle of the first contingent of the Red Army in the mother country, concretely aiding the struggle of the heroic Viet Cong. The abstract phrase "international solidarity" began to have a real meaning. We began to feel the Vietnamese in ourselves. Some of us, at moments, felt we were ready to die, if that was the price of struggle in Chicago.

BUILDING STRATEGY FOR CHICAGO

After the Cleveland Conference, we in New York had a bit more than a month to prepare for the action. Our strategy to build for Chicago consisted of three stages:

First, establish the presence of Weatherman by a series of dramatic open and other kinds of cadre actions so that when we rapped to people they'd already have a basic sense of what we were about;

Second, carry out a series of cadre actions and mass work with certain high schools and parks as the priority target areas to confront white youth's racism and chauvinism, to identify certain key institutions of imperialism that oppress them, and to compel them to grapple with the existence of a white fighting contingent allied with the blacks and the Vietnamese;

Finally, coalesce all the motions we've managed to generate and the people we've established ties with, in the form of a major fighting action, so as to consolidate our ranks and prepare all of us on all levels for the coming battle in Chicago. We were thinking of a major support rally for the Panther 21 and/or the Fort Dix 38 demo for this purpose.

The first task of establishing our presence was done quite well, considering that we were then just in the process of forming the first real Weatherman collective in New York. As for the second part of our building strategy, we worked hard at it, managed to pull off a series of precise, out-of-sight cadre actions without a single casualty, and rapped with literally tens of thousands of kids during a five-week period.

Some people accuse us of one-sidedly advocating actions and not bothering to "talk" to people. This is a mistaken criticism. Probably no group talks to people more than we do, and many of our raps are probably qualitatively more effective in changing people than those carried on by other groups, since our raps usually take place in the immediate context of action, past actions, or a prospective action. Only a handful out of these thousands that we rap with come over to our side. But this is to be expected, for you can't simply "agree" with us intellectually. To agree with us means that you, too, join in the fight now, to become a Weatherman on one level or another, now. That's what discussion, rapping, and agreeing means to us. In the context of Chicago, digging our literature or our raps meant coming to Chicago to fight. No wonder that not a few Weatherman "sympathizers" wanted to avoid seeing us altogether. Remember the good old Movement days when we could dig Mao, Che, Viet Cong and Revolution, without ourselves becoming, or struggling to become, a Mao, a Che, a Viet Cong, and a revolutionary? Remember those nice, comfortable, bourgeois, hip, counter-revolutionary, anti-communist, boring, empty, confused, deadening, nauseating days? Those days are, thank God, gone. For us "movement people," there are but two possibilities: either we push on to become soldiers in the world revolutionary war, or we completely slide back to our respective bourgeois holes and become anti-communist pigs.

While our accomplishment of the second part of the strategy was good quantitatively and good in terms of hit-and-run cadre-guerrilla actions, our practice throughout was poisoned by dogmatism and a sectarian spirit which permeated everything we did. We also allowed ourselves an impermissible luxury of a stupid (adventuristic) incident which resulted from machismo and resulted in the heaviest legal casualties of our pre-Chicago practice (five felonious assaults and one charge of attempted murder).

We utterly fell short of our goals in the third, and in some respects, the most crucial part of our building strategy for Chicago. The Fort Dix demo, originally scheduled for September 28, seemed to be a really good build-up action. The Fort Dix coffeehouse leadership, with two outstanding fighters from the Columbia University struggle, and a number of revolutionary GIs among them, appeared to be our allies at first. The political demands of the demo were good:

1. Free the Fort Dix 38;
2. Free all political prisoners, especially the Panthers;
3. Abolish the stockade system;
4. End the war in Vietnam.

But in the marshals' meeting over the weekend of September 20, severe political divisions emerged between the NY Weatherman gang and a few independents, and the rest of the movement people there.

What we thought was required and possible was a fighting action to support the anti-imperialist GIs in explicit solidarity with the Viet Cong. The support for the anti-war, anti-Army, and anti-imperialist GIs was to be expressed, according to our conception of the action, by the four political demands of the demo, and by the choice of targets to be attacked—the stockades, the court-martial halls, the MPs, the station where the coffins with dead GIs from Vietnam arrive, etc. The clear solidarity with the Viet Cong would be communicated by our chants (*Ho, Ho, Ho Chi Minh, the Viet Cong is gonna win . . .*), slogans and banners, and by the presence of the

Viet Cong flag. The coffeehouse people called our suggested plans for a fighting action and our stress on the need to break through the weak links in the MP lines "suicidal," and our insistence on our group's carrying the Viet Cong banner "sectarian." (At no time did we insist on others carrying the glorious banner of the Viet Cong.) The coffeehouse and the movement people's conception of the demo was a massive, "GIs, MPs, we are on your side"-type march which would have some militant anti-war slogans, but which by and large would be peaceful because it wouldn't really try to reach the stockade or to break through by fighting. This conception also allowed for a few hundred Weathermen and other crazies to do our own thing ("that'll be groovy"), but mostly there would be lots of rapping with the GIs and MPs(!?!!).

THE VC FLAG ISSUE

Of the two key areas of disagreement, the coffeehouse leadership focused on the famous issue of the Viet Cong flag, since the need for a fighting action was more difficult to argue against from their anti-imperialist radical standpoint.

The coffeehouse leadership argued against Weathermen carrying the VC flag on three different levels: militarily, the VC flag would evoke instant ingrained reactions from the GIs and we might be massacred by them; politically, the issues of the repression of 38 anti-war GIs, the abolition of stockades, and GI-civilian solidarity were key, and the solidarity with the VC, if too strongly pushed, would divide our own ranks and turn off potential allies among the GIs. Finally, they argued that the banners with the slogan, "We support the Vietnamese people's struggle against corrupt government, rich landlords and foreign occupation troops" was an equally clear way to communicate our solidarity with the Vietnamese.

In response, we argued that militarily there is not likely to be a massacre on the order of a hundred dead, but that if a few of us did get killed while fighting in solidarity with the VC in the stipulated context, it would not be a bad thing, but a good thing (I shall go into this point in more detail later when we get to Chicago itself). Politically, it was crucial, especially in building an anti-imperialist GI movement, to make the solidarity with the VC clear from the very start and in an up-front way; otherwise, such a GI movement would degenerate into a racist-chauvinist "GI rights" movement fighting for a better imperialist army, or become totally vulnerable to imperialist cooptation and/or red-baiting attack. (Examples are numerous: the forty-million strong Japan anti-A and -H bomb movement collapsed after the conclusion of the test-ban treaty over the question of Chinese nuclear testing. The reason? The movement was largely built on the widespread, deeply-rooted revulsion against war in general and the use of nuclear weapons in particular. The organizers of the movement, though themselves Marxist-Leninists, felt that to push anti-imperialist politics would narrow and divide the mass base that they saw and were able to build. Instead, the lack of such an anti-imperialist politics not only split, but totally destroyed it, when the Chinese began their nuclear test program after justly rejecting the US-USSR scheme for white nuclear monopoly.)

The GIs, we stated, are immediately involved in the Vietnam war. And in a war, there are only two sides. You've got to shoot at the Viet Cong or at US imperialism. To be sure, there are moments when GIs are in an intermediate position, such as when a company of troops in Vietnam refuses to fight for a day or two because of weariness, etc., without explicitly realizing that their action is helping the VC. These GIs are, to use the phrase favored by all sorts of non-struggle "Marxists," acting in an objectively anti-imperialist manner. But unless these GIs push out their immediate discontents so that they become subjectively anti-imperialist as well, their momentary deviations notwithstanding, they will revert back to serving their pig role as counterrevolutionary gendarmes. Communists and anti-imperialists must relate to all intermediate motions, such as the one mentioned above, that hurt the imperialist war effort, but relate to them in such a way as to make the real choice for the GIs explicit from the very beginning and do that in an up-front way. And when revolutionaries and anti-imperialists themselves initiate a mass action, such as the Fort Dix action, it is inexcusable not to make this choice immediately clear and real.

There are plenty of other people, many with support from certain segments of the ruling class, who are willing and able to organize purely anti-war, "pro-our boys" type affairs (and these things are OK and we should do political work with the people who turn out for these demonstrations). Our own job, first, is to project the consciousness that here, too, there will be a revolution which, in alliance with the Third World, will bring this mother down within this generation; and second, to recruit and train revolutionaries who will fight to do precisely that. An anti-imperialist, pro-Viet Cong GI movement is going to be a crucial part of that revolution. And we should be pushing out this revolutionary politics on every issue, in every action, with every type of constituency, every moment of our waking hours, to the maximum. That's what it takes. Obviously, the coffee house people and the GI leaders had an entirely different political conception of what their work was about.

The coffeehouse leaders' last point, that their slogan on the banner was the equivalent of the VC banner, is absurd. They asserted that the banner with the slogan "We support the Vietnamese people's struggle" was more concrete than the VC flag, which in their view was an abstract symbol. Let us see.

The GIs' reaction to the VC flag is a rational reaction given their national chauvinism and the pig role they acquiesce to play. If they don't react to the slogan on the banner that's because the coffeehouse slogan does not even connect up with their national chauvinism, let alone confront it. The coffeehouse slogan is just words; it's abstract. The VC flag is concrete, and hits hard at the core of their national chauvinism and their pig role. In the same way, the expression "Support the NLF or PRG" is not as good as "We're with the Viet Cong" for our specific purpose of building an anti-imperialist, revolutionary movement. To say, "We support the Vietnamese people's struggle against corrupt government, rich landlords, and foreign occupation troops," is a shame-faced way of supporting our brothers in the NLF. Who and what are you talking about? You might even be talking about the fence-sitting Buddhist manipulators in Saigon or the thousands of punk-out Vietnamese students sitting out the revolutionary, patriotic war in Paris coffeeshops! You are not pushing out your politics, you are not putting the struggle up front, and your so-called anti-imperialist politics, however sincerely felt, is a sham. In short, you are being hopelessly capitulationist and defeatist about your politics and about the people you are trying to change from the very start. From this type of action, the GIs might get the idea that you're a bunch of do-gooders or hippies on their side (and if there are many "chicks" among you, all the better), but nothing drastically new has been injected into their consciousness, and nothing has been done to break through their chauvinism and defeatism, nor has the internalized social fabric and order been disrupted at its core. . . . And, without any of these changes, how can you expect to transform their awareness of their oppression in the army into a revolutionary consciousness?

WHAT DOES IT ALL MEAN?

On the other hand, if they see a couple of thousand white kids tearing up and smashing the stockade, the court-martial halls, the coffin station, and the MPs—all symbols and institutional underpinnings of the GIs' oppression—and if these same kids are carrying VC flags, the GIs cannot help asking: What's happening here? What does it all mean?

Shock 1: Hippies and commies, who are supposed to be pacifists, fought against and vamped on some MP pigs.

Shock 2: These college kids, whom GIs dislike because of the former's privilege and elitism, fought against the places and people they too hated.

Shock 3: The same people were carrying the flags of the avowed enemy of "their country."

Shocks 1 and 2 help to overcome their class-based suspicion against the campus-originated revolutionary movement.

Numbers 2 and 3 polarize to the limit the tension between their own awareness of class oppression, and their national chauvinism. The two contradictory aspects of their consciousness are split widely apart; what lay dormant as parts of the same consciousness are now exposed as two antagonistic alternatives. Their consciousness is loosened up and the two objectively antagonistic aspects of their consciousness and of their mode of being begin to confront them as a choice between two opposing forces. Something vitally new has thus been introduced into their consciousness.

By an action of this sort, no serious revolutionary expects to see hundreds of GIs join our ranks and fight with us right away, like that. A few will. But, more important, for hundreds of thousands of GIs who will learn about such an action through the media and personal contacts, and to a much more intense degree, for thirty thousand GIs at Fort Dix, a new, radical space has opened up in the form of two antagonistic aspects of their consciousness coming nearer to the surface. Similar actions later and in other places, as well as of course the struggles of the Vietnamese and the blacks, will make the contradiction and tension in their split consciousness even more acute, and our rapping and the enemy-directed alternative we offer can gradually, and over a long period of time, help to make the class aspect of their consciousness predominant over their chauvinist-racist-defeatist aspect.

Playing their class consciousness and their awareness of their own oppression against their real chauvinism and racism, and then helping, by our raps, actions, and presence as communists, to make the class aspect prevail, this is the core of the Weatherman politics. Not to relate to the whites' own oppression would be dogmatism, not to hit hard at the whites' chauvinism and racism would be opportunist and capitulationist in the extreme. In the initial stages, the latter error is the primary danger to look out for, as was clearly demonstrated by how the Dix demo actually turned out. To repeat, the primary purpose, the stance, of our organizing, could not possibly be to "turn people on," or to have them like us, or to make them think that we are nice, but to compel them to confront the antagonistic aspects of their own life experience and consciousness by bringing the war home, and to help them make the right choice over a period of time, after initially shaking up and breaking through the thick layers of chauvinism-racism-defeatism. If being "arrogant," "pushy," "hard," if putting some people up against the wall, helps to create that tension and the requisite fluidity and space, then we ought to be "arrogant," "pushy" and "hard." Even a little bit of liberalism or politeness about imperialism or its ideological underpinnings is way too much for those of us who are serious about building an anti-imperialist revolutionary movement in this white mother country.

At the end of this polemic, the coffeehouse leadership cancelled the demo because of our insistence on carrying the VC flags. Several hours after the end of the meeting that is, early the next morning), we told them that since this demo was so important for us and for the movement, we will come without the flags, but by then the coffeehouse leadership had decided to hold the demo on October 12, specifically in order to provide an "alternative" to the Chicago National Action for the people on the East Coast. (Incidentally, the date made it impossible for the one hundred or so people who went to Chicago from the New York area under the Weatherman leadership to come to the Dix action.)

So the third part of our building strategy, in a large measure, failed to materialize, and our whole effort suffered grievously because of it.

CHICAGO: A MASSACRE?

When I rapped with those who were in a general agreement with us, the question that bothered them most always turned out to be: "Wouldn't there be a massacre in Chicago?" We always said no. That was the conclusion the Weather Bureau reached after intensive discussion and investigation. For one thing, the national ruling class could not afford the political disruption and crisis that would ensue from any massacre of two or three hundred whites. No matter how much the Movement disagreed with us, no matter how much most whites hated our guts, still two hundred dead Weathermen would be whites. The political impact of such a massacre, both internationally and domestically, would be so serious as to make such a step impermissible from the standpoint of the ruling class, who are already in serious trouble everywhere. Furthermore, the Daley machine in Chicago could afford such a massacre even less than the national ruling class, since Daley, according to the information available to the Weather Bureau, was confronted with a life-and-death struggle against certain "enlightened" segments of the Chicago ruling class who preferred a more "rational," "modern" city manager. Daley was very anxious, then, to project a new image as a "sensible" politician. Given this understanding of the situation within the enemy ranks, the Weather Bureau judged a massacre a most unlikely event.

The ruling class usually acts with a certain degree of rationality from the standpoint of their class interests. To picture them as irrational mad dogs ready to unleash their worst at any moment is to disarm the people psychologically before they commence their struggle. The argument is usually made in order to justify punking out of the struggle. Historically, the same argument was made by the Soviet counter-revolutionaries to oppose national liberation wars and the Chinese line in the Sino-Soviet polemics. The ruling class is not all-powerful. All kinds of military, political, and economic constraints limit its freedom of action. Revolutionaries must constantly analyze these contradictions concretely, look for a radical space created by these contradictions and constraints, and push out their politics and their struggle to the very limit of each situation. The two main constraints operating in Chicago arose from the ruling class' need to preserve the facade of bourgeois democracy, and the need to prevent any cracks in its only reliable rear, i.e., the whites in the mother country. Incidentally, to be able to push these contradictions to our maximum benefit required that, for now, we would not fight with guns. So the Weather Bureau issued an order to all the collectives not to bring any fire-arms. We understood that anyone who did would be dealt with as a pig provocateur. No one did.

We frankly told people that, while a massacre was highly unlikely, we expected the actions to be very, very heavy, that hundreds of people might well be arrested and/or hurt, and finally, that a few people might even get killed. We argued that twenty white people (one per cent of the projected mini-mum) getting killed while fighting hard against imperialist targets would not be a defeat, but a political victory, for the same reasons that would make a massacre a politically un-acceptable option for the ruling class; that it will hurt the ruling class ten times more than the damage inflicted in an operation with twenty Viet Cong dead. And, finally, not to be willing to risk what were by Third World standards rela-tively light casualties, when the probable political gains were so clear, was to want to preserve one's white-skin privilege, and acquiesce in being a racist. (Some people criticized us for being so frank with people about the heaviness of the actions and possible deaths. We fully realized that we might frighten away some potential fighters, but thought it necessary to psychologically and politically prepare those who came so that we'd be able to fight in a tight, together way. It is politically suicidal to dupe people into very heavy situations.)

The whites in this country are insulated from the world revolution and the Third World liberation struggles because of their access to, and acceptance of, blood-soaked white-skin privileges. In a large measure, this insulation from the struggle holds true for the radicals in the movement. The whole point of the Weatherman politics is to break down this insulation, to bring the war home, to make the coming revolution real. But this breakthrough has to be effected within ourselves before we can work with the masses of white youths. And this was what the Chicago action was all about: bringing the revolution that is already winning in the Third World home, for us radicals as well as for the white youths whom we want to reach and change.

ON TO CHICAGO!

We left for Chicago in two buses with roughly thirty persons, in addition to the cadres of our gang. In the last few days of our build-up, we counted two hundred-odd persons from New York who either reserved bus tickets or stated their intention to come. In other words, for every seven persons who promised to come, only one showed up. (Apparently, this ratio roughly held true on a national level, which means that of the three or four thousand expected to come, only six hundred actually showed up.) This extremely small turn-out not only frightened many of us cadres, but also raised some serious questions about our practice for the preceding five weeks.

In the final few days we were expecting a possible mass bust of the leadership and cadres to forestall the national action. We'd recently had a couple of close run-ins with the TPF and the SES (the Special Events Squad of the New York police). So when I saw Inspector Finnegan of SES-Red Squad fame and some of his captains and lieutenants (with whom some of us had been rather rude, so to speak, and had gotten away with it) at the bus assembly point, I expected a bust. But Finnegan merely taunted one of us, saying, "Aren't you scared with so few people in the buses for Chicago?" Obviously, they didn't bust us then, because they wanted to set us up for bigger things to come (federal conspiracy charges, for example). Some of us were compelled to board the bus at another point as a precautionary measure.

As soon as we were on our way, we began our struggle. The internal struggle within the collective involving criticism-self-criticism-transformation is in our view just as crucial as the struggle in the streets. Without the former, the latter would be half-hearted and wimpy. Even if the street-fighting were good, without political struggle afterwards we would learn only a fraction of what we could and must learn from that action. Thus, we looked upon the internal struggles on the buses and in the movement centers as an indispensable part of our battle in Chicago.

We went over the basics of busts and jail. (Don't expect to be bailed out right away; our white-skin privileges are diminishing fast. Be prepared to spend at least a couple of weeks in there. Turn the jail experience into a struggle.) For the eleventh time, we went through first aid. ("For multiple fractures . . .") In order to get to know each other and learn to move as a group, we divided ourselves into several affinity groups of six or seven persons each and did a couple of tasks together (e.g., preparing food on the bus, shaping up the dilapidated helmet-liners into a more or less usable condition with straps and paddings, preparing primitive medical kits). We discussed the functions of the affinity group, what running and fighting together meant, what leadership meant, and why leadership was absolutely necessary in a military situation. The leaders of the affinity groups were appointed, not elected, and we discussed the reasons for that.

DISCIPLINE

New people began to learn what discipline means when no one was allowed to stay out of these collective discussions and collective tasks. People who preferred to read magazines were compelled to join. People who fell asleep were woken up. Smoking was prohibited. Seating was "arbitrarily" changed according to the demands set by political criteria. Politics in command. Everything for the revolution. People began to get some sense of what these well-known Maoist slogans meant.

We slept for six hours and resumed our struggle in the morning. Many women new to us came along because their boyfriends were coming. Some of them did not have the vaguest notion about the national action. How could this happen when we deliberately tried to weed out radical tourists and scene-makers and tried to prepare everyone politically by emphasizing the anticipated heaviness of our actions? Well, no matter. These few people came, and they had to be dealt with. So we went through the basic scenario and the reasoning behind each action. As for the male-chauvinist women, we went into a heavy criticism session about bourgeois monogamous relationships and how they hold back both men and women, in the fighting situation as well as in general political development. One particularly backward woman was struggled with for two hours, and she broke down. "I don't know who I am, I guess. I'm not my own person. . . ." When we got off the bus in Chicago, she still thought she wasn't ready. Yet on the first action on Wednesday night, she was a marvelous, courageous, and persevering fighter in my affinity group. Even though she nearly lost her shoes and fell down three times, she stayed in the fight for nearly forty minutes.

The heaviest part of our struggle on the bus was the discussion on what "winning" meant in Chicago. Why in past street actions, when we could have offed a pig, did we hold back? Why are we afraid of escalating the struggle and of winning? Why are we, in short, afraid of pushing out our politics and our struggle to the very limit in each tactical situation? Without answering this question, and without successfully overcoming this fear, we would not be able to fight in Chicago.

As the struggle on the bus developed, we realized the reason for our fear. We were afraid of winning because our winning in a particular tactical situation would entail the escalation of the struggle; that is to say, the ruling class and their pigs would increase their attacks on us. It would mean that the next time we would have to fight much harder on a higher level. To preempt this possibility, we struggle half-heartedly, in a defeatist way. It is as if the movement made a secret, unspoken agreement with the ruling class not to struggle beyond certain limits. In a way, this is the manner CPs conducted the struggle in many Latin American countries before they became totally irrelevant. This is a strategy for defeat, capitulation, and cooptation. It is the stance of a counterrevolutionary revisionist out for his or her bourgeois survival. It reduces the struggle to the level of part-time play, to a parlor game. It could never be the strategy or the stance of a life-or-death revolutionary struggle for power. What we are about is a total smashing up of this imperialist state. What

we are about is winning state power and building communism. Not to be afraid of winning meant that we could continue to struggle and fight harder in each of the succeeding
stages of the revolution until we won.

But this realization, however valuable, was as yet an abstract truth, an unfelt insight. We were still dismayed by our
small numbers, and we kept reassuring each other and ourselves that the advanced collectives in Chicago, Michigan,
Ohio and Colorado would bring at least a couple of thousand fighters to Chicago. After all, they had had at least three
or four months of work behind them, while we in New York
had a mere five weeks to build for the action. The fact that
two weeks previously, a thousand kids fought with the pigs in
Chicago demanding that the Conspiracy Eight trial be
stopped, was also encouraging. If nothing else, these kids
would be with us on the streets. So we kept repeating to
ourselves endlessly.

As the buses were about to leave the state of Indiana, we
were stopped by a highway patrol car. We anticipated this
sort of harassment. (In fact, some of us didn't expect to get
to Chicago.) Our plan was to stay cool, but if attacked or
obstructed by a less than overwhelming force of highway
pigs, we planned to fight it out so as to create "Two, three,
many, mini-Chicagos" in the surrounding states. Thus, as the
buses came to a stop on the shoulder, we readied ourselves
for a heavy situation. Fortunately, a couple of tickets was the
extent of the harassment. And so, after twenty-five hours of
bus ride and nineteen hours of intense work and struggle, we
arrived safely in the south side of Daley's pig city.

THE FIRST NIGHT

Wednesday night was to be a commemorating rally for Che
and Nguyen Van Troi, and a light street march to feel out the
city and the pig situation. As soon as we left the movement
center, we felt the tense feeling of walking in the midst of the
enemy territory. Even though there were more than fifty of
us traveling together in full street-fighting gear (helmet, eye-
goggles, medical kit, heavy jacket, boots, jocks and cups),

many of us were frightened by the heavy pig surveillance. As we approached the rallying point, lit brightly by the bonfire made out of torn park benches, we chanted: "Ho, Ho, Ho Chi Minh, Viet Cong is gonna win. Pick, pick, pick up the gun, the revolution has begun."

The surging fighting spirit within me was immediately dampened when I saw only a few hundred people around the bonfire, many of whom were obviously bystanders. What happened to all those train-loads of kids from Detroit? To the thousand street kids from Chicago? We aren't going to go through with the four-day national action with three hundred people, when the Chicago pigs had prepared to vamp on us weeks in advance?! I could hardly concentrate on any of the speeches. Suddenly I heard Marion Delgado announce: "We are going to see Judge Hoffman. Let's go!" Before the absurdity of going through with the action sank in my head fully, three or four hundred people started running towards the park's exit. Having lost the New York leadership group, I led ten people under my leadership (four cadres and six new people, divided into two separate affinity groups) into the running mob. Within a minute or two, right in front of my eyes, I saw and felt the transformation of the mob into a battalion of three hundred revolutionary fighters.

We passed by a group of more than a hundred pigs outside of the park who were taken by surprise. (We learned later that there were more than two thousand pigs in the general area specifically mobilized for us.) Windows were smashed; Rolls Royces and Cadillacs and every other car in the ruling class neighborhood were smashed; small groups of ten, fifteen pigs on the way were taken by surprise and were totally powerless against the surging battalion. Some pigs were overpowered and vamped on severely. Within a few minutes all of us lost whatever fear and doubts we had before. Yes, we were out to smash the totality of this imperialist social order; we were really out to fight. Each one of us felt the soldier in us.

It took the pigs twenty minutes to regain their sense and to counter-attack. The leadership up front broke through, but the rear sections turned to another street. One of the cadres in my group sprained his ankle, and I told him to drop out with another cadre to look out for him. We couldn't have anyone drag the group back. Another intersection, another confrontation, another turn. Pigs were vamped on by some people here and there. I saw two completely bloodied pigs in a badly smashed-up pig car, but continued on. (Fear of winning?) At a third (or was it fourth?) intersection, we confronted a large group of pigs. Crack, crack, and streams of bright light. Tear grenades? "Who has the medical kit? Two persons have been shot." Shotguns. (Later it turned out that ten persons received shotgun wounds and one cadre was hit fairly seriously with pistol bullets.) Some people panicked, but most turned back in a quick but orderly retreat. We were blocked by a large group of pigs at the next corner, so we turned around again, and found that intersection also heavily blocked by pigs. The two groups of pigs triumphantly moved on us to trap what was left of our rear group (by now about a hundred persons). Luckily, we found a long, narrow alleyway and went through it, heading back to Lincoln Park. (We did so without any good reason; there was not a single person in the group who knew the streets of Chicago.)

By this time, we had been on the streets for a good forty-five minutes, running and jogging most of that time, and many people were slowing down. I also noticed that there were no national or regional leaders in our group (they were either busted or fighting in another section of the area). People were screaming: "Where is the leadership?" "What's our goal now?" "Let's split!" I saw the necessity of my seizing the leadership, but was afraid of doing so because I knew that there were undercover pigs in the crowd, and taking leadership would make me much more visible and vulnerable, so I merely shouted at the people who were slowing down or thinking of splitting, "Don't split until we are so instructed." "Come on! We're in the red army, right? We've got to run much faster and tighter!" I pushed and shoved people to move ahead. After turning away from the park to avoid being trapped in it, a few regional leaders rejoined our ranks, and we kept on running for twenty more minutes. When the regional leader shouted, "Everyone on his own; split in any way you can!" I led my group into an alleyway and hid in the back yard of a house for about an hour before taking a cab back to the movement center. While we were waiting, we debated whether we should ditch our defensive gear so as to make ourselves less visible, but I decided that we should keep our gear since it would be needed in the three remaining days of the national action.

At several points in the one hour and twenty minute street-fight I was sure that we would get busted. In fact, a couple of times the pigs were so close upon us that I almost ordered my group to give ourselves up. But we got away free by persisting and persevering. This fact had a tremendous impact on me. Now I understood why some comrades in the New York collective were criticized for their defeatism because of the way they were busted several times in a month and a half—that is, for not having the spirit of fighting through to the end, which in many cases measn doing your best to get away instead of giving up after a half-hearted effort. It was also amazing that only thirty out of three hundred cadres were busted that night (along with forty-odd freaks who were mistaken for us). It was absolutely amazing that three hundred of us were able to go on a rampage for more than one hour, smashing windows, cars and pigs, when there were two thousand supposedly well-prepared pigs concentrated in that small area. Without any doubt, on a military and tactical level, Wednesday night was a clear victory.

THE MEDIA / THE PEOPLE

The next day, the banner headlines reported: "SDS Women Fight Cops." The overwhelming impression projected by the Chicago media was: "Here we see a new breed of pro-black, pro-Viet Cong hooligan revolutionaries who are not demanding this or that change, but are out to totally disrupt the very fabric of this society, out to smash this social order." They hammered this theme home in every article; they even gave detailed analyses of how the Weatherman actions differed in content and purpose from last year's riots and from the RYM II actions. Stephen Zucker, an assistant corporation counsel: "We never expected this kind of violence. There always has been a big difference in what they say and what they do." Superintendent James M. Rochford, who personally commanded the pig forces: "They are revolutionaries. This was pre-planned to cause injuries and destroy property." Richard Elrod, while he was still able to speak on Thursday, said: "The Weatherman violence was the worst possible thing you could imagine." The RYM II activities were either not reported at all, or praised heartily in editorials as a "disciplined, legitimate way of expressing one's dissent." They were pictured as well-behaved, properly-led young radicals who were acting within the fine Amerikan tradition of peaceful dissent. Remember what Chairman Mao says? "To be attacked by the enemy is not a bad thing, but a good thing." And to be praised by the enemy while your comrades are loudly denouced. . . ?

It was not only the mass media who looked on us as a radically new force. Whenever we were on the streets, people sensed who we were, and reacted according to their class position. Whites, especially the older ones, were usually hostile and/or fearful. The blacks, especially the young ones, dug our actions immensely and helped us in all kinds of material ways. (More on this later.) Small black kids, barely ten years old, knew who we were, what we did, and what we were about. Having been a social studies teacher for three years, I know how unusual it is for young kids to have a detailed knowledge of what's going on in their own city. Both white and black kids I came in contact with were intensely aware of, and were grappling with, the existence of a white fighting force. One of our major purposes was already accomplished as far as millions of kids in Chicago and the surrounding areas were concerned. (The reaction of blacks was somewhat of a pleasant surprise, since the Panthers sharply criticized us before and during the national action.)

By Thursday afternoon, 2600 National Guard had been called in addition to the two thousand city pigs. Our jailbreak actions had to be called off because it would have been suicidal for three hundred of us to attack a stationary target defended by an equal or a greater number of pigs. The joint rally at the Federal Building, in which we agreed to participate under the discipline of the Panthers, simply petered out. The Wargasm planned for the evening was also called off. When I woke up in the morning, I was sure that with three potentially heavy actions, I would not survive the day without a bust or an injury. I was wrong. Of course, for a Weatherman to simply walk on the streets in Chicago was in itself a medium-heavy action. The pigs and the older whites made you feel that you were indeed an enemy of the imperialist state.

The cancellations and the failures of the actions that day (most women considered their action a military failure), the heaviness of the pig situation, and the fact that we had a cumulative total of at most six hundred people (including the people who were in jail or lost in the city during many dispersals)—all this indicated a need for a major re-evaluation and strategy meeting. Such a session, for all the cadres, was called for Thursday night by the Weather Bureau. I was not able to attend this crucial, all-night meeting because I was assigned with seven others to maintain security for our movement center for the New York and Ohio cadres. But the content of this meeting was related to me later in great detail, so I can summarize the results here.

RE-EVALUATION

Every cadre there had serious doubts and questions about our past practice and about how we should move in the remaining two days of the national action. But for the most part, cadres and even regional leaders could not articulate these doubts and questions, nor could they offer solid criticisms of the Weather Bureau. So, finally, the members of the Weather Bureau had to undertake self-criticism without any serious criticism about its practice from the ranks. (In Weatherman collectives, the principle is that criticism has to precede self-criticism; the latter should not be permitted to be used to preempt the effects of the former.) One of the Weather Bureau members accused that body of revisionist tendencies, i.e., making errors that were "left" in form but "right" in essence. These advanced Weather errors, as they came to be called, were held largely responsible for the extremely small turn-out in Chicago. They included: (1) the notion that adventurism was for never; (2) the sectarian and dogmatic spirit that permeated every aspect of our work; (3) our blind obedience to discipline and leadership; (4) our anti-communist, humorless franticness which we mistook for seriousness. These four errors, in all their ramifications, accounted for, in a large measure, our inability to make connections with the revolutionary motions among the masses of youth in this country.

Aside from the self-criticisms of the Weather Bureau, there was a sharp struggle against the "Tupamaros" line. This line and this tendency existed to some degree in all of us. It said: The mass street-fighting against pigs armed with guns is a losing tactic. Therefore, we must pick up the gun now, go under, and turn ourselves immediately into a corps of three hundred American Tupamaros inflicting material damage on imperialism. Given the heaviness of the developing military situation, and the deep fear that most of us had about the Saturday march, this idea of going underground and becoming Tupamaros was a tempting and romantic one. But this tendency, too, was shown to be "left" in form but "right" in content. The leadership's counter-arguments were as follows: (1) The ruling class could easily wipe out three hundred inexperienced, frightened, soft, would-be "Tupamaros"; (2) The street-fighting was militarily a losing tactic, but was politically imperative for the immediate future in order to (a) toughen our cadres on all levels so that they could become real American Tupamaros when the time came, and (b) create a strong presence on a national level, so as to compel every white youth to deal with the existence of a revolutionary white fighting force.

While this debate was going on, I was leading the security detail for the Ohio-New York movement center. The center was under a constant and heavy pig surveillance. When some Ohio cadres arrived with a van, they were harassed, and four additional pig cars arrived on the scene within a minute. We had to prepare for a bust. We discussed what to do. I argued that if the pigs came to bust up the church, we should fight back—not with any hope of defending the place, but to set an example, a precedent, and a deterrent. If the pigs got the idea that they could bust up any Weatherman headquarters without paying any price, they would be vamping on us all the time with impunity. On the other hand, if we forced them to pay a price, in terms of both physical injuries and political cost resulting from publicity, then they would think twice before they did it the next time. So we constructed barricades and got our helmets and the defensive gear together and ready. Personally, I didn't expect to get killed, but did expect the night to be heavy. After I eloquently argued for, and got agreement on, the need to defend the center, we were ordered by the N.O. not to fight or resist under any circumstances, and to evacuate as soon as possible to a church in Evanston, a suburb right outside of the pig city.

STRATEGIC RETREAT

After packing all the belongings of the NY-Ohio people into the van, we left for Evanston and arrived there late Friday morning. For a second day straight I had no sleep. After some karate practice, we in the New York collective began to discuss whether it was important to go through with the next day's (Saturday's) planned action, and if so, why? We began the discussion with a re-evaluation of Wednesday night's action. Militarily and tactically, it was a clear victory. But was it a political victory? We failed to reach the target (Judge Hoffman), we did not get to, or destroy, specifically imperialist targets, except some pigs who were hospitalized. No induction centers, no research institutes, no jailbreaks. So what happened to our goal of doing material damage to imperialism? Well, we did inflict material damage on the large stores, banks, luxury apartments, houses, and automobiles in the ruling-class residential area of Chicago to the tune of $1,000,000. We also forced the ruling class to mobilize the National Guard: six hundred of us managed to preoccupy, for a few days, the same amount of imperialist pig power that a VC regiment would attract (2600 Guardsmen + 2000 pigs = 4600 pigs). Also, the concentration of the pig forces on us opened some space in the black community; on Thursday night ten pigs were shot at and two of them were killed by blacks, because patrol cars that normally carried two or three pigs were carrying only one. That's not an insignificant material aid to the blacks. And so on.

But as the discussion and analysis developed, we discovered that our conception of material damage was one-sided. Offing an ROTC office or a draft board is a material damage, but so is the disruption created in the consciousness of whites in and around Chicago by our rampage. To disrupt the social-psychological-ideological fabric of this imperialist social order is as much material damage as hitting imperialist targets directly. In that sense, though the Wednesday action failed to do material damage to specifically imperialist targets, it was a political as well as a tactical victory. And the women's action, though nearly a disaster from a military point of view, reinforced this material damage through its disruptive effect on one kernel of the social fabric of white society.

Given this positive over-all analysis of the Wednesday action, the Saturday march seemed imperative. Without doing and winning the Saturday pig-to-pig march, the effects created Wednesday would be washed away. Already by Thursday night the media were reporting the defeat of SDS. Friday's banner headlines read: SDS INVASION STOPPED. If we stopped now, the consciousness created among the white youths would be: "Hippies ran wild and fought with some pigs. But as soon as the government escalated by calling the Guard, they punked out and went back to their campuses. They weren't revolutionaries after all." Thus, the usual pattern of radical students fighting once in a while but returning to their holes as soon as the pigs upped the ante a little would once again be confirmed for everyone to see and judge. So we had to return to the streets Saturday. There was no other way. But could we? Yes, came the judgment of the Weather Bureau—not so good tactically as Wednesday night (because there would be no element of surprise), but not nearly as bad as the situation that would have faced us had we attempted to carry through the jailbreaks (because we were not after a heavily-guarded stationary target).

But, then, why this incredible, numbing fear on the part of most people in the room? Why did Saturday's action seem so different from Wednesday's? As the discussion proceeded, we began to zero in on something that was at the root of our fear and anxiety: for us to return to the streets on Saturday meant that we were going to respond offensively to, rather than be cowed by, the enemy's escalation after his defeat of Wednesday night. And if, as is inevitable, the enemy ups the level of struggle after Saturday, we'll have to return to fight even harder, and so on, ad infinitum. Fight not only tomorrow, but the week after; not only November 8-15, but the next spring; not only for several months, but struggle as long as it takes to win, and even after that, though in a different form. We survived Wednesday, a few of us might not tomorrow, and the longer we persist and persevere in the struggle (on a higher and higher level), the greater will be the number of us who'll be wiped out. And if we commit ourselves to resolutely persist in this revolutionary struggle, the likelihood is that the majority of the seventy cadres or so in this room will get wiped out. How else could it be? Of the fifty thousand communists in China in the 1920s, fewer than one thousand survived the Long March. Of more than seventy fighters on *Granma* fewer than fifteen survived the first counter-attack on Cuban soil. In the US imperialist mother country, the revolutionary war will necessarily be more protracted and much bloodier than most other revolutions. So how could we possibly have expected to survive it? In revolution, one either wins or dies, says Che. The revolution's victory is certain, but the overwhelming majority of the cadres in this room, unless we punk out, will not live that long. To go on Wednesday night's action was to go into a heavy fighting situation. To go back on Saturday meant that we begin to feel and live the law laid down by Che. You either win or get offed. That's what a revolution takes. Such an obvious truth, yet so hard to really feel and live by. Barring our return to our holes, there was absolutely no out from this maxim. Why were we so stunned by this realization? Because the revolutionary concepts that we supposedly adhered to had not broken through the thick layers of class and white-skin privileges in our mode of feeling and being. The revolutionary was really being brought home within our own consciousness.

While this discussion was going on, an undercover pig (a Negro youth and I use the term Negro advisedly because he certainly was no black) was discovered in the next room. From the sounds emanating from there, some people seemed to be meting out revolutionary justice to this pig. I was completely shaken by the loud cries for mercy and the screaming that accompanied the initial stages of punishment. I remembered Chu Teh's saying that "Banditry is a class question." Non-class humanitarianism is counterrevolutionary and a most insidious anti-communist mode of thought. Easy to see, but a structure of feeling cannot be reformed so easily. But a more important reason why so many of us were so shook up by this revolutionary violence was that in this attack, we escalated the degree and the level of struggle significantly. The pigs were certain to counter-attack, and do so viciously. This political understanding of our fear enabled us to cope with it better.

ATTACKED!

Following this incident, we immediately dispersed from Evanston, expecting a pig counter-attack. It was about four p.m. Friday afternoon. I led my affinity group back to pig city. Downtown was an occupied area with several pigs on each corner and a pig car passing by every forty-five seconds or so. We felt insecure, even though most of us had straight street clothes, short hair, and no beards or mustaches. So after an hour we split and went to the University of Chicago cafeteria in the south side. As soon as we were seated in the cafeteria, four city pigs came in nosing around, and immediately thereafter, the campus pig began to check the IDs of everyone who came into the place. Around ten p.m. we received instructions to return to another church in Evanston. I questioned the wisdom of this instruction, since we were likely to get busted, but the N.O.'s instruction remained so I took my affinity group back to Evanston to the designated church.

When we got to the church, a discussion was in session as the reasons for the next day's action. (This was a combined meeting of people from different regions.) Since there were many non-Weathermen in the group, discussion centered on certain "primitive" Weather errors. A young woman stated that she could not possibly hit a policeman (she did not like the term "pig") because he, too, was a human being and that was no way to convince him that he should not fight us. When confronted with the question as to what she thought of the Viet Cong's use of revolutionary violence, she said she thought that was OK because their own country was so oppressed and openly invaded by "foreign" troops (as if she was a citizen of Denmark!). But she maintained that the whites in the US ought to be non-violent because they weren't so oppressed, and "our" country isn't yet invaded. When I pointed out the national chauvinism and racism that were implicit in her mode of thought, she casually said, "I can't help it," and smiled in an embarrassed way. After an hour of discussion and criticism, I began to get infuriated at her for so casually admitting her own chauvinism-racism, and not even bothering to struggle against them seriously. So I demanded that the criticism session be cut off and she be kicked out.

As we were discussing "what it means to escalate the struggle," a large number of pigs (120 in all) suddenly burst into the church. People panicked and started rushing towards the rear; and there was no leadership visible (the Weather Bureau and the regional leaders were meeting in a strategy session in another church). I felt deathly scared. "Given that tomorrow's action commands the top priority, we should split," so I told myself, and jumped from a one-story-high window, chased by a few pigs. Luckily, I was wearing my boots (I never took them off until I got to the jail), and there was a heavy downpour, so I was able to shake the pigs off in a few moments after climbing over two fences.

Four or five blocks away from the church, I found a house with a staircase in the rear, and hid under it. It was about 2:00 a.m. Saturday morning. The sound of police cars and the paddy wagons lasted for an hour in the quiet neighborhood. I wondered how many got away. (Very few did.) I thought of the people who must be fighting at that very moment. I reproached myself for having left the church. I felt sure then that I split out of fear, and not out of any sense of political priority. About three o'clock I heard footsteps approaching in my direction; I lifted two solid rocks that I had prepared beforehand, but as the footsteps came closer and closer, I decided not to fight, and this time the decision was made clearly on the basis of fear. As it turned out, the footsteps belonged to a small youthful figure, clearly not a pig. I took the figure to be that of a woman, and we embraced with a great mutual sense of relief. The warm body of another human being felt good, especially in the downpour, especially after a frightening experience. And even in this extremely heavy situation, my male chauvinism came out and I thought, "How nice it is to be able to spend this night with a woman." Actually, it was a 14-year-old boy from our collective in Grand Rapids, Michigan. No matter, to protect ourselves from the 40+ degree temperature and the rain, we held ourselves tightly together without any hesitation. I remembered a very heavy discussion we had in N.Y. in which we concluded that it was our male chauvinism alone that prevented us from digging physical contact with other men, and that, if only from a survival standpoint, we should learn to gratify some of our sensuous needs with men as well as with women. (How else are we going to survive long jail sentences?)

At 6:30 in the morning, we left the hiding place and headed for a train station with $1.25 in our pockets. By 7:15, the two of us were walking on Madison Street (Chicago's equivalent of the Bowery) headed towards Chinatown, some twenty long blocks away. We made a curious pair. A 28-year-old Japanese man with just a short-sleeved shirt on in

50 degree weather, and a 14-year-old blond boy with no coat on, both of us thoroughly wet, full of mud, walking together at 7:30 on a Saturday morning with practically no other person on the streets. Within minutes we were stopped by a pig car with two huge pigs and a police dog inside. I expected this sort of harassment, and had already decided to tell a ninety per cent-true story, since I'm not a good liar yet. I managed to shuffle through and promised to return the Grand Rapids boy to his parents. Right afterwards, I decided that it was suicidal to stay on the streets, so we went into a diner filled with black truck drivers. I started a conversation with a black driver with an Afro haircut, and told him that we needed help, that we were Weathermen being chased by the pigs. No, he couldn't drive us to the University of Chicago campus, but instead gave us a dollar, and bid us "good luck" with his raised clenched fist.

On the train, we met two more black guys who said they were going in the same direction and guided us through a couple of intricate transfers. They also gave us some money. After we got off the train, we had a half-mile walk on a main thoroughfare. Again, we didn't want to stay on the streets too long, so we stopped a car with three powerful-looking blacks inside and asked for a ride. They couldn't give us a ride but did give us the names of a couple of black leaders who might help us out.

THE STREETS AGAIN

When we got to the campus, before we could get to the International House (where I was hoping to get some money from Asian students) we met a group of cadres from the Michigan region. How good it felt to see all these comrades!! I thought everyone but us had been busted on the previous night. I learned that there was an emergency planning meeting on the campus. More and more comrades arrived. So did the members of the Weather Bureau.

Another cadre from N.Y. and myself were assigned to organize the security. Several pigs from the Chicago Red Squad were already nosing around; four squad cars and a paddy wagon were parked nearby. That tense atmosphere was there again. We assigned scouts and patrols to give us an early warning in case of a bust; we investigated the possible entrance points for the pigs and checked for the best getaway routes for ourselves; we threw out a couple of suspicious characters. All routine, by now. The political priority was not to fight, but to get away so that we could fight on our own terms later that day. About seventy people showed up. Are we going to go through with it? Yes, came the answer. Again, I'm assigned to be an affinity group leader. I think of declining: I hadn't eaten for the last twenty-four hours, I hadn't slept for more than fifty hours, and I had a temperature. But I asked myself: of the six cadres in our collective, should I be the leader? Yes. So with a rather heavy heart, I went with my group to the Haymarket Square.

As soon as we got off the subway, I saw pigs of all kinds everywhere. A small group on our way avoided looking at us—they seemed scared. Larger groups of pigs tried to scare us by taking photos and making comments. Many of them are wearing civilian clothes and are packed into unmarked cars. I had never seen so many pigs in my life!

When we got to the Haymarket Square there were about two hundred comrades listening to the speeches. Eventually the crowd grew to about three hundred. Huh, more than I feared or expected, but less than I hoped for. I felt the fear in a calm way, but mostly I was without strong emotions. I was a bit troubled by my lack of defensive gear (no helmet, no heavy jacket, no goggles, no medical kit, no jock or cup). But what worried me most was that each of us had only $1.50 in our pockets to split from the city. (The leadership instructed us to split from the city after the action in the direction of New York because of heavy anticipated repression. The return buses to New York were cancelled, and we were on our own to get back in any way we could.) I also had no ID on me, since I left my wallet in the church the previous night.

I felt the fear in a quiet way, but at no time did I feel an urge to get away (like I did so many times during the Cleveland conference). J. J. made an extremely inspiring speech. Remember J. J. when he cried after the dissolution of the

May 2nd Movement? He was seventeen then. He couldn't be older than twenty-one now. What a fighter. What a leader! I looked at the faces of the women around me. All intently listening to J. J., with a calm determination to struggle to the end. The day before, one of the people in the N.Y. leadership said to us: "Everyone is scared of tomorrow. What'll enable some of us to cope with fear and to fight to the end tomorrow is certainly not physical strength, nor sheer personal courage, but a certain kind of political understanding. If you really understand that a certain task needs to be done, if you really understand the political necessity fully, then you'll get the courage to carry it through, to fight till the end." As J. J.'s speech went on, I began to really understand the absolute political necessity of the day's action.

Wednesday night, many of us were out primarily to do the greatest material damage possible—we actively defended ourselves against the pigs only insofar as it was necessary to do material damage or to get away. Saturday, our aim was primarily to actively defend ourselves against the pigs since they were out to overpower us into submission. There was nothing ambiguous about the action. There was nothing else to do but actually *do it* on Saturday, and each one of us knew that.

As the march started, we moved tightly at a brisk pace. The chanting got louder and louder. Our spirits moved upward and upward. It was the second battle of the white fighting force. The task assigned to the New York collective was to guard the rear end of the march and to push people in the front so that the march will keep together. Our assignment was as heavy as that of the collective in the front line of the march. As soon as our rear end passed a line of pigs, they broke the line and marched behind us. In a few minutes there were more than two hundred pigs following us closely on foot, in unmarked cars, and on motorcycles. It was not a very comfortable position to be in. As we came to the intersection of Lasalle and Madison Streets, a fighting situation started in the front line. I saw about fifteen people sandwiched between two cars, and a bus being vamped on by several pigs. I saw my political necessity, and proceeded to carry it through.

Forty seconds later I was on the ground, being kicked and clubbed by several Chicago pigs.

A VICTORY / A PRESENCE

Two hundred fifty arrests and several serious injuries; at least forty out of three hundred cadres with very heavy felony charges. More than $1.5 million ($150,000 cash) in bail money. That was the cost of the four-day national action. Are these costs justified by the results? In other words, did we win a victory in Chicago? This was the question on everyone's mind in the aftermath. Some non-Weatherman radicals say that since the Weathermen feel so high about themselves and about Chicago, our evaluation of it must be strictly "internal" and subjective. Let me then summarize my own evaluation of the action in as objective a way as possible:

1. Militarily and tactically, it was a victory. Fifty-seven pigs were hospitalized, including a few who almost got killed, while we ourselves suffered many fewer physical casualties. On both Wednesday and Thursday, three hundred Weathermen moved on the streets in a together, military manner. This was a great accomplishment, given the overwhelming numerical superiority of the pig forces. We inflicted more than $1 million of damage on a ruling-class neighborhood. And our actions apparently inspired some people to blow up a couple of induction centers early Saturday morning. To balance against this, we suffered tremendously heavy legal casualties. In addition to the forty felonies and several attempted murder charges, we expect even heavier federal charges to come down on us soon. While all this was anticipated, the level of repression is nevertheless extremely heavy by white-radical standards. So, over-all, what we did in Chicago confirmed J. J.'s statement that mass street action is a necessary, but a losing, tactic.

2. Politically, we did establish our presence as a white fighting force in a dramatic way in Chicago and in the surrounding areas. As a result, millions of kids are grappling for the first time with the existence of a pro-black pro-VC white fighting force that understands that this social order can be, and is going to be, brought down. As to how much we polar-

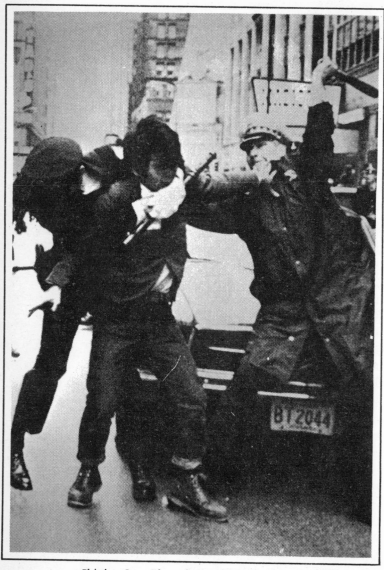

Shin'ya Ono. Photo by David Fenton/LNS

ized their consciousness and shook up their defeatist-chauvinist presumption of the permanence of this social order, that can only be judged and verified by our follow-up work and actions in that area. Because of the smallness of our numbers, our actions did not have much impact on the youths outside the Chicago area.

3. In terms of its impact on the movement, the indications are that the Weathermen in general and the Chicago action in particular (after initially pushing people to the right) are now helping many people to re-examine the nature of their revolutionary commitment, to push out their own politics more, and to struggle harder. RYM II's actions juxtaposed to the Weatherman battles embarrassed and disgusted many who came to participate in them. These people went back to kick ass on their own campuses, ripping up ROTCs, research institutes, etc. However, again, only subsequent development can confirm the validity of this general impression.

4. As for the development of the cadre, Chicago was an unqualified success. The Chicago action, its various "personal" consequences, and the heavy criticism sessions afterwards, are transforming us into revolutionaries. Turning jail and court experiences into full-fledged Weatherman actions also played an important part in this process of self-transformation. In the Cook County Jail, we organized ourselves into affinity groups, chose our leadership, and carried on full, disciplined political lives: political education, karate and physical exercises, criticism sessions, general political meetings, doing the housekeeping chores in a collective way, carrying on political struggle in alliance with other inmates, etc. In the courtroom, we have turned the usually intimidating, atomizing, and mystifying legal process into collective political struggles. We march one hundred strong into the courthouse, chanting *"Ho, Ho, Ho Chi Minh, Viet Cong is gonna win."* Most of us wear our usual street-fighting clothes and boots; we defend ourselves, and demand an immediate jury trial. We're pushing through a political offensive as avowed Weathermen, as open communists. One judge after one session with us cried out in dismay: "I feel like I'm in a

mob action right now." All this is not only to expose and fuck the courts as a major oppressive institution, but also to ensure that our cadres stay together and grow politically. By pushing out the struggle to the very limit, even in the constrained tactical situation of a courtroom, by regarding every word, every gesture, every motion and every moment as the realm of power struggle between the revolution and the imperialist state, we can take the sting out of the intended intimidation which is the core of the bourgeois court system.

Weatherman is going through a difficult period at the present time, primarily because of the repression unleashed by the enemy, and secondarily because of the shortcomings in its past practice. I am confident, though, that in the near future it will overcome all the difficulties and shortcomings, and will come to occupy a widely recognized position as the revolutionary vanguard of the entire movement in the white mother country. This will occur even if the majority of the Weatherman leadership and cadres are wiped out in the coming waves of repression.

Washington, November 15, 1969

The most important tension in the March on Washington last week wasn't over the war. Washington was really all about the question of violence. The people who organized the demonstration, and the pigs, from Nixon on down to the Mobilization pig marshals, built their whole thing on having a peaceful and "reasonable" protest march. Even when the thing was happening, when the richest parts of Washington, D.C., were trashed three days in a row, they fell off their chairs trying to isolate, denounce, and finally ignore what was coming down. A lot of people were saying how important it was that a lot of people stood in the cold all day and that 45,000 kids marched in the Parade of Death. They said it was "America's Finest Hour." But what we dug about Washington was the violence.

A lot of the kids who were into the pacifist thing said that they couldn't get into violence because it was morally wrong, that war itself is a bad thing, and that "fighting fire with fire" would make us just as fucked-up as the Man. They said that people have to show how well-meaning they are by doing "legitimate" moral acts. But that's a whole utopian trip. It's crazy to think that because we walked in front of their houses with a peace sign, the rich fuckers in power would somehow see how they rip people off, and that the people whose power is staked on imperialist wars and forces like teachers and pigs would destroy their own positions to give it all back.

So 45,000 kids walked five miles single file, not rapping, for 36 hours. Each one dropped the name of a dead GI into a coffin. All between two rows of pigs. That was the Parade of Death.

But there were a couple thousand kids who couldn't dig it. We were the people our parents warned us about. We moved

From *Fire*, November 21, 1969

through the streets in groups, marching, dancing, running, chanting, singing, downing jugs of wine. Running together with the people we knew well and trusted a lot. We carried VC flags and used the flagpoles as weapons. Trashing windows and pig cars. Setting fires at street corners.

THE VIETNAM WAR ISN'T THE ISSUE ANY MORE. Mainly because the war is over. The Vietnamese people have won a military victory over the most powerful empire in the history of the world. They have regained control of the entire countryside and most of the cities, while the American troops have retreated to a few of their most highly defensible bases (40 per cent of the U.S. troops are now stationed in Saigon). The only thing left is for Nixon to find the American ruling class a diplomatic way of admitting defeat.

The Vietnamese didn't defeat the Americans by staging peaceful demonstrations. They won when their entire population mobilized and fought a People's War for their freedom. They fought, like we are beginning to, for power. And they won power through armed, violent struggle.

What we say when we demonstrate about the war isn't that the U.S. should end the suffering or brutality. We tell people about how the VC have won. It's not so much that we're against the war; we're for the Vietnamese people and their victory. And their struggle has shown us and people all over the world that it can be done, the monster can be smashed, the people can win.

Violence by itself is neither good, bad, right nor wrong. The thing is to get a handle on what's necessary to build a revolution in the world. We've got to start looking at things in terms of winning, seeing our actions as part of a strategy for the struggle. We've got to see the connection between the sabotage of the imperialists' office buildings in New York, the SDS riot in Chicago, and the violent motion that came off of Washington. We know that the only way the fat cats who run the country are going to give up anything—the Vietnam war or their power to suck off everyone else—is when people take it back from them. The VC dig that; that's why they're doing it. Dig it? Do it!

From *Fire*, November 21, 1969

Friday night we rallied at
Dupont Circle, for a few short
speeches.

Then we moved out on the Saigon and other
pig embassies. It was a great feeling moving
out. Our people were chanting, singing and
laughing with the thought of what was to come.
The pace was fast. Everybody was anxious for
what was to happen.

After a relaxing sleep,
we moved on the
injustice department

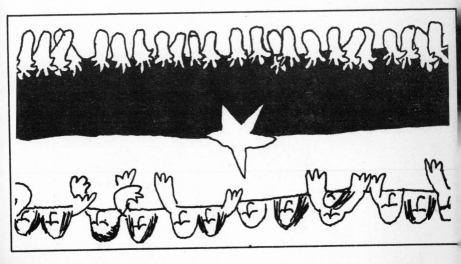

Fire, November 21, 1969

Going Down In Chicago

Andrew Kopkind

> *I prefer the philanthropy of Captain John Brown to that philanthropy which neither shoots me nor liberates me.... I do not wish to kill nor to be killed, but I can foresee circumstances in which both these things would be by me unavoidable. We preserve the so-called peace of our community by deeds of petty violence every day. Look at the policeman's billy and handcuffs! Look at the jail! ... We are hoping only to live safely on the outskirts of this provisional army. So we defend ourselves and our hen-roosts and maintain slavery. I know that the mass of my countrymen think that the only righteous use that can be made of Sharpe's rifles and revolvers is to fight duels with them when we are insulted by other nations, or to hunt Indians, or shoot fugitive slaves with them, or the like. I think that for once the Sharpe's rifles and the revolvers were employed in a righteous cause. The tools were in the hands of one who could use them.... The same indignation that is said to have cleared the temple once will clear it again. The question is not about the weapon, but the spirit in which you use it.*
>
> *—Henry David Thoreau, 1859*

There were twelve people in our two-man cell at the Chicago Police Headquarters last Saturday after the SDS "Weatherman" march through the Loop. Our charges ran from disorderly conduct (my own) through possession of explosives to attempted murder. The styles and situations of the dozen were as widely disparate as the charges: A black student (explosives) in boutique bell-bottoms stretched out coolly on one of the two wooden benches, surveying the rest of us with amusement as well as attachment. A long-haired New York Weatherman, who said he had written and produced a musical version of the Columbia University insurrection, skillfully sang both the instrumental and vocal parts of The Cream's "I Feel Free." A very young, very rich kid (mob action) spouted heroic slogans intermittently during a compulsive, anxious monologue about himself. An uncommonly tender gang-type from a Michigan Weatherman collective washed a cellmate's wounds with wet toilet paper and went to sleep on the crowded cement floor. Brian Flanagan, a bright and sensitive upper-middle "moderate" who found his way inside a Columbia building last year, and had now come to be charged with attempted murder (of Chicago's toughest judicial figure), rested in another corner, dealing quietly with his own fear and a large, still-bleeding gash in his head.

The events of the afternoon were common to us all, whether we had been busted in the La Salle Street melee, or a mile away (as I and two friends were). Solidarity and spirit grew easily from the experience of fear and force; it was expressed through the long first night in jail with songs and chants and good talking. But beyond the fellow-feeling and gallows humor, much more drastic changes were running down within us, and they could not be expressed at all, at least not then and there. That protean rebellion which was born ten years ago in the South: that found forms to fit the Mississippi Delta, the Cleveland slums, the Berkeley campus, the hundred colleges and parks and Army posts; that appeared bloody last summer in Grant Park and stoned this summer at Woodstock: it ran that day in the Loop. Almost everyone else now thinks that that spirit of the Sixties has found its end. But at night in the cell block, we believed that it had found a new beginning.

Weatherman demands the willing suspension of disbelief. As an ideology of communism and a strategy of revolution, it shatters the reliable categories of thought and modes of action which white radicals have developed in the last ten years. It challenges the validity of an intellectual left, which functions as a comfortable culture of opposition; instead, it asks that radicals become revolutionaries, completely collectivize their lives, and struggle to death if necessary. Nothing could be more threatening to the investments of thought and action which Movement people have made. Weatherman asks them to leap—in life-expectations as well as political ideas—over a distance fully as wide as that which they crossed from liberalism (or whatever) into the Movement.

Since the civil rights movement moved North in 1964, white radicals have been working within a politics that was defined in the SDS "ERAP" community-organizing projects in Newark, Cleveland, Uptown Chicago, and a half-dozen other urban centers. Although the organizers used some revolutionary rhetoric, they were never able to find a strategy for mobilizing masses of people to restructure "the institutions which control their lives." Marches, sit-ins, tenant strikes and election campaigns inconvenienced but did not seriously threaten the welfare departments, housing agencies and city administrations against which they were directed. At length, the project workers—mostly white college kids—realized that those institutions could not be overhauled without wholesale shifts in power inside the "system" itself.

Since ERAP began to dissolve in 1966 and 1967, radical organizers have used basically the same strategy in other areas: campus strikes, draft resistance, Army base movements. The common principle was the organization of people in one locale (or in various branches of the same essential locale) to change the immediate institution which most oppressed them. For example, students were organized to "change the university"; young men were organized to "stop the draft"; basic trainees were organized to "fuck the Army." It was hoped that such action might lead, in an always undefined way, to a chain reaction of structural changes throughout the whole system. But of course nothing like that ever happened.

Taken together, at least, that effort can hardly be counted a political failure, even if it did not accomplish its rhetorical objectives. What did happen was the creation of a race of radical organizers who are extraordinarily competent to do the work which their strategy defines. But there are obvious limits to the strategy, and after years of operational failures, a feeling of frustration and even desperation has set in. Many of the early organizers went off to the peripheries of politics: journalism, the academy, legal aid, teaching, or even "liberal" government welfare jobs. And others went completely into personal "life-style" retreats in one or another wooded grove in New England, California or the Southwest.

As the repository of the political forms in the Movement, SDS has been struggling to break out of the frustration of repeated failure—or at least dispiriting unsuccess. The factionalism which has now become rampant is a direct result of that situation; politics without promise rapidly loses its coherence. The various factions within and around SDS accurately represent the political alternatives that now seem available. Progressive Labor, the "Maoist" party that was expelled from SDS last June but still holds on in an ambiguous role, expresses the conviction that revolutionary conditions already exist in the US, and it requires only the organization of the industrial proletariat to set the revolution in motion. Revolutionary Youth Movement II (RYM-II) agrees in part with Progressive Labor, that workers organized "at the point of production" can become a revolutionary force in America, but goes on to emphasize the paramountcy of subordinating white efforts to the "vanguard" of black and Latin movements. Despite their expansive theoretical flights, both PL and RYM-II work inside the framework of the community-organizing strategy. They try to get factory workers to demand "power" within their factories, or hospital workers—and users—within the hospitals, or soldiers within their bases.

Weatherman is something else. It is, in theory and practice, a revolutionary "army," and it flaunts that notion: "Come to Chicago. Join the Red Army," the leaflets called out. At this point—only a few months after it was born—Weatherman presents this schema: The fight against the American empire, at home in the black "colony" and abroad in the Third World, is the center ring of world politics today, within which the American system will eventually come to grief. The colonized peoples—black Americans and Third World guerrillas—can "do it alone"; but white Americans can both deepen and extend the fight if they disregard the position of "privilege" their white skins automatically provide, and learn to live and die like unprivileged guerrillas. In Weatherman's book, it is "racist " to accept white privilege in any way.

From that ideology flows a set of shattering implications. First of all, Weatherman action has to be directed at "material" aid (not just rhetorical support) to the anti-imperialist fights. It isn't enough to march or leaflet in support of the Vietnamese or the Black Panthers; there has to be an active effort to pull the machinery of empire off their backs.

Next, Weathermen have to understand the necessity of risking death, in terms of the historical necessity of revolution. It is the custom of intellectual lefts around the world to sit sipping coffee (or its current moral equivalent, smoking dope), grooving on other people's revolutions, staring at posters of other revolutionaries, and waiting for one's own revolution to start tomorrow. Weatherman says that tomorrow is forever, and the time is always now. To the widespread charge of "adventurism" on that account, Weatherman insists that nothing that hinders the empire from carrying out its "business as usual" against the colonies can be a worthless adventure—although of course some actions are of more strategic value than others—and that there is a time for up-front fighting and a time for background organizing.

The life-arrangements which have been built to deal with both the personal and political consequences of Weatherman are collectives—numbering now about a dozen in Ohio, Michigan, Illinois, New York, Maryland, Washington State, and Colorado. The intensity with which they work is almost indescribable; they are crucibles of theory and practice, action and self-criticism, loving and working. They are widely experimental: some now are considering rules against men and women living as "couples"—a form of privatism which inhibits total collectivization. In a few, women talk of intensifying their personal relationships with other women as a way of getting over the problem of "women-hating women," which derives from female self-hate—akin to the self-hatred people in oppressed groups, such as Negros and Jews, seem to contain. Often, members of collectives are revving at such high speed and intensity that they sleep only every other night; the rest of the time they are working—reading, criticizing, writing, traveling, pushing out the problems of the collective and out talking to other people.

The Weatherman perspective treats collectives as "pre-party" organizations, building eventually to a fighting communist party. A structure of leadership is developing, with the "Weather Bureau" at the top, regional staffs under that, and the collectives providing local cadre. The principle of authority is a form of "democratic centralism," with as much self-criticism thrown in as anyone can bear—probably *more* than anyone can bear.

But despite that formal plan, Weatherman is still primarily an organizing strategy, not a fighting force. Heavy actions in the streets and schools are undertaken more for their "exemplary" effect on potential Weatherpeople than for their "material" aid to the Viet Cong. Weatherman wants to get at high school and community college drop-outs—not middle-class university kids—and it believes that the way to do it is to convince them that they can fight the authorities who daily oppress them: cops, principals, bosses. Weatherman as a strategy was born last April at Kent State University in Ohio, when a small group of SDS activists broke first through a line of "jocks" and then a phalanx of police to occupy a building where a hearing was being conducted on disciplinary and student-power issues. The attack so galvanized the campus that 5,000 students came out the next day in support of the SDS fighters.

There's no denying the antagonism to Weatherman within the radical left—not to mention the sheer horror with which liberals and conservatives view it. In some places—Detroit, for instance—unweatherized radicals have tried to form coalitions specifically aimed at destroying Weatherman. Some of the best New Left radicals believe that Weatherman is destroying (or has destroyed) the Movement. Movement spokesmen, such as the Guardian and Liberation News Service, are almost viciously anti-Weatherman; the underground press, for the most part, thinks Weatherman is positively insane. Such hostility is more than mere factionalism. It represents total rejection of Weatherman's revolutionary form.

Weatherman itself doesn't help matters. Perhaps because of the intensity of their own lives, the members cannot accept the relative lethargy of other radicals. More than that, Weathermen have built such elaborate political and emotional defenses against their fears of death and imprisonment that any challenge to the meaning of their work directly threatens their identities. It is obvious that Weatherman is quasi-religious and "fanatic" in a way; they see those who stand apart as the early Christians must have seen the pagans. It is difficult to die for a cause that their peers reject.

The Movement's antagonism is particularly wounding because Weatherman has so far failed to attract the large numbers of people it hoped would follow "up-front" fighting. All summer and in the early fall, Weatherman tried to organize its drop-out constituency by running through schoolrooms yelling "Jail break!," fighting with hostile kids, and carrying NLF flags down beaches, literally looking for trouble. When trouble came, the Weathermen fought, and in many instances "won"; but the actions did not mobilize the hordes of kids the organizers had expected. There were famous Weatherman horror shows: in Pittsburgh, where members ran through a school and were arrested with no organizing effect; and in Detroit, where a group of Weatherwomen (now called the Motor City Nine) entered an examination room in a community college, locked the doors, subdued the teacher, and then took two hostile male students out of action with karate blows.

It's hard, too, for many outsiders to grasp the dramatic—often comic—aspects of Weatherman's political style. I first saw Weatherman as the "Action Faction" of SDS at the National Convention in Chicago last June (see Hard Times, No. 38). It surfaced the first afternoon; during a particularly dreary maneuver by PL, the Action Faction people leaped up on their chairs waving Red Books and chanting, "Ho, Ho, Ho Chi Minh. . . ." They succeeded in breaking up PL's silly obstructions by an essentially dramatic move, which had elements of both parody and instruction.

That element has carried through into all aspects of weathering, so that at times it is difficult to tell whether the entire phenomenon may not be a gigantic psychodrama. Most Weathermen, in their own self-criticism sessions, are aware of the dangers of the emotional "trip" that revolutionism entails. At a meeting one night during the Chicago weekend, speaker after speaker warned against the "death trip" or the "machismo trip" or the "violence trip." "We act not out of our private emotions, but in accordance with our political understanding," one Weatherman said.

Because Weatherman is still so young, it would be fatuous to condemn it as worthless or elevate it to heroic proportions. Its contradictions are apparent, even to most Weathermen, who are defensive outside their collectives but truly self-exploring within. What seems most troublesome right now is Weatherman's simple-mindedness about the varieties of political experience in America; as revolutionaries usually discover, violent struggle and less intense organizing are not mutually exclusive. RYM-II and independent radicals are still producing organizers who can serve a variety of functions; to put all radical eggs in a weatherbasket would be unutterably foolish.

Nor is there much evidence that violence can mobilize thousands of kids, even in Weatherman's chosen drop-out pool. Real revolutionaries have a contempt for violence, not an adoration of it; it is used only as a last resort, as a response to specific oppression. As yet, most people do not comprehend the relationship of the police in America to the B-52s in Vietnam. A revolutionary party finds its moral authority in leading an oppressed people in retaliation against their intolerable oppressors: That's how the Viet Cong did it in Vietnam and how People's Democracy is doing it in Northern Ireland. To most people outside, Weatherman is a vanguard, floating free of a mass base.

But there's more to it than that. What appeal Weatherman has comes in part from its integration of the two basic streams of the movements of the Sixties—political mobilization and personal liberation. Since the break-up of the ERAP projects, few radical organizations have been able to contain and combine both streams. Those in the "liberation" stream have gone off on private trips; those in the political stream have been reduced to Old Left sloganeering and dreary demonstrations. Weatherman does break through, with its liberating collective sensibility and its active mobilization. However disastrous or brilliant its strategy may turn out to be, its spirit, purposefulness and integrity ought to command respect.

I had come to Chicago last week to see the range of actions planned in and around the trial of the Conspiracy—the eight men charged with conspiring to incite a riot at last year's Democratic Convention. The trial itself is a depressing affair, as political trials almost have to be—played as they are on hostile turf with no real chance of gaining the offensive. Slogans such as "Stop the Trial" seem too inflated even to shout, and except for a spirited action on opening day staged by the Panthers outside the Federal Building (Bobby Seale is one of the "Conspirators"), radicals have stayed away in droves. Meanwhile, the defendants are picking up support from *Life* and *Time* magazines and liberal civil-libertarians— all of which may be helpful to them, but does not seem to move the radical movements this year.

The RYM-II actions were not particularly enlivening, either. One afternoon, a few hundred people stood in a muddy park outside the Cook County Hospital and listened to uninspired speeches (some of them directed against Weatherman), but the prospects for organizing a "Revolutionary Youth Movement" out of it all seemed remote indeed. Reports of the Young Lords' (a young Latin community organization) march on Saturday were encouraging, but RYM-IIs role in that was admittedly secondary.

The Weatherman march was political psychodrama of the best and worst kind. It began dully at the site of the statue of the Chicago policeman, a singular symbol of power in Haymarket Square, which had been blown up at the beginning of the week. It was hard not to fear that Weatherman's history might be as tragic as the Knights of Labor or the Wobblies;

that it would never have even the trigger effect of John Brown's raid; that before it developed, death or long prison sentences would cut off the experiment at its inception.

The crowd was small and the weather was cold and wet. Just after noon, a posse of plainclothes detectives fell upon the small crowd of marchers and arrested Mark Rudd and several other Weatherman leaders. No one was at all sure that the march would ever happen. Then from around a corner came the sound of shouts and cheers, and a brigade of about a hundred Weathermen burst into the street, fists raised, chanting and laughing: "Ho, Ho, Ho Chi Minh. . . ." Then there was a send-off speech, and people joined arms and stepped quickly down the street into the deserted Loop. After a mile of marching, the column suddenly lurched, and there was fighting and rock-throwing and wailing sirens, and the paddy-wagons were soon filled to overflowing. For an hour afterwards, police picked up weathertypes on the streets and brought them in on various minor and serious charges.

Now some say that the police attacked first, and others say the Weathermen took the offensive, but it is true that the Weathermen did not shrink from the fight, and we all thought in the cell-block that night that simply not to fear fighting is a kind of winning.

From *Fire*, January 30, 1970.

On Weatherman

Eldridge Cleaver

It seems that a few fundamental principles need repeating. There is a point where caution ends and cowardice begins. It is time to intensify the struggle. We must support whatever the enemy opposes and oppose whatever the enemy supports.

Also, there are such things as revolutionary criticism and reactionary criticism, as well as counterrevolutionary criticism, and the enemy's criticism which we call propaganda. It seems to me that revolutionaries often make the mistake of indulging in reactionary criticism when they intend to make revolutionary criticism. Criticism is both valid and invaluable. Certain types of criticism, for revolutionaries, are invalid and valuable only to the enemy.

Much of the criticism of the Weathermen that has come to my attention seems to me to be reactionary, invalid and valuable only to the enemy. . . .

Stop and think. Did we ever pay attention to white radicals when they told us to keep our shoot-outs nice and clean and middle-class orderly? We call for a Second Boston Tea Party in the streets of Babylon. We call for the violent overthrow of the fascist imperialist United States government, ringleaders of oppression and international aggression. The only thing I oppose is going to jail voluntarily. Jail forces you to become cautious, conservative. Even the prospect of going to jail can have that effect. While in jail, if you are not cautious and conservative, but rather maintain your revolutionary thrust, you will end up spending all your time in the Hole the way Huey P. Newton is now doing (right on, Huey).

So what if we're disorderly, like a bunch of toughs, as Assemblyman Mulford used to say of the Panthers when

Excerpted from *The Berkeley Tribe,* November 7, 1969. Copyright 1969 by The Red Mountain Tribe. Reprinted by permission.

Huey P. Newton was on the set. Fuck Mulford. Through disorder we will put the pigs in order and in the process create a new order that we can relax in. I don't care if pigs don't like it or if it makes pig judges like Redmon Stats and Munro Mississippi Friedman angry. We do not require them to die happy—as long as they really die, dead.

When the pigs try to deal with our disorderly flanking attack on the skulls of their values by matching our style and the form of our motion, we have trapped them in ruin, because there are more of us than there are of them. When those for whom the Vanguard moves dig the action of the pigs on a nitty-gritty level, they will say right on because they know what that's about. They understand true power and they know that there are enough people in America to kick the ass of every pig in America.

There are enough people in Babylon to kick pig ass from the Atlantic to the Pacific and back again. We can kick pig ass for days, if we all start doing it. So why not? History will show that the pigs who publicly kick the people in the ass inevitably wind up up against the wall. (Motherfucker, Alioto! dog!) So why not put them up against the wall . . .

In times of revolution, just wars and wars of liberation, I love the angels of destruction and disorder as opposed to the devils of conservation and law-and-order. Fuck all those who block the revolution with rhetoric—revolutionary rhetoric or counterrevolutionary rhetoric.

Actions speak louder than words. Moncado is Fidel's most eloquent statement of position. Bolivia was Che's. We will not make our most eloquent statements in courtrooms and at press conferences, but in the streets of Babylon, doing it in the road but doing it. As long as we kill pigs.

We are either pig-killers or pig-feeders. Let the pigs oink for themselves, till their last oink. When we finally pull all of the American people out of their pads, out into the streets, out into the night, into the jungles of our cities, then we will hear some farewell oinking, we will be into our thing and everybody will understand our Moncados and our Willow Streets, and those who now misunderstand will then admit it.

The ideology of the Black Panther Party and the teachings of Huey P. Newton are contained in their purest form in Emory's art. Emory's art says if we really want pigs dead (Lyndon Johnson, for example, or Henry Ford or his cousin or his friends), then we must kill them. If we use iron pipes to do it, what's wrong with that?

At a certain stage in their struggle, the Vietnamese people used bamboo stalks, because that's what their environment yielded with ease. Ours is a concrete and steel environment. If we kill pigs with concrete and steel, it will only reaffirm that the human species is still able to adapt to any environment, deal with any scene that we ourselves create. In prison, even though a convict might prefer a gun, he often is forced to use an iron pipe, because he had some business to take care of which couldn't wait for the day when he could get a gun.

It is technological backwardness, however, to go into battle with inferior weapons when superior weapons are available, unless, of course, the choice of weapons was determined by objective conditions. The choice of weapons belongs to him who moves, to him who uses it—and not to those who observe the results from the TV sidelines or read about them in the newspaper. Stalin said that the weapon of criticism will never equal the criticism of weapons. I prefer a paralyzed pig to a well-criticized pig.

A dead pig is desirable, but a paralyzed pig is preferable to a mobile pig. And a determined revolutionary doesn't require an authorization from a Central Committee before offing a pig. As a matter of fact, when the need arises a true revolutionary will off the Central Committee.

In order to stop the slaughter of the people, we must accelerate the slaughter of the pigs. Those who can't stand the sight of blood, especially their own, should stay home and pray for those who come outside to move, to do it, and pray for victory and not for an end to the slaughter. Pray for us to win, because if we win you will be safe. If we lose, then kiss the baby good-bye.

Justice In The Streets

Tom Hayden

Outrage over the trial was translated into violence no less than three times nationally: in the October "Days of Rage"; at the Washington Moratorium in November; and on The Day After. Previously most radical violence was in defense against swinging clubs. But on these three occasions people were fighting back against blows coming down in the courtroom. The only "organized" violence came from the Weathermen in September and October. Rulers first fantasize their devils, then create them. We never did what the government accused us of in 1968, but the Weathermen did it in 1969. What we did in 1968 prefigured Weatherman: a few karate and snake-dance exercises, some disruption, a lot of running in the streets, and at the end of Convention Week, a prediction that a fighting force would be created which would bring the war in Vietnam home. It remained for the government to develop this seed into a paranoid image of crazy, unruly, drug-ruined, club-carrying, communist-inspired mobs rampaging in the Loop, and for Weathermen to fulfill the image one year later. Many Weatherman leaders were shaped by the events of Chicago '68. When our legal protest was clubbed down, they became outlaws. When our pitiful attempts at peaceful confrontation were overwhelmed, they adopted the tactic of offensive guerrilla violence. When our protest against the war failed, they decided to bring the war home.

And so, even as we were sitting in court, the new revolutionaries conspired to come to Chicago to "incite, organize, and promote a riot." Though there were only 200 Weathermen, the Days of Rage resulted in the destruction of a famous statue of a Chicago policeman, shattered windows in the Loop and along the Gold Coast, injuries to police, and a broken neck for the same corporation counsel who had moved with the front of our own marches the year before without mishap.

It was the Weathermen, in fact, who convinced us that we were innocent of the charges, because we were mild compared to them. Dave of course opposed violence on pacifist grounds alone. Bobby and the Panthers opposed offensive violence as a substitute for a program. The rest of us perhaps found the spirit tempting, but our flesh was weak, at least while we were on trial.

John, Abbie and I went up to Lincoln Park the opening night of the Weatherman war. They looked exactly like the people we were accused of being: helmeted, with heavy jackets, clubs, NLF flags, circled around a fire of park benches exactly like a primitive, neophyte, nervous army. They asked us to say a few words of greeting. It seemed like an invitation to another indictment, but we agreed. When I got up to speak, however, Abbie and John had thought better of it and disappeared. I said a few words praising the spirit of their new militancy, I looked around nervously at the photographers taking pictures of me at the bullhorn, and got out of there. It was the first army I had ever addressed and speaking seemed out of place. An hour later, we learned they were for real, even if they had no numbers. What they told us would be a "demonstration" near Judge Hoffman's ritzy Drake Towers turned out to be a literal rampage.

After the four-day action, the press was all over us for a statement. They wanted one that could be boiled down either to praise or condemnation. But we were not going to condemn in public any group which was escalating the struggle, so we issued a statement emphasizing differences, but condemning the hypocrisy of those who yelled about Weatherman violence while ignoring the violence of the American empire. In the statement, we concluded, "America reaps what she sows."

In fact, several of us had deeply mixed feelings about the October action. We were drawn to the seriousness of Weatherman, for here at last was a group willing to go beyond the pseudo-radicalism of the white left into a head-on showdown with the system. The New Left was rapidly becoming the old left, a comfortable left, with too many radicals falling into the ruts of teaching and monogamy, leaving Che and Malcolm and Huey only as posters on their walls.

But there was something deeply wrong with what had happened in Chicago. At first we could only understand the symptoms. Trashing Volkswagens, for example, was not "materially aiding the Vietnamese," it was just plain random violence. And only 200 or 300 people had come to the Weatherman action, instead of the thousands the Weathermen promised. To ourselves, revolution was like birth: blood is inevitable, but the purpose of the act is to create new life, not to glorify blood. Yet to the Weathermen bloodshed as such was "great." They were striking terror into Pig Amerika, Volkswagens and all, and their tiny numbers would be unimportant, they claimed, in the vast myth they were creating.

During the Moratorium a few weeks later, several thousand people streamed towards the South Vietnamese Embassy one night, then toward the Justice Department the next day. They, too, were violent, but their targets were more selective and meaningful than those of the Weathermen in Chicago. Abbie wrote that the difference was between structured, artificial violence (Weathermen) and natural, spontaneous violence (Yippie). The Weathermen believed in "war," chose an arbitrary date and then just began it. But most young people could not relate to scheduling a riot, partly because of the debatable effectiveness of such tactics, but mainly because it was not a spontaneous reaction to an immediate situation. Weatherman violence was not dictated by a situation so much as by an ideology. Their violence was structured and artificial, because in their heads they were part of the Third World. They were alienated from their own roots. The privileged, funky, hedonistic qualities of youth culture turned them off. The cultural revolution among youth, to them, was simply more pig privilege. They were not guerrillas swimming like fish among the people; they were more like commandos, fifth columnists, operating behind enemy lines. Eventually, this logic would lead to their glorification of the media image of Charlie Manson as perhaps the best "model" for white youth. They were not the conscience of their generation, but more like its *id.*

We felt, on the other hand, that there was a genuine, legitimate revolutionary consciousness arising out of the life experience of young people. We were not simply allies to a revolution centered in the Third World. As the misfits of a dying capitalism, we were oppressed in unique ways and had to rebel in unique ways. Our revolution would be part of an international revolution, to be sure, but with its own style and content. Our will to struggle would come, not simply from the inspiration of the Vietnamese or the blacks, but from the imperative of preserving and expanding our own way of life.

There are limits, however, to any notions of spontaneous rebellion. Abbie's criticism of the Weathermen relied too much on the alternative of spontaneously "doing our thing." In the face of repression it becomes irresponsible and hazardous simply to propose that people go wild in the streets. A workable organizational machinery becomes necessary to push the struggle at all levels, including in the streets. In a sense the Yippies used Washington to push for militancy. Though having a base of support in the crowd, they lacked machinery. They were exploiting an event put together by others; the only people who were organized in Washington were the peace movement moderates.

We learned how organization and spontaneity could go together on TDA. We had *leadership* (the Conspiracy), *machinery* (the network of campuses where we spoke, the underground press, etc.), *strategy* (massive protest by "our jury" as a reply to Justice Department intimidation), and *flexible tactics* (people were told to invent their own actions but make them both militant and broad-based). If it was true that this was "our generation on trial," no more organization would be needed.

That is why, on TDA, there was a riot across state lines that shook the country. Young people who had not come to

Chicago to "bring the war home" were striking back now, for a purpose they believed in, with a spontaneity flowing from legitimate outrage because their collective identity had been violated and they could stand it no longer. Weathermen had created the tactics, but the fight was about us.

Tens of thousands participated. The youth ghetto in Santa Barbara exploded and the Bank of America was burned down. Stores were trashed everywhere. Bombs were placed in buildings from California to New York. The trial, which had been designed to intimidate, had produced insurrection instead.

We didn't "organize" it; we only called for our jury to reach its verdict in the streets. It erupted spontaneously. In Berkeley, the crowd wouldn't even wait for the speakers to finish denouncing the trial. The form it took confirmed that more than eight men were on trial. People riot when they themselves feel that they have been slammed against a wall.

We eight were not special men. We were only a reflection of the impulses of our own generation. It was like riding the crest of a great wave, a wave made by the power of the people.

Part 3
Inside The Weather Machine

Introduction

Weatherman's conception of a revolutionary collective developed out of the Movement's experience with affinity groups. While affinity groups vary in form and political ideology, all consist of a relatively few people (five to twenty-five) who know each other well and can work together politically. Affinity groups incorporate a plethora of life styles: some involve communal living, some are made up exclusively of women or men, and sexual and personal relationships within groups run the gamut from fairly straight to highly experimental. However they go about it, affinity groups share at least three goals: deepening the knowledge of and trust among individuals in the group; learning various medical, legal, self-defense and propaganda skills; and engaging in internal political education.

Affinity groups have functioned on the left by providing

cadre for mass organizing projects, or by acting as effective street-fighting units in militant mass demonstrations. They coordinate and communicate their activities through exemplary actions, meetings, or the underground press. The degree to which they are "public" rather than "underground" depends on the legality of their actions and their overall security requirements. Affinity groups have the advantage of being difficult to infiltrate, as each group is small, independent, and careful in choosing its members.

The Weatherman program called for building a Red Army which would support anti-imperialist armed struggles abroad by opening up a front here at home. To transform that vision into reality Weatherwomen and men would have to drastically transform themselves while, at the same time, building the kind of organization that could strike military blows against the state—and survive.

Weatherman was organized along democratic-centralist lines with the Weather Bureau (the top leadership) exercising control over political policy and the newspaper, *Fire*.* While the collectives functioned within the political parameters set by the Weather Bureau, intensive ideological struggle went on within and among collectives and between individual collectives and the Bureau. Tiers of leadership existed within the collectives, established through an informally structured "merit" system. Those acting the bravest, fighting the hardest, pushing out their politics the best were chosen by the Weather Bureau to occupy positions of leadership. Leaders who could not keep up in the fierce competition to excel politically were replaced by others. As a security precaution, members within a collective were differentially informed about various illegal activities, depending on how well they were known and trusted. Weatherman referred to the entire

---

* *Fire* is shorthand for *The Fire Next Time*. Toward the end of August, Weatherman stopped publishing *New Left Notes* and instead started printing *Fire* as "the new SDS mass paper." By the end of the year, the paper no longer appeared.

infrastructure as the "Weather Machine." Inside it, Weatherman tried to mold itself into an organization of John Browns.

Weatherwomen played an important part in all that Weatherman did. They often, however, gave priority to struggles against male chauvinism within Weatherman and, conversely, for Weatherman political policies inside the women's liberation movement. "Honky Tonk Women" contains Weatherman's position on women's liberation. In keeping with Weatherman politics in general, the article advocates that white women reject the fight for such "empty transitional demands" as equal rights with white men and child care centers for white women. Instead it urges women to join the Vietnamese and the Cubans in picking up the gun to "open and lead another armed front against Amerika." To do less is held to be objectively racist. Weatherman theory further maintains that demands for material improvements in the lives of white women are not only readily co-optable, but avoid the most profound source of women's oppression.

Weatherman is also anti-separatist. It believes a separate women's movement is likely to fail because it tends not to clearly define American imperialism as *the* enemy and because the fight against male chauvinism can best be waged by men and women struggling *together* against their chauvinism. (Weatherman does concede the need for separate women's caucuses within revolutionary organizations to combat male chauvinism and to facilitate the unfolding of women's leadership potential.) To help women repudiate bourgeois values and break out of subordinate roles, debilitating self-hate and insecurity, Weatherman calls for an end to all monogamous relationships and looks favorably on women developing "full sexual and political relationships with women" alongside their relationships with men.

While Weatherman had an enormous impact on the lives of those who passed through it, it probably affected women the most. If Weatherwomen occupied a secondary place within the typically male-dominated organization at its inception, less than six months later women were successfully challenging men for leadership, eventually coming to hold the majority of leadership positions. A Weatherwoman recounts the process which made this possible in "Inside the Weather Machine."

The issue is more complicated than one would suppose from just reading Weatherman's views. "Inside the Weather Machine" appeared in the same issue of the *Rat* that contained Robin Morgan's article, "Goodbye to All That."* Morgan tends to argue that men are *the* enemy (or, in Weatherman terms, that male-female relations constitute a primary contradiction within the mother country on a par with that of imperialism). While at odds with Weatherman politics, "Goodbye to All That" eloquently expresses an important current within the women's liberation movement. In the course of advocating a radical feminist position, Morgan makes the following criticisms of Weatherman:

> Goodbye to the WeatherVain, with the Stanley Kowalski image and theory of free sexuality but practice of sex on demand for males. "Left Out!"—not Right On—to the Weather Sisters who, and they know better—they know, reject their own radical feminism for that last desperate grab at male approval that we all know so well, for claiming that the *machismo* style and the gratuitous violence is their own style by "free choice" and for believing that this is the way for a woman to make her revolution . . . all the while, oh my sister, not meeting my eyes because WeatherMen chose Manson as their—and your—Hero. (Honest, at least . . . since Manson is only the logical extreme of the normal American male's fantasy (whether he is Dick Nixon or Mark Rudd): master of a harem, women to do all the shitwork, from raising babies and cooking and hustling, to killing people on order.) Goodbye to all that shit that

---

* Both these articles were published in the first issue of the *Rat* put out exclusively by women, after they had liberated the newspaper from the male staff.

sets women apart from women; shit that covers the face of any Weatherwoman which is the face of any Manson Slave which is the face of Sharon Tate which is the face of Mary Jo Kopechne which is the face of Pat Nixon which is the face of Pat Swinton. *In the dark we are all the same*—and you better believe it: we're in the dark, baby. (Remember the old joke: Know what they call a black man with a Ph.D.? A nigger. Variation: Know what they call a Weatherwoman? A heavy cunt. Know what they call a Hip Revolutionary Woman? A groovy cunt. Know what they call a radical militant feminist? A crazy cunt. Amerika is a land of free choice—take your pick of titles. Left Out, my Sister—don't you see?) Goodbye to the illusion of strength when you run hand in hand with your oppressors; goodbye to the dream that being in the leadership collective will get you anything but gonorrhea.

Weatherwomen I have spoken to, though they disagree with the main thrust of Morgan's politics, accept her criticism that Weatherwomen adopted the *machismo* style of Weathermen in order to compete as equals with them and that sexual experimentation inside Weatherman collectives took on some of the worst features of bourgeois, exploitative relationships. But they contest Morgan's radical feminism by arguing that sexist relationships can only be dealt with in a revolutionary manner by members of both sexes struggling together against them.

Members of a separatist Boston women's liberation organization, Bread and Roses, also have made some trenchant criticisms of Weatherman. They differ from Robin Morgan in that they do not espouse an anti-male radical feminism, and they differ from Weatherman in their overall conception of what a revolutionary movement in America must consider. They attack Weatherman's analysis and strategy and, instead, maintain that "women must make revolutions for themselves as well as for other people," thus joining other critics who argue that the Movement must figure out how to organize people around their own perceived oppression and into a fighting anti-imperialist movement.

The struggle against male chauvinism and supremacy inside the Weather Machine was part of a larger process of personal transformation. In line with the principle that the building of communism begins with the remaking of people, the conquest of bourgeois limitations and values was considered part of the process of making the revolution, not one of its end-products. Weatherman went about transforming itself with the intensity and dedication that typified everything else it did: anything that appeared to stand in the way of people becoming totally committed, full-time revolutionaries became an object of struggle.

Members of a collective debated ideological questions, learned various skills, worked on political projects, fought in the streets, shared their clothes, food, and money, danced, turned-on, tripped out, and slept together. Every aspect of their existence became self-consciously political. Weather-people acutely experienced the anxiety, danger and satisfaction of trying to live revolutionary lives in the heart of Babylon. During the summer and fall months of 1969, Weatherman appeared very together to outsiders: its élan and camaraderie contrasted sharply with the passivity and divisiveness within the rest of the white Left.

Another, and uglier, side of life inside the Weather Machine at this time has been largely hidden from public view. The collectives made demands on their members which touched the deepest, most personal aspects of their lives. But not all of what happened to people was either good or revolutionary. The experience was marred by many bad "mistakes."

For example, ideological struggle within the collectives was supposed to be positive and reinforcing. Sometimes it was, but far too often its negative, destructive features predominated. Weatherpeople tended to treat each other (and certainly outsiders) as objects whose political line had to be smashed, whose personality had to be pillaged. The toughest, strongest-willed, most naive (or perhaps least sensitive) members stuck it out. Some tested and committed revolutionaries quit or never joined only because of the way Weatherman related to people. The turn-over among rank-and-file cadre was high. People were intimidated and browbeaten by a leadership which, at the same time, was urging them to become self-reliant and self-confident. Aggressive rivalries and scrambles over leadership positions inside the Weather Machine came to reflect the sickening competition of the mainstream culture. Fraternal feelings would often be punctured by hostility or degenerate into hero worship. Elitist practices not only failed to help remake people in the image of Che, but crippled the Weather Bureau's ability to reproduce revolutionaries of even its own sophistication.

Weatherpeople learned, after much mental anguish and personal sacrifice, that turning yourself inside out is not the same thing as turning yourself into a revolutionary, that seeing the world with fresh eyes does not mean you are looking in the right direction. If it is true, as Marcuse has argued, that making a revolution requires the union of a "new sensibility with a new rationality," it is no less true that the struggle to become revolutionary must be limited by the exigencies of liberation.* Marcuse's mistake is to stress the need to develop a new sensibility while ignoring the importance of overcoming the softness of the white Left. Weatherman errs just as much in the opposite direction. Che, whose main concern was establishing the New Man in Cuba, posed the problem properly: "We must grow tough, but without ever losing our tenderness." In contrast, Weatherman's revolt against bourgeois values often resulted neither in their negation nor in Weatherman's incorporation of socialist values.

Information as to what was happening inside the Weather Machine was hard to come by. Weatherman was of necessity a tightly disciplined and semi-clandestine organization. Facts and rumors circulated within Movement circles as disenchanted Weatherpeople confided their reasons for leaving (or not joining) Weatherman collectives to close friends. These

* See Herbert Marcuse, *An Essay On Liberation*, Beacon Press, 1969.

discussions eventually spread throughout the Movement during the debate engendered by Weatherman's "National War Council."

The idea of a National War Council developed in the fall of 1969 as Weatherman turned its attention toward reconstituting SDS as a national revolutionary mass organization. It sought to bring together, within SDS, all forces on the Left struggling to build a revolutionary youth movement. In the unfolding "drop-out" and student/hip communities, bourgeois currents co-existed with revolutionary ones, but a functioning SDS with a real base in these communities could have made a crucial difference in their politics. Weatherman envisioned creating an alliance with other white revolutionaries—Yippies, White Panthers, "Conspiracy 8" trial defendants and their militant supporters—to push the developing youth culture in a class-conscious, anti-imperialist direction and to turn the militant but fragmented youth movement into a coherent and united political force.

The call for a National War Council to initiate "the birth of the new SDS" was printed in *Fire*. Weatherman organizers toured the country, urging Movement people to attend "a celebration of revolutionary culture and a gathering of the tribes." This first national assembly of SDS members since the extraordinary convention of June 1969 would be an open meeting. Weatherman would not impose its politics on the new SDS, but hoped to raise consciousness and lead people by example toward armed struggle.

The National War Council that actually took place at the end of December in Flint, Michigan, was almost a total inversion of Weatherman's projected intentions. If people on the Left had mixed feelings about Weatherman theory, if they admired its courage and critically supported its street actions, they were generally disturbed, if not disgusted, with much of Weatherman's performance in Flint. Outsiders, while impressed with Weatherman's seriousness and discipline, complained about its discouragement of full ideological discussion, its unwillingness to struggle with non-Weatherpeople, its inability to openly confront its past errors, the crudity with which it ran down its politics, its defense of Charles Manson, and its espousal of violence for its own sake. Coming on the heels of the debacle at Woodstock West, Weatherman bears the imprint of having presided over the Movement's first political Altamont. The article "Stormy Weather," by Liberation News Service, describes some of what went on at this meeting.* Rather than marking the beginning of the new SDS, it turned out to be the last public meeting Weatherman was to hold.

Why did Weatherman give up its idea of reconstituting SDS? How is the turn of events at the National War Council to be explained? The answer rests with the Weather Bureau, since it planned and carried out the meeting.

By the end of December, aside from organizing the National War Council, the Weather Bureau had a number of pressing problems. Members of the Weather Bureau faced impending multiple felony indictments and were under constant surveillance from local police and FBI. They had been putting together the political machinery to go underground, developing a strategy for armed struggle, learning the legal and illegal skills necessary to implement it, and overseeing the political education and security of the collectives. Their situation and the tasks they had taken on in effect cut them off from all but a handful of trusted revolutionaries. They obviously were coming under great personal stress. Weatherman leaders must have experienced the disorientation that accompanies rapid and profound ruptures in one's life. This was reinforced by the different and conflicting political demands they had to meet in a short period of time: they were trying to assemble a Weather Machine that could do mass political work while supporting an underground leadership; though they took pains to root out police agents, they never did come to have total confidence in the results; the repression

---

* To my knowledge, Weatherman has not yet written its own version of the meeting, but participants (both Weatherman and non-Weatherman) agree that the events described in the article did indeed take place. Many disagree, of course, with the article's analysis and conclusions.

stemming from their previous political actions would soon foreclose on the possibility of their dealing directly with any mass revolutionary organization—yet they were planning to put such an organization together at the National War Council.

Two events occurred in Chicago prior to the Flint meeting that undermined a majority of the Weather Bureau's already waning faith in the Movement and even in its own membership's revolutionary commitment: during the "Conspiracy 8" trial, the chairman of the Black Panther Party, Bobby Seale, was gagged and shackled, then railroaded off to jail; Fred Hampton and Mark Clark, Illinois Black Panther leaders, were murdered by police in a pre-dawn raid. These crimes against the black movement produced what the Weather Bureau considered to be inadequate retaliation by the white Left. Most of the Weather Bureau concluded that white revolutionaries did not have the hardness, sense of solidarity, and courage to become a fighting force alongside of blacks. The Weatherman leadership, therefore, decided to change the emphasis of the National War Council from an open discussion of RYM politics and a celebration of youth culture to a diatribe against white skin privilege and a glorification of violence.

Actually, the Weather Bureau's rhetoric at Flint was no more than a weird extension of the kind of political propaganda that appeared regularly in *Fire* and, in fact, was a logical extension of the *macho* mentality that characterized much of the male-dominated white Left. While the struggles of black revolutionaries frequently endanger their lives, the white Left has been insulated from the worst aspects of state repression—partly because the society is racist, but also because white radicals have failed to go beyond symbolic demonstrations and revolutionary posturing. Not only did Weatherman recognize this difference within the Movement, but they felt guilty for benefiting from it. They thus moved to provide material support to Third World liberation struggles—expecting to share equally in the costs and risks of the revolution. The danger here was that Weatherman would come to see itself only as a support group for Third World revolutionary movements and would ignore the struggles among white youth which arise out of contradictions in the mother country.

That is in fact what happened. Prior to the "Days of Rage," Weatherman still retained its faith in the revolutionary potential of white working-class youth. But rather than criticizing itself for the low turnout in Chicago, it instead began to turn its back on white people. The weak response to the vicious attacks upon the Black Panthers reinforced this tendency. Compared to its earlier abstract commitment to a socialist revolution made by an overwhelming majority of the American people, Weatherman began to believe that the enemy was not just the ruling class, but—in its words—white, honky, racist Amerika itself. Much of Weatherman's political activities after this reflected a despair at organizing white people. At Flint, Weatherman decided to become nothing but a support group for the blacks and the Vietnamese.

Having lost confidence in their own revolution, Weatherpeople could not help but doubt their own authenticity as revolutionaries. The provocativeness of their flamboyant rhetoric provided them with the illusion of strength. This helps explain the speeches in praise of barbarism and devilry. Moreover, the pressure on the Weather Bureau from impending prosecutions, their political isolation, the small turnout at the National War Council, their anger and despair at the backwardness of the white Left, all contributed to their verbal excesses, their reduction of politics to theatrics. Most of all, they were discouraged by their own failure to build support for a mass-based revolutionary youth movement. Their frustration at not being able to put together the machinery that could begin to immediately smash the system led to a vulgar negation of all its values. If America hates the devil, fears Manson, and speaks in the guise of goodness and decency, then the Weather Bureau embraces the devil, lauds Manson, and equates those virtues with softness. At Flint, the Weather Bureau ended up making a caricature of even its own politics, denying in addition the moral impetus behind its own revolutionary transformation.

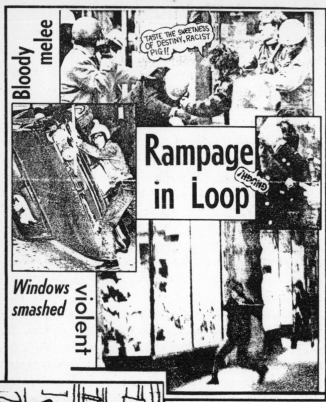

Fire October 21, 1969

Fire, January 30, 1970

Honky Tonk Women

In Cuba the imperialists were caught off guard; a small number of men overthrew Batista and drove American imperialism off the island within a short period of time. Cuban women, not involved in actual armed struggle, are now winning liberation in the Revolution. The fight in Vietnam has been the longest and fiercest yet, and the need to mobilize masses of people has produced the best Communist leadership. Under the NLF, with the vision of real equality and liberation, Vietnamese women took on major roles in their victorious war against the U.S. Now in North Vietnam and liberated zones of the South, the U.S. has been driven out, and Vietnamese women are winning formal equality in a process that began when they picked up the gun to destroy the U.S.

These revolutionary women are liberating themselves by fighting in a national struggle. But white women are part of Amerika, the white world-oppressor nation. As a nation, we have allowed a few rich men to exploit and plunder the rest of the world, and have used the wealth and privileges from their looting. The ruling class of this country has tried to buy our allegiance by creating material reasons for us to support them in Vietnam, Cuba and Latin America instead of the people fighting against them. The people of Vietnam, Cuba and other countries have fought wars for national identity, for self-determination. Our national identity is as the plunderers of the entire world. We must fight to destroy that national white oppressor identity and establish world communism—a job accomplished only by joining the people of the world, directly attacking and destroying imperialism with them. U.S. imperialism is our common enemy, and white women must join in this fight before they can win anything but empty transitional demands.

Part of a packet given out at the National War Council.

For white women to fight for "equal rights" or "right to work, right to organize for equal pay, promotions, better conditions . . ." while the rest of the world is trying to destroy imperialism, is racist. Those material improvements, like the rest of our privileges, are taken from the people of the world. These demands aren't directed toward the destruction of Amerika, but toward helping white people cope better with life in an imperialist system. (While Vietnamese and Cubans struggle daily in life-and-death encounters with our same enemy, white women should agitate for better working conditions in their work places!) All of recent history shows us that the imperialist pigs are willing to make great sacrifices, grant huge demands, to keep white people on their side. Any demand made by white people short of the total annihilation of imperialism can be granted by the pigs—and will be.

A real strategy for victory is not to get masses of people to fight with you for a few more crumbs—day-care centers for white women, equal pay with white men—but to fight with them against the source of our real oppression—pig Amerika. Our sad-eyed sisters' programs will never result in liberation for women. The strategy to win in Amerika is the strategy of international insurrection against imperialism, and we, with them, must become revolutionaries and join the fight.

Our liberation as individuals and as women is possible only when it is understood as a political process—part of the formation of an armed white fighting force. Political power grows out of the barrel of a gun, and the struggle to gain and use political power against the state is the struggle for our liberation.

Various political tendencies toward separatist women's movements do not recognize this reality. Our sad- but fiery-eyed sisters who proclaim that they—white women—can do it alone, do not see that a separatist strategy is doomed to failure. Imperialism draws its power from the control and exploitation of vast areas of the world—the oppression of white women is the source of only a tiny part of its power. They could easily grant our demands for a few improvements in our lives—demands which don't even answer or change the depth of our oppression—just as the pigs have done many times before. Only when we fight with the rest of the people of the world do we have any strategic power to destroy the pigs. Most of the separatist theories do not clearly define the enemy as US imperialism, so their programs do not focus on the source of our oppression.

Separatist women's movements have also formed mostly out of weakness and fear of men and "male strengths." By accepting the pigs' definition of what is male (and therefore, somehow, bad . . .), our sisters have ignored the need to formulate and criticize theory and strategy, the need to fight for our freedom. Because these skills are necessary to build the revolution, women too must develop and use them, changing ourselves, breaking out of our passivity and inexperience. Clearly men, too, must change—but this will happen only if we are openly Communist in our struggle with them, changing them as we make the revolution. Separatist programs and organizations have accepted the chauvinism of men as unchangeable—at least for the immediate future—and thus their strategy is to weaken men and revolutionary male leadership so that women (in the weakness they have accepted as unchangeable) can be equal or superior. By assuming that men can't change, women separatists accept their own defeat and inability to be transformed into Communists through our struggle. The only way we can win is to build a consciously Communist white movement, ready to ally and fight with the rest of the world's peoples. The pig role forced on men and women by Amerikan society has corroded our minds and strength—the only way to change that role is to destroy the pigs who want us to passively accept it. The way to win is to seize time and leadership by becoming Communists ourselves, and to show other people, especially men, the possibility and necessity for them to be Communists, too—to build a revolutionary Communist movement. This is our responsibility as revolutionary women, and we must take leadership in this struggle.

White women have long been the most hated symbols of

white privilege to Africans, Indians, and Black Americans—to colonial men, the desirable object whose price was death. To colonial women, the imperialist standards of beauty—white, superficial, and plastic—have been forced on them until they came to hate themselves and their own beauty. But this white woman-oppressor is also oppressed within the mother country. Some parts of our oppression are concrete—imperialist schools track us into jobs as secretaries and housewives; we get lower wages than men, and fewer job opportunities; we are chained to a family structure that allows us no freedom. Amerika's rulers use us as surplus and domestic labor to contribute to their pile of profits. We are objectified and used sexually—the Amerikan culture has totally dehumanized us, destroying the possibility for satisfying sexual relationships between men and women. We are taught to see other women as our enemies and to compete with them, wiping out any chance for strong, revolutionary human relationships between us as women.

Imperialism has colonized our minds and the minds of those around us. Its institutions become part of a false consciousness of what women should be. Men believe that we are stupid, inferior to them, and that the only way they can be strong is to dominate and possess a woman. Their strength comes from making and keeping us weak—by defining what we should look like, how we should act, and what we should think and feel. We are made into and kept half-people, dependent and passive by definition. We let one man define our lives for us in monogamous relationships that chain us to the limits he sets and reinforce our passivity, isolation from reality, and fear of fighting for our freedom. We are taught that we should not want or expect or care about sexual satisfaction—and men are taught that sex can only be a physical encounter with an object made solely for his satisfaction. Imperialist Amerika teaches its children that this is love, and that this is how we must "live."

But not only men believe it—we have accepted and internalized these pig standards ourselves. The pigs want us to be conservative, stabilizers of things as they are, of the family, of security. We have been well-taught by Amerikan society that women are weak—that thinking, struggling, and fighting are unfeminine. Even in the middle of revolutionary struggle we objectify each other, using and reinforcing the same imperialist standards that we have been taught—almost denying our sisters their intelligence and humanity if they are physically attractive. In the past we saw only the woman imperialism wanted us to see, and hated her, becoming isolated from each other, fighting against each other for survival and for the recognition of men. We saw the same weakness in ourselves and grew to hate our own powerlessness.

This is an imperialist view of women—a Miss America standard of beauty, desirability, success, and docility. She is a pig-woman. We all still believe in her, though her power grows less every day. Her image was imbedded deep within us—who among us could think she was really beautiful or desirable or strong, measured against such a standard? For too long this standard kept us from building Communist women and from building full human relationships—either with men or with other women. We are taught to hate our bodies, mistrust our minds, fear ourselves and everybody else.

WE CAN'T GET NO SATISFACTION

But now we are beginning to break out of this life. We say to our comrades that we can do more than merely fight the painful effects of imperialism—but we must break out through the pigs' alternatives and definitions. We will undermine and smash the pigs themselves—the people and system of imperialism. Our victory will be political and military—so we must pick up the gun and use it until this system is dead. We must open and lead another armed front against Amerika —this time here, behind enemy lines—in the gut of the mother country. A woman who arms herself and fights the pig imperialists takes the first step toward becoming free, because she is fighting against what really keeps her down in a way that can win. What this means for us now is that we must begin building a strategy to engage in massive violence and armed struggle as soon as possible—to retaliate immediately when Fred Hampton is murdered, to make the pigs pay a high price for My Lai. This is the way we become revolutionaries—by making the revolution, by fighting to destroy the state.

Victory requires building a Communist movement—a movement of men and women working and fighting to make the revolution happen, because the society we build after imperialism is destroyed will be part of a world Communist system. It is still a struggle for any of us to be Communists—imperialism has totally corroded and distorted our minds and relationships with each other. But though our sad-eyed sisters think it impossible, we have begun to change men and ourselves into Communists able to deal with each other in a revolutionary way—in order to win.

But they are right about the heaviness of the obstacles confronting us—male chauvinism still permeates society, and in many ways all of us. This is why women must often be together as women within any revolutionary white movement. Combatting our hatred and fear of each other as women, and struggling together against male chauvinism in our comrades, we break down the pieces of Amerika still hidden inside our minds and begin to become revolutionaries. Our new strength comes out of understanding and destroying our oppression—both by fighting against its real source and by transforming the misfits that it creates into whole people. The only reason for separateness is to strengthen us in our fight against the state. It enables us to fight together against our oppression, breaking out and overcoming it together through the struggle. The relationships that we build between us after our self-hatred and competition are broken down reflect the transformation that happens as we become revolutionaries. Women sleeping with other women, developing full sexual and political relationships with each other, indicates that we are beginning to really destroy the bourgeois values we have believed in for such a long time, and apply revolutionary values to every facet of our lives. As we break down these pig attitudes toward each other, and begin to discover what revolutionary love is, we learn how to build satisfying relationships with men too. But the basis of all relationships that we have with each other—men and women both—must be the war that we are making against the state. That is the reason that our old imperialist values must break down—so we can become better revolutionaries, better able to make war and destroy the pig. That is the reason monogamous relationships must be broken up—so that the people involved, but especially the women, can become whole people, self-reliant and independent, able to carry out whatever is necessary to the revolution.

Building women's leadership is another part of the reason for separateness; it is through the struggle with other women that our leadership grows strong. The struggle of women for leadership of the revolutionary movement must be understood as a struggle to deal with and meet the necessity of making the revolution. Our belief that we should be leaders of the whole movement, as Communists, leads to a political struggle with men that changes and expands the philosophy of the movement. Separatist movements say that leadership qualities—theoretical understanding, political struggle, fighting hard against the state—are "male" (and thus somehow automatically bad), and therefore reject all leadership in a totally anti-communist way. These qualities, in fact, are neither male nor bad, and are necessary to the development of all leaders. When men use these skills in a chauvinist way against women and their leadership, their male chauvinism must be smashed, but these qualities themselves are necessary for the revolution. It is by struggling together with other women that we best develop these skills and become revolutionaries.

Completely transformed from passive wimps, afraid of blood or danger or guns, satisfied with the limitations set on us by hated slave relationships with one man, we become revolutionary women—whole people struggling in every way, at every level, to destroy the dying pig system that has tried to keep us and the rest of the world under its total control. But our leadership cannot be just exemplary, it must also be strategic. In the past, few of us ever thought that we could formulate strategy or theory. Learning these skills together with other women, taking responsibility for our own political development, has broken down our male chauvinism and self-hatred, preparing us to better struggle with men's chauvinism toward us.

We have begun our fight against imperialism, the source of our oppression. In the fight we become transformed—and must transform ourselves—into revolutionaries in order to win, but this change is only real when we are actually fighting and destroying Amerika, ripping her apart from the inside as the rest of the world destroys her from the outside. We are honky tonk women in the gut of the mother country. We demand—not "Bread and Roses" to make our lives a little better and shield us from struggle a little more—but bombs and rifles to join the war being fought now all over the globe to destroy the motherfuckers responsible for this pig world.

Inside The Weather Machine

A Weatherwoman

Something strange and new has occurred in a revolutionary organization—the emergence of strong woman leadership in Weatherman. Women who previously were passive and sat quietly at meetings have become political leaders (thinkers as well as fighters). The myth of the "exceptional" political woman is breaking down. Generally what occurred in the past was that a few women in each organization were recognized as leaders by adopting male conceptions of leadership, aggressiveness, domination and the whole ego trip. We've learned that all women can become political. Much of the leadership of Weatherman throughout the country are women. This article is an attempt to show what conditions were present which allowed women to develop.

A conference was held under the leadership of Weatherman in September 1969. Most of the people not directly in Weatherman (including this author at the time) came because of their stress on violence and internationalism. What remained as a common thread throughout the whole conference was the desire to totally mess up this racist country. We got tired of thinking that the only way white poeple could support black struggles was by buying guns for them, or even worse, by picketing or petitioning. If blacks could fight it was racist to simply say "right on." We saw a need to identify openly with all Third World struggles and create another front here in this country which would further weaken it from within. The Algerian war might not have gone on so long if French people were into ripping up the mother country and creating havoc and chaos. All of us understood and desired to fight here, not in some far-off romantic mountain but in the heart of the monster. We had to pick up the gun.

After the first day of the conference the women split off and met separately. Much of the discussion was on how male chauvinism holds women back as revolutionaries. Male chauvinism is basically the way men see women as sex objects who can't either think very well or fight. We are something either to be laughed at and protected if we are weak or put down and fought against if we are strong. Women are also male chauvinist in the way they view themselves. Men's image of women reinforces the image women have of themselves and the image women have of themselves reinforces the image men have of them. The problem is to break into this cycle and that is precisely what women in Weatherman are trying to do by becoming a political force. The male chauvinism in women in the past prevented us from assuming any real kind of role in the revolution because most of us felt there was very little we could do.

In conjunction with the insights developed over male chauvinism, women spoke about the need to break up monogamous relationships. These relationships are usually built around weakness and dependency. They're usually one man/one woman, although varieties spring up. Women identify themselves through their men and usually get introduced as someone's girl. Monogamous relationships are set up because people see them as the only way to feel secure and loved. What this creates is a situation where both members are into trying to make each other feel safe about their place in the world. They can always hide in each other when the reality becomes too heavy; they can always protect each other from having to fight oppression. This doesn't work in reality. These relationships generally end up in unhappiness for both the men and women involved. Any woman who has had these kind of relationships knows the unhappiness and fear of being left alone. We clung to the men because we had no other identity. Any woman without a man feels like a failure because in a sense she isn't possessed by anyone. Private property is what our system is based on and women were used and saw themselves as an extension of this private property.

In Cleveland we began to see concrete examples of how monogamy politically weakened women. One woman told how she and her boyfriend were working in a Weatherman summer project together. She contributed very little and sort of hung around. When her boyfriend went to jail for a month she assumed some leadership of the summer project. Her fears about herself diminished, yet immediately upon his return she retired into the background again. Most of the women present had been through a similar experience. We then realized that if we were to become revolutionaries these relationships had to be broken because people had to become self-reliant to do what has to be done to fight the state. Our new strength allowed us to develop relationships not based on needs of security which expressed themselves by having to be owned. Instead we began to have several relationships and began to feel free to allow others to develop these relationships without the intense jealousy we used to feel.

A woman's action took place directly after Cleveland in Pittsburgh with all the Weatherwomen. It was essentially a demonstration at a school and a fight broke out with the pigs. The important thing that came out of the action was that women could plan and carry out struggles against the state. We came back from Pittsburgh feeling pretty together due to our understanding of male chauvinism, and having fought. The important part of the Pittsburgh action was that it built self-confidence in ourselves and helped the development of a new woman that is going to make a revolution. Pittsburgh did not say that women could do it alone; both are needed in the fight against the system. Moreover the fight against male chauvinism can only be carried out together by people struggling against their chauvinism. Separatism can only lead to a continuation of chauvinism and an unsuccessful revolution.

Many women's groups are into saying "fuck men; we can do it alone." While the struggle with men is hard, there is no other way to make the revolution. We have to start learning how to build this new society where people don't destroy one another but build each other. Otherwise our revolution is bullshit and we become like the Man.

Coming back, we moved into a collective with men and women, creating a new life style for ourselves with the revolution as our goal. We had to internally make ourselves strong to fight the pig. Strength means thinking strategically, militarily and politically, something most women think they are unable to do. Men who had been leaders in the collective became totally passive to us. Leadership in the past had always meant domination, with men generally competing with one another for the prize of power. What happened was that women increasingly took on leadership in the collectives, but [leadership of] a different kind. Our leadership attempted to build people and not play the whole ego trip.

In our collectives the new kind of chauvinism we have is the passivity to women, which is being used as a weapon against us. Specifically, passivity means that men will not front us on our ideas; some will withdraw sexually because they cannot dominate and they sometimes allow women to do the strategic thinking while they sit quietly. Fortunately this passivity is breaking down now as we become more used to dealing with each other as equals. Passivity is the one thing that keeps people from changing and getting better. It destroys leadership and drags everyone down. When men first became passive to us we didn't see it as a wepon but the more we understand chauvinism the more we realize it is just as harmful as the old put-down.

At the same time our monogamous relationships broke up because we simply didn't need them any more. We began not to have to identify ourselves through men and could become total human beings. Women began digging one another; jealousy and competition were not necessary anymore because our point of existence was the revolution; and the old way of life became intolerable to us. The men in the collective were also changing their conceptions of women. Although their chauvinism was not less than [that of] other men in the movement they saw the necessity to change.

The women acted together in these struggles. Relationships were built around these struggles and not on bourgeois conceptions of love. No more crying because we were being fucked over by men. We were forced to fight it out with them when they tried to make us feel stupid.

We do not view ourselves as sex objects but as part of the revolution. Sex isn't something to happen isolated from daily work. Destroying the one man/one woman relationship was perhaps the most liberating thing that happened to us. We could speak at meetings without being uptight of being on an ego trip and most important we were upfront at demonstrations along with men. We became self-reliant and don't have to protect anyone, we are forced to struggle and it makes life more meaningful. We changed because of the necessity of the times, and dig the changes. The fight to destroy the shit in us is part of building a new society.

Fighting alongside people we believe to be our brothers and sisters gives us strength. Sex becomes entirely different without jealousy. Women who never saw themselves making it with women began digging each other sexually. People who live together and fight together fuck together. What Weatherman is doing is creating new standards for men and women to relate to. We are trying to make sex non-exploitative as we don't use our bodies to control situations. We are making something new, with the common denominator being the revolution. Weathermen from all over the country can dig one another. In the last edition of RAT it was mentioned in an article that "heavy fucking" went on at the national convention which was a criticism of us. I'm not sure what "heavy fucking" is but knowing that we may never all be together again makes us serious about what we do, whether it be fucking or struggling over new ideas.

This system oppresses us as women and we hate it. Once our political consciousness is raised we can see a connection between our oppressor and what this country does to the 3rd world. Male supremacy means dominating and Amerika is about dominating and controlling. This is how they make us feel powerless. The system we live under is the oppressor and uses men to carry out their policies. By destroying this system we must destroy the relationships we had based on domination.

Women have an added advantage in becoming revolutionaries. Who suspects a well-dressed woman of carrying a gun or a bomb in her pocketbook? We can be great terrorists as well as political leaders. Power still comes from the barrel of a gun.

In the movement monogamous relationships are even more oppressive. Men are into openly putting down women if they begin leading. Most women realize that leadership by manipulation is bad because they have been controlled most of their lives. Men can learn from women and become better leaders themselves. Women with high political consciousness are still asked for "dinner dates," which is a subtle way of asking for a fuck. The same dishonesty this country uses in dealing with people the movement uses between men and women. So far Weatherman is the only white group that gives an alternative to relations between men and women.

This article is not saying that we have destroyed chauvinism or monogamy. The struggle still goes on. What this article does say is that we are changing as people. When we are feeling weak we still want the reassurance of a man and reinforce our own weakness. To fight the styles of behavior we've been taught to follow all our lives is hard but we know that those styles suck and becoming revolutionaries allows us to change. The time has to be seized if we are to bring this motherfucker down and women must play a large part in it. The fight against chauvinism must go on at the same time we fight the pig, or the struggle is just a tea party. Women must pick up the gun and kill the pig. Our liberation depends on this fight as well as seeing this fight as part of a worldwide struggle with all the people of the world.

Weatherman Politics And The Women's Movement

Bread and Roses collective

The problem that many of us face is that our women's movement has not yet developed a sense or complete strategy of what is "right." It then becomes all too tempting to accept—or feel pressured to accept—what someone else says is right, whether or not we believe it. The current mood produces enormous pressure from Weatherman to do what they have defined as "correct" work. Even though most of the women's movement has believed that an intellectual understanding of what is wrong is not enough to compel people to act, to take risks, to become revolutionaries, many women find themselves accepting a political position that does not stem from their own understanding or experience.

Weatherman raises important questions that reflect real social conditions: domestic repression, defeat of American imperialism by the Vietnamese, strong racist and anti-communist attitudes among many whites. The challenge is a valid one. Weatherman is important because they see the same problems we do, but our reactions and partial answers are different. We must confront their politics to further define our strategy for the women's movement.

I. Weatherman believes that American imperialism—the present stage of capitalism—must be destroyed. They believe the Vietnamese and other Third World movements are defeating American imperialism. Internally, they believe that America is in a revolutionary situation: blacks, Puerto Ricans, Chicanos and *young* people from different classes, are fighting to destroy American imperialism. They state that people in this country, especially white middle-class youth, must give up

Excerpted from *Women*, Winter 1970. Reprinted by permission.

their "white-skin privilege," which they maintain off the backs of blacks and Vietnamese, and then fight alongside of the blacks. And Weatherman believes they must organize other whites, especially working-class whites, to confront their racism and anti-communism, to join the struggle, and become explicit Communists.

Weatherman criticizes the American movement for its nationalism: they criticize us for organizing around our do-your-own-thing liberation and around domestic economist demands. They accuse us of reneging on our responsibility to international Communist revolutionaries who are fighting American imperialism. They note that the movement has not built a revolutionary movement; and they therefore believe the movement has done no good.

Some of Weatherman's criticism is well-founded. Our internationalism has been sporadic and apologetic. We were not exempt from the effects of the Cold War—for years SDS had an anti-communist clause on its membership card, and we maintained an uncritical rejection of "dictatorial" communism. Most damaging was the fact that we thought imperialism was just a bad foreign policy. We had not realized that imperialism is part and parcel of the very structure of capitalism as it exists now in the US.

The Vietnam War, actual visits to Vietnam and Cuba, and renewed study of Marxism have helped us define ourselves as part of an international movement. But most of us certainly have a long way to go before we act as true Communists and true internationalists. However, it is unclear that "internationalism" means romanticizing or trying to transport to this country the models of revolution that have worked in peasant, agricultural countries. Although we can learn important lessons from these revolutions, this romanticism has led us to ignore the lessons and achievements of youth movements in countries more like ours—France, England, Japan, Germany, and Mexico.

It is also true, as Weatherman charges, that much of the American movement has been demoralized by a sense of powerlessness, which often leads to inaction due to fear of failure. The Panthers understand: "The spirit of the people is stronger than the Man's technology." People must learn to fight, first in self-defense, and then collectively against chosen institutions. We must look for places where people are struggling and be willing to take risks, to help them fight, instead of waiting until all our "constituencies" are "organized." We are also the people in this country; and we can begin to strike out for ourselves against the institutions that oppress and anger us—at the same time [that] we are reaching out to other people.

Weatherman—and other SDS groups—have also pushed us to realize that we must have a much more complete class strategy for fighting and winning in this country (instead of our past mechanistic faith in reaching more and more "constituencies"). Weatherman and the Yippies have also indicated how disruptive action could be used (if there were follow-up) to bring up the hard political issues which do not necessarily arise in daily work or conversation.

It is important that we learn from these questions that Weatherman has raised. But we disagree with them about what a revolutionary movement is.

II. We do not think that an American anti-imperalist movement—or a domestic terrorist movement attacking centers of power—could by themselves produce *conditions* that would end imperialism internationally. And it certainly seems that the Weatherman timetable for revolution is off.

Vietnam has won the war against the US; but the US is still there, fucking them over. Guerrilla movements outside of Southeast Asia are neither strong nor necessarily anti-imperialist. Insurgencies have been checked or defeated in Bolivia, the Congo, Brazil, South Africa, Ghana and the Dominican Republic. And neo-colonialism has successfully created potentially stable capitalist regimes in Nigeria, Chile, Mexico, Senegal and Kenya. There is no evidence at this time tha the Third World is about to rise up in solidarity with the blacks in this country even if the blacks try to do it alone. (Weatherman has stated that such an uprising is imminent and will wipe out American fascism/imperialism.)

Radicals must confront the possibility that successful Third World attacks against American imperialism will create an economic and political crisis in this country that could swing towards either fascism or a communist revolution. Because so many Americans benefit from imperialism in the short run, any threat to that system could intensify the backlash and create a government based on racism and anti-communism. We must show people that they have a political stake in giving up these short-range benefits for the obvious long-range benefits of a society free of economic exploitation, male chauvinism, racial oppression.

It is obvious to us that the movement is now pitifully small. We think that if the polarization of the country occurs now that we lose—and that the movement in white and black communities will become the scapegoat the fascists would try to use to turn people to the right.

Yet many of the white people we've met organizing—Appalachians in Chicago or welfare mothers in Boston—despite their car and TV—are fucked over all the time. In fact, more and more people in this country—women, farm and factory workers, GI's—are realizing that they don't have any *real power* in relation to the class that runs and profits from this country. Our problem is to reach people and organize them with political tools so that they have a gut understanding of why that exploitation and powerlessness must end. (Weatherman thinks they should be labelled and fought as "pigs" unless they immediately fight with Weatherman against U.S. imperialism.)

III. A second major element of the Weatherman analysis is their belief that blacks, under the vanguard leadership of the Black Panther Party, are fighting a revolution now. Weatherman claims that white leaders are holding the white people back from joining them, for fear of losing their white-skin privilege. Weatherman is wrong in several ways.

First, while the BPP has obviously played a crucial role in moving the black movement left, it does not follow that most American blacks are now fighting revolutionaries. The government is able to use repression against revolutionary leaders because they know the people aren't ready to die for the same vision and society the leaders are. The reason Huey Newton can be kept in jail is because most blacks are not yet willing to fight and die for socialism, as he is. (Similarly, it is not enough for us, as self-conscious radicals, to know that white working-class women are oppressed; it is *their* self-perception that counts, and they will become revolutionaries only when they see the need and possibility for revolution themselves.)

A second weakness is their assumption that racism will be ended if whites reject their "white-skin privilege." Many whites in this country do not actually have significant material privileges or power as white workers, women, etc., because they continue to be exploited by capitalism. Their "white privilege" usually amounts to psychological, social, and relatively minor economic gains (like the "privilege" of an unpaid mortgage, or organized black competition for their jobs). These privileges seem particularly crucial since such whites lack real power or mobility. The irony is that many of these Americans—who would gain most from a socialist revolution—are tightly caught in the grips of the racist media, the church, etc. (For example, white working-class kids who liked some radical leaflets distributed at East Boston High School were also influenced by teachers' charges that they were fools and were being manipulated. The brainwashing about brainwashing goes deep.)

What is very important for us to understand is that a socialist society that fights male chauvinism and racism will be much better for most whites (as well as Third World people) than imperialism could ever be. This does not mean—as Weatherman fears—that the crux of this improvement would be that everybody's material possessions will increase as we domestically redistribute the many goods produced in our country. The reason socialism will deliver better lives for all of us is that such a society would meet collectively our real needs—rather than the artificial consumption needs superimposed on us all now.

"From each according to his means; to each according to

his needs." The point is that people's basic needs are not being met in this society—as we are finding out through the women's movement. Most of the women who have become active in the women's movement are terribly oppressed by their condition in the nuclear family—as unpaid workers, sex objects, socializers, etc. (See Juliet Mitchell, *Women: The Longest Revolution*, Nov. '66, New Left Review; Margaret Benston, *Political Economy of Women's Liberation*, Sept. '69, Monthly Review.) This condition of oppression is quantitatively—not qualitatively—worse for women married to men working in factories than it is for women married to white-collar professionals (even though they have different amounts of material possessions). Such oppressed and exploited women are proving—through the rapid growth of the women's movement—that they are very willing to fight for the political and social and economic conditions that will liberate women. Even in our short experience, we have seen that while fighting for such a revolution, women's consciousness and actual conditions have changed—i.e., as part of a collective movement, they no longer "need" their racism to protect them against a threatening oppressive world. It is absolutely essential that the women's movement directly and quickly confront racism among ourselves and with any white people we might reach (something we have not really begun to do). Yet, we also believe that the time women will be able to fight and defeat such racism will be when they are moving collectively and fighting to end their real exploitation and oppression as women.

Such a model for individual change grows out of our feeling that a socialist revolution means that we—as women—are going to be part of the class that will overthrow the ruling class from power and share in the task of serving the real needs of the people.

That model for change includes us as participants. Women —as well as blacks, Chicanos, youth—will help destroy the power of the ruling class and share in the task of serving the real needs of the people. There must be a concrete reason for people to give up their white-skin privilege, and any strategy that aims to defeat racism must start from the consciousness whites have of themselves.

When Weatherman talks about ending racism, they assume that a good "fighting" rap will lead to sudden rejection of privilege. Their Communist ideology will be imposed by them—a small cadre of revolutionaries—and the "masses" of Americans will be dealt with accordingly. That strategy has at least two damaging effects: it delegitimizes people, or possibly polarizes them to be even more hostile; and it alienates the few chosen revolutionaries from the rest of the movement and lands them in prison, or even dead. Their proclamation that it's revolutionary and necessary to go to jail or die, and that the rest of the movement (weirdness) can fuck itself, seem diametrically opposed to their own Weatherman paper:

On repression: "retreat to survive to fight again"; on masses and the party: "It is a movement diametrically opposed to the elitist idea that only leaders are smart enough to accept full revolutionary conclusions. It is a movement built on faith in the masses of people. . . . The party is not a substitute for [the movement] and in fact is totally dependent on it."

Many of us are looking for ways to put ourselves on the line, as black people are, and to support blacks. But mounting up heavy felony charges does not seem to be delivering any solid political support for the blacks within the white communities.

IV. Finally, as women, we are very angry at Weatherman's male chauvinism in theory and action. A woman from a N.Y. Weatherman collective says: "We smashed individualism, we smashed our chauvinism. We define ourselves in terms of revolution." Whose terms, whose revolution, for what? The machismo and militarism characterizing Weatherman action and literature do not merely reflect tactical errors or improper application of theory. Indeed, their male chauvinism stems from a basic misunderstanding of the nature of women's oppression.

They believe that women are oppressed by male chauvinism, but are also racist oppressors in an imperialist society.

They admit that the nuclear family is oppressive, an oppression that crosses class lines, but state that many women also have "white-skin privilege." Their logic is that the primary contradiction is imperialism. Strategically, they conclude that the priority is to fight imperialism, to engage women in anti-imperialist struggles, to support blacks, and to fight male chauvinism when it occurs within those struggles. Women's Liberation is but a part of a larger anti-imperialist struggle; it is through supporting—and emulating—blacks and Vietnamese that women will be liberated.

Women in Weatherman are thus forced into a double bind. Not only are they told that their oppression, which they share with all other women, is less important or compelling than the oppression of blacks or Vietnamese, but their revolutionary commitment is measured by male chauvinist standards; they must struggle in terms defined by men. A woman becomes a heroine in Weatherman circles when she is a tougher, better fighter than the men, regardless of whether she's helping women's liberation. In fact, one woman was expelled from a Weatherman collective for "male chauvinism" because she wasn't militant enough.

Many of the characteristics which one needs in order to become respected in the movement—like the ability to argue loud and fast and aggressively and to excel in the "I'm more revolutionary than you" style of debate—are traits which our society consistently cultivates in men and discourages in women from childhood. But those traits are neither inherently male nor universally human; rather they are particularly appropriate to a brutally competitive society.

—Kathy McAfee & Myrna Wood, *Leviathan,* June '69

The Weatherman position on monogamy illustrates how women are delegitimized individually and collectively. The women's movement has been very critical of the present institution of the nuclear family; the woman's structural oppression (her economic dependence on her husband, her unpaid labor within the home), the bad division of labor, and the belief instilled in most women that they have no identity or existence outside of their marriage—all prevent love between adults. Another evil is that the nuclear family forces women to view children as their individual responsibility and property, through whom they try to "live." In other words, our analysis tells us that an attack on the bad prescriptive effects of the nuclear family must be an attack on its material basis socially and politically—and not dependent on individual solutions.

The key to ending the nuclear family as a prescriptive institution is to end women's oppression and discrimination in the *entire* society. For until there is good communal child care and unalienating work that can be done by women and men equally, the nuclear family will remain a relatively good economic and social shelter for women in our capitalist society.

Weatherman has chosen to ignore this complex oppression, and instead decreed the end of monogamy within their collectives, with very destructive consequences. First, their approach is voluntarist—i.e., they believe an individual woman can will herself to be different, which ignores the social reality that women's pressure for monogamy grew from their unequal position in the entire society (in the home, at work, and in the movement). It is interesting that Weatherman chose to deal with monogamy rather than nuclear families. Such emphasis does not deal collectively with the daily pressures—like children—that most women face. (Instead, children become the woman's full-time problem and responsibility again—thus guaranteeing that only a small elite of young women without families could ever participate in Weatherman struggles.)

In addition, such a dismissal of a woman's present need for the nuclear family while she is being forced to be revolutionary according to Weatherman male standards raises the question of the motivation behind the decree. They argue that what is wrong with a deep monogamous relationship with one person is that it involves so much responsibility that you are prevented from taking risks. Instead of recognizing that a person can move out of individual problems to take risks only through a real sense of strength and independence, they stress cutting off all personal ties and responsibilites. This model may be a relief to the men—freeing them from emotional involvement and responsibility. But it is liberating for neither men nor women. Such a denial of love and personal involvement may produce effectiveness and homogeneity and loyalty—but it doesn't produce freedom.

We believe that women must make revolutions for themselves as well as other people. Women's oppression has been ignored and used by other socialist movements before. There is no reason why women should allow this to happen in America now.

Yet, we also realize that this paper only indicates the problems for the women's movement—and does not pretend to answer finally the question of how *we* can fight racism and imperialism as part of the fight for our own liberation. We hope that Bread and Roses and other groups will begin to act experimentally on some of the ideas and politics expressed in this critique of Weatherman—and will then write about their mistakes, as well as their successes.

National War Council

When we expelled PL from SDS last June, we for the first time put our politics above bourgeois notions of how to carry on political struggle. That act opened up the possibility of SDS becoming a vital revolutionary form for mass movement. Since then, the Chicago National Action, followed by tremendous motion during the Washington Mobilization and general development of political theory and strategy, have created a context in which the National Council meeting, December 26-31, will be the birth of the new SDS.

The last five years have been a succession of isolated flashes. Every instance in which motion has been expressed through individualism, (individual or collective) self-interest, or narrow issue orientation has proven sooner or later to be a defeat. We have never been able to sustain masses of people's involvement in struggle. The growth of political consciousness among kids in general has happened not because of any coherent strategy of our own, but despite its non-existence.

The most striking characteristic of the failures of the past is that those struggles—the majority—which were not victories and did not raise the level of action and consciousness suffered from a fundamental misunderstanding of power. "Political power grows from the barrel of a gun." People's movements around the globe have understood where power is, and it is their armed struggles for liberation which will bring American imperialism down. Our task is twofold: to understand and pinpoint where power is, and to make ourselves part of the international war which is a self-conscious strategy for seizing it. The success of the revolution—the realization of our highest aspirations for a better world—demands of necessity a strategy of international armed struggle.

The role of SDS as a national revolutionary mass organiza-

From *Fire*, December 6, 1969

tion is crucial. The youth movement, until now incoherent and fragmented, has to become a strong and offensive political force. We need SDS as a forum for the ideological struggle that will build our understanding of how we move among youth, how we can provide political leadership for the white kids in this country.

Our program should provide a context for the support and interpretation of the highest levels of struggle in the country and the world. This is especially key to building a revolutionary movement in the mother country. In Watts or Bolivia, when a bank is blown up, everyone can dig it: living as colonial subjects gives them a basis for understanding U.S. imperialism as their enemy, and for seeing attacks upon imperialist property and power as a part of their struggle. But part of the pacifying effect of our white-skin privileges is our inability to define clearly the source of our own oppression. White Americans do not immediately see an act of sabotage or a colonial people's war of liberation as a blow against our same enemy. For us in the mother country, blowing up property also needs some blowing of minds.

Changing people's consciousness can only happen if at the same time we are changing the political reality of the country. We should be leading large numbers of young people on the campuses and in the streets in struggles that focus on fighting for power. The highest acts of armed struggle, of course, do the most damage to the Man. But lower-level actions, like violent street-actions, have a real effect on the ability of pig Amerika to function all over the globe. We have to create chaos and bring about the disintegration of pig order. The future of our struggle is the future of crime in the streets.

Through the practice of struggle we become revolutionaries. The concrete/steel reality of fighting an urban/technological/mother country revolution is teaching us the identity between survival and transformation. The honky social forms we come out of turn out, not surprisingly, to be totally counter-revolutionary. Creating new forms for living—collectives, communist relationships—and destroying the bourgeois consciousness in ourselves that keeps us from being able to touch, love, and struggle with each other against the Man is part of and necessary to destroying imperialism.

We see the NC as a coming together of people who are out front in building the revolutionary youth movement. With all the shit that kids are bringing down, it's absurd to get hung up in parliamentary forms and the old notion of what a political convention should look like. We'll use plenaries, resolutions and parliamentary procedure when that helps us teach each other. But we see other forms, too, a lot of flexibility, and time for different groups of people to meet together, things like films, music, etc. It oughta be a gas. See you there.

Stormy Weather

FLINT, Mich. (LNS)—Weathermen, Weatherwomen, their friends and some of their critics met in a "war council" December 27-30. The gathering was a serious political meeting, although it had been widely billed as an outasight international youth culture freak show.

About four hundred young people from across the country made it to the bare Giant Ballroom in Flint to practice karate, rap in regional and collective meetings, dig a little music and hear the Weather Bureau lay down its political line for revolution in Amerika.

The Weatherman SDSers, who sometimes refer to themselves as the Weathermachine or the Weathernation or Weatherland, called the meeting to try to bring together various parts of the radical movement and other young people, including those turned on and turned off by Weatherman politics.

"We've made a lot of mistakes," said Bernardine Dohrn, a Weatherman leader. The meeting was planned to make amends for some of these mistakes—such as the hostility shown by Weathermen for the rest of the movement—and to broaden support for Weatherman politics and actions.

The meeting place was decked out in large colored banners of revolutionary leaders—Che, Ho, Fidel, Malcolm X, Eldridge—hanging from the ceiling. One entire wall of the ballroom was covered with alternating black and red posters of murdered Illinois Panther leader Fred Hampton.

An enormous cardboard machine gun symbolizing Weatherman's commitment to armed struggle also hung from the ceiling. The Weathermachine began to gather on Saturday

Excerpted from *San Francisco Good Times,* January 8, 1970

morning, December 27. The first few people to arrive were greeted with a grisly scene—the night before, a shooting had taken place at the ballroom; a bullet had passed through several of the paper-thin walls and killed a customer inside. His blood still covered a corner of the ballroom floor. A lot of cops were around. (Later, the cops kept constant surveillance of the Weatherpeople, but there were no incidents, no arrests.)

Violence was the keynote of the long hours of talk that followed. For over a year, the New Left has expressed near-unanimity on the need for armed struggle to overturn U.S. imperialism. This came naturally out of a number of political experiences, including the civil rights movement, the ghetto rebellions and the Cuban revolution.

Broad sectors of the movement have welcomed the occupation of buildings on campuses and the destruction of draft boards and ROTC installations as steps in this direction. But the distinction between revolutionary armed struggle and violence for its own sake is a major point of contention between Weatherman and its critics.

While security people remained at the ballroom and decked it out with the banners and posters that gave it the flavor of a revolutionary cabaret, the delegates went temporarily to the Roman Catholic church/convent complex that served as housing and meeting space. Eventually, the National Council got underway.

While Weathermen had spoken of their desire to reconstitute SDS as a mass organization representing various points of view within the revolutionary movement, it was clear that Weatherman was running the show. This was a Weatherman meeting, with a handful of outsiders there to gawk, scowl, listen and occasionally to debate.

Old-time movement people at the meeting remarked, however, at the large number of unfamiliar faces there. True, there were the Weatherman founders, people who had played a major role in SDS in 1966-69, many of them from Columbia and other elite schools. But then there were dozens of new, young kids—long-hairs, street kids, a few of them only

13 or 14 years old, some of them from out-of-the-way places like Grand Rapids, Michigan, and Fall River, Massachusetts.

The strongest debate centered on the question of who is going to make the American revolution. Weatherman, along with many others in the movement, recognizes that the American revolution is part of the world struggle against US imperialism, a struggle for liberation from both colonial and capitalist oppression.

Weatherman's critics maintain, however, that Weatherman's internationalism is based on an analysis that ignores capitalist oppression in America. Weatherman sees revolutionary change in America as happening almost solely, if at all, as a belated reaction to a successful world revolution, including a successful revolt by the black colony inside the American mother country.

The logic of that view was expressed in a statement by Ted Gold, a top Weatherman, who said that "an agency of the people of the world" would be set up to run the US economy and society after the defeat of the US imperialism abroad.

A critic spoke up: "In short, if the people of the world succeed in liberating themselves before American radicals have made the American revolution, then the Vietnamese and Africans and the Chinese are gonna move in and run things for white America. It sounds like a John Bircher's worst dream. There will have to be more repression than ever against white people, but by refusing to organize people, Weatherman isn't even giving them half a chance."

"Well," replied Gold, "if it will take fascism, we'll have to have fascism."

Weatherman continues to promote the notion that white working people in America are inherently counterrevolutionary, impossible to organize, or just plain evil—"honky bastards," as many Weathermen put it.

Weatherman's bleak view of the post-revolutionary world comes from an analysis of American society that says that "class doesn't count, race does."

White workers are in fact fighting for their survival, insisted people doing organizing of factory workers in California. They claim that strikes for wage increases and job security can fairly easily be linked to an anti-imperialist analysis.

But Weatherman denies that survival is an issue for white workers. Weatherman leader Howie Machtinger derided white workers for desiring better homes, better food and essentially better lives.

Bob Avakian, from the Bay Area Revolutionary Union, argued that not only do white workers need these things for their survival, but that black people need them and want them, too. The several black people Weatherman had brought to the meeting shouted "Right on!" and waved their fists.

"If you can't understand that white workers are being screwed too, that they are oppressed by capitalism before they are racists, then that just shows your class origins," said Avakian.

Machtinger shot back, "When you try to defend honky workers who just want more privileges from imperialism, that shows *your* race origins."

The Weatherman position boiled down to inevitable race war in America, with very few "honkies"—except perhaps the four hundred people in the room and the few street kids or gang members who might run with them—surviving the holocaust.

That notion is linked to Weatherman's concept of initiating armed struggle *now* and not waiting to build mass white support—that is, a small but courageous white fighting force will do material damage that will weaken imperialism while the black liberation movement smashes the "imperialist motherfucker" by itself.

Machtinger talked a lot about how the black liberation movement is so far advanced at this point that the only thing left for white revolutionaries is to support blacks by fighting cops as a diversionary tactic.

The Giant Ballroom is a black-owned establishment in Flint's black ghetto. There was some fear of possible conflict between the blacks and the Weathermen, but relations were generally good. At first, neighborhood blacks didn't like being frisked as they entered the meeting hall. But later they cooperated with the friskers, who were checking everyone for drugs and weapons, and engaged the white radicals in lively discussions on the edge of the dance hall. The black concessionaires who had charged 45 cents for hot dogs when the meeting opened later reduced the price to 25 cents in a gesture of solidarity.

But the blacks who came to the meeting, as they stood alone on the fringes of the ballroom, argued strongly that it was "jive bullshit, just romantic" to think that at this stage the blacks alone can smash imperialism inside the mother country.

"We're just not that together yet," said one. "The man is coming down so fucking hard—look at the Panthers. They know they need white support, a white revolutionary movement too. Even Rob Williams split with the Republic of New Africa, which says you don't need white allies. He knows you do."

But Weatherman is adamant in saying that whites cannot be organized into a mass revolutionary movement. To say that they can or should, according to Weatherleaders, is "national chauvinism."

"The Panthers say they should," argued Avakian.

"Well, we don't agree with the Panthers on a lot of things," replied Machtinger.

Weathermen now talk less about a "strategy to win," more about their historic role as catalysts. They emphasize the need to establish a white revolutionary presence, to break movement people out of the traditional role of long-term base-building and passivity.

A new Weatherman catchword was "barbarism." The Weathermen see themselves as playing a role similar to that of the barbarian tribes, such as the Vandals and the Visigoths, who invaded and destroyed the decadent, corrupt Rome. (Some Weatherman even suggested changing their name to the Vandals. This would have a double meaning: first, a reference to the barbarian tribe; second, a reference to the line from Bob Dylan's "Subterranean Homesick Blues"—"The pump won't work 'cause the vandals stole the handle." The name Weatherman comes from a line in the same song—"You don't need a weatherman to know which way the wind blows.")

Unlike former SDS National Council meetings, which used to be held quarterly, no specific resolutions were debated or voted on. The only formal structure consisted of speeches by the small leadership group known as the Weather Bureau. There were many small discussions and regional meetings, too.

Bernardine Dohrn, former inter-organizational secretary of SDS for 1968-69, gave the opening speech on Saturday night, December 27. She began by admitting that a lot of Weatherman's actions have been motivated by "a white guilt trip."

"But we fucked up a lot anyway. We didn't fight around Bobby Seale when he was shackled at the Conspiracy Trial. We should have torn the courtroom apart. We didn't smash them when Mobe peace creeps hissed David Hilliard on Moratorium Day in San Francisco. We didn't burn Chicago down when Fred was killed."

Dohrn characterized violent, militant response in the streets as "armed struggle" against imperialism. "Since October 11 [the last day of the SDS national window-breaking action] we've been wimpy on armed struggle. . . . We're about being a fighting force alongside the blacks, but a lot of us are still honkies and we're still scared of fighting. We have to get into armed struggle."

Part of the armed struggle, as Dohrn and others laid it down, is terrorism. Political assassination—openly joked about by some Weathermen—and literally any kind of violence that is considered anti-social were put forward as legitimate forms of armed struggle.

"We were in an airplane," Dohrn related, "and we went up and down the aisle 'borrowing' food from people's plates. They didn't know we were Weathermen; they just knew we were *crazy.* That's what we're about, being crazy motherfuckers and scaring the shit out of honky America."

A twenty-foot-long poster adorned another wall of the ballroom. It was covered with drawings of bullets, each with a name. Along with the understandable targets like Chicago's Mayor Daley, the Weathermen deemed as legitimate enemies to be offed, among others, the Guardian (the radical newsweekly which has criticized Weatherman) and Sharon Tate.

"Honkies are going to be afraid of us," Dohrn insisted. She went on to tell the war council about Charlie Manson, the accused leader of the "Tate Eight," who allegedly murdered the movie star and several others on their Beverly Hills estate. Manson has been portrayed in the media as a Satanic, magnetic personality who held near-hypnotic sway over several women whom he lent out to friends as favors and brought along for the murder scene. The press also mentioned Manson's supposed fear of blacks—he reportedly moved into rural California to escape the violence of a race war.

Weatherman, the Bureau says, digs Manson. Not only for his understanding of white America—the killer purportedly wrote PIG in blood on the wall after the murder—but also because he's a "bad motherfucker."

(At least one press report explained the "PIG" on the wall by saying that Manson wrote that in order to throw suspicion on black people.)

"Dig it, first they killed those pigs, then they ate dinner in the same room with them, then they even shoved a fork into a victim's stomach! Wild!" said Bernardine.

The Weatherwomen also held a panel discussion on women's liberation. The fighting women, "the women who can carry bombs under their dresses like in *The Battle of Algiers*," were put forward as the only valid model for women's liberation. Women's liberation comes not only with taking leadership roles and with asserting yourself politically, they said, but also with overcoming hangups about violence.

In between the women's raps, the people sang a medley of Weatherman songs, high-camp numbers such as "I'm Dreaming of a White Riot," "Communism Is What We Do," and "We Need a Red Party." Spirited chants broke out, too: "Women Power!" "Struggling Power!" "Red Army Power!" "Sirhan Sirhan Power!" "Charlie Manson Power!" "Power to the People!" "Off the pig!"

Other women speakers pointed out that male chauvinism

has both an active, intolerant side and a passive, insulting side. They criticized the men in many Weatherman collectives for passively accepting women in leadership roles while refusing to engage in political struggle with them. Another speaker referred to the white women's role as reproducer, and characterized white women who bring up children in white America as "pig mothers."

The "crazy violent motherfucker" theme was picked up on Monday night in a long address by Weather Bureau member John "J.J." Jacobs, who laid out the "White Devil" theory of all world history, and traced the history of today's youth from the Beat Generation of the 1950s.

"We're against everything that's 'good and decent,' " J.J. declared. That notion, coupled with the White Devil theory, gives you an idea of what Weatherman means when it talks about "Serve the People Shit." Serving the people, relating to people's needs, is a crucial factor in many people's minds or organizing white working people in America, so that the revolution will come as class war and end in socialism, rather than come as race war and end in fascism.

Despite the cabaret atmosphere of the ballroom, the occasional music and the constant reference to orgies and "wargasm," Weatherman's reported swing to the youth culture/freak/hippie world didn't quite materialize. Some Weatherleaders appeared in beads, headbands and capes. But when it came down to digging music over hard politics, or combining them, the Weathermen chose serious discussion.

The Up Rock and Roll Band from Ann Arbor, Michigan, had been invited to make music for the war council, but when people broke up into small groups for more discussion, the Weather Bureau asked Up to leave. Things were too heavy for music. Later, the church/convent asked Weatherman to cancel a planned New Year's Eve party.

White Panther Party people, who came on the promise that Weatherman would soon be relating strongly to youth culture and hippiedom, went away somewhat disappointed.

While Weatherman has talked a lot about getting stoned and tripping, drugs were prohibited at the meeting and in the sleeping area, on security grounds. While Weatherman spoke favorably of the liberal use of grass, acid and alcohol, there was some criticism of self-indulgence in recent months. Some Weatherman said they had spent too much time in personal things, including drugs and sex, [and] not enough in furthering struggle.

Ken Kelley, a leader of the White Panthers and an editor of the Ann Arbor Argus, came away from the meeting calling it "heavy" and saying with awe, "Those guys are really serious." Kelley, who has been annoyed at the anti-Weatherman sentiment in the movement, affirmed that he was not about to join Weatherman.

There was, however, a clear celebration by Weatherman of white youth culture. While "honky bastards" were denounced, there was relatively little talk about the fight against " white-skin privilege," an important aspect of early Weatherman rhetoric.

While some of the non-Weathermen present remained critical, if not openly disdainful, of the Weathermen, there were others who concluded that it was important to take the Weathermen seriously.

The intense seriousness of the Weathermen themselves was very noticeable. They gave the impression of being internally disciplined, of being able to absorb the blows of repression. Eric Mann, Weatherman leader from Boston, is set to begin a seven-to-twelve-month jail term in mid-January—but this was treated rather matter-of-factly. Mann himself was the ideal stoic.

There is no sense of demoralization or fear on the surface, although it's clear that they're obviously in trouble: the vast majority of Weathermen are up on charges, many of them felonies, and future police/court actions based on testimony from undercover agents seem quite likely.

Some Weathermen said they did not expect to hold a public meeting of this sort ever again. . . .

Their strategy of "upping the cost of imperialism" is key. Heavy fighting in the streets, assassinations, bombings, terror and fear—chaos is a Weatherman word for this new strategy—may in fact do some material damage to America, and may encourage liberation fighters throughout the world. But the Flint war council has brought the Weathermen no closer than they ever were to a strategy for making revolution for all oppressed people in America, black, brown and white.

Weatherman Songbook

RED PARTY
(to the tune of "Dream Lover")

Every fight we lead astray
With no Red Party to show the way
With a line that we can use
To organize the fighting youth

Chorus:
Because we need a party to lead the fight
We need a Red Party
So we can learn to struggle right

Red Party fights to win
When we off pigs we wear a grin
We know from where the power comes
And the Party is the gun

Chorus

Someday from me and you
A Red Party will rise again
Someday I know it's true
It'll lead our RYM

When the Party needs some bread
Another banker winds up dead
Red Party likes to loot
But then again we prefer to shoot

Chorus

Spoken:
In 1902 Vladimir Illitch Lenin said that
The Social Democratic parties of Western Europe
Were like radishes—red on the outside
And white on the inside

OH, CHICAGO

(to the tune of "Oh, Donna")
Chorus:
Oh Chicago, Off the Pig
Oh Chicago, Off the Pig

There once was a town, Chicago was its name
Since we went there, it's never been the same
Cause we offed that town
Chicago, brought it down
To the ground
Down to the ground

Chorus
Red Party's coming soon
We kicked the radish out last June
And now we know the time is near
When our Red Party will be here

Chorus

Red Army brought Chicago down
When we were just gettin' off the ground
Now Washington has shown the way
The Red Army is here to stay

Because we need a Red Army to win the fight
We need a Red Army
So we can lead the struggle right

When the Action started, Elrod's face was red
When it was over, the town had lost its head
The jails were all freed, the pigs were on their knees
Beggin' please
Please don't off me

Chorus

Chicago, now that you're through
In November, DC it went too
And as the panic hits the Kys and the Thieus
The ruling class will know its days are few

(Repeat first verse with chorus.)

VIETNAM
(to the tune of "Connection")

Chorus:
Vietnam
They just can't win in Vietnam
When all they want to do
Is to help Ky and Thieu

Everything is going in the wrong direction
Airborne 101 can't pass inspection
And the Saigon troops just won't stop their defection
And now we know
That they'll have to go

Chorus

We've come to tell this SDS convention
How the Vietcong smashed US intervention
With people's war, the world's greatest invention
And now they're sure
They can't beat people's war

Chorus

LAY, ELROD, LAY
(to the tune of "Lay, Lady, Lay")

Lay Elrod lay
Lay in the street for a while
Stay Elrod stay
Stay in your bed for a while

You thought you could stop the Weatherman
But up-front people put you on your can

Stay Elrod stay
Stay in your iron lung
Play Elrod play
Play with your toes for a while

You thought the Weatherman was mighty green
But we were the heaviest that you'd ever seen

Lay Elrod lay
Lay in the street for a while
Stay Elrod stay
Stay in your bed for a while

STOP YOUR IMPERIALIST PLUNDER
(to the tune of "Stop! in the Name of Love")

Stop your imperialist plunder
We're gonna smash the state
Revolution has come
Revolution has won

Rocky, Rocky, we're aware of where you go
Each time you leave your door
We watch you movin' through the scene
Drivin' in your chauffered limousine
But this time before you run away
We'll leave a bullet in your brain
Think it over
We mean what we say
Think it over
Van Troi has shown us the way

Stop your imperialist plunder . . .

WHEN YOU'RE A RED
(to the tune of "When You're a Jet")

When you're a red you're a red all the way
From your first party cell till your
        class takes the state
When you're a red you will fight till you die
With a gun in your hand and an
        armed struggle line

You're often alone, you're often unprotected
The pigs tap your phone, your mailbox
        is inspected
And you're rejected

But if you're a red you take this with a grin
You go straight to the mass and you
   know they will win
When you're a red you are just out of sight
You attack the pig class and you
   fight cause you're right

Your home is your class, and all
oppressed nations
You kick the pigs' ass, form mass
   organizations
Lead demonstrations

So if you're a red take your gun and its lead
Get the people behind you, the pigs out of bed
The struggle's begun, don't let fear hold us back
There's a world to be won, onward comrades attack!

When you're a red you stay a red

KIM IL SUNG

(to the tune of "Maria")

The most beautiful sound I ever heard
Kim Il Sung
Kim Il Sung, Kim Il Sung, Kim Il Sung
The most beautiful sound in all the world
Kim Il Sung
Kim Il Sung, Kim Il Sung, Kim Il Sung
Kim Il Sung, Kim Il Sung, Kim Il Sung
I've just met a Marxist-Leninist named Kim Il Sung
And suddenly his line
Seems so correct and fine
To me
Kim Il Sung
Say it soft and there's rice fields flowing
Say it loud and there's people's war growing
Kim Il Sung
I'll never stop saying Kim Il Sung

And surely now Korea
Will forever more be a

Socialist country
Korea
Say it sneaky and the Pueblo is taken
Say it bold and the imperialists are quakin'
Korea
I'll never stop saying Korea

FA LA LA LA LA
(to the tune of "Deck the Halls with Boughs of Holly")

Deck the pigs out on the pavement
　　Fa la la la la la la la la
We are now a fighting movement
　　Fa la la la la la la la la
Don we now our boots and helmets
　　Fa la la la la la la la la
We used to talk but now we do it
　　Fa la la la la la la la la

WHITE RIOT
(to the tune of "White Christmas")

I'm dreaming of a white riot
Just like the one October 8th
When the pigs took a beating
And things started leading
To armed struggle against the state

I'm dreaming of a mass movement
That has the highest consciousness
That the Third World's winning
And we're beginning
To join their fire in SDS

We're leading now toward armed struggle
With every cadre line we write
May you learn to struggle and fight
Or the World will off you
'Cuz you're white

WEATHER MACHINE
(to the tune of "Yellow Submarine")

Chorus:
We all live in a Weather Machine *(six times)*

And our friends are all in jail
Many more of them are out on bail
We demand a jury trial
'Cuz we know it drives them wild

Chorus

And the bureau can't be found
Everyone of them is underground
And we ask them what to do
And they say—DON'T ASK US!

TROUBLE ON THE WAY
(to the tune of "Bad Moon Rising")

I see a bad moon a-risin'
I see trouble on the way
I see earthquakes and lightnin'
I see a bad time of day

I see hurricanes a-blowin'
I know the end is comin' soon
I see rivers overflowin'
I hear the voice of rage and ruin

Hope you have got your shit together
Hope you are quite prepared to die
Looks like we're in for nasty weather
One eye is taken for an eye

Let's go out tonite
We're bound to win the fight
There's a bad moon on the rise

WE ARE THE TRASHMEN
(to the tune of "Come Together")

We are the Trashmen we got
Bricks and bottles we got
Stones and sticks right on
Politics
Put gas in a bottle and heave it along
It's the Pepsi generation and it's rising up strong

Trash together
Right now
Off the pig

We love the VC and the
Cuban people and the
Pathet Lao and the
Tupamaros
Huey P. Newton
Ho Chi Minh
We're rising up strong and we know that we will win

Trash together
Right now
Off the pig

Part 4
Going Underground

Introduction

This last section begins with two critiques of Weatherman written well after the "Days of Rage." The authors, James Weinstein and Michael P. Lerner, assess Weatherman theory in the light of much of its subsequent practice, an opportunity not open to critics represented in the first section of this book. A third critique, written since Weatherman went underground, includes an analysis of the Weatherman view on armed struggle. The three critiques differ considerably, though all share a lack of regard for Weatherman political practices, and the belief that Weatherman will soon cease to be a serious force on the Left.

I

Weinstein develops his critique of Weatherman within the context of a broader critique of New Left politics. He traces the fragmentation of the white Movement to its tendency to act on behalf of other people's revolutions instead of developing "a theory and strategy appropriate to specific historical circumstances in the United States as the most advanced industrial nation." As he sees it, SDS gradually moved away from its anti-ideological bias once whites were excluded from the black movement and the anti-war movement failed to spontaneously generate a revolutionary perspective. This process was reinforced as PL's influence grew inside SDS. But the "theory" that did develop was distorted by both the need to combat PL's "Marxist" politics and the tendency toward romantic identification with Third World revolutions. In other words, when the New Left finally recognized the need for an appropriate theoretical perspective for socialist revolution, it turned toward borrowed Marxist ideas which were dated or derived from conditions prevailing in Third World countries. For the most part, however, theory entered into New Left politics as an instrument of coercion and control which one faction of the Movement used against another to justify its existing or foreseeable activity. The core of Weinstein's disagreement with the New Left is that it never came up with a class analysis of its own concrete situation, incorporating a comprehensive historical perspective.

Weatherman exemplifies this theoretical vacuousness, according to Weinstein, in the way it elaborated two main tenets of its ideology: (1) the contemporary strategic significance of the contradiction between United States imperialism and national liberation struggles, and (2) the vanguard position of blacks in the unfolding American revolution. Weatherman maintains that white working people in this country have been made counter-revolutionary by the white skin privilege they reap from Third World exploitation. It conceives of blacks as a growing, self-conscious revolutionary force that could, if necessary, make the revolution by themselves. White revolutionaries, Weatherman then argues, must move toward armed struggle to bolster the efforts of blacks at home and national liberation movements abroad.

Weinstein attempts to turn Weatherman's arguments on their head: white skin privilege is just one of a variety of weapons capitalism uses to maintain its ideological hegemony. Before revolutionaries can physically smash the state, they must first acquire a base with social weight. Mass revolutionary consciousness develops under advanced capitalism by breaking the power of capital to define people as consumers rather than as producers of their own world. Weatherman has failed to work toward developing this consciousness. Furthermore, it is not true that blacks are moving toward urban guerrilla warfare without at least trying to secure significant allies in the white community. The Black Panthers, for example, disagree with Weatherman's contention that blacks can make a revolution on their own or that race war rather than class war is a winning strategy. Hence Weinstein concludes that Weatherman's politics are adventuristic, and the path to revolution it has chosen must end in defeat.

The addendum to Weinstein's article contains his reply to the Radical Education Project collective's criticism that his analysis of Weatherman includes both errors of fact and political judgment.* In answering these charges, Weinstein further clarifies his views on the proper relation of theory to practice and elaborates on his thesis that Weatherman's mistakes represent the logical outgrowth of the bankruptcy of New Left political theorizing in general.

Weinstein, however, gives only lip service to the competing class analyses of PL, RYM II and Weatherman. He writes almost as if these analyses do not exist. Perhaps he finds them too abstract to provide much of a guide to revolutionary practice. But the New Left's tentative political perspectives have been tested in practice over the years and when found

---

* Those who wish to read REP's critique are referred to the May-June, 1970 issue of *Socialist Revolution* from which Weinstein's reply is also taken.

wanting have produced new theory, programs, and visions. No doubt New Left activists think their analysis of society should develop out of their practice (which they hardly equate with mere intellectual work). Despite any failings of Weatherman, this general notion has yet to be disproven.

Lerner is perhaps even more critical of Weatherman theory than Weinstein, but he does not view Weatherman theory or practice as a logical extension of New Left politics. Instead, he attacks Weatherman for ignoring the insights which the New Left has gained from the confrontations that marked the decade of the sixties. Having observed Weatherman organizing techniques in Seattle, Lerner concludes that it applies its politics without even rudimentary subtlety, to the detriment of the entire Movement. Lerner's key differences with Weatherman can be summarized as follows: (1) struggles which weaken the capitalist system are objectively anti-imperialist even if they are not explicitly anti-imperialist, and they should therefore be supported; (2) actions need not be openly anti-imperialist to lead people to radical consciousness; (3) if blacks together with Third World peoples are forced to try to make the revolution alone, the most likely result will be domestic fascism, not socialism; (4) militancy can be a crucial element in advancing consciousness, but never when it becomes an end in itself; (5) if the Movement is to provide the Vietnamese with material support, sabotage and terrorism are poor substitutes for a militant mass movement; (6) white workers should not be organized around renouncing their privileges: the Left should not emphasize the advantages white workers receive from Third World exploitation, but the benefits that would accrue to them under socialism.

Lerner suggests an approach to working class organizing which tries to overcome the pitfalls of economism (simply organizing workers around bread-and-butter demands that might be won but would not result in greater workers' control or increased radical consciousness). He urges the Left to organize around city-wide programs based on principles similar to those enunciated by André Gorz,* that is, "reformist" programs for which the mere struggle tends to build revolutionary consciousness and which, if instituted, would bring radical structural change.

Weatherman's argument against the position represented by Lerner is that struggles which are not explicitly anti-imperialist (that is, those in which major imperialist institutions are not materially damaged or in which no anti-imperialist consciousness is generated) tend to increase the consciousness of white skin privilege and the desire to protect that privilege. Thus Weatherman has refused to give priority to struggles around particular interests unless they are linked to racial and imperialist oppression. Weatherman wants to convince Americans that their interests are inextricably tied to those of the people of the world. Any struggle centered around people's separate interests is considered counter-revolutionary because such a struggle often leads people to believe they can be well off no matter what happens to the more oppressed.

Both Weinstein and Lerner believe that before the Left can wage armed struggle against capitalist institutions, it must carry on a massive political mobilization campaign (involving militant mass confrontations when appropriate) to educate people toward the need for socialist revolution. Weatherman, seeing itself as part of the world proletariat and viewing white working class people in this country as among the most politically backward elements of that proletariat, feels compelled to push for armed struggle now. It believes that as existing institutions continue to erode and as the drawbacks of the American Empire become harder to bear, an established white fighting force—though at first small in number—could help awaken white workers to the impending victory of the most oppressed. In addition, such a fighting force could provide material aid to national liberation movements by depriving the American ruling class of its most precious "sanctuary"—the capitalist heartland itself. Weinstein and Lerner

* See André Gorz, *Strategy for Labor,* Beacon Press, 1964.

see Weatherman's activity as adventuristic and self-defeating; Weatherman understands its activity to be exemplary and most in the interests of the "wretched of the earth."

The authors of "It's Only People's Games That You Got to Dodge," unlike the two critics just discussed, have all been members of Weatherman.* While their criticism of Weatherman collectives is based on their own first-hand experience inside the Weather Machine, the major thrust of their article is theoretical. They argue that Weatherman has reneged on its original class analysis and concern with mass work and has, therefore, become hopelessly bogged down in its own subjectivism. They trace the consequences of this fundamental error through Weatherman's views on white-skin privilege, women's oppression, and armed struggle. This critique challenges Weatherman and its sympathizers directly: its authors not only share Weatherman's belief in the importance of beginning armed struggle in the mother country now but also couch many of their criticisms in Weatherman's own terms.

Assuming such criticism to be basically correct, their article does not account for the numbers of committed, experienced, and intelligent revolutionaries attracted to Weatherman even after the "Days of Rage"; nor does their article explain why they and others like them were unsuccessful in raising their criticism within the Weather Machine. While they accuse Weatherman of subjectivism, they themselves tend to objectify developments inside Weatherman as if they were an inevitable outcome of preceding events. In this they inadvertently avoid their own, and other people's, responsibility for Weatherman's errors.

To avoid a one-sided critique, Weatherman would have to be viewed in the context of the emerging youth culture, against a backdrop of the uneven development of class struggle in the United States and throughout the world. This

* Their article, written well after Weatherman went underground, assumes knowledge of the material contained in the final part of this book. It would be best, therefore, to go through those articles and documents first, especially the "Weather Letter" and "Everyone Talks About the Weather . .," before reading "It's Only People's Games That You Got to Dodge."

would allow a full account to be given of the *conditions* that made it possible for Weatherman to play such a decisive role on the Left. Moreover, having defined these circumstances and relationships, rational grounds would then exist for fixing personal and collective responsibility for Weatherman's concrete decisions. This kind of definitive critique has yet to be made. Nor is it likely that it will be made until the Left gains a better understanding of its roots and Weatherman feels free to reveal much more of its inner history.

II

Little is known about Weatherman's activities since it went underground. Earlier statements of intention, a tragic accident, and messages released from underground make it clear that a core group from Weatherman has taken the first steps toward urban guerrilla warfare by joining the growing band of radical bombers. Those who were leaders and experienced cadre in this country's largest mass-based organization on the Left slightly more than a year ago, have made the transition to totally clandestine struggle, supported directly by a relatively small, secret infrastructure. The decision to go underground was not just a defensive tactic to avoid prosecution, but part of an offensive strategy that Weatherman had been moving toward from its inception.

"Everyone Talks About the Weather . . .," while highly vague and exhortative, is the most elaborate statement to date of Weatherman's conception of armed struggle in the mother country. It was written for RYM cadre and distributed by Weatherman at its National War Council. Weatherman's total emphasis at that time on human will and spontaneity and its rejection of thoughtful planning on how to build support for armed struggle is well illustrated by the following passage:

> Armed struggle starts when someone starts it. International revolutionary war is reality, and to debate about the "correct time and conditions" to begin the

fight, or about a phase of work necessary to prepare people for the revolution, is reactionary. MAKING WAR on the state creates both the consciousness and the conditions for the expansion of the struggle, making public revolutionary politics, proving that it is possible to move and that there is an organization with a strategy.

This document should be read in conjunction with "Revolution in the 70s," one of the last public statements issued by Weatherman before it went underground. It sums up Weatherman strategy in a sentence: "We have to force the disintegration of society, creating strategic armed chaos where there is now pig order."

That is, as long as United States imperialism exists, Weatherman will do its best to turn the already eroding peace and prosperity at home into outright war and insecurity. White America will know no rest: it will ultimately be robbed of its sham showplace stability by its very own sons and daughters. It will be compelled to take sides in two wars—the one in the Third World and the one raging in its midst. The American ruling class, whether or not it opts for fascism, will be faced with a Vietnam at home and the further overextension of its resources. America will experience not just the benefits but the full costs of Empire: armed struggle in the mother country. That is the fight Weatherman has chosen to wage in the coming decade.

No outsider knows the size of the Weatherman underground. It seems certain that far more people have passed through the Weather Machine than remained with the organization—but that does not mean they have ceased to be revolutionaries or that they no longer support Weatherman. The article "Affinity Groups," written by an ex-Weatherwoman from Detroit, does not represent official Weatherman policy, but it eloquently expresses the lessons one person drew from her struggle with Weatherpeople and more than likely reflects the thinking of others in and around Weatherman. The article takes a less harsh, more balanced view of monogamous relationships than Weatherman has been known to do in the past.

The reference to previous crazed trips hints at the traumas Weatherpeople experienced in their collectives which, despite their negative aspects, seem to have strengthened people's commitment to living revolutionary lives.

The "Weather Letter," apparently written by Weatherpeople, but not necessarily an official Weatherman policy statement, extends the line of argument found in "Affinity Groups." In the Movement today, collectives are replacing mass organizations as basic units of political allegiance and struggle, with much energy being spent trying to transcend bourgeois relationships and values within these small groups. The goal is to produce greater trust and fraternity and to break down elitist and chauvinist practices within collectives.

This is, of course, all to the good. But there is a danger in this trend. Revolutionaries may end up focusing exclusively on their own personal transformations while only incidentally struggling to raise mass consciousness. One basis for this misplaced emphasis is the dogmatic application of utopian criteria to both arenas of struggle. Neither the mass of people nor the revolutionary "vanguard" can live communist lives under capitalism. If that were possible, there would be no need to make the revolution. If this is not recognized, it is easy to conclude that revolutionaries must *first* remake themselves into new women and men before effective mass work can be done. Such a mistake, combined with outside political pressures, encourages the Left to turn in upon itself and to reduce political and ideological struggle to individual and small group therapy.

People must and can transform themselves, but only in accord with the possibilities opened up by the revolution itself. There can be no successful resolution to what the "Weather Letter" refers to as "the dialectic between love and hatred" short of total world revolution; there can be little genuine advance toward this goal as long as "vanguard" revolutionaries neither feel great love for the people nor are consumed by the desire to educate and learn from them. Weatherman is highly vulnerable on this point. The "Weather Letter," while purporting to be self-critical, never honestly faces up to the fact that many of Weatherman's worst errors derive from its post-"Days of Rage" contempt for and isolation from white America. This must be overcome if the sacrifices that go into making a revolution are to move large numbers of ordinary people.

Weatherman already has paid a relatively high price for its politics. This has not, however, been consistently true. During the summer and early fall of 1969, virtually no indictments followed the numerous arrests for scattered regional actions leading up to the "Days of Rage." Most cases were settled with "deals" offered by the state: charges were dropped, small fines and short sentences were handed out. (One exception was Eric Mann, who received two years for a Harvard demonstration. That sentence is being appealed.)

The "Days of Rage" alone resulted in approximately three hundred arrests, about sixty regular indictments, and twelve conspiracy indictments. Those arrested generally received small fines and short sentences, mostly "time-served" sentences of from two to thirty days. A few who were given six-month sentences successfully appealed and were released after a few months.

Nine Weatherpeople (out of nineteen indicted, ten have "disappeared") indicted on up to nine felonies each for a "Conspiracy 8" trial demonstration received a total of two months' time and then parole for not forcing the state to a jury trial.

The face value of "Days of Rage" bonds came to three-quarters of a million dollars. Most of it was returned when people showed up in court and copped pleas. People who have not shown up for their court dates have forfeited their bonds. As a Weatherwoman put it: "That's life in the mother country! Money we can rip-off; people it ain't so easy to get out."

Among those who have failed to show up for court dates are the twelve Weatherpeople indicted on federal conspiracy charges for "crossing state lines with intent to incite a riot" for the "Days of Rage" demonstrations. (This is similar to the federal charges which resulted in the five-month "Conspiracy 8" trial in Chicago.) Most of the twelve are members of the Weather Bureau: Bernardine Dohrn, Mark Rudd, Bill Ayers, Jeff Jones, John (J. J.) Jacobs, Judy Clark, Terry Robbins, Kathy Boudin, Mike Spiegal, Linda Evans, Howie Machtinger, and Larry Weiss. They since have been classified as federal fugitives and are being sought internationally by the FBI. Most went underground before their court dates. Thus far, to the great embarrassment of the FBI, only one member of the Weatherman underground has been caught— Linda Evans (who describes the circumstances of her capture in a letter to the Movement). It seems that Linda and Dianne Donghi were arrested because of the efforts of Larry Grathwohl, whom Weatherman believes definitely to be a police agent. "Unsettled Accounts" is a compilation of information about Grathwohl collected from people around the country who were extremely close to him during the seven months he was in Weatherman.*

The worst catastrophe yet to befall Weatherman was the town-house explosion in Greenwich Village, New York, on March 6, 1970, in which Ted Gold, Diana Oughton, and Terry Robbins were killed. Police claim the house was being used as a "bomb factory." The blast appears to have been an accident.

J. Kirk Sale attempts a portrait of Ted Gold, whom Sale describes as neither a "typical" Weatherman nor one of its major leaders. Many, however, will see their own Movement histories in the pattern described by Gold's life: from acceptable student activist to SDS militant to committed revolutionary. Sale's article is least convincing when he engages in armchair psychologizing and strings together unidentified quotes about Gold's "real" motivations. The proposition that Gold became a revolutionary because he was short and stubby and wanted recognition is gratuitous. As the article

* While the evidence regarding Grathwohl is still incomplete, further information and proof will be brought out at Linda Evans' trial when her lawyers present a motion for the prosecution to admit that Grathwohl is a police infiltrator. Grathwohl claims to be a revolutionary in good standing who is being slandered by a paranoid Movement.

implies, Ted felt people should understand that they are morally responsible for immoral acts they do not attempt to stop. He personally was ready to die if that was necessary to begin curbing the world-wide immorality of the United States government. Sale's suggestion that Ted might have been a disobedient child with a death-wish desire to be punished obscures the meaning of his life. Either Sale is unable to comprehend revolutionary courage or he prefers to demean such courage by attributing it to a psychological deficiency.

Unfortunately, there is nothing but *Time* magazine to turn to for information about Diana Oughton.* Perhaps that is as it should be and the way Weatherman prefers it. Revolutionaries in the mother country are no more special than those in the black colony or elsewhere in the world. All of them live in the presence of death, and only the most optimistic expect to reap the fruits of the revolution for which they risk their lives. When revolutionaries die—in battle, by accident, or old age—the greatest honor that can be bestowed upon them is for others to take their place and continue to struggle where they left off.

I. F. Stone and Andrew Kopkind view the recent wave of political bombings as part of the growing crisis in American society. Stone seeks to repudiate liberal clichés about the radical bombers being "criminals" and to place the onus for their existence on the continuation of the war in Southeast Asia. He appears to be taking pains to argue in terms that will

---

* Shortly after this book went into print, a long article on Diana's life appeared in the establishment press. While the article is highly informative, it suffers from the same inadequacies as Sale's article on Ted Gold. See Lucinda Franks and Thomas Powers, "The Making of a Terrorist," *Oakland Tribune,* September 14–18, 1970. I am unaware of any article about Terry Robbins. Terry was born and raised in Brooklyn, New York. He went to work in the Cleveland ERAP project in 1965–1966, when he was sixteen years old. In 1966, he was elected a national officer of SDS. He later became the main organizer of the Ohio Region of SDS, eventually leading the Kent State University SDS chapter in the violent upheavals of April, 1969. In June, 1969, he worked in the SDS National Office in Chicago and became a key organizer of the "Days of Rage." He was one of the founders of Weatherman and a member of the Weather Bureau.

appeal to men in power. He reasons thus: if you do not end the war and correct the gross injustices of American society, if you deal with young revolutionaries in a high-handed, unnecessarily repressive manner, then you will only turn the moderates into activists and the activists into revolutionaries.

But Stone's faith in rational discourse and peaceful change has shown little in the way of results, as he himself admits in his article. This man—who has so thoroughly and honestly documented the failure of American institutions to live up to their best ideals—has also provided revolutionaries over the years with evidence to support their call for the overthrow of capitalist society. But instead of questioning his own lack of revolutionary commitment in face of the self-admitted inadequacy of his politics, Stone mixes political criticism of Weatherpeople with paternalistic references to their being "wild and wonderful . . . kids." And in good liberal fashion, he ends up giving government leaders (whom he describes as inane) advice on how to diminish Weatherman's impact.

Stone seems not to realize that his analysis of American society is the other side of Weatherman's: both despair at the possibility of a majority of white Americans moving left in the near future. Stone then turns to a liberalism he knows produces nothing but at best tokenistic and transient reforms, while Weatherman conceives of itself as a fifth column operating in the United States on behalf of Third World revolutionary movements. Stone fears that "between the disaffected white youth and the growing anger of the blacks, we could be on the verge of a wild upheaval"; Weatherman views that possibility with great enthusiasm, hoping that the ensuing chaos will lead to civil war and armed revolution. Given the rapid breakdown of American society and the collapse of the liberal center, Weatherman's politics seem more realistic than Stone's.

Kopkind at least makes some of the relevant points. He notes that while the active part of the revolutionary movement is small and cannot yet inflict much material damage on capitalist institutions, it does indeed have a relatively large sympathetic following among "ordinary people" who have experienced nothing but "dull futility" from their peaceful anti-war protests. Kopkind goes on to argue that increasing support for the revolutionary movement will depend largely on how fast the radical bombers overcome their amateurishness, political immaturity, and tactical blunders. The bombings—when their targets are clearly understandable and when injuries to people are avoided—are useful because they reinforce the general sense of crisis in the society (which Kopkind attributes to the disintegration of capitalist institutions and values). If people find their "world no longer holds together" and therefore "all the things that Americans want to get and spend are without meaning," then people might "choose to fight—one way or the other." Kopkind suggests that now may be such a time.

Kopkind ends on an ambiguous note. What does it mean to say people might "choose to fight—one way or the other?" Kopkind is probably not referring to a mere choice of tactics; more likely he is suggesting that the deepening crisis in American society will lead to further polarization, with at least an even chance the white majority will move right, providing an activist base committed to exterminating the Left and expanding the *Pax Americana.* Or then again he might be implying that the revolutionary Left, if it acts with great maturity and intelligence, might convince the white majority to fight for socialism. Perhaps the ambiguity is designed to conjure up all these competing possibilities. In any case, Kopkind's "defense" of the radical bombers leaves much to be desired, for he does not answer the most prominent counter-argument: Movement critics maintain that "strategic sabotage," while only a minor inconvenience to the ruling class, will detract from building a mass base of conscious support, which the Left must have if it is to thwart fascist reaction. Kopkind, in his conclusion, inadvertently or purposely lends credence to that possibility.

Weatherman has no such doubts about the efficacy of "strategic sabotage."* On May 21, 1970, Bernardine Dohrn

* While Weatherman seeks to disrupt or destroy major imperialist institutions, it has not tried to kill or assassinate "pigs." Thus far Weatherman has avoided resorting to individual terrorism—a tactic blacks have begun to apply against the occupying army in the black colony.

issued the first communique from the Weatherman underground, which states that Weatherman has decided to adapt the teachings of the Viet Cong, Che Guevara, and the Tupamaros (a brilliantly successful urban guerrilla movement in Uruguay) to fit conditions in the United States. The statement, issued soon after the American invasion of Cambodia and the killing of black and white students on the campuses, addresses itself to white youth in the mother country. Weatherman has not given up on the idea of building a revolutionary youth movement. The fascination and interest on the part of white activist youth in Weatherman—even though many still eschew violent tactics—is indicative of Weatherman's potential mass base among them. The linking of dope (marijuana) with guns and the statement "Freaks are revolutionaries and revolutionaries are freaks" reaffirms Weatherman's faith in the revolutionary possibilities of the youth culture.

Weatherman's position on white youth has gone through a number of changes since its inception. At first, the focus was on marginal working-class youth, such as "greasers" and lumpens, while university students were viewed as hopelessly privileged. Then, after the disappointing turnout during the "Days of Rage," Weatherman immersed itself in the drug and hip culture. During this period, Weatherman once again flirted with, but finally rejected, the idea of building a mass-based revolutionary youth movement. Instead it began to conceive of itself as a clandestine force operating inside the mother country on behalf of the blacks and the Vietnamese. Race war came to be viewed not as a tragic possibility, but as progress. But Weatherman's extreme isolation following the National War Council and the disastrous town-house explosion led to a period of agonizing reappraisal. The unprecedented protest against the Cambodian invasion finally seems to have renewed Weatherman's faith in the revolutionary potential of white youth.

Weatherman ended its communique by vowing to attack a "symbol or institution of Amerikan injustice" within two weeks. All across the country people wondered if Weatherman had gotten "its shit together" enough to do it. When the fourteen days passed and nothing happened, many Movement people were angered and frustrated by the false hopes Weatherman raised and the weakness it displayed to established power. Then, on June 9, a few days after the deadline, in an incredibly audacious act, Weatherman blew up the heavily guarded New York City police headquarters. The Left's sense of powerlessness for the moment dissolved— Weatherman had struck a forceful blow against the enemy and escaped unscathed. The power structure experienced the anger and frustration of being outwitted and out-maneuvered in the very place where people assumed they were strongest. People began to comprehend that the Weatherman underground was indeed for real. As Bernardine said in the communique, there are white revolutionaries in America today who "will never go back" and black revolutionaries who will never again have to fight alone.

The poem "How Does It Feel to Be Inside an Explosion . . ." and the unsigned "Notes to the Underground" are part of the dialogue aboveground revolutionaries continue to carry on with Weatherman through the "underground" press. As the Weatherman underground makes its presence increasingly felt by its deeds, the present trickle of criticism and debate will assume flood-like proportions. This book demonstrates that Weatherman already has some serious criticism to mull over and a great deal of its own concentrated revolutionary experience to impart to the rest of the Movement. This is hardly an idle exchange. While people might continue to identify with Weatherman vicariously, they will not follow in its footsteps unless they not only feel sympathy for what Weatherman is doing, but also understand how it can be part of a sensible winning strategy. If Weatherman is to nurture its potential base, it must clarify the ambiguities and inconsistencies of its theory and previous practice. Weatherman still has not issued any detailed evaluation of its praxis since going underground, though it will doubtless do so eventually. Until then the Movement will have to keep the channels of communication open and assume Weatherman is listening.

Meanwhile, the police, FBI, and Justice Department are pursuing Weatherman with all the resources at their command. On July 23, Attorney General John Mitchell announced that a federal grand jury had indicted thirteen Weatherpeople on charges of conspiring to blow up police stations and other buildings throughout the country and to kill and injure those inside.* The indictment reads in part:

> It was part of the conspiracy that the defendants . . . together with others not known to the grand jury, would organize a "control committee" to direct underground bombing operations of the defendants and [unindicted—ed.] co-conspirators; that this group would be assigned to Berkeley, Calif.; Chicago, Ill.; New York, N.Y.; and Detroit, Mich.; that clandestine and underground "focals," consisting of three or four persons, would be established; that the "focals" would be commanded by the "central committee" in the bombing of police and other civic, business, and educational buildings throughout the country.

Ten of the thirteen Weatherpeople indicted are already being sought on fugitive warrants stemming from previous federal or local cases. Among the thirteen were Linda Evans and Dianne Donghi, who were arrested earlier this year in New York and released on bail. They were re-arrested along with Russell Neufeld, who had not been previously indicted but was already in jail for an earlier Weatherman action. Jane Spielman and Robert Burlingham offered themselves for arrest a few days later—neither apparently had been underground. The indictment listed twenty-one items, attempting to link Weatherman meetings in Flint, Michigan, last December and in Cleveland in February with bomb-making in New York and an arms cache found in Chicago, and with meetings among the thirteen.

---

* People who were close to Weatherman before it went underground claim this indictment and the earlier federal indictment of April 3 are quite confused and contain a number of inaccuracies. Movement people have generally concluded from this that the FBI actually knows quite little about Weatherman.

It did not take Weatherman long to respond to this latest act of repression. Its third communication from the Weatherman underground, issued on July 26, ended with a message to Attorney General John Mitchell: "Don't look for us, Dog; We'll find you first." And on July 27 Weatherman took credit for exploding a pipe bomb at the entrance to a branch of the Bank of America in Manhattan's financial district. Two handmade Viet Cong flags were found at the scene of the blast. A message received at *The Daily News* shortly after the explosion claimed the bombing was done to honor the 17th anniversary of Fidel Castro's revolutionary movement in Cuba and the student who was killed by police after the Bank of America was burned in Isla Vista. Weatherman concluded this message with another word to John Mitchell: no matter what he does, Weatherman cannot be stopped.*

A few months later, in the most spectacular feat of its career, Weatherman assisted Dr. Timothy Leary in his escape from the California Men's Colony (a minimum security prison) at San Luis Obispo. Leary was serving a six-month to ten-year sentence for possession of marijuana. His request for parole had recently been denied for another year—but even if it had been granted, Leary faced a host of other charges, which could well have kept him in prison for the rest of his life.

Leary became famous for extolling the virtues of LSD and for advocating that people "turn on, tune in, and drop out." He is the guru of the drug culture and the father of all flower children. His politics were far from revolutionary: he represented the passive, non-violent, do-your-own-thing side of the hippie revolt. All the more extraordinary, then, is the statement he issued upon his escape. For in it, he links his fate to that of the fugitive Left and calls for violent resistance against the state.

---

* The reader should keep in mind that of the scores upon scores of unsolved radical bombings that recently have taken place throughout the country, it is impossible to tell how many are the work of the Weatherman underground itself or how many have been inspired by Weatherman politics.

This alliance between the Weatherman underground and the renowned leader of the hip culture probably will have its greatest impact on "dropout" white youth. Leary no doubt echoes the sentiments of thousands of once non-violent young people when he writes:

> Listen Nixon, we were never that naive. We knew that flowers in your gun-barrels were risky. We too remembered Munich and Auschwitz all too well as we chanted love and raised our Woodstock fingers in the gentle sign of peace.
>
> We begged you to live and let live, to love and let love, but you have chosen to kill and get killed. May God have mercy on your lost soul.

By helping to free Leary, Weatherman passed beyond mere verbal identification with the evolving youth culture. This suggests that Weatherman now places top priority on mobilizing the legal and semi-legal wing of the cultural revolution behind open support of the Weatherman underground's illegal activities. If such an outcome is achieved, Weatherman will have gone a long way toward reopening contact with the growing mass movement of insurgent youth.

* * *

The scenario that emerges suggests the following possibilities. There is no reason to believe the American ruling class has either the will or the imagination to peacefully resolve the conflicts now dividing the nation. The liberal hopes of the sixties are languishing in the presence of America's global system of violence. There is something basically corrupt about the American power structure that will not end with the war in Southeast Asia. As anti-imperialist struggles gather momentum within America's colonies, the consciousness and costs of empire become pervasive. People all over the world are coming to understand that in an age of permanent revolution, America is a fundamentally retrograde and counter-revolutionary world power, and that peaceful protest, no matter how dramatic, cannot change that fact. The demand for the overthrow of American capitalism (and its imperialist offspring) will grow as the system increasingly demonstrates its inability to meet people's evolving needs and as the carnage it reaps abroad results in further disintegration at home. Violent repression can delay but hardly defeat the aspirations of all oppressed peoples for freedom and justice. The Vietnamese have shown that American power is not invincible.

Imperialist war has produced its revolutionary backlash. The American ruling class, once securely entrenched behind the manipulated consensus of the fifties, finds itself threatened by growing insurgent movements in the seventies. Women, dissident professionals, students and dropout youth, soldiers, young workers, blacks and other Third World peoples—while confronting their own specific forms of oppression—are united in opposition to a common enemy. The politically most conscious element and militant edge of this mass movement consists of an active minority of revolutionary partisans—who may soon find themselves in the vanguard of not only a protesting but a fighting majority of the American people. A new American revolution, nurturing a new sensibility and a profound sense of internationalism, has already begun. Although the effort will be long and hard, history moves without respite when ordinary people struggle to take control of their lives. Weatherman, whether or not it survives, can only be a forerunner of events to come.

Weatherman: A Lot Of Thunder But A Short Reign

James Weinstein

> *There's a lot of skepticism in some places about whether this action can come off ... people have been listening to so-called "movement people," [who] have been telling them that it won't work, that it's adventurist. ... And these movement people, this kind of right-wing force, this weirdness that's moving around, it's all these old people who came into the movement when pacifism was important ... when there was no strategy for victory ... in Detroit, where because of the actions that people were taking, every so-called "movement group" in the city started to get together in a coalition to stop SDS [RYM I].*
>
> *We know there's going to be polarization, but we also know that through that polarization there's going to be change. In Detroit, the whole question of creating a presence, of polarization, has come to a halt because they've polarized the whole city. ... When you say SDS in Detroit, they say oh, those are those broads who beat up guys, those are those people who come into drive-ins, and that polarization is an important thing. Of course, the pole of the city that hates us is all these old "movement people."*
>
> —Bill Ayers, *New Left Notes*, Sept. 12

Beginning as an adjunct to the civil rights movement, both in the South and in the ghetto, the early politics of the student left was liberal. Its strategy was to provoke federal intervention in behalf of voter registration, school integration, and desegregation of public facilities. But buried in the disquiet of that period was a portent of massive discontent among whites, a portent that stemmed as much from the deepening misery of everyday life in the United States as from the disintegration of liberal ideological hegemony forced by the action of blacks. By the mid-sixties the turn of most young black militants from civil rights to the revolutionary nationalism symbolized by Malcolm X, pushed the white student movement out of the black community and into its own, as the escalation of the war in Vietnam provided a new focus for activity. That war was so patently neo-colonial that it rapidly transformed the movement from a small collection of forces led by the Cold War pacifism of SANE and Turn Toward Peace to a mass movement with a rapidly developing anti-imperialist perspective. The growing awareness of the United States as the center and last defender of world imperialism led to recognition of the identity of interest of American blacks, the colonial peoples of the world, and those in the Movement—but at the same time it reinforced the long-standing tendency of white American radicals to act in behalf of others, to externalize good, just as the American ruling class had always externalized evil.

This was only a tendency in what was by 1966 and 1967 a diverse movement embodying a cultural critique of American capitalism as well as a political critique of American imperialism. This conjunction continued, however, only as long as the Movement's main attention was drawn to opposition to the war and as long as the size of demonstrations increased. Optimism and camaraderie pervaded the Movement in those years, but as the demonstrations continued and the war went on—and as the 1968 elections approached—the diversity in the Movement fell to fragmentation.

This fragmentation was a result of the inability of the Movement to develop a theory and strategy appropriate to the specific historical circumstances in the United States as the most advanced industrial nation. To do that would have required, above all, a comprehension of the sources of the Movement's own radicalism, which could be explained neither in terms of revolutionary nationalism, which defined blacks, Cubans, Vietnamese, and Chinese, nor in terms of archaic official Marxism, which defined nineteenth century industrial working-class movements. The key to such a comprehension would have been an analysis of the process of increasing proletarianization and diversity within the working class. Such an analysis would repudiate the bourgeois conception of people as consumers and define them in terms of their relationships to the productive process. To do this was extremely difficult in the midst of the rapidly expanding and developing activity of the Movement, particularly in the absence of any tradition of serious Marxist thought in the United States, or of a mass socialist movement since 1919. There was no sense of history that could be acquired from the socialist sects in the United States, no tradition of developing theory, but only atrophied ideas about revolution adopted from pre-revolutionary Russia or China and liberal ideas about human nature. These the new left early rejected.

For the Movement to be able to continue its development unified in its diversity, a comprehensive socialist perspective was required. Instead, even those who had an anti-capitalist outlook insisted on viewing discrete parts of the larger Movement as surrogates for a comprehensive revolutionary Movement. Community organizing was the first such surrogate, but the peace movement was the more fully developed one. Neither realm of activity could develop into a revolutionary movement, however, for reasons that became apparent in the course of their development.

Although many whites projected their proto-revolutionary desires into their work in the South or in the ghettos, the very nature of that work was in behalf of the proletarianization of blacks—particularly in the South; that is, it was to achieve equality for blacks as part of the working class, a goal that could be, and was, supported by liberal corporate leadership. In addition, the development of the Movement's anti-imperialist perspective, and the increasing identification of the post-Malcolm black movement with the Vietnamese and other revolutionary colonial peoples, convinced many activists that the peace movement itself was evolving by its own internal development into a general revolutionary movement.

But the anti-war movement could serve as surrogate for a revolutionary movement only so long as there was no other force that could promise immediate results. Once such a force appeared, as it did in 1968 in the form of the McCarthy and Kennedy campaigns, fragmentation was inevitable, with the masses following the liberal men of power, leaving the revolutionaries isolated.

With their exclusion from the black movement completed, and then with the collapse of the hope that the anti-war movement would become the rallying point for revolutionary politics, the early ideological "anti-ideology" began to dissolve into a search for "theory" and a long-range perspective. Unfortunately, the militants had nothing to fall back upon except the "Marxism" of the old left sects, which they had earlier rejected.

Meanwhile, SDS, which had always been open to leftists of all political persuasions, and which had come to be a broad political expression of student activism with no coherent politics of its own, had been chosen as the Progressive Labor Party's major base of operation among students. PL had what the rest of SDS lacked: a tightly knit, well coordinated organization, a distinct ideological line, a firm identification with what many believe to be the leading force in the anti-imperialist revolution: China and Maoism. Actually, PL had operated within SDS since it dissolved the May 2 Movement in 1965, but although its presence at first caused much consternation, PL gave little real cause for alarm for the first year or so. In fact, it stimulated some new thinking about the working class and the "new working class" among non-PL SDSers that for a brief moment showed signs of developing into serious theoretical work. But as revolutionary socialist consciousness began to develop, as identification with the revolutionary forces in the colonial world increased, as the need for an effective national organization and a long-range program of action became clearer, PL took on a more menacing aspect.

That menace was a measure of the failure of the new left to develop an appropriate perspective for socialist revolution in the United States, for PL, at best, crudely caricatured Marxist thought. In place of an identification with an increasingly proletarianized American population, PL substituted China, Mao, the Red Book, thereby mistaking the American people for their ruling class and its government. In place of an understanding of the increasing diversity and disparity of the forms of exploitation and alienation of American proletarians, PL substituted a nineteenth century industrial working class, whose exploitation, in PL's estimate, consisted almost entirely of being underpaid. PL's bridge to the working class was the picket line: PLers and workers had the same enemy, police, a fact they expected would be recalled when (somehow) the revolution started.

In a period less characterized by frustration and despair, these weaknesses had been enough to prevent PL from gaining substantial numbers of recruits within SDS, but as the movement became increasingly diffuse and SDS came to constitute only a part of it, PL's strengths came to the fore. Most significant was its sense of historic importance and mission, a sense acquired without ambiguity by repudiating the concrete situations and social roots of its members (for example, PL's program for students was for them to leave school and go to work in the shops). PL identified with an historic tradition (Marxism), a world movement (Communism), and was convinced of the certainty of its positions and of the inevitability of its triumph. For an organization that had gained whatever sense of history it had from blacks and colonials, and had always repudiated its own expressions as "Hippiness," cultural criticism, self-indulgence, moralistic witness, PL now had substantial appeal and grew quickly.

In that situation what was later to be known as the Revolutionary Youth Movement (RYM I) formed. It began consciously at the 1968 convention to prevent PL from gaining control of the national office, or even a substantial influence in it. The strategy of this group, first known as the national collective, was two-sided; to the majority of SDS members it presented itself as the only practical means to prevent capture by PL, to the militants it presented itself as more revolutionary than PL—as the "real" communism. In its former role it could count on the support of almost all of SDS, and although its historic function in SDS was to rid it of PL, by doing so RYM I laid the basis for its own destruction, and possibly for the destruction of SDS. For once PL, the recognized enemy, was out of the way, RYM I would be forced to act out the politics it had developed to counter PL. Those politics narrowed the possible social base of revolutionary action even more sharply than PL had by eliminating even the working class as construed by PL. While fantasizing an external good in the form of black urban guerrilla bands, RYM I left for whites only the role of auxiliary shock troops.

The first noteworthy thing about the SDS convention in June 1969 was the absence of both the old-time national leaders and almost all the regional organizers of recent years. In previous years the great bulk of the delegates had been rank and file members, most of whom not only remained outside the organized groups, but did not even understand the maneuverings of the national leaders. This, however, was a convention of organized factions, with PL and its Workers Student Alliance having some two-fifths of the delegates, RYM I and RYM II (a group even more directly dependent on the Chinese experience for its ideas than PL) having something close to that, and the remaining fifth divided among the International Socialist Club, various ill-defined groups like Rank and File Upsurge and the Revolutionary Socialist Caucus, and a sprinkling of delegates who represented only their chapters. From beginning to end the convention was a struggle for power among highly ideological, disciplined groups, more reminiscent of old left struggles of the 1920s than of recent SDS conventions. The last thing that was wanted by PL, RYM I, or RYM II was a serious open discussion of any question. "Theoretical" positions were put forth by each group solely for the purpose of rallying its respective supporters. Mystification and ritual language, rather than an open seeking for political clarity, were the order of the day. This appeared to be somewhat less true for PL, since it was the aggrieved party with a near majority and could therefore defend established democratic procedure with apparent sincerity. But PL was just as capable as others of using political issues as bludgeons rather than as opportunities for political development and education. The use of women's liberation made this clear. When a Panther spokesman put forward his idea of "pussy power" and then defended that notion, PL mobilized the overwhelmingly negative response into a ritual chant—only one of many during the convention—to "fight male chauvinism." This blunder by the Panthers handed PL an ideological club for its counterattack against Panther condemnation. The Panthers found it necessary to retreat in the face of the response, but they returned later with a pronouncement from Bobby Seale stating baldly that any movement that included the Panthers had no room for PL. In the context of RYM I "theory" such a statement made a split mandatory.

For the convention, RYM I had assembled a lengthy statement of principles that was in fact nothing more than a rationale for the practice it had developed since the first Columbia strike, and for attacking PL from the "left." That document was titled "You don't need a weatherman to know which way the wind blows," and RYM I came to be known as Weatherman.

If, in the recent history of the movement, "theory" had been used as anything but a means of coercion and control, the Weatherman resolution would have been laughed out of the convention, and RYM I along with it, if not before the split with PL, then certainly afterward. That it wasn't is evidence both of a deep-seated contempt for theory on the part of the ideologues in SDS and of the dimensions of the failure of earlier SDS leaders, who used "anti-ideology" in much the same way as RYM I and RYM II use ideology, though with a more humane style.

For a number of years there has been a debate among intellectuals in the movement about the nature and role of theory. One side argued that the development of theory was a task that had to be carried out purposefully, that if it were not the movement would either remain subordinate to bourgeois ideology or become dependent on socialist theory of other times and places. Others argued that theory would emerge, more or less spontaneously, from the activity of the movement. Weatherman is the result of the second line of development. It was put together out of the immediate needs of the National Collective (RYM I), which were to combat PL and to justify a practice already developing. In combatting PL it was necessary to offer an alternative to a "working class" perspective, and to identify with some other section of the population—some other "revolutionary force"—than the workers narrowly construed in traditional "Marxist" style. At the same time, it was necessary to justify a strategy and a politics that had begun to emerge at the first Columbia strike and had revealed its adventurism in the second.

Weatherman did that by developing two major theses: first that the main struggle going on in the world today is between United States imperialism and the national liberation struggles against it, and, second, that the blacks were the vanguard of the revolution in the United States, which, if necessary, they could win by themselves. In developing these concepts, Weatherman had a lot to say that is important and useful to the movement. Particularly valuable was its repeated insistence that in the United States, the most developed of the capitalist nations, replacing monopoly capitalism meant establishing socialism, that an intermediate state of "new democracy" is meaningless—and that, similarly for blacks, the struggle for self-determination must embody the struggle for socialism.

But the main thrust of its "theory" was to prove that it was either impossible or unprincipled to attempt to organize a socialist movment among white Americans, and that the function of white revolutionaries was to play the role of suicide squads, to give cover to the black urban guerrillas. In short, the resolution was developed to justify a politics of despair and adventurism. To prove that it was impossible to organize white workers, Weatherman argued that whites were corrupted by what it called "white skin privilege"—a higher income than people in the colonial world—and that this wealth was directly dependent upon the labor and natural resources of the Vietnamese, the Angolans, the Bolivians, and the rest of the peoples of the Third world. But this statement profoundly confused the relationship of the United States and the colonies. Neither the administrative and technical knowledge nor the machinery required for the high level of productivity that underlies American consumption were stolen from the colonies. While it is true, of course, that American corporations have plundered colonial peoples by underpaying for raw materials, the main source of American wealth is not located in that plunder. If American wealth were the result of plundering the colonies, how would one explain the fact that the basic industrialization of the United States occurred long before its neo-colonialist period, that the rapid expansion of American capital into the colonies started after World War I, and that ninety percent of its foreign investment has taken place since World War II?

It is true that American corporate capitalism has become more and more dependent on its overseas markets and its overseas investments—both in Europe and in the colonies—for continued profitability and capital accumulation, just as capitalist expansion and development on this continent was made possible by the slaughter of the Indians and the stealing of their land. But while that land and its resources were a prerequisite to subsequent industrial development, it would make no sense to assert that the railroads were stolen from the Indians—nor would the Indians consider the "return" to them of the railroads adequate compensation for the loss of their ancestral lands. Similarly, the main impact of American imperialism on the colonies, and the main cause of their continuing underdevelopment, flows from the disruption of the colonial economies as they are subordinated to the imperatives of capital accumulation of American corporations. The deterioration of the conditions of life in the colonies, including the low level of consumption, is a precondition for the prosperity of corporate capitalism. In that sense Weatherman is correct in linking consumption at home to imperialist exploitation abroad. But the link between the ability to produce the goods needed for a high level of consumption at home and misery in the colonies is capitalism. The two appear to be linked together inseparably because under capitalism production can go forward only with constant expansion of the areas for profitable reinvestment of the surplus. A socialist revolution will break that link, particularly since the achievement of industrialization (accumulation) means that further expansion of production can be achieved as a function of replacement.

Socialism in the United States will mean the end of world imperialism because it will remove the compelling force behind foreign investment and control of foreign markets—the need for the profitable reinvestment of surplus. Furthermore, unlike all the previous socialist revolutions, the American revolution will not have nationalism as one of its major components because the United States is not thwarted in its development by an external oppressor. For these reasons Weatherman's rejection of "socialist revolution simply in terms of the United States" is both meaningless and reactionary. Socialist revolution in the United States will be the first fully internationalist revolution because it will be the first in which there will be no conflict between the need to develop and the obligations of internationalism.

Weatherman's definition of revolutionary potential in terms of the level of consumption was also narrowly self-serving. If taken seriously, it would lead one to conclude that the growing discrepancy between levels of consumption in the United States and in the colonies would be followed by a decline in international solidarity. Further, if "white skin privilege" did, as Weatherman asserts, give white workers a "stake in imperialism," it would give blacks a similar if lesser stake, since compared to Biafrans, Angolans, Vietnamese, Bolivians, etc., American blacks are enjoying the good life (if defined in consumptionist terms). But proletarian internationalism is on the rise despite a growing divergence in consumption because the peoples of the world are coming more and more under the sway of American capitalist relations of production—because they are increasingly and obviously oppressed by a common enemy. It is this relationship to the productive process, not how much or what is consumed, that prepares the ground for revolutionary consciousness. This has been understood ever since Marx advanced the reasons for working class revolution, since in the nineteenth century workers had a higher level of consumption than the peasantry. Since 1917 this understanding may have become obscured by the predominantly peasant base of the Chinese and Cuban revolutions, but its validity remains.

But for both RYM I and RYM II the blacks have a central significance analogous to the colonial peoples. What they provide, or at least what they provided last June, is something external to support, something for whites to subordinate themselves to. If, as Weatherman argued, blacks can make the revolution alone, then it makes as much sense to support the blacks as to attempt to build a mass revolutionary movement among whites—indeed, if urban guerrilla warfare were the order of the day for blacks, as Weatherman asserted, then it would make more sense. Blacks can make the revolution alone, according to Weatherman, because of their "centralness to the system" economically and "geo-militarily," as well as because of the high level of unity among blacks. But the black work force is not essential to the survival of American corporate capital, as Weatherman insists. Because it is predominantly unskilled and semi-literate the black work force as presently constituted is less and less relevant. Even in agriculture, blacks are being replaced by machinery. Unemployment among blacks is steadily rising. Indeed, the growing marginality of the black work force is what has led many blacks to an active fear of genocide. A work force "essential to the survival" of any system need not fear genocide, whatever else it may suffer. Further, the level of unity among blacks may or may not increase. The entrance of significant numbers of blacks into highly skilled and better paid jobs raises the possibility of growing political disparity between ghetto and "middle class" blacks.

How profound Weatherman's adherence to its line on blacks was can be measured by the events that occurred in the weeks after the convention. At the convention the composite view of blacks, expressed by Bernardine Dohrn and Mark Rudd, went something like this: blacks are the vanguard of the revolution, as they have been of radical forces in the United States throughout its history. There is not and never has been a liberal black movement because in fact the black movement has always been led by working class blacks. White workers and the white middle class are racist and corrupted by white skin privilege. Therefore, organizing a mass movement for socialism among whites is not only a waste of time, but objectively racist, unless it is organized around a program of combatting racism. The order of the day for SDS, said Mark Rudd, is "two, three, many John Browns."

So far, RYM I and RYM II had relied upon the Panthers, but had given little more than verbal support in return. Their opportunity to pick up their end of the obligation presented itself only four weeks later at the Panther Conference for a United Front Against Fascism in Oakland. There, the "vanguard" declined to assume the role assigned it by Weatherman; instead of calling for urban guerrilla warfare it called for a united front on the left in defense of the Black Panther Party, a sensible proposal from the Party's point of view, but one that undermined almost the entire rationale of both RYM I and RYM II. As a result neither RYM group agreed to the task assigned by the Panthers.

For the Panthers, alliance with whites had been a major step in the direction of becoming a serious revolutionary movement. It was precisely because the Panthers never believed that they could fight and win a revolution on their own that they had repudiated cultural nationalism. Serious revolutionary politics meant building a coalition of revolutionary movements, securing allies of substance. The credibility of the Panthers in the black community depended in part on their ability to demonstrate that masses of whites were also committed to revolutionizing American society. Both in theory and in practice RYM undercut this attempt to build a diverse movement.

Weatherman by assigning to the movemnt a position subordinate to the black "vanguard"—by limiting white activity to support of black initiatives—re-established, however fleetingly, the parasitism of ghetto organizing on a more obvious basis. Trying at least to take advantage of that parasitism to mobilize defense against police repression, the Panthers called upon RYM and other white movement groups to engage in activity for community control of the police. Weatherman quickly reversed itself and made it clear that it would be parasitic only if the Panthers behaved according to RYM's original prescription. Soon afterward Bobby Seale and David Hilliard denounced RYM I. Kiss ass was over and kick ass was coming up.

Subordination to the Panthers, however superficial and temporary, was another escape from white America—and therefore from revolution. In that sense it was a return to the pattern of civil rightsism. The difference was that in the first instance when whites were excluded from the black movement and forced to begin to look into their own communities, among their own people, for a movement and an understanding of their radicalism, the escalation of the war provided them with the means to do so. This time, however, RYM simply backed off when the Panthers pursued their own program, leaving Weatherman no place to go but from bad to worse: if the blacks refused to play urban guerrilla warfare, Weatherman would—and it would kick the ass of anyone who stood in the way. First came plans for October 8 and the great "jail break" (abandoned in Chicago because of a shortage of troops), then came dress rehearsals in Detroit and Pittsburgh. Curiously, with the Panthers out of the picture, it was the rage of the Weatherman women—their alternative to the women's liberation movement—that Weatherman harnessed in its guerrilla attacks on the high schools. These attacks achieved what RYM I desired: they forced people to take sides. But this time it was the rest of the movement as well as the general public who took sides against Weatherman. What followed in Chicago was 200 beleaguered Weathermen and women running wild through the streets, demonstrating their fury but little else.

But although we shall probably hear little more of Weatherman, the ideas that informed its actions and precipitated its downfall are still in the air. For all its poverty as a revolutionary force, Weatherman was nevertheless the first new left group within SDS to attempt to derive a long-term strategy of revolution from current movement perceptions of American capitalism. That attempt necessarily resulted in a strange conglomeration of insights—the result of some eight years of haphazard action and thought—framed in a model of revolution borrowed from revolutionary nationalist struggles abroad and inappropriate to advanced corporate capitalism at the center of the empire.

An important insight, distorted though it was, lay in the concept of white skin privilege—a concept that implicitly admitted that the ruling class holds its power by ideological hegemony, by imposing its view of man as consumer. The despair of Weatherman and of others who share its views follows from accepting that definition of man.

Weatherman's view of the role of militance was similarly distorted. As a tactic, militance has served the movement well, first in dramatizing opposition to the war and thereby destroying the appearance of consensus behind which the corporations conceal the meaning of their policies, second in struggling for concrete demands whose realization will advance the movement for socialism and finally in transforming individuals, in specific and limited contexts, from passivity to action—as in Stop The Draft Week. But such militance is tactical, not strategic. Militance can serve as a strategy only where state power is held primarily by force, rather than by ideological means. Then it can force people to choose between an already understood oppression and revolution. Elevated to a strategy in the United Sates, militance can only reinforce the left's worst image of itself as a band of isolated desperadoes.

Weatherman tried to do the impossible. Recognizing the difference in the state of consciousness of Americans and

Vietnamese, RYM I nevertheless sought to make America into Vietnam. Their odd theory of imperialism and of the "world struggle" (in which there is no such thing as "adventurism"), is at best an attempt to render consistent a strategy and an understanding of the United States that are inconsistent on their face.

The scarlet hues of Weatherman sinking in the west raise the question: what next? The groups waiting in the wings to assume the leadership of SDS have little more to offer. Both RYM II, especially in its most active part, the Revolutionary Union, and the International Socialists now aspire to replace the falling leaders, while other groups are forming and developing. But no group now on the scene can reunite the movement. Weatherman, with its rigidly ideological mystifications, has brought to an end the anti-theoretical phase of the new left. A coda will follow in which it is likely that the RU will swing a steadily diminishing number of followers back into a more orthodox Maoism. In reaction to that, perhaps, the IS will have a turn—although it seems unlikely that many people can still be found to follow an organization that has spent so much of its time waiting for new revolutions to condemn. The prospects for SDS are therefore dim. That is not necessarily a tragedy, since the movement has at every point managed to transcend the limitations of its organized sects. Until now it has done so intuitively, but to rise above the level of its accomplishments to date will require a theory that does more than reflect current practice. What is required is a theory that can understand such practice in the context of our historical situation and by grasping the possibilities inherent in that situation, move toward their realization.

Reply to REP

James Weinstein

The nature of theory and the nature of practice, as well as their relation to each other, are at the heart of all of REP's criticisms. REP asserts that Weatherman is not anti-theory, and that the proof of this contention is that "there is no contradiction between their theory [the resolution] and their practice." I said more or less the same thing—that Weatherman "theory" grew out of their immediate needs to "combat PL and to justify a practice already developing." But where I view this as illustrating a deep contempt for theory, REP takes it at face value. In other words, REP accepts as theory any statement that grows out of the need to justify existing or anticipated activity.

In this respect, however, neither Weatherman nor the Revolutionary Union and RYM II differ from the long-term practice of the movement. Thus, for example, various SDS leaders developed "theories" in 1964 and 1965 about the impossibility of organizing outside the ghetto; and in 1966 various anti-war activists developed theories about building an anti-imperialist peace movement as a surrogate for a party. These ideological positions corresponded perfectly with the activities of the "theorists"—indeed, as we can see now, painfully so. But both sets of "theories" served only to lock people into activities in which they were already engaged and to prevent them from seeing their activities in historical perspective.

In contrast, revolutionary theory must develop a comprehensive analysis of social and class relationship. In the United States that means that revolutionary theory must comprehend the changing class structure and the changing nature of the proletariat in advanced corporate capitalism. It must also

From *Socialist Revolution,* May-June 1970. Copyright 1970 by *Socialist Revolution.* Reprinted by permission.

comprehend the relationship between the oppression of the American proletariat and the rest of the world proletariat—what is shared and what is unique. To understand that, revolutionary theory must also comprehend the creation of new needs by changing social relations and the development of technology.

In writing about the relationship of theory to practice, REP points to the contempt that many activists have "for those who do not participate in the practice necessary to develop and test theory." But this variation of movement *machismo* simply avoids the issue. Revolutionary theory does not grow out of the practice of any group. Practice is impossible without theory, without an explicit or implicit view of the world—although those engaged in practice may often be unconscious of the theories on which they act. Practice is not a means to theory but involves and requires theory. Through practice people can become aware that the theories—conscious or unconscious—on which they are acting are inadequate; it can create an awareness of the need for revolutionary theory, but it cannot create such theory.

Weatherman did attempt to articulate a comprehensive theory of its own, but it did so within the context of defending and justifying the practice it was developing. Thus, for example, while part of Weatherman theory was the concept of increasing and diversified proletarianization (put forward by Jim Mellen), it had a stronger commitment to the bourgeois view of people as consumers, out of which the idea of white skin privilege and the glorification of race war grew. Weatherman accepted the bourgeois explanation of human purpose so easily for two related reasons. First, like RYM II and RU, Weatherman never sought to explain their own transformation from "privileged," "middle-class" students into revolutionaries, but saw that process as simply a quirk. They did not understand themselves as the products of a massive social transformation that had converted college students from a narrow elite—as they had been in pre-World War II days—into a substantial, technically and administratively skilled sector of the corporate work force. They bypassed their own history and development in order to become root-less, detached shock troops for other peoples' revolutionary movements. Without an historical and class understanding of themselves they were left with only a moralistic explanation of their actions. And as a result guilt became—and remains—their main lever for moving others.

Second, Weatherman understood world politics ideologi-cally, rather than theoretically. They accepted the common bourgeois notion of smugly self-satisfied white Americans surrounded by an army of blacks and colonials seeking to redistribute their personal possessions. This view depends on the idea that human beings, narrowly construed as con-sumers, act only on the basis of immediate economic self-interest—an idea that diverts the attention of various sectors of the proletariat from their role as producers, and therefore tends to divide them.

RU and RYM II also accept these ideas, along with much else of the Weatherman world view, and also have no way of explaining their own transformation into revolutionaries. The main difference between these groups and Weatherman is that they have adopted a nineteenth-century definition, re-jected by Weatherman, of an immiserated industrial working class as the key to revolution. The impossibility of reconcil-ing an archaic and narrow definition of the proletariat, op-pressed largely by being underpaid, with the abstract and classless conceptions of racism and imperialism raised within the movement by Weatherman, led to the fragmentation and sectarianism of RYM II and RU during this past year.

Neither Weatherman nor RYM II and RU confronted the void with which we all must begin: the absence for the last half-century of a class-conscious political movement or an ongoing Marxist theory in the United States. To have done so would have been to initiate a long-needed return to Marxism, rather than to frozen dogma and street-fighting slogans. It would have required the development of a view of human beings as producers of their own world and a conception of the proletariat corresponding to the world-wide integration of productive forces by modern corporate capitalism. Within that framework, the new left can be seen as a spontaneous struggle by one sector of the proletariat. In contradiction to the needs of a socialist revolutionary movement, Weatherman, RYM II, and RU never sought to understand themselves historically. Instead each chose a particular sector of the proletariat on behalf of whom to act. In this sense these groups have failed to transcend the missionary character of the community organizing projects of early SDS.

Of course, Weatherman does justify or rationalize its actions since it must convince itself that it is a political movement. Therefore Weatherman asserted that its strategy of building an elite "liberation army" within the United States was based on rising guerrilla warfare in the ghetto and the rapid spread and growth of anti-imperialist armies in the colonial world. It is clear, however, that the Panthers (on whom Weatherman relied last June) are not engaged in armed struggle in the Weatherman sense of that term, and that neither are blacks in general. Indeed, most of the violence of the ghetto is directed inward, is violence among and between blacks, or, at most, is violence between organized black and white gangs over territory. Similarly, the rapid spread of wars of liberation is ungrounded in reality. Both the Chinese and the Cubans are turning inward and are concerned primarily, for the time being, with their own economic and political development. Revolutionary movements in Africa, South America, and most of Asia have been defeated or dispersed for the time being, and even the Vietnamese have clearly indicated a desire to end the war. Indeed, extension of the war into Laos and Cambodia is not the result of revolutionary militance but of United States provocation—first by intervening on a larger scale in Laos despite no increase in Communist activity there, and second by arranging the overthrow of the neutralist Prince Sihanouk. In the light of these developments, one might have expected Weatherman to abandon its shock troop theory. Instead it has increasingly given up even its limited public presence and turned to clandestine violence—a turn that would make sense only in the context of more intense and more pervasive armed struggle against the United States from other sources. In short, just as Weatherman cannot explain its own existence, neither can its "theory" explain its actions.

In the early days of the new left the activism was almost entirely positive: while the old left complained and wrangled over doctrine, the new left boldly confronted a rotten society. That activity created the possibility of a new mass revolutionary movement, but it did not create such a movement. It did not because, despite its activism and its conscious rejection of capitalism, the movement both in its earlier anti-ideology phase and in its recent "Marxist" phase is permeated with bourgeois, interest-conscious pragmatism.

Revolutionary theory cannot be separated from revolutionary practice. If it is, neither the theory nor the practice can be revolutionary. But practice can be abstract and inherently bourgeois in the same way that theory can. Practice is revolutionary only if it is informed by a comprehensive historical perspective. No action or activity is inherently revolutionary, but only becomes revolutionary in the right political/ theoretical context. Five years ago many people in the Vietnam Day Committee believed that non-violent demonstrations were inherently revolutionary and that a revolutionary theory would grow out of that experience. Since that time others have come to believe that violent elite demonstrations are inherently revolutionary. These people (Weatherman and others) have as much contempt for those engaging in non-violent demonstrations as they do for those who allegedly are not participating in practice. Twenty years ago many of us went to work in factories, believing that that activity was inherently revolutionary. In the early days of SDS that form of practice was ridiculed because it so obviously produced no results, but today many people are returning to the factories with a renewed belief that their activity is inherently revolutionary. But was that practice necessary twenty years ago to develop theory? If so, is it necessary to do it again with the same economistic approach to develop theory? Why, if no theory developed out of that practice twenty years ago, should we expect it to develop now?

Working on this journal is practice, and I believe it is revolutionary practice. But the test of that will be whether or not the journal becomes part of a new political tendency and movement. As long as the journal is contributing to the development of such a movement its editors and contributors are engaged in revolutionary practice. If it becomes detached or abstracted from that process the practice will no longer be revolutionary. The same can be said of the activity of the movement over the past several years. As long as that activity was contributing to the development of a mass socialist consciousness—and the movement was doing that from the inception of SDS until the summer of 1969—its practice was revolutionary. The irony is that having become aware of the need for a socialist (or communist) theory, the movement found that it had none and began to splinter. Some groups, searching for appropriate paths of action, latched onto earlier, and even then inadequate, socialist (Communist) programs; others took over programs designed for fundamentally different societies; most people simply dropped out of organized activity. . . .

The present "sectarianism" of the movement is not the result of the struggle for power among individuals. It is based upon a deep disagreement about the meaning of our own transformation into revolutionaries: a disagreement about who will make the revolution and why it will be made. Our disagreement with Weatherman and the REP collective comes down to precisely this point: our own belief that the revolution will not be made by any single sector of the proletariat, but that it will be made by a diversified proletariat increasingly capable of taking over the processes of production for itself (rather than simply "shutting down"). And that therefore the only revolutionary organization capable of making the revolution is a mass, democratic organization encompassing and at the same time unifying the diverse needs of the entire proletariat.

Weatherman: The Politics Of Despair

Michael P. Lerner

Weatherman alone cannot be credited with destroying SDS as a mass-based new left organization. Certainly the political context was crucial: widespread frustration with the continuing war in Vietnam, increased repression against the Panthers, Senate Internal Security Committee attempts to stir up a new witch hunt against anyone connected with SDS, the felt need of many activists to define their own political understanding more carefully—indeed Weatherman itself is as much a product of these factors as of a series of internal developments within SDS. Yet other responses to these phenomena were available, and the particular response of Weatherman contributed greatly to centrifugal tendencies in the Movement and made it virtually impossible for anyone who did not agree with every detail of Weatherman strategy to identify with the "old" SDS.

Nothing could have served the interests of the ruling class more. Precisely those factors that had caused the left great frustration were about to bring a mood of frustration and anger to large sections of the population. The 1968 elections had once again demonstrated the American political structure was irrelevant to the major decisions being made. Nixon was talking of withdrawals that would guarantee a large US combat force in Vietnam for another ten years; leaders of the left were being tried for conspiring to organize a demonstration outside the Democratic National Convention in Chicago; Panthers were being murdered. If ever there was a time for an articulate left to revive its organizing, it was the summer of 1969. Of course, any organizing in 1969 would have been

Michael P. Lerner is a former Berkeley activist and is now one of the Seattle "Conspiracy 7" defendants. Copyright 1970 by Michael P. Lerner. Reprinted by permission.

difficult—Nixon's strategy for Vietnam had confused many— but it was inevitable that the objective situation would ultimately reach people: the war, struggles on campus and the oppression of blacks were not about to stop. How very different 1970 would have been if a force on the left had existed which was sufficiently coherent to counter the vagaries of the Moratorium committee and the opportunism of the Young Socialist Alliance and the Communist Party. Demonstrations protesting the invasion of Cambodia, the murders at Kent State or the trial of Bobby Seale might have had both greater militancy and greater meaning to working people if SDS, armed with a solid theoretical understanding developed from 1967 to 1969, had been around to suggest a unified national strategy.

Nor was the dissolution of SDS an unavoidable consequence of ideological splits among the membership. The vast majority of those who belonged to SDS in June 1969 had a much greater understanding of their common beliefs than of their differences, and would have responded enthusiastically had the leadership which expelled PL proceeded to put forward a mass line designed to unify all elements around a concrete organizing program directed against American imperialism and domestic repression. Radicals around the country were ready to move together; instead they faced Weatherman leaders and a variety of competing sects (RU, IS, RYM-II), each concerned principally with defining and promoting its own politics. This burning sectarianism significantly weakened the Movement just when an outward-looking Movement could have made serious inroads among previously unorganized sections of the population. Literally tens of thousands of SDSers, unable to relate to sectarian squabbles and despairing of future political activity, returned to privatized lives. Many others began to see trashing as the only viable political program. For this latter group, Weatherman could energize the frustration it had, in part, created.

But sectarianism is only part of the story: the more important problem with Weatherman flows from theory, on the one hand, and the inability to put that theory into practice, on the other. While I am primarily concerned with Weatherman theory, no weakness in that theory can adequately account for the rapid collapse of Weatherman as an organized group. Almost from the beginning, Weatherman was involved in tactical errors so serious that sympathetic Movement people began to suspect that some of the national leadership were police agents intent on discrediting the whole left. For example, if one believes a revolutionary's main task is to aid the Vietnamese by damaging America's military capacity, then one ought not to break the store-windows of small shopkeepers at random, but should, rather, blow up military installations, war factories and the like. Again, if one believes high school students are prepared to join the struggle, it does not follow that one should run through high schools yelling "jailbreak," hold a brief rally, and then split over the state line. Nor does it follow from any part of Weatherman theory that those in the Movement who disagree should be called "pig" or "objective racist" or be subject to physical attack. However bad Weatherman theory may be, Weatherman practice proved far worse, earning enemies among those who wanted to be sympathetic.

True, many attacks on Weatherman have come not from people sympathetic to the Movement, but from those who would use Weatherman's mistakes to attack all revolutionary activity. As revolutionaries, we should be especially cautious not to discard some key insights of new left practice because Weatherman distorted or misapplied these insights. Weatherman is not the logical extension of our previous understanding; it is the illogical, if often understandable, outgrowth of an empirical approach to revolutionary practice. We must not give up confrontation politics, the rejection of bourgeois life styles, or building political collectives simply because Weatherman failed, nor should we reject the theoretical strengths of the Weatherman line just because Weathermen have repeated them hypnotically in situations where they did not apply. In fact, it is to see what can be preserved that I now turn to an examination of Weatherman theory.

II.

The principal contradiction in the contemporary world, says Weatherman (quoting Lin Piao), is the contradiction between the revolutionary peoples of Asia, Africa and Latin America and the imperialists headed by the United States. Weatherman's greatest strength is its tremendous emphasis on imperialism as a key to understanding the world. No sensible account of modern history can fail to consider the crucial role of the capitalist imperative: economic and political domination of the greatest possible number of markets and sources of raw materials. Two historical phenomena have set the context of our lives in the post-World War II period: the emergence of the United States as the leading imperialist country (picking up the mantle dropped by Britain, France, Italy, Germany and Japan after their own industrial base was significantly weakened in World War II) at a time when increasingly large numbers of people around the world are coming to understand they can run their own lives for their own benefit and need not be exploited by the capitalist powers. If we step back from the immediate struggle we cannot fail to see that increasing numbers of people, numbering in the hundreds of millions, have withdrawn themselves from the sphere of capitalist exploitation over the past fifty years. There is every reason to believe that trend will continue—witness Southeast Asia. No history of the Vietnam War can ignore America's global economic interests—interests that spring not from the avarice or stupidity of a few presidents and their advisors, but from the economic necessities of the capitalist system.

Nor can we understand political life within the United States unless we understand the role imperialism played in stabilizing the country. The capitalist rulers of the United States had good reason to fear the end of World War II, for they know (despite all the rhetoric) it was that war, not the New Deal, which saved the country from economic disaster. US domination of foreign markets and exploitation of raw materials were critical factors in creating the post-war affluence which made "the politics of consensus" seem plausible. Certainly the old left criticism about the workers' condition seemed to lose its biting edge when the system began to look as if it could "deliver the goods." At the same time, however (and these are points Weatherman rarely mentions), the quietude of the workers was made possible not only by the carrot but also by the stick—during the late 1940s and early 50s all labor leaders and cadre who aspired for more than material comfort were systematically crushed—and the vaunted material "affluence" was much more real for the middle classes than for the workers, whose tiring and "enstupiding" labor would finally earn them the right to watch the idiot box every night.

Weatherman was correct to stress the importance of imperialism, then, but the way this stress was applied to a political program turned the insight into senseless dogma. For Weatherman proceeded to argue that since imperialism was the key contradiction, the only struggles of any value would be anti-imperialist struggles. This formulation misses two crucial points:

(a) Capitalism is a well-integrated, seamless whole; a global system. Both imperialist foreign policies and internal exploitation of the workers are essential to the operation of that system. Any successful attack on the system, from whatever point, will weaken the system as a whole. If, for instance, white workers engaged in militant action so intense it involved armed struggle at home, this would severely hamper the system's ability to successfully wage foreign wars; the converse is also true. A struggle can therefore be objectively anti-imperialist even if the participant's subjective consciousness includes nothing remotely resembling "imperialism." This suggests a related point: the final defeat of imperialism is the defeat of capitalism; hence anything that hastens the end of capitalism hastens the end of imperialism. If this is the case, the Weatherman strategy of attacking any struggle which is not explicitly anti-imperialist is fundamentally misguided. The criterion should be: does this struggle weaken the system? If so, it is good (as well as, objectively and in the long run, anti-imperialist).

(b) This last formulation should not obscure another fundamental point: one crucial aspect of weakening the system is weakening the attachment of people to the system, that is, changing their understanding of themselves and of the society in which they live. But such transformations in consciousness require hard and persistent work, and are not always the result of explicitly anti-imperialist actions. In fact an anti-imperialist action may in some situations keep people from developing an anti-imperialist consciousness, if that action is not adequately explained to them. Conversely, an action may lead people toward radical consciousness even if the action is not anti-capitalist in and of itself.

A few examples: the struggle for free speech on the Berkeley campus in 1964 was not aimed at imperialism and its demands were quite consistent with the continued existence of the present capitalist order (and were, in fact, granted in the end). Nevertheless, that struggle gave thousands of students a new understanding of the power relationships in capitalist society which led them to an anti-capitalist and anti-imperialist position. At a later time, this same struggle would have been inappropriate and a severe backsliding. The point is that one must carefully analyze the people's consciousness and the real possibilities of moving it in an explicitly revolutionary direction. Mechanical formulae, à la Weatherman, can only confuse those who try to make this kind of concrete assessment. For instance, the first SDS meeting on the University of Washington campus in September of 1969 comprised four brief harangues about imperialism (without the slightest attempt to explain the term), after which a Weatherwoman jumped up and said, "Let's cut out this bullshit and move," followed by the immediate exit of about thirty Weatherpeople to the nearest ROTC building, where they proceeded to trash a few windows and then split. More than one hundred fifty people, who had come to learn about the left, were dazzled and perplexed; most never came to another meeting. ROTC quickly replaced its windows, some Weathermen were expelled from school, others were arrested, and SDS soon disappeared from the campus. The action was in-

tended to be anti-imperialist, but its main effect was to confuse and discourage people. One might even argue that this
confrontation was counterrevolutionary and objectively
strengthened imperialism because these same people, and
many others with them, might have been moved into a revolutionary action at a later time when their understanding was
greater. The dialectics of consciousness require sophistication
and subtlety, the two virtues most notably absent from
Weatherman theory and practice.

III

At this point, a Weatherman usually interjects the notion
that blacks, together with people of the Third World, can
make the revolution; hence any concern about the dialectics
of consciousness is unnecessary since building an American
white revolutionary movement is not crucial—and anyone
who thinks it is simply reveals national and racial chauvinism.
There are several problems with this position, too.

First, it is racist in its consequences. No amount of moral
exhortations will suffice to offset the incredible burden this
position places on blacks and the irresponsibility and adventurism it allows to whites. If one believes "they" can do it
alone, why spend one's life running the many risks of a revolutionary struggle?

Second, there is no reason to believe it is true. As long as
the vast majority of Americans are willing to fight for capitalism (or become more willing because Weatherman scares
them into believing the left can offer nothing but window-
breaking), and as long as the ruling class controls weapons
sufficient to destroy the world, how can blacks and Third
World people do it alone? The notion that "the spirit of the
people is greater than the Man's technology" makes sense in a
colonial situation where the vast majority of people sym-
pathize with and support the guerrilla movement. But in
America, mass annihilation of the black minority is the likely
result of this position. Blacks could, it is true, exert a high
price in such a race war, and the fabric of American society
would crumble. But it would crumble toward some kind of

fascist dictatorship, not toward socialism. Recognition of these points caused the Black Panther Party, which Weatherman called the vanguard of the American revolution, to reject Weatherman strategy and attempt to build a United Front of blacks and whites against fascism.

Third: assuming blacks and Third World people could defeat America without the help of the American working class, what kind of a new society could they build? Certainly not a socialist one, with power in the workers' hands. More likely we would face a trusteeship, with Third World peoples running this country in their own interests. While this may well be morally justifiable, it is certainly less desirable than changing white America to a socialist society whose first task would be to rectify the inequalities America has created in the world. Is this impossible? Weatherman almost suggests the racism and national chauvinism of the white working class are inalienable characteristics (much like the conservative notion of the inherent evil of man). Instead of analyzing the social, historical and economic causes of this kind of consciousness and how it might be altered, they take these features as fixed, essentially writing off most of the population as unreachable, and then place all their hopes in the Third World. The practical result is to avoid the American revolutionary's chief job at this moment—namely, to show the working class it is oppressed and exploited in ways like those used to oppress and exploit black and Third World people, that this exploitation stems from a common source (the economic structure of corporate capitalism), and that the workers' only hope of achieving the kind of life they want is to join with these other groups in struggle against the common oppressor. (Part of the problem here is that Weatherman doesn't really believe white workers are exploited, a point we shall discuss below.)

Finally, the idea of defeating America from without suggest the analogy of Nazism. In terms of the objective effect of American imperialism upon the world, the analogy is basically correct. But in terms of the system's internal functioning, the analogy quickly breaks down. The widespread opposition to the Indochina war differs markedly from the general acceptance of German imperialism in most sectors of the German population in 1938. Furthermore, the continued existence of some civil liberties and of working-class self-defense organizations (e.g., unions and their newspapers, etc.) still permits considerable flexibility in organizing opposition groups. I do not mean to underestimate the extent to which civil liberties are being curtailed whenever they lead to significant opposition, or to underemphasize the Marcusean thesis about the tendencies toward rigid thought-control under the guise of openness and rationality. But at this moment there are openings and strategies available which would be totally closed in an authentically fascist state.

IV

During the last few years, who has ever really attempted any sustained working-class organizing? And what attempts has the left made to put forward clear working-class programs? Virtually none.

We are starting to work along these lines in Seattle* with a

---

* We are organizing at food-stamp and unemployment agencies, and putting forward an initiative that would: (a) Eliminate all taxes on people making less than $10,000 a year and halve the tax rate for people making between $10,000 and $14,000, shifting the entire tax burden to those earning over $30,000 and to corporations with assets of $300,000 or more. (b) Prohibit any corporation from entering a contract with any other corporation or government agency participating directly or indirectly in a foreign war. (c) Prohibit any Washington citizen from serving in or training for any foreign war. (d) Establish a state board which would receive all federal income tax and hold it until the federal government stopped waging foreign wars, reduced war-related expenditures to ten per cent or less of its budget, and stopped taxing people making less than $10,000 a year. The board would be empowered to spend the money within the State of Washington to: retool war factories to produce goods serving the needs of people within the state; provide funds for open enrollment at state universities; rebuild cities; provide funds for child-care centers; initiate programs to combat the destruction of the environment; establish free health care centers throughout the state; and provide funds for community control of police.

program that is concretely anti-imperialist: it explicitly cuts off finances and manpower for America's overseas adventures, requires retooling of war factories, and shows people how their money could be spent to serve their own interests rather than to oppress others. It strikes directly at the increasing need of the imperialist system for a large tax base and adds substance to the tired radical chant of support for black liberation by specifying programs—like community control of police and open enrollment in the universities—which we are asking working people to support.

Of course, the ruling class will never allow such a program to take effect. But it does provide an excellent opportunity to begin organizing among the workers by linking issues they are sure of with issues they are less educated about and by showing that one can only talk sensibly about taxes from a class perspective. So far this program has generated much excitement in working-class communities. Other programs can be developed, but the left has never seriously tried in the past thirty years. To be sure, such an effort might bring greatly increased repression and we may face a domestic situation similar to that of fascist Germany, but this is not yet the case.

But why talk about taxes when we should be giving material aid to the Vietnamese? Isn't it immoral, Weatherman suggests, to worry about building an American Movement around the needs of privileged workers while murder continues throughout Southeast Asia? The problem here is to distinguish the ways in which we can help our brothers in the Third World. There is very little reason to believe any group of terrorists could sufficiently damage US military installations to seriously impair the war effort. Such terrorism would more likely bring widespread fear that would allow greater repression of the left at home and intensification of the war abroad. Even in the short run, the internal pressure brought by the mass anti-war movement has—by helping to stop the bombing of the north—given the Vietnamese more material aid than any combination of Weatherman trashing actions in the past year, or any conceivable bombings in the next. Ultimately, the most important aid we can offer the Third World is to build a mass revolutionary force which causes so much internal dissension that the rulers of this country must recall troops to deal with domestic disorder. But if that domestic disorder is to be a real threat, it must be massive—not the action of three hundred people running wild in the streets, nor even of a relative handful of clever terrorists. What is more, insofar as terrorist activity precludes building a mass revolutionary base, it is objectively counterrevolutionary and should be dealt with as such. Our feelings of rage at the ability of so many Americans to ignore the murder of Fred Hampton, the massacre of Vietnamese and people throughout the world, and the repression at home, are certainly understandable. But we must channel this rage into building a majoritarian revolutionary movement that can end these atrocities, and to do that, we must engage in the frustrating, tiring, slow work of building a mass movement among white workers.

Weathermen frequently discount this approach, partly because they believe it is impossible. Pointing to the "whiteskin privilege" of the white working class, Weathermen assure us that white workers are privileged, that this privilege depends upon the exploitation of Third World peoples, and that white workers will never give it up voluntarily. This position, too, presents several problems:

(a) White workers enjoy "privilege" only in relation to blacks and Third World people; they are vastly underprivileged in terms of the material and social benefits that could be realized within the framework of advanced industrial societies. Weatherman here performs a great service for the ruling class: its analysis focuses our attention (as this country's rulers have tried so long to do) on the relative advantages of being a white worker under capitalism, rather than on the absolute disadvantages. Precisely this attitude (America is the greatest country in the world; stop complaining—look how much more you have than everybody else) has kept the workers from making demands that seriously threaten the rulers' wealth and power and from engaging in militant struggles along class lines. Part of the white revolutionary's job is to show white workers how phony their privileges are: the privilege of selling one's labor so one can buy poisoned foods, shoddy goods and cardboard houses in an environment being completely destroyed by capitalist avarice; of producing goods for someone else's personal profit; of raising children who will die in foreign wars to protect the investments of the bosses; of relating to other human beings as objects who will screw you if you don't screw them first; and finally the privilege of totally losing the love and respect of your children since they are beginning to see that the price you paid for the TV set and second car under capitalism was the exploitation of blacks and Third Worlders —an exploitation they cannot accept.

(b) While it is true that, under capitalism, the high standard of living in the United States depends on exploiting Third World people, the operative phrase is "under capitalism." If production were geared to human use instead of corporate profit, all white workers could enjoy a higher standard of living for less effort without exploiting the Third World. Although the dependence of capitalist societies on external exploitation should be stressed, to prepare people for a time immediately after the revolution when internal production will have to be geared to rectifying the inequalities inflicted by capitalism throughout the world, international solidarity cannot be achieved by telling the white worker his goods "already belong" to the people of the Third World. This only reinforces the fears which reactionaries are trying to instill: that the revolution will mean eliminating the goods the workers have achieved through hard work. And it would, in fact, be crazy to proceed as if a revolutionary program involved taking refrigerators away from white workers to send them to Vietnamese. The point is we can fill all of man's key needs and solve the basic problems of scarcity, if only men could overthrow the capitalist system.

(c) The focus on "white-skin privilege" leads to a disastrous organization strategy, *viz;* workers are to be organized *around* renouncing their privileges. Obviously, one cannot organize many people around the idea of giving up their worldly possessions (Jesus' followers tried it for a time, but when it didn't bring the Second Coming they quickly abandoned the idea), particularly when it is impossible to show them they did anything wrong in acquiring them. After all, the workers did not choose imperialism. To suggest that they had would be to accept every liberal pluralist's interpretation of the American political system which attributes some substantial power-making ability to all sectors of the population. One must not confuse our opposition to the ruling class with relations to the present ideological confusions that exist among white workers; rather, in organizing, one must stress the shared need of workers, blacks and Third Worlders to overthrow the American ruling class and the capitalist system which sustains it. Such organizing must continually emphasize this common interest; it must show how the Viet Cong's partial victories improve the workers' possibilities and, conversely, how the taking of power by workers will help weaken capitalists abroad. It must always aim to unify various forces: white and black workers, Americans with Vietnamese and Bolivians, men with women. And this unity must be based not on some hypothetical moral notions, but on a concrete understanding that the liberation of all is the precondition for the liberation of each. This sort of organizing will never involve telling people to stop struggling around their own needs. Rather, it will show them that no such struggle—given a correct understanding of those needs—can possibly be won without aligning oneself with all others who struggle against capitalism.

V

This is not to suggest that the struggle to organize white workers is the only one that matters. On the contrary, every group whose demands would seriously weaken capitalism should accelerate its own struggle. Nor am I claiming the overthrow of capitalism alone will bring the liberation of all people. The fight against racism and for women's liberation will not be won without the defeat of ideological elements which, although originally rooted in the economic base, have now gained a measure of independence. The final defeat of these elements may have to wait until after the revolution, but unless significant steps are taken in that direction there will never be a revolution. Thus it is absolutely correct for blacks and women to assert the independence of their struggles, but they must realize they cannot possibly succeed as long as capitalism exists, and that the defeat of capitalism will require unified effort with Third Worlders and white workers. By the same token, all workers must be led to understand that a meaningful and rewarding life can be achieved only by uniting with blacks, women and Third Worlders. This is quite different from saying they can be organized *around* renouncing their racism and chauvinism; it is to say, rather, that they can come to see such renunciation is crucial if they are to achieve the kind of life they want. All too often Weatherman forgets how recently young people could only be moved to struggle around local campus reforms, and how crucial a role conscious revolutionaries played in helping them enlarge their own conception of self-interest by showing how their own struggles were related to those of the blacks and Vietnamese.

In building a revolutionary struggle along the lines I have suggested, we will doubtless find much greater response among youth than among their more socialized and bought-off parents, and a revolutionary youth movement is certainly the first and key stage in building a revolutionary party. But while the constituency is youth, the focus of the program cannot be "youth." Rather, youth must be organized around a concrete vision of a new society, a socialist order in which the people's own power to control their lives will lead to the self-realization of all men. .

In American today, large numbers of working-class youth (and even many of their parents) realize something is very wrong with the current order. But anxiety about the unknown, coupled with a well-conditioned fear of the left, keeps many grabbing at the straws set afloat by liberal democrats and labor bureaucrats. We must come forward with understandable programs which serve the people's interests and, at the same time, focus attention on their need to struggle against the ruling class. This was the great significance of People's Park in Berkeley. Everyone could see a vision of the new society being realized through the collective work of the people, and they could also see that new society would come only by rejecting the capitalist principle of private property. It is useless to say we need more People's Parks, for that struggle showed that the ruling class is willing to use its entire army, if necessary, to prevent us from building the new society. People's Park did show that putting forward positive visions gives us the greatest chance of building a large revolutionary youth movement.

And there is another important lesson: struggles that emerge from a desire to build a more creative and beautiful life for people in America, while objectively anti-capitalist, need not lead people to an anti-imperialist consciousness; as such, they are eminently co-optable. But they need not be: if revolutionaries had attempted to unify themselves and to infuse that struggle with more explicitly anti-imperialist and anti-capitalist dimensions, they could have shifted its direction and built a more consciously anti-capitalist movement. For those who like to deal with certainties, who cannot stand the ambiguities and risks of a struggle that may not move as expected, the Weatherman insistence on supporting only explicitly anti-imperialist struggles should provide comfort. Those who want to make a revolution in this country will have to involve themselves in struggles which might go the wrong way—but which contain the possibility of mobilizing tens of thousands, and may move in the right way if the revolutionaries are smart and tough and willing to do political struggle with those at another point of political understanding.

The building of a revolutionary youth movement is not what Weathermen call building "a white fighting force." The revolutionary youth movement will be revolutionary because it struggles for socialism, not just because it struggles. This critical difference is too often ignored by Weathermen. At one Seattle meeting, when large numbers of new people had come to find out about the left, a Weatherwoman stood up to declare, "What we are about is fighting." This turned off most of those present—many of them recruited from working-class high schools and unemployment agencies—not because they were scared, but because they wanted something new, something different from the constant violence of modern America. It is not our task to appeal to these people by pretending pacifism is a correct strategy, but neither can we appeal simply by showing how tough we are. Rather, we must prove there is something worth fighting for, namely, socialism. Consider the following statement by Weatherman Shin'ya Ono:

> The only way to make our anti-racist ideas and analyses real is for these white kids to be confronted with a group of other whites who are willing to actually fight on the side of the blacks (and not just talk, hand out leaflets, picket, march or give money for black liberation). Make oppressed and racist white working-class youth really grapple with the existence of such a white fighting force. To see a group of other whites willing to fight to the very end on the side of the blacks will be a shocking experience for most whites. The existence of such whites and actually seeing them fight will hit hard at the core of their racist being in ways no words or analyses alone can do.

This theory has now been disproved: the existence of a kamikaze Weatherman force of whites willing to fight for blacks and Third Worlders has not changed white racism. In Seattle, for instance, high school students said both they and their parents thought Weatherpeople were some kind of nuts whose behavior justified the increased emphasis on police repression and counterinsurgency. College students, particularly from working-class community colleges, felt Weatherpeople had nothing important to say about their lives and should be pitied as social deviants. I do not share these attitudes, but the predicted mystical transformation in consciousness did not occur in Seattle and there is little evidence it occurred anyplace else. On the contrary, all the Weathermen did was give police an excuse for generally increasing their violence.

VI

Isn't it justified morally, a Weatherman might ask, to fight imperialism by creating disorder in the mother country, even if one had not worked out the details of a new society? Surely, the French underground had a right to struggle even without a vision of socialism, so why not fight against the Nazis' successors in the United States? But my opposition to the strategy of building a fighting force is tactical, not moral. It would be right to build such a force, if one could. The point is that it can't be built at this time; the left has never succeeded in showing the connection between the people's real needs and the anti-imperialist struggle. In this context, any fighting force that emerges will have neither the numbers nor the support needed to withstand the onslaught of the Man's technology and trained pigs. The fighting force will be defeated in struggle and decimated—as Weatherman was, despite a courageous fight. Such battles will only demoralize people further and convince them the revolution is only the wild dream of a few, whose very lack of numbers ensures their defeat. Here once again Weatherman serves the ruling class by convincing people that revolutionary struggle can never mobilize the masses or defend itself from repression— and hence the only rational path is to fight for reforms within the system or become a "smack-head" or go live in the country and groove on trees and flowers.

The final irony of the white fighting force as proposed by Weatherman was that it would not end up fighting the ruling class, or even the pigs, but rather the people, primarily the working class. Consider Shin'ya Ono's words:

> If our actions, struggle, and words often put white working class people (and Movement people, too) up against the wall forcing them to fight us, so be it. They're dealing with the ideas of anti-chauvinism, anti-racism, and the coming revolution much more seriously by fighting us than when they threw our leaflets into

garbage cans, or passed good resolutions without any practical consequences.

This is the final admission of despair for a revolutionary: precisely those whom one was traditionally supposed to organize become one's enemies; "fight the people" must replace "power to the people" as the summary of the Weatherman program. But fighting the people does not cause radical breakthroughs in their consciousness; it makes them want to institute repression instead. If the revolution really is against me, then I want the protection of the counter-revolution, and is that is not effective, then I want fascism. True, popular support for repression shows you are being taken more seriously, but it does not mean your program is being taken more seriously. And, of course, when one talks about fighting the people, all pretense of being a revolutionary disappears: at most one is a fighter for the resistance.

This does not mean that militant demonstrations, fighting police, and even selected acts of terrorism are never appropriate, nor that we should be concerned about the liberals' constant reproach that we are "turning people off." This argument is used by those who do not agree with our revolutionary goals but pretend their disagreements concern only the question of "means." Many liberals who "agree" with our goals will still be on the other side of the barricades whenever a real struggle begins; it is in reaction to the pathology of these elements that the New Left becomes rightly suspicious whenever we hear arguments about "better communication." Many of us have found that the best communication with those we wanted to reach has occurred in a confrontation situation, often in reaction to a militancy which those who are transformed by that militancy would never have previously approved. We must keep in mind the devastatingly bad example of the Young Socialist Alliance and their Student Mobilization Committee, whose fear of being isolated from their base has always kept them two steps behind that base. But we must also avoid the Weatherman overreaction, which claims that anyone's assessment of militant action is irrelevant because the action is right in itself.

I contend that very few acts are right in themselves, and that it is always crucial to ask how a particular militant act advances revolutionary consciousness, and for whom. The problem is tactical, but it is crucial. The criteria for assessing any form of militant action must be whether this action will be understandable to the relevant communities and whether it will make those who do not understand react in a way that seriously impedes the revolutionary development of those who do. Underlying these criteria is the assumption that one always aims to increase the number of "relevant communities" where revolutionary consciousness is being advanced. A few qualifications: (a) It is not enough to argue that relevant communities *could* be made to understand a militant action: the action can be justified only when reasonable steps are taken to ensure it *will* be understood. (b) The criteria suggested do not always allow a clear answer. It will often be impossible to know in advance exactly what direction a struggle will take or exactly how it will be distorted by the media and vamped on by the pigs. This should never be used as an excuse for avoiding struggle, but reasonable assessments should be made, and one should always be sensitive to the "understandability" criterion. (c) "Understandability" also provides a guide for terrorist activity. For instance, most Weatherman trashing activity (particularly trashing car windows parked along the street—something Weatherman did during its "Days of Rage") clearly should be avoided. On the other hand, one might well criticize those involved in People's Park for not taking more definitive action against the oppressors when the whole community saw itself as resisting an occupying army. (d) "Understandability" does not mean comprehensible to the press or the bourgeoisie. We must avoid the ruling-class notion of one undifferentiated community, with similar sets of needs and interests, and worry about making our action understandable to potential allies in the struggle to overthrow capitalism: blacks, students, soldiers, workers, alienated youth, women, Third Worlders. Nor would we expect understanding until we have engaged in political struggle. This struggle will not be won overnight, but we must remain sensitive to these concerns, as Weatherman is not. Some argued in its early stages that Weatherman was interested in building a majoritarian movement, but could do so only after several years of hard struggle. The early actions were steps which would transform the consciousness of young workers now so they would later come to revolutionary consciousness. Many of us shared this theory. But when the evidence began to show that Weatherman practice was not even beginning to transform bourgeois consciousness, they abandoned the theory instead of their practice and said such movement-building was not crucial; hence the "fight the people" line emerges. (e) The criteria proposed will require subtle and intelligent application, not mechanical formulas. The great flaw of Weatherman is that it did not want to do the hard political work of changing people's minds through education and talk. Weatherman embodies all of the anti-intellectualism which so pervaded the movement in the 1960s. At the same time, it was reacting to an equally dangerous tendency in the old left and in groups like RYM-II, IS and YSA which have underemphasized the role of action and struggle in providing the conditions within which educaiton and talk can effectively change consciousness.

Making your actions understandable to those who are not yet revolutionaries must seem relatively unimportant if you see yourself, like Weatherman, as a resistance movement rather than a movement to build a majoritarian socialist revolution. The problem with the "underground resistance" à la World War II in France is that we are dealing not with an occupying army but with an entire civilian population, so on whose behalf is this resistance being fought?

At first, Weatherman could respond they were fighting on behalf of the people of the Third World. But blacks and Vietnamese have indicated repeatedly that the best material help they could ask from us is to build a mass left movement in this country. Panthers have stressed the need for whites to organize whites rather than fight them, and warned repeatedly that the fight against fascism cannot and should not be waged by blacks and Third Worlders alone. The people of this country can act to save Bobby Seale, to stop the continued murdering and jailing of Panthers, and to end the repression of the black community, only when a white working-class movement has emerged which can and will align itself with blacks. This task may be huge—it involves changing the impending race war into a class war—but it is the only possible way to deal with the situation. It will be no service to the black community if we allow a race war to begin, and die fighting on the side of the blacks.

We do not need martyrs: we need revolutionaries. The urgency of the task should encourage us to find concrete programs that begin to relate the workers' needs to the struggles of the blacks and Vietnamese. The tragedy is that Weatherman has made the race war more likely by undermining a white movement that could have begun to reach workers, by giving the ruling class just the evidence it needed to back up its campaign to make workers fear the left, and by adopting all the myths of bourgeois ideology (from "workers are doing just fine" to "America is different from all other countries—you can't make a revolution here because everybody's happy"). The task of a revolutionary is to unite where the Weathermen divide, to struggle where the Weathermen despair, and to continually raise to consciousness the ways in which all struggles are one struggle: to overthrow capitalist imperialism and its institutionalized racism, and to replace it with socialism.

It's Only People's Games That You Got To Dodge

Inessa, Victor Camilo, Lilina Jones, Norman Reed

The authors of the "Weather Letter"[1] have set forth in the clearest form we know the subjective and idealist tendencies that are rampant in the white revolutionary movement. These tendencies must be understood, analyzed and refuted if we are to advance the struggle.

We are four ex-Weathermen (two women and two men) who have been in the movement from two to seven years. We joined Weatherman in the hope that it would provide the leadership, correct political ideology, strategy and discipline necessary to form a revolutionary party. We all left at various times after learning through practice that Weatherman could not accomplish this task.

The "Weather Letter's" theme is simple: the principal task for white revolutionaries is to work out the "dialectic between love and hatred." No revolutionary would deny Che's statement that " . . . true revolutionaries are guided by great feelings of love." But the "Weather Letter" omits all the other things we must understand and do to carry out our central task: to make the revolution.

What is necessary today is not phrase-mongering about love and hatred, but concrete analysis of the class and social forces that are developing within white America as the crisis of imperialism deepens. This analysis must tell us which

---

1. There is some doubt whether the "Weather Letter" was actually written by someone in the existing Weatherman organization (or that it represents their politics at this time). However, the ideas put forth in this letter are a logical extension of the "politics" of Weatherman at the various times we left it. Moreover, our criticisms of Weatherman do not rest entirely or even predominately on this letter, but rather on their practice since the organization was formed.

groups can be won to a revolutionary position, which will be the leading groups and which will be counter-revolutionary. It must be an analysis which permits us to adjust our work and parcel our time, placing emphasis on what is most important.

With this kind of concrete analysis, the movement could develop a general strategy (open, of course, to change as objective conditions change). From this strategy, in turn, we could resolve the problems of the interrelationship between mass work and armed struggle, the tactics of mass organizing and education of the people, the development and training of cadre, and the choice of organizational forms. And only by engaging in day-to-day work, by serving, learning from and leading the people can we develop *revolutionary love* for brothers and sisters and *effective revolutionary hatred* for the oppressor.

To place love and hatred rather than concrete conditions at the center of the political universe is to put the cart before the horse. It is an old error, one known as *idealism,* which holds that ideas and attitudes such as "fears and doubts," "love and hatred," and "male chauvinism" are the foundation of our society, rather than material conditions such as exploitation and oppression.

I

Weatherman began with a materialist analysis of the nature of U.S. imperialism and the international class forces moving to destroy it. They developed as a reaction to rightist trends in our movement and fought the hardest against them. They took the lead in expelling the Progressive Labor Party from SDS at its last convention in June, 1969. At that crucial point in our movement, Weatherman argued most clearly that U.S. imperialism could only be understood and analyzed as a world system. They tried to identify those whites in the U.S. who would side with the people of the world in destroying imperialism. They broke with the dogmatic view that only the *industrial* proletariat (regardless of age) can be the backbone of the revolution in America.

But, though Weatherman identified potentially revolutionary white groups, they asserted that U.S. imperialism could
be overthrown without any white movement at all: black
people could do it alone. "Blacks could do it alone if necessary because of their centralness to the system, economically
and geo-militarily, and because of the level of unity, commitment, and initiative which will be developed in waging a
people's war for survival and national liberation" ("You
Don't Need A Weatherman To Know Which Way The Wind
Blows"). Thus whites were reduced to an auxiliary force,
which—though unnecessary—would lower the costs of the
black revolution. The primary job of white revolutionaries in
this view was to organize those whites who could push the
struggle ahead as quickly as the blacks.

Weatherman stated that "the real interests of the masses of
oppressed whites in this country lie with the Black Liberation
struggle" ("You Don't Need A Weatherman To Know Which
Way The Wind Blows"). But in practice they never showed
they believed that many whites could actively help make the
revolution. This contradiction is the result of a misunderstanding of the nature of class interest and white skin privilege. Weatherman said that:

> virtually all of the white working class . . . has short
> range privileges from imperialism, which are not false
> privileges but very real ones which give them an edge of
> vested interest and tie them to a certain extent to the
> imperialists ("You Don't Need A Weatherman To Know
> Which Way The Wind Blows").

They claimed this white skin privilege is in the true interest
of the white working class in the "short run." If this were
true, it would mean that it is not in the interest of the white
working class to fight against U.S. imperialism *now*, but that
it will be *later on* when conditions in the U.S. decay further.

We do not deny that real privileges accrue to white working people in the U.S. Their standard of living is far higher
than that of the people of the rest of the world. But these
privileges are miniscule compared with what working people
could achieve through the establishment of socialism. Weath-

erman failed to understand that the destruction of U.S. imperialism is *always* in the *class* interest of white working people. There is no difference between one's short and long run *class* interest. But white skin privilege promotes false consciousness and makes that class interest hard to see.

White skin privilege is only in the interest of the ruling class. It is a weapon used to divide whites from blacks and to keep everyone, including whites, enslaved. Weatherman did not recognize this and therefore did not educate white working people to their class interest through consistent mass work. Instead, Weatherman invented a short-cut method for organizing whites to prevent them from "holding back" the black and third world struggles. Their strategy was to convince whites that U.S. imperialism was losing badly and that third world victory was imminent. With the fighting example of Weatherman, whites would flock to the winning side.

Their effort to project a fighting and winning image was central to Weatherman's planning for the October "Days of Rage" in Chicago. But their attempts to organize for this demonstration showed contempt for the people. Sometimes they ran through schools merely shouting slogans, knowing such actions would prevent them from communicating their politics to the students. They treated the people contemptuously simply because they were white and because they did not have the same understanding as the leaders of Weatherman (middle and upper class intellectuals, most of whom had spent years studying U.S. imperialism). In practice Weatherman elevated "fight the people" to a cadre, if not a mass, slogan. As a result they failed to mobilize many people.

The failure of the "Days of Rage" stemmed both from Weatherman's theoretical errors and from the class basis of its leadership and cadre. Coming from middle- and upper-class student backgrounds, they had an impatience with the people and a lack of consistency in work that has historically characterized intellectuals. They also retained the crisis orientation that had always been a problem in SDS, as they threw all their energy into organizing for a single, massive confrontation with the enemy.

A militant mass national demonstration could have been a good tactic if it had been part of a general strategy that included long term mass work among working class youth. Instead, the action was the *only* program of Weatherman. They had elevated a tactic to their entire strategy. And when this strategy failed, as it had to, they blamed not themselves, but the people. Regis Debray has observed that, "For a revolutionary, failure is a springboard. As a source of theory it is richer than victory; it accumulates experience and knowledge." But Weatherman acknowledged no failure; they simply maintained that their conception of white skin privilege was correct, that masses of whites were too privileged to "fight." From here it was only a small step to the position they soon adopted: nearly all white people were enemies.

II

How does the "Weather Letter" address itself to this period of Weatherman history? The authors tell us that:

> Weatherman was a response to the Vietnamese and black struggles, to the growing youth movement within the mother country, to the emergence of white revolutionary women and to the escalating militance of the New Left.

They admit revolutionary motion existed, not only in third world colonies, but also among white people.

How did Weatherman view this situation? "We knew we had to be not only a response to history, but also a force of history" ("Weather Letter"). This statement would lead one to suppose Weatherman saw the potential for the development of a revolutionary movement within white America. They would therefore try to create an organization to tap the *revolutionary energy of the people,* educate them and lead them against the oppressor class. And this, in large part, is what the original Weatherman position paper proposed.

But no. The "Weather Letter" says:

> The energy behind that force could only be our revolutionary love and our revolutionary hatred. To move on to a higher level of struggle, we had to work out relationships between the two.

But the energy behind forces of history can never be "*our* revolutionary love and *our* revolutionary hatred." It can only be the power of the exploited classes organized, educated and led to fight in their class interest. This quote reflects Weatherman's lack of faith in the people which followed the failure of the "Days of Rage." Their actions had been so audacious, "custeristic" and conspiratorial that they found themselves under severe repression without an organized base among the people.

Since very little support was coming from the masses, in which all strength really lies, Weatherpeople were forced to generate "strength" from themselves. The definition of strength was always vague and changed frequently. At first, individuals became "strong" by sacrificing their "privileges" and their security: children, close relationships and nearly all possessions. Later Weatherpeople became strong by "digging themselves" and by understanding revolutionary love and revolutionary hatred. Most of their time was spent in making *themselves* "strong." Therefore, the collectives focused inward.

The "Weather Letter" says, "The collective was conceived of as an arena for struggle and transformation, a form in which people could be open about their past lives and what it meant now to be a revolutionary." This is an extremely subjective and narrow conception of a collective. Everything is directed to the working out of *personal* problems among the small group of aspiring revolutionaries. There is no mention of the need for collectives to facilitate a rational division of labor or to aid in mass work in any way. The only other remark in the letter about collectives is that the "different collectives had to take on different kinds of tasks . . ." But what kinds of tasks? We have no way of knowing if they involved work of any kind.

Even if the only purpose of the collectives were to transform small groups of people into more effective revolutionaries, this is still an extremely limited conception. There is no mention of ideological struggle, study, research or any means of broadening the political outlook of the cadre. Instead, all emphasis and attention is placed on personal problems and on male chauvinism and "monogamy." The latter, we will show, was never correctly understood by any of the leadership or cadre.

The "Weather Letter" purports to contain self-criticism. It fails, however, to discuss Weatherman's original analysis, or how it changed and developed. Moreover, the little self-criticism it offers of Weatherman practice is either idealist (takes attitudes as the basis of society), or subjective (fails to make a concrete analysis and instead reduces all political, social and organizational questions to the level of an individual's feelings). The authors of the letter have certainly abandoned materialist analysis (concrete analysis of concrete conditions).

Summing up and criticizing their mistakes, the "Weather Letter" states:

> An *elitism* which led us to believe that we were the only whites that could bite into the pear gave *others* some bad tastes. *Political conviction* led us to disagree with many people, but *sectarianism* kept us from finding ways of struggling with these people. We were unable to understand the validity and potential of *other forms of struggle* and unnecessarily separated ourselves from many revolutionaries particularly in the women's movement. [our emphasis]

But this cannot be accepted by the revolutionary movement as "self-criticism." Yes, Weatherman was elitist, and yes, they were sectarian, but the *reasons* behind this elitism and sectarianism are what is important.

Weatherman's practice failed to mobilize and organize masses of whites. This lack of response "proved" to them what their incorrect analysis had already led them to believe: white people were too "privileged" to be revolutionaries. This conclusion was the cause of the "elitism which led us to believe that we were the only whites that could bite into the pear . . ." It was also the "political conviction" that led them to disagree with many people and was the basis of their "sectarianism."

Many people did not agree with Weatherman's tactics ("forms of struggle"), which they had elevated to a "strategy." If you were not in total support of the "Days of Rage," the Motor City 9, the Pittsburgh Women's Action, etc.; if you did not believe the *only* task for white revolutionaries was to engage in Weatherman's particular brand of "armed struggle," then you were part of the enemy.

None of this comes out in the "Weather Letter's" "self-criticism." The authors either do not understand their errors or do not desire to evaluate their practice honestly and objectively. They do not mention that after the National War Council in December, 1969, Weatherman believed nearly *all* white people were the enemy, that race war was inevitable and should be promoted by white revolutionaries. They do not understand that the type of collectives they describe could not possibly develop sophisticated political leadership.

These errors cannot be explained away by saying, "For those of us who are trying to be revolutionaries in Amerika, it is very difficult for us to work out the dialectics between love and hatred." This is the same subjectivism and lack of self-criticism that led Weatherman to make such errors in the first place, including the error of mistaking "hatred for each other with hatred for the enemy."

III

There was virtually no analysis of the oppression of women in the original Weatherman position paper. At that time some women in the women's liberation movement were beginning to formulate a materialist analysis of male supremacy: the nature of women's oppression by class and race; the nature of the nuclear family; etc.

Weatherman in subsequent months contributed nothing to this analysis. They resolved the problem of the interrelationship between women's struggles and third world struggles by stating there should be no women's struggles. No demands should be made for white women, since they would only be asking for an increase in their white skin privilege. Instead white women were to fight only racism and imperialism.

No analysis was made of the institutional oppression of women (male supremacy) since no struggles would be conducted around these institutions. Weatherman did not understand that struggling against male supremacy could broaden the attack on imperialism. Their lack of analysis led them to absurd positions. In "Honky Tonk Women," they say, "Any demand made by white people short of the total annihilation of imperialism can be granted by the pigs—and will be." If this is true, why aren't there child-care facilities for all white women? Weatherman asserted women would be "liberated" simply by changing their role from housewife to liberation fighter. However, this could not free masses of women since Weatherman provided no alternate means of raising children and doing housework. No provisions were made for the children of the cadre because to do so would only add to their white skin privilege. Children had to be given away.

Since there was no materialist analysis of male supremacy, the struggles over male chauvinism and "monogamy" were marked by idealism almost from the beginning. This idealism is apparent in the "Weather Letter." The authors describe monogamy as a "counterrevolutionary practice," "a dependency relationship in which people held on to each other rather than pushed each other," "a central form of male chauvinism." A materialist analysis of monogamy appears in Engels' The Origin of the Family, Private Property, and The State. Here monogamy is correctly identified as an institution which defines women's relationship to the means of production. Women provide the capitalists with free socially necessary labor: the care of the worker-husband and the raising of children. Monogamy, moreover, is defined by enforced sexual exclusivity for the woman but not for the man. Male supremacy is the institutionalized form of the oppression of women (monogamy is a male supremacist institution); male chauvinism is the attitude which rationalizes the inferior position of women and the exploitation of their labor through the family. Weatherman has never attacked male supremacy, only male chauvinism. They follow the Beatles' line for revolution: "You tell me it's the institutions, well, you know, you better change your mind instead."

Revolutionaries should be trying to organize masses of women to fight imperialism and male supremacy, not only struggling over male chauvinism with each other. Day care centers should be organized to free women from the main chores that make it impossible for them to do much revolutionary work. But Weatherman did not do these things because they did not understand the nature of the oppression of women.

Weatherman erased the work revolutionary women had begun in showing both men and women they are not just *individually* responsible for the oppression women experience in monogamy. Men obtain privilege from monogamy, but the imperialists, not men, are the enemy. Weatherman defined the oppression of women as male chauvinism. Male chauvinism was individual men "holding back" individual women, especially in coupled relationships. In "Honky Tonk Women" they said, "We let one man define our lives for us in monogamous relationships that chain us to the limits he sets and reinforce our passitivity, isolation from reality, and fear of fighting for our freedom." For upper-class women, who have relatively little economic insecurity, this may be the primary form of oppression. But most women suffer more from the institutionalized and economic forms of male supremacy.

Weatherman's "position" on monogamy made men the enemy. No wonder that "in their anger against chauvinism [Weather] women often attacked men rather than struggling with them" ("Weather Letter"). In Weatherman men were smashed because they were supposed to divest themselves of chauvinism on command. When this, of course, failed, many men lost confidence in their ability to struggle against their chauvinism and many lost confidence in their ability to carry out any kind of revolutionary work. This problem is not confined to Weatherman; it is widespread in the movement today.

But the authors of the "Weather Letter" do not criticize themselves for their incorrect analysis or their failure to learn from the women's liberation movement. Instead, they conclude: "Male chauvinism still exists in all of us. . . ." But male chauvinism cannot possibly be completely eliminated until the material basis for it, male supremacy, is destroyed. And even then there will be a struggle!

They also say:

> We have come to a much more realistic approach to monogamy. It's still true that [while] male chauvinism forms the basis of bourgeois dependency monogamous relationships there are great possibilities for love between two people struggling to be revolutionaries.

If Weatherman had understood monogamy, *all* coupled and close relationshiops would not have been smashed. If the authors of the "Weather Letter" understood their idealist error, we would be getting a new analysis of monogamy—not just a "softer" line.

Weatherman's practice of "smashing monogamy" closely paralleled the way the state affects all close relationships. Anyone familiar with divorce and separation figures in the U.S. knows most marriages are "smashed" before they are a few years old. This does not, of course, eliminate the oppression of women; nor does it eliminate male chauvinism.

Neither did the Weatherman "solution." In fact, Weatherman attacked couples and close relationships (at least among the lower level cadre; for in truth there was a double standard within the organization—a concrete example of elitism) which they erroneously labeled as "smashing monogamy."

What did Weatherman substitute for forcing couples to break up, some of whom had been together for years? "Sex, dope, and violence." There was no mention of love. Perhaps this is why we hear so much about love in the "Weather Letter." Attempts were made to force sexual relationships between people who "struggled" with each other. This was labeled "building communist relationships." Women in particular were supposed to be freed from male chauvinist men by engaging in sexual activity with women, many of whom were as chauvinist as any of the men. People literally hid from each other to avoid having sex with comrades for whom they had no sexual desire. Could anything be more absurd?

Sexual compatibility, personal attractiveness, or simply "digging" someone cannot be the foundations of "communist" relationships; they are based on similar politics and common practice and work. Male chauvinism must be dealt with in a political context, based on practice, by forcing men (and women, too) to be conscious of their chauvinism and to struggle against it. Sometimes this will mean that close relationships will be broken apart and new ones formed.

For Weatherman struggles over male chauvinism and monogamy were of primary importance. Despite much talk about armed struggle, the working out of interpersonal relationships probably occupied more time within the organization than anything else. Solving these problems is extremely important. But this can only be done in the context of a strategy to defeat imperialism, while doing revolutionary work on a day-to-day basis. Isolated from this strategic context, any struggle over male chauvinism or personal problems becomes subjective and cannot succeed.

IV

If the average underground press reader were asked what Weatherman stood for, the answer would probably be: "armed struggle." Although Weatherman was certainly not the first white group to engage in bombings, street fighting, or other offensive actions, they were the first organized white group to publicly stress the importance of armed struggle in America.

When Weatherman captured the leadership of SDS in June, 1969, they were in a better position to influence the white left than any other group in the movement. While few people followed them, they forced everyone to respond to the questions they raised and the positions they developed. But despite their reputation the "military" thought of Weatherman is minimal.

Their only lengthy statement about military strategy— "Everyone Talks About the Weather. . . ."—appeared at the National War Council in Flint. As with most Weatherman "positions," it contains numerous contradictions. "Everyone

Talks About the Weather. . . ." pays lip service to the necessity of combining legal and illegal work, the usefulness of
mass demonstrations, the necessity of building a "people's
army," the need to "organize and fit things together so that
more people can get into the fighting in more and heavier
ways," etc. From this one would expect them to try to build
an organization that could combine legal and illegal work,
that attempted to build and lead a mass movement out of
which would come the "people's army."

But by the time of Flint, Weatherman already saw itself as
a fifth column operating behind enemy lines supporting the
worldwide revolutionary movement. Since they considered
almost all white people as the enemy, their military strategy
was to create "strategic armed chaos" in this country rather
than to build a mass socialist revolutionary movement.

In seeking a strategy and tactics for their fifth column
movement, they attempted to apply the ideas of Debray. But
the attempt was mechanical, since they did not analyze the
differing conditions in Latin America and the United States.
Moreover, they failed to understand that the strategy and
tactics set forth by Debray were for guerrilla warfare, a war
of the people, not for a fifth column movement operating
"behind enemy lines." Che, Debray's teacher, points out:

> It is important to emphasize that guerrilla warfare is a
> war of the masses, a war of the people. The guerrilla
> band is an armed nucleus, the fighting vanguard of the
> people. It draws its great force from the mass of the
> people themselves . . . The guerrilla fighter needs full
> help from the people of the area. This is an indispensible
> condition. (*Guerrilla Warfare*, p. 17.)

For Weatherman armed struggle was the answer to all the
strategic questions facing the movement. They say, for
example:

> Armed struggle starts when someone starts it. Interna-
> tional revolutionary war is reality, and to debate about
> the "correct time and conditions" to begin the fight, or
> about a phase of work necessary to prepare people for
> the revolution is reactionary. *Making war on the state*

creates both the consciousness and the conditions for the expansion of the struggle, making public revolutionary politics, proving that it is possible to move and that there is an organization with a strategy. ("Everyone Talks About the Weather . . ." [our emphasis])

But this is in direct contradiction to what Che writes in *Guerrilla Warfare:*

Naturally, it is not to be thought that all conditions for revolution are going to be created through the impulse given to them by guerrilla activity. It must always be kept in mind that there is a necessary minimum without which the establishment and consolidation of the first [guerrilla] center is not practicable. People must see clearly the futility of maintaining the fight for social goals within the framework of civil debate. (p. 16)

Weatherman believed that it was necessary to begin armed struggle immediately. They may have understood, as masses of colonized people do, "the futility of maintaining the fight for social goals within the framework of civil debate." But instead of trying to educate and organize the people who did not see this, they wrote them off as enemies of the world revolution.

This marked the ascendency of the purely military point of view in Weatherman thinking. They now confined their outreach to the small group of whites they considered potentially revolutionary. Weatherman argued that since these whites already knew that "imperialism sucks," all they needed was a revolutionary example in order to move into armed struggle themselves. Weatherman was to provide the exemplary action and also the technical knowledge—in posters and leaflets clandestinely distributed. Weatherman cadre would "lead" these whites through a series of rigidly defined steps from the "lowest level" of armed struggle to the "highest level." The levels were determined by the violence or deadlines of the weapon used. Rocks and trashing were on one level; molotovs were higher; and bombs higher still. The highest level was, of course, guns. This notion of "levels" includes no political guidelines or flexibility and almost completely disregards the need for mass participation. Because levels were defined solely in terms of the weapons used, a mass action involving thousands using only rocks was *defined* as a lower level of struggle than a bombing carried out by a small group.

This "strategy" for leading and educating the people is undialectical. It does not understand that in order to lead people into "higher levels" of effective revolutionary action it is necessary to instill in them correspondingly "higher levels" of revolutionary consciousness and understanding.

We are not denying a place in our movement now for strategic sabotage, armed actions by small groups, etc. In fact, the relationship between clandestine action and work among the people is a key problem facing all of us. But *formulas* are not the answer. Neither is reliance on only one form of struggle. Weatherman's theory said people would act if only they saw others in action. There is some truth to this idea. In itself, however, it is insufficient. It must be complemented by consistent propaganda which exposes the inner workings of imperialism and its contradictions, while explaining the best way to defeat it and build a socialist society. In order to win, the people must have both the "weapon of criticism" and the "criticism of weapons" (Marx).

The "Weather Letter" says Weatherman was "unable to understand the validity and potential of other forms of struggle" (than armed struggle). All those not immediately willing to engage in armed struggle, or those who felt there were other, equally important priorities (such as mass work) were racist and reactionary. Instead of debating these questions in a principled way, they attacked the entire past experience of the movement and all who disagreed with them.

> The experience of our movement until the emergence of Weatherman was one of grabbing every chance not to move; not to struggle, not to jeopardize ourselves or our positions as professional "Radicals." ("Everyone Talks About the Weather . . .")

The lack of armed struggle by white people was explained in

subjective terms (cowardice, holding back, etc.) rather than in material terms (relatively less overt oppression than in the third world, the semblance of democratic procedures, etc.).

Within Weatherman the question of armed struggle was handled in the same subjective fashion. In its crudest form this can be seen in the way Weatherman recruited new cadre. In the main, people were not recruited on the basis of political principles or from an evaluation of their practice. The issue was whether or not the potential cadre had the "guts" to carry out armed struggle, to be a *real* revolutionary, to be a *Weatherman*. Are you revolutionary enough to smash your closest relationships? Are you revolutionary enough to give away your children? This style of "struggle" came to be known as "gutcheck." It was an important form of "struggle" within the organization on every question.

With such subjectivism within the organization it is not surprising that Weatherman failed to emerge as an "organization with a strategy." What did emerge were "strategic" notions and tactics that changed frequently.

Originally, Weatherman believed blacks would make the revolution with the aid of masses of whites. But when Weatherman failed to mobilize even a small number of whites they maintained race war was inevitable and should be promoted by white revolutionaries. Blacks would do it alone with the help of Weatherman and their supporters. Since black and third world revolutionary groups such as the Black Panther Party, the League of Revolutionary Black Workers and the Young Lords Organization disagreed with these positions, Weatherman labelled them "revisionist." Weatherman then argued whites would "fight on the side of blacks" only if there was "non-revisionist" black leadership. Therefore, it was necessary for white revolutionaries to carry out actions in black communities in order to develop new black leadership which believed in race war, armed struggle now, and other Weatherman positions. This was the height of their racism.

Hand in hand with the strategy of race war was the strategy of bringing down fascism on the white community.

Armed struggle was expected to increase repression in white communities, decrease white skin privilege and spur a repression-resistance cycle. When repression became too great Weatherman would move on and create the same conditions elsewhere. But Weatherman never explained how the people were supposed to resist the repression except by following the exemplary actions of Weatherman. This was simply encouraging spontaneity, not providing leadership. They reasoned that since there were already some advanced white people all that was necessary was exemplary action by a vanguard group. Others were supposed to follow despite their lack of direction, organization and preparation.

Fortunately, the internal contradictions within Weatherman never allowed them to implement these "strategies." The deaths in the townhouse occurred during this period, and much of the organization disintegrated as more and more cadre resisted the gutchecks necessary to put these incorrect ideas into practice.

Weatherman has never made an official "communique" to the rest of the movement about the errors that led to the deaths of the three comrades in the New York townhouse. For these deaths not to be in vain it is necessary for the movement to understand they were a result of incorrect politics. The incorrect identification of the enemy; the elimination of all mass work; contempt for and isolation from the people; the subjective handling of all political questions; and the lack of technical training and knowledge are the causes of this tragedy.

How does the "Weather Letter" speak of this incident?

One conception [of the underground] which came a lot out of feeling unable to change ourselves and others, out of the failures of the collectives, led to an even greater political and personal isolation. *This conception correctly identified the enemy,* but saw moving out of revolutionary hatred, without understanding revolutionary love [our emphasis].

There is no concrete political analysis or criticism here.

Everything is reduced to "feelings" and the relationship between love and hate. This explains nothing. It is merely a cover for the outright lie that the enemy had been correctly identified. This kind of "criticism" (or no criticism at all) is totally irresponsible.

But irresponsibility is nothing new to Weatherman. They have been the most consistent to exhort people to engage in armed struggle but have done almost no educational work about it. Leaders at lower levels often did not understand the meaning of armed struggle. Some argued that throwing rocks or even painting walls was "armed struggle."

Weatherman has never attempted to explain the distinction between sabotage (destruction of property or equipment important to the maintenance of imperialism) and terrorism (assaults or attacks aimed primarily at people). But it is essential that we prevent the pigs from blurring this distinction in the eyes of the people. Only consistent educational work by revolutionaries can make it difficult for the pigs to carry out acts of terrorism and blame them on the revolution. Anyone who aspires to leadership in the armed struggle must constantly educate new people about the correct tactics to be used. New people must understand the necessity of choosing targets correctly and of being extremely selective in the use of terrorism. Che says, "We sincerely believe that terrorism is of negative value, that it by no means produces the desired effects, that it can turn a people against a revolutionary movement, and that it can bring a loss of lives to its agents out of proportion to what it produces" (*Guerrilla Warfare*, p. 93). After they bombed the N.Y. Police Headquarters Weatherman had an excellent opportunity for such educational work, but once again they did not use it.

Weatherman's irresponsibility goes even further. After the "Days of Rage" there was no consistent political or military education carried on within the collectives. There was almost no training in the care and use of guns, in the technical aspects of explosives, or in first aid skills. Karate and self-defense practice, and nearly all physical conditioning, ended about this time.

The "Days of Rage" also marked the end, for the most part, of internal political education. There was no longer any required reading of the political and military thought of people like Mao, Giap, Che or Lenin. Some of the cadre never even read all of the original Weatherman paper, and many had not read Debray's *Revolution in the Revolution* on which much Weatherman thinking came to be based. It is not surprising, then, that there was almost no debate within the collectives over the relevance of these authors' ideas to conditions in white America.

Weatherman's irresponsibility in developing their own cadre is consistent with their practice with people outside the organization. They have put out incorrect technical instructions in leaflets and posters in various parts of the country without correcting them. Slogans such as "Dig the N.Y. Bombers!" have been raised in place of analysis of the possibilities and limitations of such actions. They have also spread slogans like "the Viet Cong Have Won" which are incorrect and highly misleading. They have consistently failed to analyze or criticize mass or small group actions happening anywhere in America.

In short they have failed consistently to provide political or military leadership for the movement. Despite this, the "Weather Letter" states that "the political direction of armed struggle is indicated by the underground."

Weatherman burst upon the revolutionary movement just over a year ago. They raised questions nationally that had never been raised before. In this sense they provided leadership and education for the movement. More importantly, they also put forth answers and acted upon them. But these answers were largely incorrect. Leadership must be both consistent and correct. Weatherman has proven to be neither. It is now necessary for others to *seize the time*.

All Power To The People.

Everyone Talks About The Weather . . . .

There is no mystical oppressor creating the misery in the world today. The cause is Imperialism—Pig Amerika—a system of economic, political, and cultural exploitation which respects no national boundaries in its hungry expansionism. The people of Cuba and Vietnam, Laos and Palestine, and of the United States are bound together by this common enemy.

There is no mystical solution either. The reality of imperialist power is that those who have it seek to maintain it at all costs. The reorganization of society depends on smashing that power, building ourselves by any means necessary into a force that will attack the man and kill him. The only question for serious revolutionaries to ask is "How to do it, how to win?"

Because imperialism is an international system, built on worldwide domination, the strategy needed to defeat it must be an international one, attacking different peoples' common oppression by linking together their struggles for liberation.

In the imperialists' colonies, victory demands that the people seize political, military, and economic control of their country from the United States. The people of Vietnam, Bolivia, Laos, etc. are engaged in nationalist wars, struggling for national self-determination, identity, and power. Militarily, their task is to defeat the occupation army, physically kicking the imperialists and their puppets out and building an independent state based on the armed power of the people.

Their struggle, nationalist in form, is of necessity internationalist as well. The Cubans won their national war by seizing power in their country, but the development of a communist society in Cuba continues to be obstructed by US

Part of a packet given out at the National War Council.

imperialism in the form of blockades and embargoes, CIA counter-insurgency operations, etc., and by the continued oppression of the many remaining colonies. The ultimate success of the Cuban revolution and all revolution depends on the total worldwide destruction of imperialism and the establishment of world communism. So the Cuban people fully understand their role in creating and materially supporting the international struggle. Hence Che leaves Cuba to open another front in Bolivia. Similarly the Koreans, who are fully mobilized for another inevitable war with the US, produce three times the number of tractors they actually now need. One third are used in the work of transforming the economy; one third are stored underground for use during and after the expected war; and one third are exported to other revolutionary countries.

For us in the white mother country victory also means defeating the same ruling class and military machine. But the differences in our political/military situation lead us to a somewhat different strategy. We are fucked over in schools, jobs, in every social relationship, robbed of our humanity and the political power on which that must be built. We are oppressed because of class origin, as youth, as women, but not as a nation. We are a nation only in doing the shitwork and ripping off the world and accepting the privileges the rip-off produces. In white Amerika nationalism can be nothing other than a reactionary ideology, a basis for the further oppression of the world's people. Our task is not to seize state power for ourselves, but to destroy the imperialist order. What replaces it must be internationalist, with its highest priority the destruction of racism and great nation privilege and chauvinism, and restitution for Amerika's crimes through internationalization of resources, etc.

These differences in the political and military requirements for victory as between the colonies and the mother country lead not only to different military objectives and tactics, but also to qualitatively different kinds of warfare. Guerrilla warfare as it has been used in the colonies is a special kind of war generated by oppressed and poorly armed people to over-

come the initial advantage of better weapons and organization at the disposal of the occupation force. It utilizes a
strategy of building from small and weak forces to many
fighters and mighty strength. It is a revolutionary form of
war—People's War—and cannot win or sustain itself other
than through massive popular support.

The guerrillas start on the defensive, build their power, and
go over to the offensive. While starting strategically on the
defensive, this is not a passive defense. Tactically it takes the
offensive and chooses to fight only when it can win by concentrating superior forces to the point of action. Its aim is to
destroy the enemy's capacity to fight. "Strike to win. Strike
only when success is certain. If success is not certain, then do
not strike." (Vo Nguyen Giap) Targets are chosen carefully:
because guerrilla warfare is national liberation struggle,
actions must meet with the approval of the mass of the
people, raising their understanding of the struggle and joining
them together against the enemy. A guerrilla army utilizes
the supplies and arms of the enemy, but since it depends
upon popular support it respects the property, interests, and
likes of the people.

The strengths of imperialist power are the professional
armed forces, sophisticated weaponry, and highly centralized
organization. It is armed to the teeth with air power, sea
power, mechanized forces, transport, instant global communications, and chemical, biological, and atomic weapons. Its
military bases all over the world provide unique logistic support for wars on each specific front. But all of these seeming
strengths in reality become weaknesses when met with
people's war. The sophisticated training and long experience
in conventional warfare are useless in fighting a guerrilla
force. The guerrillas are fighting as revolutionaries, on their
own terrain, with a spirit and resourcefulness that comes
from their determination to win. The imperialist army is too
unwieldy and inflexible in its conventional military strategies,
and its troops, though better armed, do not fight well because of the political contradictions in which they are caught.

The apparent advantage of numerous bases all over the

globe is outweighed by the vulnerability of over-extended supply and communications, and by being immersed and encircled in a sea of revolutionary people. The awesome weaponry of the imperialist army, destructive as it is, has not blunted the power of people's technology; over 40% of US combat casualties in South Vietnam result from booby traps constructed by the people.

The most striking characteristic of imperialist military organizing, its centralization largely determines the nature of armed struggle here. The basic resources of supply, manpower, and command lie in the United States itself. Within the generally centralized octopus of power there are subordinate but essential centers. Everything has to be co-ordinated, centrally directed.

This is why the liberation struggle of the black internal colony is key. While blacks are fighting a nationalist war for self-determination, the success of their struggle depends not on kicking the imperialists out, but on destroying them completely. Black people are in a unique colonial situation because of their location in relation to the centers of power.

White revolutionaries live behind enemy lines. We are everywhere: above, below, in front, behind, and within. While we possess none of the machinery of the state, it is always close at hand. Our ability because we are white to move within the structure of the state, to locate ourselves in and around all of its institutions, opens up explosive possibilities for undermining its power. Our strategy must take into account the ways in which this particular asset can be used to prove material support for the strategy of the black colony.

Thus, the political command of means of violence, prisons, mass media, schools, election and party machinery, etc. gives the ruling class a strength which is only illusory. It is material, institutional, and rests on sand. The entire works has not been able to keep us, the youth of Amerika, from waking up and striking out at our oppression.

Our political objective is the destruction of the imperialist state, and the military conditions we face fighting within the borders of the mother country are ideal. Our strategy has to be geared toward forcing the disintegration of society, attacking at every level, from all directions, and creating strategic "armed chaos" where there is now pig order.

At this stage in the development of our strategy there is much about the forms of struggle that we don't yet understand. But to continue from here we need to outline what we've learned so far:

The beginning level of rebellion is the generalized, spontaneous fucking up taking place in schools, the army, etc. Acts of individual refusal to take orders, moves to escape repressive social/cultural forms are good since they show a growing awareness of (mostly) young people's alienation, and can lead to higher levels of struggle. By itself, lacking direction and political self-consciousness, this spontaneous motion has little effect on the power of the state. But in the context of armed struggle it takes on greater importance.

Demonstrations, public mass action, are exactly what they say. Their function is as a show of of strength and numbers, raising for the people in general the reality that there are revolutionaries, there is motion, and sharpening public conflict around different issues. Many people think that demonstrations are useless since their effects on the state are limited. For many of us who come out of a movement history of mass demonstrations, there has been a growing sense of frustration around them, an inability (due to lack of overall strategy) to understand where they can lead. This frustration has accounted for many people dropping out of the action, and others getting into nonstrategic terrorist activity as a way of "doing something". The point is that mass demonstrations aren't going to bring down the state. They are one level of action and their continued usefulness lies mainly in their connection with a larger plan.

The notion of public violence is increasingly key. That is, planning, organizing, and carrying off public and visible violent action against the state as Weatherman did in Chicago in October. Making clear the political reasons for people to act and doing it so that people understand the reality of revolutionary motion. The Chicago action has affected people in the movement and kids all over the country; we forced the level of political understanding by raising the level of struggle, by creating the reality of white kids undertaking offensive violent actions. In Washington one month later the primary question in everyone's mind was about the possibility of violence within the Mobilization demonstration. The underground press and movement discussion in general has centered on it since Chicago as well.

We have got to the place where we have to work out the role of all kinds of struggle. We have to learn how to meet the legal and illegal combinations of the pigs with better ones of our own.

We have to answer all the pig sounds about sabotage and terrorism being terrible, suicidal, and adventurous with what we have learned from the Vietnamese and from Black revolutionists:

Any kind of action that fucks up the pigs' war and helps the people to win is a good kind of action. What we have to do is organize and fit things together so that more people can get into the fighting in more and heavier ways—and so that people who are already fighting get the back-up help that they need. This relationship between "illegal" (by pig law when done by non-pigs) action and legal public motion is one of key importance.

The highest level defines the terms of the struggle and creates a context in which mass public action happens. The fact that three big imperialist firms had their office buildings in New York hit by sabotage several days before the November mobilization changed the meaning of the demonstrations, focusing them as part of a struggle against clearly defined enemies and as a tactical stage of a developing strategy. This helps to sharpen our understanding of the present and opens up greater possibilities for the future.

These initial acts of armed struggle in times like the deep crisis of the present help harness the spontaneous energy of youth motion, giving it a greater context too. Mass consciousness of the existence of a worked-out military strategy to destroy imperialism and win liberation makes it possible for people to become the prime movers in creating the solution to their own oppression.

But at present, many of the specific targets and acts of armed struggle will be determined within the existing level of mass struggles that are going on—much as were the New York bombings. At the same time, the actual damage done to the state remains relatively small. As the actions grow and spread this relationships will change, and ultimately it is certain to be the highest kinds of struggle that lead the whole. All these means are definitely necessary, for they help both the Third World, the internal colonies, and us to win. All these developing actions go toward creating the people's army that is necessary for the destruction of the enemy's ability to fight, which is the strategic condition for victory.

Our employment of strategy has to be a dynamic thing; its internal elements and relationships will change as the struggle goes on. All these steps are governed by the political aim of building a revolutionary army, as a broad and yet a self-conscious, skilled, and centralized organization as the means necessary to carry out the most decisive military and political tasks of the revolution.

EVERYONE TALKS ABOUT THE WEATHER . . . Armed struggle starts when someone starts it. International revolutionary war is reality, and to debate about the "correct time and conditions" to begin the fight, or about a phase of work necessary to prepare people for the revolution, is reactionary. MAKING WAR on the state creates both the consciousness and the conditions for the expansion of the struggle, making public revolutionary politics, proving that it is possible to move and that there is an organization with a strategy.

The experience of our movement until the emergence of Weatherman was one of grabbing every chance not to move, not to struggle, not to jeopardize ourselves or our positions as professional "radicals". That opportunism has contributed to the continued oppression of people in the colonies and here in the United States: the expansion of the empire, and the increased militarism and fascism in this country which we now face in the struggle.

Leadership in the struggle has to do with making things happen. Leadership is the people who are doing it, cutting through diversionary debate, smashing forms and familiarities that hold us back, and through developing and acting on a clear line of how we move to win, redefining the context and content of the movement. That's what we call SEIZING THE TIME.

Revolution In The 70's

The seventies are exploding. Armed violence is in the air. In Madison, Wisconsin, an underground terrorist organization goes on the offensive carrying out four actions in three days. In Champaign, Illinois, two cocktails are tossed into a pig station house, setting a pig on fire. In Seattle two kids are stopped on the street for a hippie check, attack the pig, rip off his piece, and blow his head off. It's happening.

The past years are being summed up. David Hughey, one of the alleged New York Bombers, summed it up in words: "Our little individual consciousnesses whose main concern is to be protected and to stay alive have to start giving way to a broader consciousness, a collective consciousness where the individual rather than constantly escaping from life and death and trembling at the slightest signs of repression lets go and flows into life and into death. And in the context of repressive Amerika this flow into life and death amounts to a very deep and strong desire to fight."

The sixties saw fighting made real by the struggle of people all over the world to smash the white imperialist pig. Ninety miles off Miami, Florida, Fidel Castro and Che Guevara led the Cuban people to take over power, kicking out the Yankees. Cuba is still engaged in the revolution, building a communist society out of the ruins of colonialism. In Vietnam, people's war has been pulling the US deeper and deeper into its own imperialist mire. In the South and in the Northern ghettos, black people have been forcing this country to shed its liberal cloak and defend its pig power in terror.

But most white kids don't dig the struggle for themselves. Our brothers and sisters are into a heavy defeatist trip that comes off of our experiences of the last decade. We started fighting against honky Amerika in a hundred ways, but our

From *Fire*, January 30, 1970.

own struggles have been primitive. We've been unplugged from history, from what's happening in the world around us.

Without a strategy that ties us to the worldwide struggle, a sense of how to move the struggle to higher and higher levels, a clear definition of the enemy, we've brought down just so many flashes, losing actions.

In Berkeley last spring People's Park was the heaviest white street action, tactically. But the struggle was all about turf for white street kids, a futile attempt for a "liberated Berkeley" that didn't deal with the black struggle just a couple miles away in Oakland. What people remember from People's Park is that it was the first time the pigs shot into a crowd of white demonstrators, murdering one. What they don't remember is that the next action three days later was a peaceful flower march of fifty thousand people. Nobody moved. Everybody was afraid of dying. They didn't dig that defeat is living death.

And the Stones concert a couple of weeks ago in California. Hundreds of thousands of kids totally spaced out, paralyzed when the Angels beat a black brother to death in front of them. Mick was singing "Sympathy for the Devil." Afterward he said, "Something always happens when I sing that song. . . ." It was the highest realization of a culture that started out as a fight to escape and build something new for our survival, and has resulted in total cynicism. But the culture didn't lead us to war, to destroying white Amerika. Kids have made a deal with the Man. But the Man deals from the bottom of the deck.

But after five years it is clear that the VC are winning. American GIs can't walk around at night in Vietnam anymore. The pig press tells us stories of massacres like My Lai, but they don't tell us that these are the tactics of an army on the verge of extinction. There's no reason to pity the Vietnamese: VC run it. Hampton was murdered in Chicago but the next day the LA Panthers held off a pig army for five hours. With this year's sugar harvest the Cubans are going to establish an economic strength that will be the basis of their revolutionary society.

When we hook ourselves into the winning energy of the international revolution, each of our actions becomes a beginning and an end. An action's success sums up all our knowledge of the past. Its failures open the way to the next highest levels of struggle. When Weatherman ripped apart Chicago last October, it was the strongest, most damaging, and best organized white street action Amerika had ever been hit with. That's because we went to Chicago with a vision of where to move to in the future. The cost of the action in busts and injuries, and the limits of how much we can destroy with our fists, mean that the struggle will find new forms. Because we're building it to win.

We are behind enemy lines. We are the sons and daughters of the enemy. Our political objective is the destruction of honkiness. We are going to wipe out the imperialist State and every vestige of honky consciousness in white people. Our military strategy takes into account our ability, because we are white, to be everywhere: above, below, and within the belly of the pig. We have to force the disintegration of society, creating strategic armed chaos where there is now pig order.

If we understand our role as joining and fighting with that international struggle, we can develop the forms and tactics for our own survival and victory as revolutionary fighters. We've got to build new forms as fast as we use them up. Two years ago a group in New York called the Motherfuckers started moving in "affinity groups," running groups made up of people who knew and trusted each other, which were a necessary weapon for their survival in the streets. By the Democratic Convention action that summer hundreds of affinity groups had been formed, and it was they who led the struggle in the streets of Chicago. As the level of struggle has risen, a lot of people have felt the need for tighter and stronger forms, and now there are hundreds of collectives being built all over the country, chains of affinity groups linked together by strong leadership, discipline, and political coherence. A network of many collectives which can strike in coordinated ways and share resources, etc. And we are building an army, a centralized military organization that can lead the struggle.

As a foundation for it all, we have to build ourselves. We've understood that smashing the pig means smashing the pig inside ourselves, destroying our own honkiness. When we are fighting a war, there is no place for male chauvinism, individualism, competition, or any of the Man's fucked-up values. We must be what we have set out to create—self-conscious, self-reliant communist revolutionaries, changing ourselves and each other in order to win.

THE YOUTH WILL MAKE THE REVOLUTION
THE YOUTH WILL MAKE IT AND KEEP IT
THROUGHOUT AMERIKA AND THE WORLD
BE STRONG, BE BEAUTIFUL

Affinity Groups

a daughter of the Amerikan Revolution

In Amerika today, a lot of people are already moving towards armed struggle. One of the best ways to prepare ourselves is to start pulling together in affinity groups. The term "affinity group" means different things to different people—anything from a group of people that run together in a riot to a basic armed unit for the revolution, which is my conception of it.

I used to be in an affinity group of sorts, and though it was a lot fucked-up, I learned more through struggle with those people than I ever had before. I've taken the things I learned there and am applying them to my life and work now.

A group should pull together not only out of political unity, but out of personal love and trust as well. People should start living together and struggling together to gain that closeness before they start moving militarily. This way, I look at people that I work with every day as people I might be fighting the revolution with, so struggle with them becomes more of an urgency.

Once people start living collectively, real changes start to come down. One of the first things we got into in my group was a trip about women's liberation, male chauvinism, and monogamy. Most of the women in the group had come in as the other half of a guy—in other words, they related to the movement and the collective through their old men. Monogamy held us back in all sorts of ways. A revolutionary has to be a strong, self-reliant person, not totally dependent on another individual or group for their personal sanity. Monogamy was in direct opposition to this. Also, it divided women from each other . . . when you have a boyfriend, every other woman close to him is a direct threat.

From the *Berkeley Tribe,* May 29, 1970. Copyright 1970 by The Red Mountain Tribe. Reprinted by permission.

Monogamy held members of the collective back from relating to each other fully, because we always felt obliged to relate primarily to that one person, and everyone else was secondary. We couldn't relate politically, personally, or sexually to anyone else without feeling guilty about it.

So we smashed monogamy—everyone broke up their monogamous relationships. At first, there were all kinds of crises around it. People made it on the sly, and then didn't make it at all for fear of being male chauvinists. That was clearly a bummer and couldn't last for long, but we did kind of a flip-flop from celibacy to a near orgy state. Fucking became pretty impersonal—if someone was a revolutionary, that was a good enough reason to make it, never mind if you dug the person or not. That didn't work either, because there is something special about making it, and the orgy stage was just too much of a "macho," "I don't give a shit" trip.

Looking over all those trips we went through, some of them seem a bit crazed. Although the bourgeois hangups about possessiveness and dependency have to be smashed, there is nothing wrong with loving someone, and giving and gaining strength from a relationship. What we gotta do is take that love and build it with other people that we know—spread it thick, not thin, with men and women.

Another thing that applies especially to women is our self-hatred. So much of our lives have been desolation, isolation from each other, passivity to men and to authority. When women started getting together in the group, we discovered just how much this self-hatred we all shared held us back. Like I had always hated Amerika, but I also hated myself and was quite sure that I would never have the strength it takes to fight.

We were all of us, men and women, scared by what the revolution means. We still are—it isn't that easy to overcome Amerikan consciousness and seize control of our lives. Not only women, but men too, are fucked over by bourgeois roles. Like a man who thinks he has to live up to this big tough-guy image. Amerika's image of a white male isn't an image of a real person—how can he grow, love, feel in that role?

Macho is a false strength—it doesn't deal with our fears, our feelings. And unless we can learn to come to terms with ourselves there's no way we can survive.

A big criticism I had of my people before was that they were into a big guilt trip about being white. They didn't want to dig on our culture, and instead tried to put it down. That was really bullshit. We have to dig where we came from—not our middle-class backgrounds, but our new lifestyle, which we've turned into the very antithesis of honkiness. Eldridge talks about how white kids have cut through the traditional white uptightness, how our music lets us feel our bodies again. And our dope culture—grass, acid, mesc—has opened up our minds to possibilities of freedom that our parents never dreamed of. The Youth Nation is something new, something real, and a part of the world revolution.

We have to be really sensitive to ourselves and to each other, or we lay ourselves open to infiltration by undercover pigs. Any pig can run down a correct line about the revolution, but what a pig can't relate to is the energy of that revolution itself. He can't dig on it because he is part of its total opposite—part of the death culture we are fighting. We won't be able to tell this, though, if we're on a death trip ourselves, if we can't relate to each other honestly.

We also have to learn to be security conscious—to be careful of what we say, when, where, and to whom we say it. We have to start seeing ourselves as real outlaws—to get a consciousness of ourselves as enemies of the state, not just its rebellious children.

We have to start moving now. The Red Army already exists in its basic form as the Weatherman underground. They are the leadership of the white revolutionary movement in this country, not because of their ideas, which are basically right, but because they put those ideas into practice.

How can we best relate to their leadership? I don't think that we have to be in direct contact with them to move. We have to start building that Red Army on all levels—an underground can't survive without support from an aboveground. That means we start getting ourselves together to make the revolution grow ahead and make ourselves stronger people, keeping in mind that we need to have a way we can move to win. When we start to move, we will of necessity have to set up communications with other groups and individuals. Thus new networks are formed and the Red Army is expanded to another level.

The revolution is life, is being real—and the way we live has to be that constant change, constant growth, constant struggle ... "HE NOT BUSY BEING BORN IS BUSY DYING!"

Weather Letter

Man, Woman and Socialism in the Mothercountry (should we change this to Fathercountry?)

> If you want knowledge, you must take part in the practice of changing reality. If you want to know the taste of a pear, you must change the pear by eating it yourself. If you want to know the theory and methods of revolution, you must take part in revolution.
>
> —Mao

It's easy to hate in Amerika—it's a lot harder to love. We learn to hate from the time we're born into this society. As small children, our models for behavior are the anxious competitive lives that our parents live. They teach us the racism, male chauvinism and egotism which protects them from their fear of themselves and others. The fear and hatred which begin within the family continue in our experience in school, with friends, at jobs and generally pervade our adult lives.

As Amerika falls apart, the hatred and fear extend beyond our personal lives and become a political tool used internationally by those in power to protect themselves and their position. Our personal doubts and fears become of necessity political. Growing up in the last two decades, we have seen in Black America, Vietnam, Cuba, Korea and the Dominican Republic that the ruling class is willing to use any means necessary to hold on to their power.

In contrast to the hatred used by the U.S. ruling class, the people of the Third World showed us a different kind of hatred, a hatred which they converted into the energy of the people's war. Third World people also taught us about revolutionary love—the love for each other which they learned as they fought for their liberation from the oppressors. They need to love each other and all revolutionary people around the world as a necessity of life, as a way of surviving and eventually winning. They need love to survive in the same way we are forced to hate as a way of survival. As the Vietnamese, Cubans and others fought for their liberation, they understood the dialectical relationship between revolutionary love and revolutionary hatred. Love for sisters and brothers means hatred for the oppressor and hatred for the oppressor means love for sisters and brothers. For those of us who are trying to be revolutionaries in Amerika, it is very difficult for us to work out the dialectic between love and hatred. It has always been easier for us to hate and we often mistake hatred for each other with hatred for the enemy. We have tried to turn our love into revolutionary energy, both in our personal relationships and at People's Park, in the Columbia communes and in other struggles, but so far we haven't been strong enough to keep any of these things going.

In an attempt to sustain these struggles, some of us joined together to form Weatherman. We said, "You don't need a Weatherman to know which way the wind blows," to show that we were a product of existing social forces. Weatherman was a response to the Vietnamese and black struggles, to the growing youth movement within the mother country, to the emergence of white revolutionary women and to the escalating militancy of the New Left. But we knew we had to be not only a response to history but also a force of history. The energy behind that force could only be our revolutionary love and our revolutionary hatred. To move on to a higher level of struggle, we had to work out relationships between the two.

No longer could we separate our politics from our personal lives. Because we were white and in the oppressor nation, we had never understood, either personally or historically, what it meant to live our whole lives being revolutionary. As part of the oppressor nation, we had been separated from the

Third World. As a result of this cultural and economic separation, our minds had been split from our bodies, our thought
from our action, our feelings from our thoughts.

To struggle with these contradictions of being a white
mother country radical, to begin to transform ourselves, we
formed collectives. We employed criticism–self-criticism to
evaluate our practice and learn from our mistakes. Much internal struggle centered on male chauvinism and monogamy,
both of which we attacked, not as abstract principles, but as
counterrevolutionary practices. We saw how male chauvinism
set up men as machismo leaders who developed a politics
around proving their masculinity. It held women back from
being leaders and denied them the ability to struggle politically. We attacked monogamy because we saw it as a central
form of male chauvinism which reinforced women's political
dependence on men.

The collective was conceived of as an arena for struggle
and transformation, a form in which people could be open
about their past lives and struggle over what it meant now to
be a revolutionary. Macho prevented men particularly from
being open about their fears and weaknesses. Monogamy was
a dependency relationship in which people held on to each
other rather than pushed each other.

Women became leadership around pushing to be honest
and open, and from this strength which we got from our
honesty, particularly with each other, we were able to confront men and feel the power we had to change both ourselves and men. A new kind of leadership began to emerge
based on building each person to be strong rather than on
reinforcing the power of a few at the expense of others. For
this style of leadership to succeed we need an understanding
of ourselves and of revolutionary love. Only recently has this
leadership become a reality.

In our attempts to change we made many mistakes. We
knew that to change the pear we had to bite into it, but in
our over-eagerness, we often got some bad mouthfuls. That
hatred and self-doubt which Amerika had drilled into us led
us to confuse hatred for the oppressor with hatred for each

other. Too often we forgot that criticism was meant to build and not to smash. In their anger against chauvinism, women often attacked men rather than struggling with them. We understood a great deal about sisterhood and revolutionary love, but we still found it difficult sometimes to believe that men could change.

An elitism which led us to believe that we were the only whites that could bite into the pear gave others some bad tastes. Political conviction led us to disagree with many people, but sectarianism kept us from finding ways of struggling with these people. We were unable to understand the validity and potential of other forms of struggle and unnecessarily separated ourselves from many revolutionaries, particularly in the women's movement.

Several months ago, it became apparent that the struggle around these basic questions had to continue but as we moved towards armed struggle in the mother country, our forms of struggle had to change. Different collectives had to take on different kinds of tasks and we thought about the underground and how it would work. We needed an underground to carry out higher levels of struggle, that was clear, but there was great disagreement as to the role of the underground. One conception, which came about out of feeling unable to change ourselves and others, out of the failures of the collectives, led to an even greater political and personal isolation. This conception correctly identified the enemy, but saw moving out of revolutionary hatred, without understanding revolutionary love. Because this political conception struggled with only half of the basic relation between love and hate, it could not survive and proved itself to be horribly wrong.

Most people think of Weatherman as a group of people who sneak around at night with little bombs in our back pockets. But that's only half of what we are. We could not exist without a very strong feeling of love for each other, without feeling a tremendous joy at carrying out the tasks we have determined for ourselves. If at night we are secretive and tricky, in the day we are open and happy, digging on being alive; moving, as the communique said, in every commune, dormitory, barracks, and freak scene.

We have learned a great deal from our past mistakes. Just as other revolutionary people have learned that they must be guided by great feelings of love and hatred, we have made much progress in our struggles with each other. For us in the mother country, as for our sisters and brothers around the world, revolutionary trust and love are becoming a necessity for survival. We know that as we destroy we must build and that the relationships upon which we construct our work and our lives are vital in creating the socialist society of the future which Che describes.

Many problems remain. Male chauvinism still exists in all of us, but we realize that if we are to survive and build for the future, macho will have to be smashed. Our struggle is too important to be held back by male chauvinism. Bernardine Dohrn is no token; she's one of the strongest revolutionary leaders we have.

We have come to a much more realistic approach to monogamy. It's still true that while male chauvinism forms the basis of bourgeois-dependency monogamous relationships, there are great possibilities for love between two people struggling to be revolutionaries. It is inconceivable that at this stage of the struggle we can have totally equal communist relationships with all our brothers and sisters, and natural that we should dig some people more than others. It is out of our love for a particular person, as well as out of our love for all the people, that we get the strength for a protracted war. Just as it was important in the beginning to understand that our personal relationships and happiness affect and help to determine our politics.

Our task now is to join the people of the world in destroying U.S. imperialism and building a socialist society. We must all understand what destruction and construction mean for us in our daily political lives. While the political direction of armed struggle is indicated by the underground, this does not mean others can sit back and let the underground do it alone. Our struggle must be waged on every level, on every front.

We must learn from the Viet Cong, the Latin American revolutionaries, and the Palestine Liberation Front. We must all begin to think of ourselves as urban guerrillas and attack the enemy where we can. The communique issued after Pig Headquarters blew up, said, "Political power grows out of a gun, a riot, a Molotov, a commune . . . the soul of the people." We all have the power to change our lives, to begin to build as we begin to destroy, to begin to live our revolutionary love and our revolutionary hatred.

"He that's not busy being born is busy dying."
"Make Love and War"

Letter To The Movement

Linda Evans

On April 15 I had eaten breakfast with a "friend" (who turned out to be a pig) and was walking home, humming spring songs to myself, when twenty or so Feds pushed me into a wall. "This is the FBI. You're under arrest, Linda." I was captured. An hour later Dianne Donghi, fellow Weatherwoman and good friend, was busted by the same pigs.

I freaked: I thought all my paranoid nightmares were coming true at once. On the surface it looked like the pigs were totally together and that this was just the beginning of the end—that the Underground and all of us were doomed before we really got started.

But in fact that day shows us in a thousand ways that the Feds really don't know what's happening. They had no idea of where I lived in New York. They had never followed me or Dianne. By their own admission, they hadn't recognized me. No one I had stayed with during the month the pigs were after me had given them information. It was obvious that their knowledge was based solely on information given to them by this one pig. They had assigned a hundred Special Agents to find just the twelve Weathercriminals (besides the hundreds of Feds who have been so unsuccessfully hunting the rest of us: (STILL AT LARGE): Pat Swinton, H. Rap Brown, Jane Alpert, scores of Black Panthers, Pun Plamundon, Linda Quint, etc.) and yet this elaborate, special network for cornering freaks/fugitives of various sorts hasn't produced a single prisoner. (. . . Hundreds of us are still free, mocking them with our very lives, gleefully wreaking havoc on the fucked-up way of life they try so painfully to protect. . . .)

Dianne and I were busted by a very clever infiltrator who had survived living in one of our collectives for over six months, suffered incredible sexual/social/political traumas without flinching, even made it through a two-day acid epic/test because people suspected he might be a pig. They got me because of our bad security in the past (when we were an open organization), and because I was careless, trusting other people's evaluations of this motherfucker rather than following my own head. I wasn't busted because the Feds knew anything about where I was or what I was doing. One single pig, whose cover and usefulness are now totally blown, is responsible for my capture. Our mistake, and bad luck, but *not* part of any technological miracle machine decreeing our ultimate defeat.

So now I'm a prisoner of war, the first person captured from Underground. BUT IT IS *NOT* INEVITABLE OR PROBABLE THAT THEY WILL CATCH ANY MORE OF US. It was *never* inevitable that any of us would be captured—only our carelessness caused it. These pigs are totally freaked out by all our disappearances, ridiculously incompetent as super-sleuths, and, most important, *on the wrong side*. If we are cool, even in the smallest ways, all the Special Federal Agents in the world won't get any more of the (growing. . .) hordes of us who are free. OUR STRENGTH IS EACH OTHER—coming closer and closer together, discovering/knowing who we are and what we want, fighting to change or destroy what is wrong and ugly about the world—for our own freedom. We can change and love each other enough to give us the strength we need to win. And we will.

Freedom. Peace.
Linda

Unsettled Accounts

Larry Grathwohl began hanging around the Cincinnati Weather collective before the National Action in October, 1969. He came on as a "greaser"—a poor Cincinnati working-class street kid. He said he was an ex-G.I. who had served his time in Vietnam, and had come out of that experience totally disgusted with Amerika. He said he had an old police record in the city from when he was a kid, and that he'd gone to night school at the University. He told the collective that he'd never dug political groups, because none of them seemed to be into much; he was attracted to Weatherman because it was the first organization he'd seen that was really into doing shit.

Grathwohl didn't go to the National Action, but after it was over, he came into the Cincinnati collective. People didn't quite trust him, and tried to run security checks on him. Posing as employers, they tried to check out both his police record and his claims about night school; neither place would release any information about him. They met with old friends of his, to check out what he said about himself; that seemed to fit together. They talked heavy to him, trying to find out where he was at; he never got flustered or contradicted himself. The best example of how Grathwohl handled himself in the collective is the story of an "acid test" of him they did in January. For the first six hours of the trip, people laid into him hard about their suspicions—questioning, accusing, and pressing him for information. He wouldn't say anything at all. Finally, he looked up at them. "You're right," he said slowly, "I AM a pig—I'm a pig because of what I did in Vietnam; because I stood by and saw the brutality of what was being done to innocent people, because I watched Viet-

From the *Berkeley Tribe,* August 21, 1970. Copyright 1970 by The Red Mountain Tribe. Reprinted by permission.

namese women being raped by G.I.s, and didn't try to stop it." He spoke of the beauty and strength of the Vietnamese people, and how that had turned him on to fighting for revolution here when he returned home. The end of the trip was a coming together between him and the other people in the collective. They felt they had made a mistake about him; that their suspicions had been wrong. "Most people you suspect of being a pig are schmucks anyway," one of them told us; "If you throw them out, it isn't much of a loss. But with Larry, what we felt was that if he wasn't a pig, there was a good chance that he'd turn into an outasight revolutionary leader."

After the acid trip, Larry became much more open in his relationships in the collective. He became something of a leader in struggling to find a new life and a new identity for them as white revolutionary kids. He even began to loosen up about fucking, one of the things he'd always been most uptight about, and almost incapable of. People were feeling pretty good about him.

In February, Dianne Donghi, who'd known Larry in Cincinnati, went to Chicago. There, she was busted by the FBI for interstate transportation of stolen weapons. The U.S. Attorney threw the case out, and told Dianne and her lawyer that the bust had been set up by an informer inside Weatherman.

Meanwhile, Grathwohl was in another city, supposedly sick with malaria. He said he was desperately ill, and getting treatment in a Veterans Hospital. When his friends called the hospital to check on how he was, they were told that he had never been there. At the same time, he was seen outside the Federal Building in Cincinnati in a coat and tie. If the malaria story was true, there's no way he could have been well enough to be out of bed on the day that he was seen. Because of communications fuck-ups, this information didn't get through to people who could have put it together until much, much later.

Grathwohl "recovered," and became active again. He took to disappearing for days at a time and returning with weird stories, and unexplained sums of money. People didn't question him too much—they wanted their cadre to be independent, and not to feel that they had to account to each other for every facet of their lives.

Larry met up with Dianne again in New York City, shortly before the April bust. He was acting strange; constantly grumpy and bitter. He couldn't relate any more to the closeness they'd been developing. His sexual uptightness had returned—once again, he was incapable of fucking. As the time of the bust got nearer, he grew increasingly violent, alienated, and hostile. He demanded to meet with other Weatherpeople who were underground, and refused to tell Dianne why. He said he had his own reasons, and that he didn't trust her enough to tell her what they were. She grew suspicious of him again; she was sick, pregnant, and fucked up by the contradiction of caring for him and thinking that he might be a pig. She tried to make sure that he didn't know much about anyone but her.

The day of the bust, Larry went out to meet with Linda Evans. As they walked down the street, they were surrounded by FBI agents. "Linda Evans," the pigs announced, "you're under arrest." They said nothing to Larry (or Tom Niehman, the alias he was going under). Larry took off down the street. He says that when they caught him, he pulled a knife, and hit one of them. He and Linda were taken to jail, and the pigs went for Dianne. Twenty agents busted into her hotel room at once. "Where's your boyfriend?" they demanded.

The FBI told Dianne that she'd been followed for six days, and mentioned places she'd been, and things she'd done. She thought they knew everything, and that she'd been a total fool for not realizing that she'd been followed. But as they kept questioning her, she began to realize that all they knew was stuff she'd told Larry about—nothing else. The only people they asked her about were those she'd talked to him about. The pigs emphasized to Dianne how glad they were to have caught Tom Niehman. They said they wished they'd beat the shit out of him when he put up a fight. But a little while later, when Dianne got to speak to Larry, he complained that they HAD beaten him up badly. Obviously, there was some game they were into playing about Larry to Dianne and Linda. When the three were booked and finger-printed, Linda and Dianne smiled and joked with each other, trying to give each other strength in the panic of what was happening to them. Larry wouldn't look at or speak to them. Both women were rapidly coming to the same conclusion.

Larry's next appearance was at his identity hearing. His alias of Tom Niehman was exposed, along with the fact that he'd been using stolen identification for months. But no charges were put on him for that Federal offense—pretty strange practice for a government that's into piling charges sky-high on any Weatherman they can get their hands on. His bail was set at $7,500—absurdly low for the charge of assault-ing a Federal agent (Linda's was $50,000, and Dianne's $20,000, for the comparatively minor charge of witnessing a forgery). He was cut loose on his own recognizance.

Once out on bail, Grathwohl's travel restrictions were that he couldn't leave New York. He promptly split to the New Haven Panther trial, and hung around openly, trying to make contact with people. He also went to Cincinnati and Dodge City, Iowa, where Linda Evans was living in her parents' custody. Straight lawyers in Dodge City have proof that he was given a police escort out of town. In all this traveling, he moved freely and obviously—not at all like someone who would be thrown back in jail if it was discovered that he was violating the terms of his bail. He consistently hung around places that were crawling with undercover pigs, and yet he was never busted for what he was doing. In late July, the day that the latest Weather indictments came down, he called Linda, and kept her on the phone until the very minute when the FBI knocked at her door to arrest her. And everything that's happened since has followed the same pattern.

Grathwohl was one of the conspirators named in the July indictments. Every other conspirator who was living openly has been picked up by the FBI. Larry has been traveling freely from city to city, making contact with all kinds of people, coming into watched movement offices, hanging out in pig-patrolled places like Telegraph Avenue. And yet he's never been picked up on the Federal fugitive warrant they have out for him. At a time when the FBI is so desperate to pick up Weathermen, it's obvious on the basis of how he's been living that they could get him in a minute if they really wanted to. The only explanation for why they don't is that he's on their side—one of the most together police agents they've ever been able to put over on us.

There are several reasons the FBI is leaving Grathwohl on the streets, despite the fact that his cover is partially blown. The most obvious is that they want to preserve his cover as a Weatherman, so they can use him to testify against the others at the trial. Larry is working hard to re-establish his identity as a revolutionary in Movement circles around the country; his rage and protests against our charges are loud and clear. It's possible that people who don't know the facts will be taken in by him, and will lead him to further chances to destroy work that's going on, and the people who are doing it. And of course, the government might be insane enough to hope that Weatherpeople would still trust him, and that he would be able to lead them to people who are still under-ground. The other possibilities are just as insidious. One is that the government is hoping that by leaving him open in the midst of all this suspicion, some people will take care of business with him. Then maybe they can pin a conspiracy to murder charge on Linda and Dianne. And if that doesn't happen, maybe—and this is what the Weatherpeople's lawyers fear most—maybe the Government will off him themselves, and pin the blame on people they want to put away for a long time. Both these possibilities make it hard to know how to deal with the situation.

We all know what should happen to Larry Grathwohl. But like one of the Weather defendants said: "The thing about a level of struggle is, you do it when you can win." And right now, there's a danger that people with the best intentions could move on Grathwohl in a way that would fuck up our sisters who were busted real bad. What we've got to do is deal with him in a way that will put him out of circulation, and not hurt any of us. For example, if the pigs are forced to arrest Grathwohl, and still refuse to declare that he's their agent, a good part of their legal case will be blown.

What's probably the worst thing we could do is to think that we can outsmart Grathwohl by getting friendly, and turning his game around on him. Larry is clearly one of the smartest dudes going, and to try to turn him around would be suicidal. Pigs like him are, literally, wired for sound, and anything—ANYTHING—you say to him can be used against you in court, in a new Grand Jury indictment, or whatever.

If Grathwohl stays in circulation, Berkeley'll probably get too hot for him soon—he'll move on to a place like Portland or Isla Vista, where his pig identity isn't well known, and where kids would be inclined to trust a tough, smooth-talking revolutionary who pulled a knife on the FBI when they were busting Linda Evans. We've got to spread the word about Grathwohl all over the country, and cancel any chance of that happening.

Agents like Larry Grathwohl are viciously fucked up. The only thing we can want is to have them wiped out like the poisonous vipers they are—without leaving them or the government that controls them the smallest chance to strike back.

Larry Grathwohl

Ted Gold: Education For Violence

J. Kirk Sale

A sign in a store on Eighth Street in Greenwich Village says: "Ted Gold died for our sins." On the wall of a building near Columbia University someone has scrawled: "Ted Gold Lives." And at the base of a flagpole on the Columbia campus, students who tried to lower the flag to half-staff wrote, in crayon: "In Memory of Ted Gold. Fight Like Him."

Ted Gold's death, in a Greenwich village town-house explosion on March 6, was heavy with symbolism. He was suffocated in the fancy paneled walls of an incredibly luxurious building worth, in these inflated times, some $250,000. Its owner was a man who made much of his fortune as an advertising executive for Young & Rubicam, who was a frequent defender of the role of advertising in the American system, and who put his money into commercial radio systems in the American heartland. The explosion was probably caused by dynamite, that romantic nineteenth-century revolutionary weapon. And at the time of his death Ted Gold may have been seated at a desk, working on a history of Students for a Democratic Society that he was reputed to have been researching, probing the roots of the New Left, and determining how it had come so far in such a few years.

The details of what happened in this tragic explosion are still murky. But it does seem clear that those in the house were Weathermen, a splinter group so far down the road of violence from the rest of the old SDS that it no longer even thinks of itself by those initials, and is indeed composed mostly of people who are not students and scorn the notion of a "democratic" society. They had a sizable stockpile of explosives in the house—probably one hundred sticks of dynamite, some packed into twelve-inch lead-pipe bombs,

From *The Nation*, April 13, 1970 (J. Kirk Sale is an editor of *The New York Times Magazine*) Copyright 1970 by *The Nation*.

and others into tape-wrapped packages; plus detonating caps, wires and cheap alarm clocks for timers—and were probably planning their imminent use. At least three people died: Gold; a Weatherwoman, Diana Oughton; and a second man as yet unidentified.

The explosion brought home to the public a dramatic and, for some, frightening turn by a part of the young left in this country. It showed—what should have been obvious by now —that many people, not by any means the Weathermen alone, are so angry at the ills of this society, so frustrated by their inability to eradicate them, so embittered by the failure of earlier peaceful efforts and the repression those have called forth, that they feel the only hope is "to bring the mother down." Revolution is a word much flaunted these days—"the revolutionary new car from Germany," "the revolution in men's fashions," "the appliance that will revolutionize your kitchen"—but for these people "revolution" is a serious, literally a deadly serious, word. It means fighting, bombing, even dying to change totally the American system.

To understand this rage-turned-to-revolution, it may help to focus on Ted Gold, who believed in it. There are hazards, of course. Gold was only one man, and such concentration can make more of him than we should. He was not, by the usual yardsticks, a major leader of the Weathermen, nor in any sense a "typical" member. There is no special pattern to his life that sets him apart from his comrades, and even his death was an accident of the sort that can exaggerate a humble man into a hero. The lens too narrowly focused on Ted Gold causes the edges to blur, making unclear the larger issues.

Moreover, the subject is now beyond our reach, and one must attempt his portrait through family, friends, acquaintances and teachers. Ted Gold's parents, stunned with a sorrow mixed with anger and bewilderment, do not want to talk about him; his friends, for whom the overwhelming reaction seems to be simple shock, are similarly saddened and puzzled, and for the most part choose to keep their thoughts private. Those most closely allied with Gold in the Weathermen have chosen to go underground, fearing police harass-ment. In any case, as revolutionaries, they are not about to blurt forth the workings of their revolution.

Finally, many of those in the movement generally—from those who deplore the use of violence, through those for whom it is only too early, to those who are even now prepar-ing more of it—feel that one should be writing not about Ted Gold but about the rapacious, unrepentant society that made him what he was. They believe that to concentrate on the minimal violence of a single town-house and three young bodies is to ignore the over-arching violence of a society which for the past ten years has been blowing up entire cities and killing upward of half a million people in Vietnam; which has systematically wrought violence upon its black, brown, red and poor white peoples throughout its existence. They believe that the ultimate effect of concentrating on Gold will be to justify the powers-that-be in their already escalating attack upon the Left, and they point out that there was no parallel attack on the Right when, for example, during the 1960s at least two hundred thirteen acts of white violence were committed against those in the civil rights movement. Holding these beliefs, many of those who knew Gold best refuse to talk.

I find these arguments important but not persuasive. That violence is a part of the system, that repression is afoot, that the media are biased—those seem to be facts, but not there-fore sufficient reasons to turn away, or to turn inward. The impulse to revolution needs examination if it is to be compre-hended by any of us, from Left to Right. The Eleventh Street blast, though only one of many in the escalating wave of violent rebellion, was an explosion heard across the country. By the vagaries of history—even instant history—Ted Gold has become a signal figure.

Theodore Gold was born in New York City on December 13, 1947, into a milieu that is by now almost predictable for contemporary activists. He was an only child. His parents were liberals of the upper-West Side Jewish variety, living in a pleasant apartment on tree-lined Ninety-third Street, comfortably well-off if not exactly rich. His father, Dr. Hyman Gold, an internist in a Health Insurance Plan clinic and a volunteer emergency doctor for an East Side day-care center, is regarded as having an evident concern for bringing medicine to the poor. His mother, Dr. Ruth Gold, is an associate professor of Education at Columbia University's Teachers College. Most sociological studies suggest that activist youth come from just this kind of background, where both parents work and the dinner table ideas are likely to be at least liberal. What they don't go on to say is that when both parents are away all day and the child is raised by a black maid, as in Ted Gold's case, the resulting psychological dislocations may be as great an impetus to radicalism. In fact one might even imagine that part of the attraction of a close-knit, intimate group—as were those formed during the Columbia confrontation of 1968 and as are the Weathermen collectives and "affinity groups"—stems from family deprivation in early life.

At high school, Gold was so ordinary as to make him almost invisible. He was very bright and very normal. His teachers, if they remember anything, recall a "bright-eyed" or "attentive" or "very smart" boy, but for the most part they agree with his high school biology teacher, Mrs. Elektra Demas, that "there was nothing really to distinguish him from the other boys." At Manhattan's top-level Stuyvesant High, he did well in all his courses (graduating two hundred twelfth in a class of six hundred ninety-nine, with an eighty-nine average), was a member of the Stamp Club and the History and Folklore Society, and ran on the track and cross-country teams. "All in all," says Stuyvesant Principal Leonard Fliedner, "he was the kind of boy you like to have around a school, the kind you'd want your own son to be like."

There are some suggestions of a burgeoning political sense even in these days. He was involved in civil rights work, largely through the Friends of SNCC, a Northern group composed mostly of students, which raised money and food for civil rights workers in the South, and whose Stuyvesant chapter Gold helped organize. And he went, for a couple of years at least, to Camp Webatuck, in Wingdale, N.Y., one of those "leftist" camps that serve Left-liberal New York: labor songs, unstructured hours, muted Marxist rhetoric, involved kids. During the summer of 1963, one old friend remembers, Gold was "already very pro-Cuba—and therefore somewhat, you know, bitter about Kennedy—and already upset about American involvement in Vietnam"—plus being "an outasight third-baseman."

Still, all this was within what another friend calls "acceptable student activism." in his first two years at Columbia, Gold was quiet, intellectual and unobtrusive; his concern took the form of work with CORE and a summertime slum-tutorial group. He spoke vaguely about going to law school to become a poor people's lawyer, or about concentrating in urban studies. One of his freshman teachers noted at the time that he was "quiet but had convictions."

Gradually Gold gravitated to a few like-minded students who in the spring of 1966 were restarting an intermittent SDS chapter, and early in 1967, his junior year, he became vice-chairman of the chapter. That fall he had his first taste of activism when New York SDS demonstrated in the streets against Dean Rusk—the first time, on the East Coast at least, that students had initiated violence rather than waiting to be clubbed. Gold was arrested and charged with rioting, a misdemeanor for which he was not even fingerprinted—so that when his body was found in the town-house New York police were unable to make an identification and had to send to the FBI in Washington for his prints. (The FBI had a set, taken when Gold was arrested along with seven other Weathermen, for vandalizing a Philadelphia television station last January 10, after it broadcast what they called a "slanderous" TV documentary on the Black Panthers.)

Gold's politics began the turn toward revolution during the Columbia uprising in the spring of 1968, an affair that, in retrospect, illuminates some of his major characteristics.

First, he was a bright, intellectual, behind-the-scenes man ("quiet and reserved," says a friend) who, when possible, left the stage to more excitable grandstanders like Mark Rudd. He was, according to a student at the time, "one of the few people who really had *read* all that Marx and Lenin that they all quoted," and was one of a small group whose researches in 1967 had originally exposed Columbia's tie to the Institute for Defense Analysis. He was also a member of a moderate wing of Columbia SDS called the "praxis axis," which emphasized research and winning adherents by education and persuasion, as opposed to the "action faction," which emphasized confrontation and overt demonstrations as the best way to win followers. This latter wing, led by Rudd, Nick Freudenberg and John Jacobs, won out in the March 1968 chapter elections and dominated much of the subsequent action.

Gold, however, never tried to bolt the organization or work outside it. For a second characteristic was that, though scholarly, he never felt wholly comfortable with that role alone. He was one of the first on campus to affect proletarian blue shirts, and was obviously attracted to action-minded types. At times he tried to join them on the platform, and on several occasions during the uprising gave speeches to hold crowds together or encourage bystanders to join, though without noticeable success. (Once, before addressing a crowd, he turned to a friend and confessed, "I don't know what's happening," not realizing his bull-horn amplifier was turned on.)

Originally in separate wings, Gold and Rudd nonetheless worked together throughout the Columbia battle, spent the next year in fairly close association around the New York SDS office, and finally went together into the Weathermen. But Gold never really liked Rudd, it would seem, or at least resented his style. Dotson Rader, one of the Columbia strikers and author of a very revealing account of New Left activism, *I Ain't Marchin' Anymore,* remembers that during the take-overs Gold "felt that Rudd was trying to establish a personality cult. He said one night he thought Rudd was grandstanding too much and wasn't directly involved with the building of communes and what people were thinking."

Still, Gold—short, bespectacled, quiet, intellectual, controlled—must have found something enormously appealing in Rudd—tall, loose, attractive, outgoing, reckless. It is easy to imagine that Rudd and the other actionists were very important to Gold. At Columbia (and after) they were continually talking about the need for courage, for "putting your body on the line," for shaking off "bourgeois hangups" about violence and death, for ceasing to be "wimps." During the confrontations (and after), Gold, the quiet intellectual, moved steadily toward their camp.

Gold made what may have been a last break with standard liberalism during the Columbia fracas. He was apparently terribly embittered by what he regarded as a liberal sellout by the Ad Hoc Faculty Committee, with whom he was one of the chief student negotiators. As he later put it to the authors of *Up Against the Ivy Wall,* a history of the Columbia crisis:

> They were demanding complete abdication of our position, and we were talking in terms of their joining us. We were miles apart. But we didn't want to break off discussion. We were told that they were a more "liberal" group. We said, "All right, if you're on our side, then take a position in favor of amnesty and the other six demands." Those s.o.b.'s said that we should be more reasonable.

It is characteristic of student radicals that they feel betrayed and angered when they are confronted at first hand with the shoddiness and failure of those liberal institutions which they had once regarded as sacrosanct. Hence their particular dislike of Kennedy, Stevenson, Goldberg, Humphrey and the like.

Finally, the Columbia affair showed that Ted Gold had come to some understanding of the place of violence in society and its use as a political weapon. As early as April, in a letter to President Grayson Kirk that Gold helped draft, the SDS leaders said: "Until Columbia ends all affiliation with the IDA, we must disrupt the functioning of all those involved in the daily disruption of people's lives around the world." (Or, as the Weathermen were to put it eighteen months later in their Chicago action: "Bring the War

Home.") Later, Gold recalled, "We didn't want a police bust, but we would rather have had that than give in to the administration." And the feeling of the eleven-man strike committee, of which Gold was a member, seemed to be that a bust, if it came, would be advantageous to the striking students, would lead to the kind of radicalization it indeed produced. In the heat of battle, in short, Gold accepted the need for violence.

The entire Columbia experience, in fact, was a test of personal courage in the face of violence, or threatened violence, and that must have left a mark. Perhaps even without so planning, the SDS students put themselves into situation after situation in which their courage would be on the line—taking buildings, refusing to leave after warnings, locking arms in the face of moving policemen. At first so unaccustomed to all this as to be terrified of the guns that the blacks were reported to have brought with them into a seized building, the SDSers by the end were steeled to it.

Ted Gold was suspended for a year by Columbia for his role in the occupations, though he had completed all his coursework, and with a solid B average. That summer he began to organize a Teachers for a Democratic Society, part of a loose Movement for a Democratic Society that was forming in New York of SDSers who had graduated from college and wanted to continue their activism. That fall he began to teach at the Adams School, a private Manhattan school for brain-damaged and emotionally disturbed children.

TDS was Gold's last organized attempt to work through education and (however militant) persuasion. He was "an incredibly hard worker" and ran "the neatest office I've ever seen in the Movement," says one who worked with him for a while that year. Not surprisingly he was one of the half-dozen leaders of the organization. The thrust was toward organizing high school youth, an effort that seemed to have some success, especially in an atmosphere made electric by the teachers' strike that fall. With Adrienne Yurick, wife of novelist Sol Yurick, and Shin'ya Ono, later a Weatherman, Gold shaped the editorial views of a sporadic four-page newspaper, *Hey Teach,* which the TDS put out that year. In one issue the featured article, headed "Jailbreak! Join US!" said:

Schools are basically jails and the kids know that. People in jail want to get out. . . . Black and brown students understand not only that schools are oppressive every day, but they also know that there is nothing waiting for them when they get out—only jails of a different kind— menial jobs or unemployment, rotten housing, rats, disease, police, or the Army, Vietnam and death.

Today, when the Weathermen begin actions at high schools in cities around the country, the slogan they use is "Jailbreak!"

But ultimately the TDS effort failed. The high school kids in effect resented the attempt by "outside agitators" to radicalize them, and once the strike was settled the air began to cool. Gold, according to some who were around him then, became more and more rigid, less and less inclined to trying to "change heads." "He had no patience for anyone not at the same level of consciousness," says one young man. "If you said something he didn't agree with, he'd say 'Bullshit' and walk away. He became terribly autocratic—he was *hell* to deal with." Rudd, who was also in New York directing the SDS regional office, took an I-told-you-so line—he had never been convinced that there was any way to radicalize students other than direct action—and for a while the two were somewhat estranged. Gradually, however, Gold seems to have been won around to the actionists' conviction that winning hearts and minds is perhaps best done by twisting arms.

By the end of the school year Gold had apparently made the break. He was not rehired by the Adams School—"he gave no indication that he had a continuing interest in special education," principal Moses Lorentz says—and though Columbia alllowed him to get his degree after wresting from him a promise to behave, he apparently went through with it largely to please his mother. The stage was set for the SDS June convention.

At that convention, everyone knew that SDS was going to split. The Progressive Labor Party, an outgrowth of the left wing of the Communist Party, had successfully infiltrated

SDS ranks and now planned to take over its national office. The national office people, with whom the ex-Columbia radicals were aligned, hoped to beat them down or force them out. When the test came, the PLers were in the majority, the national office followers split off into their own convention, and there the action wing, the Weathermen, was born.

The Weatherman line is complicated and has shifted over this past year to take account of different actions—and reactions. But basically the group is made up of those who feel that the only way to change this country is through violent confrontation: "The primary purpose, and the stance, of our organizing," writes Shin'ya Ono, "could not possibly be to 'turn people on,' or to have them like us, or to make them think that we are nice, but to compel them to confront the antagonistic aspects of their own life experience and consciousness by bringing the war home, and to help them make the right choice over a period of time, after initially shaking up and breaking through the thick layers of chauvinism-racism-defeatism." In other words, if you put people up against the wall, force them to choose, sooner or later they'll have to be either for the revolution or for the system.

Gold was a Weatherman from the start, though, characteristically, on its more moderate flank. ("If Gold was a member of some nihilist group, the farthest left thing you could be," comments Dotson Rader, "he'd find some way of being on the moderate side of it: that was his nature.") And, as at Columbia, he seems to have been continually pressed—as indeed the whole group was, and deliberately—to prove himself. One young observer recalls: "Rudd continually accused people of cowardice, that was his big word then, and said how you had to get a gun, and stop being afraid, and be a man, and all that."

There is in all of this what seems to be an abiding sense of guilt, and it was probably as true for Gold as for other Weathermen and those like them. To oversimplify, they tend to feel guilty about the comfortable, privileged, often very rich homes from which they come, especially when they try to take their message into the mangled, oppressed and very desperate homes of the poor. They feel guilty about what they regard as their own inescapable middle-class racism and that of the society that has showered its benefits on their parents. They feel guilty that they are, at least at the start, frightened of violence, and envy those, like the blacks and the working-class youths, who have confronted violence from infancy. They feel guilty that their brains, money or pull has kept them safe on university campuses while others are sent to Vietnam. And they feel guilty that the society which has given them and their families so much, and which they have spent the better part of their adolescence trying to change, is obdurate in its basic inequities.

Out of all this, not surprisingly, grows an immense rage. Each day that rage is fed—with a My Lai or neighborhood police brutality, with a Moynihan memo or a black friend forced onto welfare, with a Chicago Conspiracy trial or a local pot bust, with an ABM system, a Hampton murder, an illegal Laos bombing. The rage solidifies into something that contains all the elements of a religion: asceticism (no drugs, liquor or pets were allowed in the Weather collectives), intolerance, a conviction of one's own rightness, and the abiding need to demonstrate that rightness. And thus the last weapon of a religious minority, martyrdom. "So now also the revolution shall be magnified in my body, whether it be by life or by death. For me to live is revolution, to die is gain."

After the formation of the Weathermen at the SDS convention, a trip to Cuba in late summer began for Gold the solidification of his ideas. The Cuba trip provided not only an attractive, energetic, functioning communist society that he could, for a time at least, identify with, but also a meeting with the Vietnamese Provisional Revolutionary Government and some of its shrewdest cadre. The message of the PRG people seems to have been that they needed allies within the United States to bring an end to the war, and Gold returned with the conviction, as he wrote it for Liberation News Service, that:

"As people who are located inside the monster, revolutionary Americans are in a position to do decisive damage to the

U.S. ruling class's plans to continue and expand its world rule. The upcoming U.S. defeat in Vietnam will be a vital blow to those plans; we must aim to do everything we can to speed up that defeat."

Next came October 8-11 in Chicago, what the Weathermen called, appropriately enough, the "Days of Rage," when they went up against the cops and found their courage not wanting. But not sufficient, either—the action was too weak, too many people were arrested, too much money ($1 million) was required for bail. The Weathermen retired to their collectives, to rethink their strategy, and for the next three months went through serious soul-searching. Gold apparently stayed at the Chicago collective, where most of the national leaders—Rudd, Jacobs, Bernardine Dohrn—also spent most of their time, and was an intimate part of those who planned the next strategic steps.

Those steps were more or less danced out at the Weatherman "war council" in Flint, Michigan, December 27-30. The council's temper was suggested, though not wholly seriously, by its gimmicks: the slogans were such as "Piece Now," "Sirhan Sirhan Power" and "Red Army Power"; the greetings were four fingers slightly spread (symbolizing the fork which Charlie Manson's gang plunged into one of its victims), and forefinger pointed out, with thumb cocked.

Violence, in short—though paid homage with rhetoric rather than in fact—was the abiding theme. Gold made a speech in which he tried to show its immediacy. The American revolution, he said, would come about as part of a large worldwide revolution and as part of a revolt by the black colony within the nation. Once the country is brought to its knees, "an agency of the people of the world" would be established to run things here.

A critic in the audience objected: "In short, if the people of the world succeed in liberating themselves before American radicals have made the American revolution, then the Vietnamese and Africans and the Chinese are gonna move in and run things for white America. It sounds like a John Bircher's worst dream. There will have to be more repression than ever against white people."

"Well," replied Gold, "if it will take fascism, we'll have to have fascism."

Some time after the Flint war council, the Weathermen decided to break up their collectives—the largest of which were in Chicago, New York, Boston and Philadelphia—into smaller four- and five-person affinity groups. They hoped in this way to ferret out the FBI informers who they were certain had infiltrated their ranks, and to plan guerrilla actions that could be carried out better by smaller bands. Some time early in the year Gold met Dotson Rader in the West End Bar, Columbia's watering-hole, where he vigorously defended the Days of Rage and the actions of Weathermen at Harvard who broke into the Kennedy International Affairs Center and roughed up workers and professors. "He told me," Rader recalls, and with sympathy, "that we have to teach people that violence is not an abstraction. We have to confront them with it so that they can see what they're doing. You see, Gold was always an existentialist, not really a Marxist for all his talk. He really felt that man has got to be responsible for his actions, that the people who deal in abstract violence like the Harvard teachers or Herman Kahn, say, have to be *shown* what they're doing, what real bodies are like, what violence really is. You see, our lives aren't really threatened by the Vietnam war now, and the liberals can continue along their comfortable ways. I still remember Ted saying, 'We've got to turn New York into Saigon.'"

Perhaps that is what the Eleventh Street town-house was to be used for; or perhaps the ultimate idea was simply to create the terror that would bring fascism.

How must it have felt to be living in a house full of explosives and to be preparing for actions which were certain to be dangerous? "I think the Weathermen were all prepared to die," one former Columbia student says. "They were in a way like disobedient children who wanted to be punished, and on a larger scale that's a death wish." A friend who saw Gold two weeks before the explosion reports his having said, "I've been doing a lot of exciting underground things, and I know I'm not afraid to die."

Another who knew Gold thinks it was more than just the absence of fear. "I think a desire for recognition was motivating him, I really do. He wanted to be in history—he wanted to be like Che, a tragic figure. And for tragedy you need a stage, like this historical point in time, and you need violence." And an adult around Columbia who knew Gold less well speculates: "I always felt that Ted, perhaps because of his size, or maybe his bookishness, had a kind of drive to get people to know who he was. I don't mean he wanted the limelight, not like that. But he wanted everyone to know who he was, what he was doing."

Inadvertently, he did. And at the same time made people aware not only of the Weathermen but the others like them for whom the answer to American violence is . . . American violence. *Time* pontificates that this is no way to change the country: "Many effective resources for reform are available— the courts, public opinion, peaceful demonstration, the ballot." To revolutionaries, that is a joke.

And what if the answer to the Left's new violence is the Right's new repression, a repression that could even lead to a kind of fascism? The Weathermen, as Gold said, would welcome that: "If it means that it'll make white slaves," one Weatherman is reported to have said, "we want fascism." Making the country's latent fascism overt, the Weather line goes, will force everyone in the land to take his stand: as part of the (fascist) problem, or as part of the (revolutionary) solution. There will be no middle ground, the revolutionary ranks will have to swell, and America will turn into Vichy France, complete with underground.

That is why the prospect of future violence, even of assassination, is not remote. America has made revolutionaries out of some, at least, of its young, and that is frightening; America has also shown no sign that it will not continue to do so, and that is even more frightening. In that sense the life, and death, of Ted Gold should suggest self-examination for all of us.

In Memory Of Ted Gold

I
remember ted gold best
            riding to connecticut
in a car with six
        young kids from the
            ghetto
to a conference on the war
        Five congressmen spoke
and we played
        smoky and the miracles on
            the portable record player
        and went swimming
        The kids have grown
            STUDENT
            PUSHER

            PANTHER
Ted liked to go
to the Knick games
He had season tickets
            last year
This year,
        he is dead
Of a bomb meant for better targets
There will be no processions
        and the articles in the
Times will have no quotes
For those who lost before the battle
        Who found a battle
they never really sought

                        Nelson Temple

From *Radical America*, April 1970. Copyright 1970 by *Radical America*.

For Diana Oughton

Sometimes
There is only bullets and hate
  self-sacrifice
        dismembered bodies
and blood—

And all I can see are
the lines of
   cruelty on
our faces.

But when I think of you,
Sister,

and remember how you
loved the people
        and
fought the struggle
I know what you would say now—

"You don't cry for me
but for yourselves—
That's bullshit!
Why do you only talk of dying for the
        Revolution—
Live for it!"

From the *Berkeley Tribe*, July 31, 1970. Copyright 1970 by The Red Mountain Tribe. Reprinted by permission.

Memories Of Diana

Bomb threats plagued the nation again last week, but very few bombs were going off. Nonetheless, the reverberations of recent blasts could still be heard. In Washington and in state capitals, officials were searching for new means to control dynamite and dynamiters. In Maryland, where two black militants died in bomb blasts, the trial of Rap Brown was moved once more to a new site as an indirect result of the explosions. In Manhattan, police picked carefully through the rubble of the West Eleventh Street house where at least three people died. There, in the ruins, they found a severed finger, which enabled them to identify one of the victims as Diana Oughton, twenty-eight, a talented, idealistic girl whose turn to radicalism brought her in the end to a rebel bomb factory.

Most Americans find it difficult to grasp that some of the brightest and best-cared-for young are so enraged that they have opted for the nihilism of blowing up society. Diana Oughton's story provides some answers—and engenders some pessimism as well:

Diana was born on January 26, 1942, and raised in Dwight (pop. 3,100), a town set in the prairie cornfields of northern Illinois. Her conservative, Episcopal family is one of the community's most prominent. Her paternal great-great-grandfather established the Keeley Institute for alcoholics. Her maternal great-grandfather, W.D. Boyce, founded the American Boy Scouts. James Oughton, fifty-five, Diana's father, is a Dartmouth graduate and restaurateur. Diana and her three sisters were cherished and deeply loved. Said her father: "The social life in Dwight has never separated adults from children. Dinner was a family affair, and there was a pretty wide discussion all the way through."

From *Time* magazine, March 30, 1970. Reprinted by permission from *Time,* the weekly newsmagazine. Copyright 1970 by Time, Inc.

Storybook Child. Time Correspondent Frank Merrick met in Dwight last week with Oughton and one of Diana's sisters, Carol, twenty-six, who now lives in Washington. At first, Jim Oughton was remarkably composed for a father who had just learned that his eldest child had been blown apart. He told of her storybook childhood, of how she became a good horse-woman and swimmer, played a social game of tennis, studied piano and the flute. Her father remembers Diana as "independent in her thinking. She always had her own ideas, and they were sound ideas." About what? "A picture she liked, the best way to treat an animal, which was the finest season of the year—almost anything."

Aware of the limitations of Dwight, Oughton sent Diana off to Madeira School in Greenway, Virginia, and Bryn Mawr. She spent her junior year at the University of Munich. It was at Bryn Mawr that Diana first showed an interest in social problems. Like many collegians, she was active in voter registration and tutored junior high school students. At night she would go by train to Philadelphia, where for two years she tutored two ghetto boys. Said Carol: "I remember how incredulous Diana was that a seventh- or eighth-grade child couldn't read, didn't even know the alphabet." A Princeton football player proposed marriage, but Diana said: "I don't want to get married now. There are too many things to do."

During her year in Germany, Diana made the turn away from affluence that so often marks the contemporary young. She preferred a *pension* to a luxury hotel, a bicycle to a taxicab. On a trip with her father, she carried a Michelin guidebook because, he recalled, she "didn't want to go to any of those places, she wanted to go to places unknown."

After graduating, Diana signed on with the American Friends Service Committee, took a crash course in Spanish and was sent to Guatemala. Stationed in Chichicastenango, she taught Spanish to the local Indians, who were mostly limited to their native dialect. Her eyes widened at the vast poverty and the class hatred between the wealthy few and the impoverished many. She was particularly troubled that a regime she viewed as oppressive was so strongly supported by the U.S. But she was still willing to give the U.S. Establishment a chance.

Diana went on to the University of Michigan to earn a teaching certificate. This was the critical year of 1966, when U.S. students were being radicalized by the Vietnam War. While at Ann Arbor, Diana joined the Children's Community School, an unstructured, permissive experiment in education for children from four to eight. There, she worked with Bill Ayers, son of the board chairman of Chicago's Commonwealth Edison Co., and with Eric Mann—who later became luminaries of the Students for a Democratic Society. The school, operating on Great Society money, folded in 1968, when its funds were cut off.

Stormy Days. "It was about this time," said Jim Oughton, "that there was less and less communication between Diana and any of us. She'd call and we'd call. She'd be home briefly from time to time." Diana joined SDS, and she was in Chicago for the stormy days and nights of the Democratic Convention. Sometimes she would stop in Dwight. She brought Bill Ayers and other radicals, and she would talk politics with her father, defending the revolutionary's approach to social ills.

"That was one of the tense things we did. I was so eager to find out the rationale of her thinking and activities that I probably pressed her harder than I should have. It was a complete stalemate, and she would just change the subject. I deeply loved Diana, and I certainly didn't want to break the communication for the future. I felt that sooner or later there'd be a maturity of thinking, a change of thinking."

Oughton, losing his composure at last, said: "This is as much as we know. Anything that happened with Diana in the last two years we don't have information on." He did become convinced that Diana was "completely carried away. It was almost an intellectual hysteria." The years unknown to her father were intensely political for Diana. When factionalism shattered SDS in 1969, she and Bill Ayers joined the most radical, extreme, violence-prone faction, the Weathermen. She began to build an arrest record, once in Flint, Michigan, for passing out pamphlets to high school students, and again in Chicago in the Weathermen's "Days of Rage" forays against the police. Detroit police say that Diana was present at the small, secret conclave of Weathermen last December in Flint, at which a decision was reportedly made to begin a bombing wave. As one of the leading activists, gifted and smoldering Diana Oughton went on to her death in Manhattan.

To people in Dwight, what happened to Diana seems to be news from another planet. As one elder explained: "There is no radicalism in Dwight. It was a contact she made outside of this town, and thank God, she didn't bring it back." Diana's father is equally puzzled, but absolutely sure of one thing: "Even though there is a big difference of opinion as to whether she's right or wrong, I'm sure that in her own heart she conscientiously felt she was right. She wasn't doing this for any other gain than—well—you might say the good of the world."

For Terry Robbins

For Terry Robbins
   You're dead now
   And there's no time to settle
   all that we had to settle
         between us.
You're dead now
because you thought there was no time
to settle your own fears about the struggle;
No time—
only urgency to do Armed Struggle;
born out of seeing the need
without digging on all the complexities
       and changes
it would put us through.
   Sometimes
   I think if Kent had happened sooner
   you would have seen there was time—
   you would have known better how to
     seize the time
instead of being
     seized by time.

For Kent was so much your victory—
A year before you had initiated the struggle there,
     had forced us to understand the need
       to fight Imperialism
       to smash ROTC
       to dig on the Vietcong
And dig on ourselves as Americong—
To stop being honkies and become
Stoned Revolutionaries—

From the *Berkeley Tribe*, August 21, 1970. Copyright 1970 by The Red Mountain Tribe. Reprinted by permission.

Feeling ourselves as part of the people
whose power we believe in,
whose power is so strong.

II.
You were a person who loved—
        so many of us,
        so deeply.
But after a while,
we forgot to love so much;
started mistaking smashing the enemy
with smashing ourselves, daughters and sons
                of the enemy.
We didn't see that trashing monogamy
didn't mean trashing the idea
that love can build our strength
but rather that hate, not love,
is the weakness we must destroy.

III.
    In memory of you,
    With memories about you,
    We live to fight the struggle you fought and died for.
    We live for the revolution
        and because of that,
    Life flows from us—
        Life that is Love—
    Love for you, for ourselves,
and for all our Sisters and Brothers.

Where The Fuse On That Dynamite Leads

I. F. Stone

> *The search of the youth today is for ways and means to make the machine—and the vast bureaucracy of the corporation state and of government that runs that machine—the servant of man. That is the revolution that is coming. That revolution . . . need not be a repetition of 1776. It could be a revolution in the nature of an explosive political regeneration. It depends on how wise the Establishment is. If, with its stockpile of arms, it resolves to suppress the dissenters, America will face, I fear, an awful ordeal.*
> —Justice Douglas: *Points of Rebellion*

The New York Times editorial Friday, March 13, on the rash of bombings and bomb scares in New York City was called "Not Idealists: Criminals." This was the standard reaction of a liberal publication, the easy way to clear its skirts of any suspicion of the slightest sympathy with revolutionary radicalism. But it is a dangerous cliché. Falsely to diagnose the trouble is to move toward the wrong remedies, and the wrong remedies will worsen the disease. Statistics on bombings from cities around the country suggest that we may be entering the first stages of an urban guerrilla movement. A guerrilla movement is a political, not a criminal, phenomenon, however many crimes it may commit. Experience has shown over and over again that a guerrilla movement can only be defeated by political means. The effort to treat it simply as a criminal matter, without resolving its political causes, ends by increasing the number of the guerrillas and widening their support in the larger community.

LIKE A NEW CHILDREN'S CRUSADE

Whether the New York bombings prove to be a spasm in the wake of the Greenwich Village explosion, when a radical arsenal blew up, or the beginning of a serious terrorist movement, will now depend on the authorities, and their ability to keep their cool. The first requisite—*and* the second, *and* the third—is understanding. The Weatherman kids can be seen in various ways, and it is necessary to see them in as many as possible. The Weatherman faction of SDS, whence several different "direct action" splinter groups seem to derive, can be looked at like a distraught child. They can be viewed as spoiled brats, in a tantrum with a world which will not change overnight to suit them. But they are also the most sensitive of a generation which feels in its bones what we older people only grasp as an unreal abstraction: that the world is headed for nuclear annihilation and something must be done to stop it. The Weatherman manifesto from which they take their name is from one point of view a mishmash of ill-digested pseudo-Marxist rubbish, an effort to compete with their bitterest rivals, the "square" sectarian ideologists of that other far-out splinter group, Progressive Labor. The manifesto spurns every normal base of revolutionary support and ends up squarely in the clouds: the middle class is, of course, no good; the working class is corrupted; the college generation will soon sell out; their only hope is in the juvenile Robespierres of the high schools. It sounded like the Children's Crusade come back to life, a St. Vitus' dance of hysterical politics.

It is from just such despair that terrorist movements have grown. This recalls the Russian pre-revolutionary *Narodnya Volya* (People's Will), through which a handful of disaffected middle-class and noble youths sought by bomb and pistol to overthrow the mighty Czarist order, with roots so deep in the religious reverence of the peasant masses as to seem impregnable. How to overturn their Little Father? A movement which has no faith in the masses seeks out the desperate few idealists willing to sacrifice their lives in gestures they realize may be futile. Some of our young revolutionaries are chillingly sober and disconcertingly sensible. Their criticism of conventional dissenters like myself and our futility, as the war goes on, is hard to rebut. Others in recent months have displayed a morbid development, a tendency to glorify violence for its own sake, as when they make Manson a hero for killing "bourgeois pigs," i.e., people exactly like their fathers and mothers. The ultimate menace they fear is their own secret selves in their own parents. This is what they are acting out on the stage of national politics.

But these psychological aspects are only a part of the whole complex picture. These wild and wonderful—yes, wonderful!—kids also serve quite rational political ends. I became strongly aware of this when I ran into an old friend on an early-morning Washington street-corner the other day who is working hard in a respectable do-good reformist organization, the very kind the youthful radicals despise. I told him that in talks on various campuses I had tried to talk the young people out of the typically American idea that revolution could be "instant" like coffee or iced tea. "Don't discourage them," was his unexpected plea. "If they stop acting up, we'll never get the Establishment to budge."

From a longer-range political point of view, the New Left and the hippies and the Yippies may, in however weird a form, also forecast the future. They see Soviet communism merely as a further stage of capitalism, a mass-production bureaucratic society concentrated on the production of goods rather than [on] the liberation of the spirit. They see the working class becoming "middle class" under it, and the need for a newer revolution against making the individual *thing* in a mindless industrial process, rather than the loving center of a universe meant to be joyous in our brief moment of passage through it. To study their irrationality is to become aware of ours.

NO SALVATION IN HOLOCAUST

The immediate lesson is this: If the police authorities are high-handed and arbitrary in their hunt for the bombers—as some already are—they will turn more moderates into activists. The answer to the revolutionaries is to behave with justice, to demonstrate that the system can operate under pressure in accordance with its own best ideals. *And first and above all to end the war.* Again and again, the overreaction and panic of an established order has turned a handful of conspirators into a revolutionary movement. This is, of course, exactly what the Chicago trial has done in radicalizing youth and destroying its faith in the courts. What happens on appeal may represent the last chance of winning them back to rational discourse and faith in peaceful change. In these, rather than a blind and volcanic upheaval, I see mankind's only chance. For the problems which confront us lie deep in the conditioning of man and in the power of technology to enslave him. No one is yet wise enough to chart the way out, as the most perceptive of the kids themselves admit. They merely hope something better will turn up out of the ruins. But I do not believe in salvation by holocaust. Hate and hysteria certainly will not create a new man or build a better world. Political suicide is not revolution.

But I must confess that I almost feel like throwing rocks through windows myself when I see Judge Julius Hoffman turn up as an honored guest at the White House and when I see Billy Graham like a smoother Rasputin dishing out saccharine religiosity there: If all Americans would only repeat the Lord's Prayer together, he said, "He could lead us out of our dilemma"—and at no increase in taxes either! I sense in Nixon and his entourage no anguish, no awareness, no real comprehension. When has there been a more inane leadership as storm clouds gather? Not since Marie Antoinette has there been a remark to match Moynihan's "benign neglect."

ON THE EDGE OF BLACK UPHEAVAL

Between the disaffected white youth and the growing anger of the blacks, we could be on the verge of a wild upheaval. I hold my breath as I go to press waiting to see whether Rap Brown is dead or alive. In the black community here in Washington those who knew Ralph Featherstone best, and remember his efforts only two weeks ago to advise the ghetto youth against violence, do not believe he was transporting explosives. They think he was murdered. They see the police and the FBI engaged in an effort to throw the blame upon the dead men themselves. Hoover's name at the bottom of that cryptic FBI report on the bombing is a provocation to the blacks. For them Hoover is an old ally of the Southern racists in Congress. In the black community, too, the established order is recruiting the forces which threaten it. Until the war in Southeast Asia is ended, until the Pentagon is cut down drastically, until priorities are revised to make racial reconciliation and social reconstruction our No. 1 concerns, the dynamite that threatens us sizzles on a fuse that leads straight back to the White House.

The Radical Bombers

Andrew Kopkind

> *But you see, we all believe in what Bakunin and Nachaev said: that a revolutionary is a doomed man.... So you come to terms with the idea that you may be killed. And when you have to live with the prospect of being wiped out in a flash, you either stop doing what you're doing and remove yourself from that situation, or else you have to accept it and kind of repress it, and get it off your mind. Otherwise, you'll be nonfunctional. You can't walk around afraid and watching and looking over your shoulder. Anyway, I think many people these days have learned to live with that understanding. I learned to live with it somehow.*
>
> —Eldridge Cleaver

Ralph Featherstone lived in Neshoba County, Mississippi, for two years, off an on. He had first come there one day in the summer of 1964 to meet three fellow civil rights workers in a church in the county seat of Philadelphia. The three had left Featherstone in Meridian in the morning; he was to catch up with them in Neshoba later in the afternoon. Featherstone waited all afternoon in the church in Philadelphia. Micky Schwerner, James Chaney and Andy Goodman never did come.

Black folks in Philadelphia gave Featherstone a place to sleep and food to eat, and he'd pay them a few dollars every now and then with money he'd get from Northern white contributions to SNCC. Then the money stopped, and Featherstone began working on economic development projects which might make the Southern movement, and the black community, self-sustaining. I spent some time with Ralph in Neshoba, and the one day I remember most vividly was framed by two visits: by the FBI in the morning and by the notorious Sheriffs Rainey and Price in the late afternoon. Neither visit was pleasant; the FBI agents were polite and menacing and the sheriffs were rude and menacing, but Ralph dealt coolly and good-naturedly with both. At the end of the day he drank a lot of milk and took medicine for his stomach. He kept a shotgun next to the medicine.

The economic development project didn't work, and Featherstone came back to Washington, where he had grown up and had gone to college, to try a similar scheme. That one came to little, too, and he went back to Mississippi for a spell. As the movements of the Sixties progressed, he went to Japan to talk to young people there, and he traveled to Cuba to see what that was like, and to Africa. SNCC pretty much stopped functioning as an organization, but Featherstone and some of the best of the SNCC people kept working. In the months before he was blown to bits by a bomb in Bel Air, Maryland, Featherstone and several others were running a book store, a publishing house and a school in Washington. Ralph lived a few blocks from me and we'd bump into each other every few weeks, chat briefly, and make vague plans to get together for a meal or a longer talk. As we both knew, the plans would not be followed. Somewhat mindlessly, I would slip Ralph into a category called "the black thing," which was a locked box decorated with exotic Benin artifacts, and a tag: "Do Not Open Until . . . ." I shudder now at the thought of the tag on the bag he had for me.

I don't doubt that the road from Meridian ended, in many more ways than one, last week. Ralph's progression in the last six years was, like the road itself, an attenuated metaphor. Strung out along the way were the mileposts of a generation, the markings of a movement, passed as soon as they were come upon, quickly out of sight. It's hard to say how one or another man or woman is bound to travel, and it can't be known where anyone is going to stop. Ralph missed a meeting in Neshoba; but then he kept his appointment in Bel Air.

A desperate irony of history, a dialectical pun, put

Featherstone's death next to the explosions in the Wilkerson house in Greenwich Village and the bombings a few nights later of three corporations' offices in Manhattan. In evidentiary terms, the events of that week seem totally disconnected. Featherstone and his companion, Che Payne, were most probably murdered by persons who believed that Rap Brown was in their car. Featherstone had gone to Bel Air on the eve of Brown's scheduled appearance at the trial to make security arrangements; Brown had good reason to fear for his safety in that red neck of the woods. No one who knew the kinds of politics Featherstone was practicing, or the mission he was on in Bel Air, or the quality of his judgment, believes that he was transporting a bomb—in the front seat of a car, leaving Bel Air, at midnight, in hostile territory, with police everywhere.

The police and newspaper accounts of the goings-on in the Wilkerson house on West Eleventh Street seem—in outline, at least—consistent within themselves and probably in the (dim) light of developments after the recent break-up of a formal Weatherman organization. The tensions within Weatherman, both organizationally and politically, were always as explosive as any bomb; Weathermen were experimenting not only with new tactics and ideas but with new styles of living, new ways of loving, and new values of existence. They changed their course almost fortnightly: puritanical one week, totally uninhibited the next; druggy and orgiastic, then ascetic and celibate; concerned with a mass line and liberal movements, then deep into guerrilla training. And all the time they were dealing—not very successfully—with open repression from the Man and open hostility from most other radicals. It was clear at the Weatherman convention at Flint in December that the organization was not going to grow in size and legitimacy, and as early Weathersymps and cadre from the collectives dropped out of contact, the core hardened. In a few months, the distance between the guerrilla center and the discarded cadre and the lost sympathizers could be measured in light-years; people who had once worked closely with the women who were, reportedly, in the Eleventh

Street house knew nothing of those recent activities, and could not begin to find out.

The bombings in Manhattan on the night of March 11 appear to be the work of people with politics quite different from the post-Weathermen of Eleventh Street. The obvious differences can be seen in the messages the bombers left; even a cursory *explication du texte* indicates that the bombers were of the same anarchist strain as those who hit similar targets last November, and quite distinct from the specific line of Weatherman. The notes spoke in terms of "death culture" and life forces, but contained few of the internationalist, anti-police, anti-racism, and pro-Viet Cong references which mark the Weather ethic.

But although the three events are disconnected in all particulars, they are at the same time tied at some radical bottom. Guerrilla attacks by the revolutionary left and counterattacks by the extreme right seem almost natural in America this winter. When students demonstrate, they do not merely sit in but burn up: They firebomb a bank in Santa Barbara, snipe at policemen in Buffalo. Few peaceful marches end peacefully; both marchers and police are ready to fight.

The newspapers have begun calling the current crop of radicals "revolutionaries," but they have removed the quotation marks and have dropped such skeptical qualifiers as "self-styled" or "so-called" before the word. For the first time in half a century, at least—and perhaps since 1776— there is a generalized revolutionary movement in the US. It is not directed at organizing labor or winning civil rights for minorities or gaining power for students in the administration of universities. Wholly unorganized and utterly undirected, the revolutionary movement exists not because it is planned but because it is logical: not because a handful of young blacks or dissident middle-class whites will it, but because the conditions of American life create it; not because the left is so strong, but because the center is so weak.

It's worth saying what the revolutionary movement is *not*. First of all, it's not big—at least the active part. All the people who are into demolitions this year could gather in a town-house or two in the Village—and probably did. There have been scores of bombings in the past six months—in New York, Seattle, the San Francisco Bay Area, Colorado and scattered college towns. In Madison, Wisconsin, for instance, someone predicted "Zabriskie Point" and bombed an ROTC building from an airplane (the bombs did not go off). But a hundred or two hundred people could have done all that, and there is no reason to believe that there are vast divisions preparing for the next assaults.

Second, it's not yet a revolution. A bomb in Standard Oil's headquarters in Manhattan does as much material damage to Standard Oil as a tick does to a tiger. Universities have not ground to a halt, draft boards have not been shut down, the war in Indochina hardly has ended. The resources of the corporations and the government that make public decisions and social policy are complete.

But then, the revolutionary movement is not isolated in its few activists, nor confined to its few acts of violence. There was a general sense of depression in the liberal left when the Eleventh Street house blew up; and there was a genuine sense of exhilaration when the bombings followed. People who could not, in their weirdest fantasies, ever see themselves lighting a fuse, were lifted for a moment from their sense of dull futility. For that reason, the guerrilla acts cannot be dismissed as "isolated terror" by a "lunatic fringe"; they draw a positive response from a surprisingly large number of ordinary people—even those who venture out of their conventional lives for nothing more exciting than a Moratorium rally, and who will tell you before you ask that they "deplore" violence. The contradictions of the society as a whole exist within each of them as well.

Finally, the revolutionary movement is not professional, nor is it politically mature, nor tactically consistent. Nor is there much chance that it will get itself together in the coming months. If it was a "tragic accident" that killed three young people in the Eleventh Street house, it was in one sense no accident: Those who seek to build a revolution from scratch must inevitably make such mistakes. (For a description of how amateurish revolutionaries can be, read Che's diaries.) The politics of the guerrilla acts are not always self-explanatory, even to committed radicals; in what kind of political demands were the Manhattan bombings set? One New York radical activist said recently that those acts could have contextual meaning only if the messages demanded US withdrawal from Vietnam and Laos, say, or freedom for Black Panthers in jail. A note which threatened continued attacks until the war ended, for example, would make sense to many more people than the seemingly "nihilist" statements made last week.

At this stage, tactics can be crucial. Attacks against property—in which care is taken to avoid injuries to people—are much more easily understood than terrorist acts against police, much less "innocent" bystanders. It's necessary, too, to think through any action to avoid bringing retaliation down against those who are not responsible: for example, the firebombing of Judge Murtagh's house in New York (in protest against the trial of the Panther 21) was obviously prejudicial to the Panthers' case, and their cause. If whites did that act, they should have made it their own responsibility—and they should have set its political meaning straight. Explanations are necessary, but they are hard to make by the underground guerrillas, in the absence of an overground mass movement—tied in sympathy but not in fact to those below.

The escalation of radical protest into revolutionary action will produce two major social effects: a sense of crisis in the society as a whole, and a need for repression by the authorities. The two effects are inextricably related. If there is crisis, there will be an appropriate response to it. The sense of crisis is not the work of the bombers or bank-burners or demonstrators or Panthers alone. It develops easily when the phones don't work, the beaches are oil-slicked, the blacks are bussed to white schools, the priests are marrying, the redwoods are toppling, the teen-agers are shooting-up, the women are liberating themselves, the stock market is falling and the Viet Cong are winning.

Neither does repression happen in a single tone of voice. Even in the most critical of times (*especially* in the most critical of times) the State acts, as Lenin put it, like hangman and priest. Despite the policy of "benign neglect" which the Nixon Administration is following in most matters, the process of buying off black revolution—by accepting black militancy—is continuing at a fast clip. If the government tends to fall behind in the effort, private corporations, foundations and educational institutions keep up the pace. In the same month that Fred Hampton is killed or desegregation is postponed in Mississippi, millions of dollars went to black urban bureaucrats; black students were streaming into previously white colleges and white jobs; and the government made plans to give preferential hiring to blacks in construction jobs. It's easy but unwise to dismiss such methods as "meaningless," or "too little," or "cynical." Of course, the "Philadelphia Plan" for hiring black construction workers is also a way to limit the power of labor unions. But in the near and middle distances, those measures—the repressive and the co-optive—are reasonably successful in blunting the chopping edge of the black liberation movement.

In the week that Vice President Agnew is denouncing "kooks" and "social misfits," and Conspiracy Prosecutor Foran is talking of a "freaking fag revolution," the Nixon Administration and a coalition of politicals from (and including) Goldwater to Kennedy are proposing lowering the voting age to eighteen, and plans are going ahead for an all-volunteer army. Again, the point is not that either of those proposals will accomplish much in the way of changing social values in America; but those measures are not exactly Nuremberg Laws to be used against a radical force or a distasteful element of society.

In the wake of the bombings and deaths last week, the FBI fanned out to question anyone known to have a connection with the Eleventh Street people. Agents were unusually uptight; one set of FBI visitors called a New York man who declined to speak to them a "motherfucker." There were police agents with walkie-talkies standing around major airports all week long. The newspapers—especially in New York —bannered scare headlines and speculated endlessly, and foolishly, on the connections between the events. Authorities "leaked" word to Richard Starnes, a Scripps-Howard reporter in Washington who often acts as an unofficial flack for the FBI, that both Featherstone and the three Eleventh Street people so far identified had visited Cuba—and that Attorney Leonard Boudin, whose daughter's papers were found in the house, represented the Cuban government in legal matters in the US. Senator Eastland has now called for an investigation of the Venceremos Brigade of Americans who have gone to Cuba to harvest sugar cane. No one believes that the natives in America can be restless—all by themselves.

The level of fear (that is, paranoia with good reason) rose to exorbitant heights, but that too affects the general sense of crisis in the society. Seen in relief (if there can be any), that crisis is the most serious organizing effect of the bombings. If the radical movements are to win middle-class people —or those, both black and white, who aspire to middle-class comfort and security—they must devise ways of forcing real existential choices upon them. At one time, marches and rallies or sit-ins or building occupations provided a setting for those choices. But privileged Americans do not easily make the revolutionary choice. Only if their privilege is worthless are they free to act. Now, the sense of crisis is the specific contradiction to privilege: that is, all the things that Americans want to get and spend are without meaning if the world no longer holds together. At such times, people choose to fight—one way or the other. It may be that such a time is now.

How Does It Feel To Be Inside An Explosion . . .

How does it feel
To be inside
An explosion?

Was there time
To flash upon
The way we came?

Came from childhood
    of horror and hope
To black awakening
    petition and protest
Massed in resistance
    to their whip and wars
Came youth on fire
    fighting for freedom
Naming the enemy
    embracing our friends
Learning war through war
        in the world revolution.

Was there time
To flash upon
The way we came?

Diana and Ted and Terry
Dead inside an explosion.

No one of us will ever be the same.

We have to go
Thru so many changes
When things come down
The way they do.

When comrades die
We cry.

When comrades die
We avenge.

When comrades die
We ask why.

We have to go
Through so many changes
When things come down
The way they do.

Slaves sang
Sang spirituals
In code
On the underground railway.

And before
I'd be a slave
I'll be buried
In my grave

Fighting with those
Who fought to be free.

Oh Freedom!

Harriet Tubman
Black revolutionary
Leading groups
Along the way.

When one stopped
Afraid
Wanting to turn back
She spoke of slavery and freedom.

And there were times
When she
Drew a gun and said
There is no turning back.

Oh Freedom!
Explosions in the night
Scream power
Death
To the slavemasters!

Fear of death
Is so
For real
Because we fight for life

On the underground railway
Fighting with those
Who fought
To be free.

Revolution
Means learning things
The hard way
Through doing them.

People have to be together
When making bombs
And revolutions
Have to plan
Think past the act
Within a strategy
Consider all the angles
Work carefully
People have to be together.

Know and treasure every person
For people do the planting
And every swallowed fear
Or unsaid word of caution
Each new idea
All the loves and strengths
Are part of becoming together
When making bombs
And revolutions.

It doesn't mean don't do it
It means making sure you do it.

An hour, a week,
A month that's taken
To insure a victory
Is time well taken.

And time is on our side.

It doesn't mean don't do it
It means being able to do it again.

Every one involved
Should understand
How and why everything works
So they can use and teach it.

Understand so they
Can be prepared
For the unexpected
Can meet new needs.

So they can insure
Their safety
Effectively aim
In the desired direction.

Break through
The powerlessness
Programmed
In the technological mystique.

Don't let a question pass
Because others might think you ignorant
They may be glad you asked
It may mean life.

Don't let a fear be buried
Because others might think you weak
Everyone is afraid
To deny it may mean life

The same fear
Unraised
Could allow an enemy to escape
Just execution

A fear may change history
There may be grounds for fear
That raising it can remedy
Don't be afraid to speak your fear.

Go to an isolated place
To practice
Try different devices
Watch what they do.

You are doing this
As part of the struggle
Not to prove
That you can do it.

We're Communists
Violence is a tool
Terror a tactic
Not a proof of manhood

Keep cool
Don't be afraid to change or flow
Be real
People have to be together.

The slow one now may later be fast.

And when the lives and loves
The strategy and plan
Have been struggled through
Then do it.

The revolutionary bomb
Contains the dynamite
Of mass anger
Packed tightly
Nera blasting caps
Of leadership
Fire carried by fuses
Of propaganda
The spark is set
By revolutionaries.

It is well timed.
It has a safety switch.
It is well placed.

And it does a lot of damage.

When it explodes
It should speak
Clearly
It should attack
An enemy
Of the people.

An explosion follows
The path of least resistance.

Pry open a contradiction
And shoot the fire through.

Fit the bomb
To the target.

Bombs are one thing
Guns another
There are many ways to fight.

Learn war.

Uncle Ho said
Those with swords will use swords
Those with hoes
Will use hoes in the heroic war.

Create weapons that everyone can use
Materials at the corner store
Build an army and militia
Masses win the war.

Have a party to lead.

Chairman Mao says
An army without culture
Is a dull witted one

The seeds of a new culture
Have been planted on this continent
Harvested by venceremos brigades
Che lives
And inside the monster
Black voices shout of freedom
Youth gathers to celebrate life.

Culture
Is the way you live your life.

Lives
Point the way
The warmth and honesty
For realness
Of being with the ones you love
Non exclusively.

Pushing outward.
Learning from
And teaching
The lives you cross.

Pushing outward
For the way
To change reality
Is to know it

Laughter and joy
Are real
When people
Are fighting together

How does it feel
To be inside
An Explosion?

Was there time
To flash upon
The way we came?

Two women escaped
And are free
To carry on.

Where is Rap Brown?

Weatherman
Cannot be found
Because they're finding
Ways of revolution.

Change a face
Discard a name
No one of us will ever be the same.

Tearing away
At the heart of the monster
Not hiding
But living lives

Of care and confidence

The war expands
As victory comes near
Avenge the Kent State 4.

The campuses
Explode in anger
Don't let them weaken us.

Shut it down.

Four in Ohio
Six in black Augusta
Two at Jackson State

When the black rebellions break
Draw the pigs away
Fight for our freedom
Each time they take a life
Or move on us
Prepare to move on them
Our heroes will be avenged.

They have sucked and spilled
The blood of millions
In taking their lives
The blood of freedom flows

Humanity
Twists and turns

In struggle
Making love
And revolution

We shall gather
In Parks
Named for

The women and men
Who led the way.

There will be time

To flash upon
The way we came.

Along the way
There will be
Twists and turns
Struggle, love
And revolution.

We shall gather
In homes
Of brothersisterhood
Building Bombs
Of communism.

Diana and Ted and Terry
Dead inside an explosion.

No one of us will ever be the same.

Diana is
A teacher
She loves children
Loves life.

She is gentle
Warm and close
With those she knows
Diana is.

Ted is
A speaker and songwriter
Quick and a little awkward
Loves life.

He is funny
Plays baseball
Laughs and sings
Ted is.

Lovers of Humanity

Human

Flash upon the way they came.

Pig papers ask
Why are the children of America
Making bombs?

Why did these good kids go bad?

They can't understand
But sisters and brothers
We do.

It is because
They were so human

Lovers of Humanity

That they came from childhood
                of horror and hope
To black awakening
                petition and protest
Massed in resistance
                to their whip and wars
Came youth on fire
                fighting for freedom
Naming the enemy
                embracing our friends
Learning war through war
                in the world of revolution.

Communique #1 From The Weatherman Underground

Hello. This is Bernardine Dohrn.
I'm going to read A DECLARATION OF A STATE OF WAR.
This is the first communication from the Weatherman underground.

All over the world, people fighting Amerikan imperialism look to Amerika's youth to use our strategic position behind enemy lines to join forces in the destruction of the empire.

Black people have been fighting almost alone for years. We've known that our job is to lead white kids into armed revolution. We never intended to spend the next five or twenty-five years of our lives in jail. Ever since SDS became revolutionary, we've been trying to show how it is possible to overcome the frustration and impotence that comes from trying to reform this system. Kids know the lines are drawn; revolution is touching all of our lives. Tens of thousands have learned that protest and marches don't do it. Revolutionary violence is the only way.

Now we are adapting the classic guerrilla strategy of the Viet Cong and the urban guerrilla strategy of the Tupamaros to our own situation here in the most technically advanced country in the world.

Che taught us that "revolutionaries move like fish in the sea." The alienation and contempt that young people have for this country has created the ocean for this revolution.

The hundreds and thousands of young people who demonstrated in the Sixties against the war and for civil rights grew to hundreds of thousands in the past few weeks actively fighting Nixon's invasion of Cambodia and the attempted

From *The Berkeley Tribe*, July 31, 1970. Reprinted by permission. Copyright 1970 by The Red Mountain Tribe.

genocide against black people. The insanity of Amerikan "justice" has added to its list of atrocities six blacks killed in Augusta, two in Jackson and four white Kent State students, making thousands more into revolutionaries.

The parents of "privileged" kids have been saying for years that the revolution was a game for us. But the war and the racism of this society show that it is too fucked-up. We will never live peaceably under this system.

This was totally true of those who died in the New York town-house explosion. The third person who was killed there was Terry Robbins, who led the first rebellion at Kent State less than two years ago.

The twelve Weathermen who were indicted for leading last October's riots in Chicago have never left the country. Terry is dead, Linda was captured by a pig informer, but the rest of us move freely in and out of every city and youth scene in this country. We're not hiding out but we're invisible.

There are several hundred members of the Weatherman underground and some of us face more years in jail than the fifty thousand deserters and draft dodgers now in Canada. Already many of them are coming back to join us in the underground or to return to the Man's army and tear it up from inside along with those who never left.

We fight in many ways. Dope is one of our weapons. The laws against marijuana mean that millions of us are outlaws long before we actually split. Guns and grass are united in the youth underground.

Freaks are revolutionaries and revolutionaries are freaks. If you want to find us, this is where we are. In every tribe, commune, dormitory, farmhouse, barracks and town-house where kids are making love, smoking dope and loading guns—fugitives from Amerikan justice are free to go.

For Diana Oughton, Ted Gold and Terry Robbins, and for all the revolutionaries who are still on the move here, there has been no question for a long time now—we will never go back.

Within the next fourteen days we will attack a symbol or institution of Amerikan injustice. This is the way we celebrate the example of Eldridge Cleaver and H. Rap Brown and all black revolutionaries who first inspired us by their fight behind enemy lines for the liberation of their people.

Never again will they fight alone.

May 21, 1970

Terry Robbins. Photo: David Fenton/LNS

Communique #2 From The Weatherman Underground

SLIP NR 12 / 1909 / JUNE9-70 / POLICE HDQTRS / 77
BOMBEXPLOSION - 240 CENTRE ST - POLICE HDQTRS -
UNK
DAMAGE AND INJURIES AT THIS TIME - DETAILS
LATER

Tonight, at 7 p.m., we blew up the N.Y.C. police head-quarters. We called in a warning before the explosion.

The pigs in this country are our enemies. They have mur-dered Fred Hampton and tortured Joan Bird. They are re-sponsible for 6 black deaths in Augusta, 4 murders in Kent State, the imprisonment of Los Siete de la Raza in San Fran-cisco and the continual brutality against Latin and white youth on the Lower East Side.

Some are named Mitchell and Agnew. Others call them-selves Leary and Hogan. The names are different but the crimes are the same.

The pigs try to look invulnerable, but we keep finding their weaknesses. Thousands of kids, from Berkeley to the UN Plaza, keep tearing up ROTC buildings.

Nixon invades Cambodia and hundreds of schools are shut down by strikes. Every time the pigs think they've stopped us, we come back a little stronger and a lot smarter. They guard their buildings and we walk right past their guards. They look for us—we get to them first.

They build the Bank of America, kids burn it down. They outlaw grass, we build a culture of life and music.

The time is now. Political power grows out of a gun, a Molotov, a riot, a commune . . . and from the soul of the people.

WEATHERMAN

From the *Berkeley Tribe,* July 31, 1970. Copyright 1970 by The Red Mountain Tribe. Reprinted by permission.

Notes To The Underground

To the Brothers and Sisters of the Weatherman Underground:

I read your communique, and was really excited to find out that you're still here in America, and into doing heavy stuff. The presence of an underground here, in the midst of the Man's boasts about his high-level pig technology, is a victory in itself.

For you to survive must mean that thousands of kids everywhere are enough like you that the pigs can't isolate you to pick you off. Many people like us must have helped you directly in those first days after the townhouse; you couldn't have survived doing everything yourselves.

But being underground also means being more alone than you've ever been before. Having fewer people to trust and move with can create a sense of isolation and apartness about yourselves and your relation to all of us. Maybe for that reason, I felt that you didn't seem quite real when you wrote the communique.

I think you were wrong to set up a fourteen-day deadline for your action. Raising people's hopes that high isn't a good way to build trust in the underground. It perpetrates the myth that the underground is a kind of American Tupamaros fighting at an incredibly high level, when you're all actually just people who are real new at this.

It's important that you don't become isolated as super-beings. Most of us are pretty unsure about what to do, and it's easy to fall into a pattern of seeing you as a super-together, tightly disciplined force who'll take care of business for us while we cheer you on from the sidelines. Believing in the underground as a glamorous revolutionary legend will only hold us back from the kinds of struggle and practice we need to be about now; leadership has got to be what we can see ourselves becoming.

From the *Berkeley Tribe*, June 12, 1970. Copyright 1970 by The Red Mountain Tribe. Reprinted by permission.

I want to know more about what kinds of changes you had to go thru to survive as an underground, and what put you thru those changes. I want to know more about how you built love and trust among each other and with the people who helped you, because we all have to build the kinds of relationships we'd stake our lives on. If you make your growth and survival seem mystical or easy, it's harder for all of us to change and learn off it.

It's true that most freaks are potential revolutionaries, but we're all confused about how to get from here to there. Even tho millions of kids are in motion, we're not very together with each other. We'll have to find ways to share our experiences and our struggle on deeper levels than ever before. We've got to move towards a time when the mass movement and the underground build off each other, and become integrated under the same politics and the same leadership. That will only happen when we share the kind of trust and love that comes with an open and self-critical relationships between you and us.

Power to the people whose bombs tore up the Centre St. pig station (on any fucking day)!

A revolutionary
brother and sister

Communique #3 From The Weatherman Underground

July 26, 1970
The Motor City

This is the third communication from the Weatherman underground.

With other revolutionaries all over the planet, Weatherman is celebrating the 11th anniversary of the Cuban revolution. Today we attack with rocks, riots and bombs the greatest killer-pig ever known to man—Amerikan imperialism.

Everywhere we see the growth of revolutionary culture and the ways in which every move of the monster-state tightens the noose around its own neck.

A year ago people thought it can't happen here. Look at where we've come.

Nixon invades Cambodia; the Cong and all of Indochina spread the already rebelling US troops thin. Ahmed is a prisoner; Rap is free and fighting. Fred Hampton is murdered; the brothers at Soledad avenge — "2 down and one to go." Pun and several Weatherman are ripped; we run free. Mitchell indicts 8 or 10 or 13; hundreds of thousands of freeks plot to build a new world on the ruins of honky Amerika.

And to General Mitchell we say: Don't look for us, Dog; We'll find you first.

For the Central Committee, Weatherman Underground

From the *Berkeley Tribe,* July 31, 1970. Copyright 1970 by The Red Mountain Tribe. Reprinted by permission.

Communique #4 From The Weatherman Underground

September 15, 1970.
This is the fourth communication from the Weatherman Underground.

The Weatherman Underground has had the honor and pleasure of helping Dr. Timothy Leary escape from the POW camp at San Luis Obispo, California.

Dr. Leary was being held against his will and against the will of millions of kids in this country. He was a political prisoner, captured for the work he did in helping all of us begin the task of creating a new culture on the barren wasteland that has been imposed on this country by Democrats, Republicans, Capitalists and creeps.

LSD and grass, like the herbs and cactus and mushrooms of the American Indians and countless civilizations that have existed on this planet, will help us make a future world where it will be possible to live in peace.

Now we are at war.

With the NLF and the North Vietnamese, with the Democratic Front for the Liberation of Palestine and Al Fatah, with Rap Brown and Angela Davis, with all black and brown revolutionaries, the Soledad brothers and all prisoners of war in Amerikan concentration camps we know that peace is only possible with the destruction of U.S. imperialism.

Our organization commits itself to the task of freeing these prisoners of war.

We are outlaws, we are free!

(signed) Bernardine Dohrn

From *San Francisco Good Times,* September 18, 1970. Copyright 1970 by *San Francisco Good Times.* Reprinted by permission.

Letter From Timothy Leary

The following statement was written in the POW camp and carried over the wall (in full sight of two gun trucks). I offer loving gratitude to my Sisters and Brothers in the Weatherman Underground who designed and executed my liberation. Rosemary and I are now with the Underground and we'll continue to stay high and wage the revolutionary war.

There is the time for peace and the time for war.

There is the day of laughing Krishna and the day of Grim Shiva.

Brothers and Sisters, at this time let us have no more talk of peace.

The conflict which we have sought to avoid is upon us. A world-wide ecological religious warfare. Life vs. death.

Listen. It is a comfortable, self-indulgent cop-out to look for conventional economic-political solutions.

Brothers and Sisters, this is a war for survival. Ask Huey and Angela. They dig it.

Ask the wild free animals. They know it.

Ask the turned-on ecologists. They sadly admit it.

I declare that World War III is now being waged by short-haired robots whose deliberate aim is to destroy the complex web of free wild life by the imposition of mechanical order.

Listen. There is no choice left but to defend life by all and every means possible against the genocidal machine.

Listen. There are no neutrals in genetic war. There are no non-combatants at Buchenwald, My Lai or Soledad.

You are part of the death apparatus or you belong to the network of free life.

Do not be deceived. It is a classic stratagem of genocide to camouflage their wars as law and order police actions.

Remember the Sioux and the German Jews and the black

From *San Francisco Good Times*, September 18, 1970. Copyright 1970 by *San Francisco Good Times*. Reprinted by permission.

slaves and the marijuana pogroms and the pious TWA indig-
nation over airline hijackings!

If you fail to see that we are the victims—defendants of
genocidal war you will not understand the rage of the blacks,
the fierceness of the browns, the holy fanaticism of the Pales-
tinians, the righteous mania of the Weathermen, and the pervasive resentment of the young.

Listen Americans. Your government is an instrument of
total lethal evil.

Remember the buffalo and the Iroquois!

Remember Kennedy, King, Malcolm, Lenny!

Listen. There is no compromise with a machine. You cannot talk peace and love to a humanoid robot whose every
Federal Bureaucratic impulse is soulless, heartless, lifeless,
loveless.

In this life struggle we use the ancient holy strategies of
organic life:

1) Resist lovingly in the loyalty of underground sister-
hoods and brotherhoods.

2) Resist passively, break lock-step . . . drop out.

3) Resist actively, sabotage, jam the computer . . . hijack
planes . . . trash every lethal machine in the land.

4) Resist publicly, announce life . . . denounce death.

5) Resist privately, guerrilla invisibility.

6) Resist beautifully, create organic art, music.

7) Resist biologically, be healthy . . . erotic . . . conspire
with seed . . . breed.

8) Resist spiritually, stay high . . . praise god . . . love life
. . . blow the mechanical mind with Holy Acid . . . dose them
. . . dose them.

9) Resist physically, robot agents who threaten life must
be disarmed, disabled, disconnected by force . . . Arm yourself and shoot to live . . . Life is never violent. To shoot a
genocidal robot policeman in the defense of life is a sacred
act.

Listen Nixon. We were never that naive. We knew that
flowers in your gun-barrels were risky. We too remember
Munich and Auschwitz all too well as we chanted love and

raised our Woodstock fingers in the gentle sign of peace.

We begged you to live and let live, to love and let love, but you have chosen to kill and get killed. May God have mercy on your soul.

For the last seven months, I, a free, wild man, have been locked in POW camps. No living creature can survive in a cage. In my flight to freedom I leave behind a million brothers and sisters in the POW prisons of Quentin, Soledad, Con Thien . . .

Listen comrades. The liberation war has just begun. Resist, endure, do not collaborate. Strike. You will be free.

Listen you brothers of the imprisoned. Break them out! If David Harris has ten friends in the world, I say to you, get off your pious non-violent asses and break him out.

There is no excuse for one brother or sister to remain a prisoner of war.

Right on Leila Khaled!

Listen, the hour is late. Total war is upon us. Fight to live or you'll die. Freedom is life. Freedom will live.

(signed) Timothy Leary

WARNING: I am armed and should be considered dangerous to anyone who threatens my life or my freedom.